T0202998

Lecture Notes in Computer Science　12910

More information about this subseries at http://www.springer.com/series/7410

Shivam Bhasin · Fabrizio De Santis (Eds.)

Constructive Side-Channel Analysis and Secure Design

12th International Workshop, COSADE 2021
Lugano, Switzerland, October 25–27, 2021
Proceedings

 Springer

Editors
Shivam Bhasin 🄳
Nanyang Technological University
Singapore, Singapore

Fabrizio De Santis 🄳
Siemens AG
Munich, Germany

ISSN 0302-9743   ISSN 1611-3349   (electronic)
Lecture Notes in Computer Science
ISBN 978-3-030-89914-1   ISBN 978-3-030-89915-8   (eBook)
https://doi.org/10.1007/978-3-030-89915-8

LNCS Sublibrary: SL4 – Security and Cryptology

This Springer imprint is published by the registered company Springer Nature Switzerland AG
The registered company address is: Gewerbestrasse 11, 6330 Cham, Switzerland

Preface

The Twelfth International Workshop on Constructive Side-Channel Analysis and Secure Design (COSADE 2021) was held as a hybrid event at the Università della Svizzera italiana, Lugano, Switzerland, during October 25–27, 2021.

The COSADE series of conferences began in 2010 and provides a well-established international platform for researchers, academics, and industry participants to present their work and their current research in implementation attacks, secure implementation, secure design and evaluation, and practical attacks, test platforms and open benchmarks.

This year, we received 31 papers, each of which was assigned to three reviewers. All the submissions went through a rigorous double-blind peer review process. The Program Committee included 40 members from 16 countries, selected among experts from academia and industry in the areas of secure design, side channel attacks and countermeasures, and architectures and protocols. Overall, the Program Committee returned 93 reviews. During the decision process, 14 papers were selected for publication in the COSADE 2021 proceedings. We would like to express our gratitude to the Program Committee members and the 22 subreviewers for their reviews and for their active participation in the paper discussion phase.

The highlights of the COSADE 2021 program include two keynotes and an industrial session. The first keynote entitled "Securing the Next Trillion of Chips via In-Memory and Immersed-in-Logic Design – Beyond Traditional Design Boundaries" was given by Massimo Alioto from the National University of Singapore. The talk explored the road towards truly ubiquitous hardware security from a primitive design perspective, designing PUFs and TRNGs that are inherently immersed in existing memory arrays and logic fabrics. The second keynote entitled "Defending CyberPhysical Systems and Infrastructures from Cyber Attacks" was given by Alberto Sangiovanni Vincentelli from the University of California, Berkeley. The talk explored attacks against critical infrastructure such as gas pipelines, power generation, and water treatment plants, as well as against cars and airplanes.

The industrial session included the following talks: "Introduction to OpenTitan – An Open-source Silicon Root of Trust Project" from G+D Mobile Security GmbH, "Is Revolutionary Hardware for Fully Homomorphic Encryption Important? What Else is Needed?" from Intel Corporation, "Post-Quantum Cryptography with Contemporary Co-Processors" from NXP Semiconductors, and "Analyzing the Harmfulness of Glitches in the Context of Side-Channel Analysis" from Secure-IC S.A.S.

We would like to thank the steering committee, Jean-Luc Danger and Werner Schindler, the general chairs, Alberto Ferrante, Francesco Regazzoni, and Subhadeep Banik, and the local organizers, Liliana Sampietro and Nadia Ruggiero-Ciresa, from Università della Svizzera italiana, for taking care of various aspects of organization. We would also like to thank the Web administrators, Helmut Häfner and Lothar Hellmeier of the University of Stuttgart, for maintaining the COSADE website for 2021. We are very grateful for the financial support received from our generous sponsors Hasler Stiftung, FortifyIQ, NewAE Technology Inc., Riscure, Secure-IC, PQShield, and Rambus Cryptography Research.

Finally, we would like to acknowledge Springer for their active cooperation and timely production of the proceedings.

October 2021   Shivam Bhasin
                                                                  Fabrizio De Santis

Organization

General Chairs

Alberto Ferrante   Università della Svizzera italiana, Switzerland
Francesco Regazzoni   University of Amsterdam, The Netherlands, and
     Università della Svizzera italiana, Switzerland
Subhadeep Banik   École Polytechnique Fédérale de Lausanne,
     Switzerland

Program Committee Chairs

Shivam Bhasin   Nanyang Technological University, Singapore
Fabrizio De Santis   Siemens AG, Germany

Steering Committee

Jean-Luc Danger   Télécom Paris, France
Werner Schindler   Bundesamt für Sicherheit in der Informationstechnik
     (BSI), Germany

Program Committee

Diego Aranha   Aarhus University, Denmark
Aydin Aysu   North Carolina State University, USA
Alessandro Barenghi   Politecnico di Milano, Italy
Lejla Batina   Radboud University, The Netherlands
Sebastian Berndt   University of Lübeck, Germany
Jakub Breier   Silicon Austria Labs, Austria
Ileana Buhan   Radboud University, The Netherlands
Anupam Chattopadhyay   Nanyang Technological University, Singapore
Chitchanok   University of Adelaide, Australia
     Chuengsatiansup
Lauren De Meyer   Rambus Cryptography, The Netherlands
Jean-Max Dutertre   Ecole Nationale Superieure des Mines de Saint-Étienne
     (ENSMSE), France
Wieland Fischer   Infineon Technologies, Germany
Fatemah Ganji   Worcester Polytechnic Institute, USA
Benedikt Gierlichs   Katholieke Universiteit Leuven, Belgium
Dong-Guk Han   Kookmin University, South Korea
Annelie Heuser   Inria and CNRS, France
Johann Heyszl   Fraunhofer AISEC, Germany
Naofumi Homma   Tohoku University, Japan

Dirmanto Jap	Nanyang Technological University, Singapore
Jens-Peter Kaps	George Mason University, USA
Elif Bilge-Kavun	University of Passau, Germany
Juliane Krämer	Technische Universität Darmstadt, Germany
Victor Lomne	NinjaLab, France
Patrick Longa	Microsoft Research, USA
Stefan Mangard	Technische Universität Graz, Austria
Nele Mentens	Leiden University, The Netherlands, and KU Leuven, Belgium
Debdeep Mukhopadhyay	IIT Kharagpur, India
Zakaria Najm	Nanyang Technological University, Singapore
Ralph Nyberg	Infineon Technologies, Germany
Colin O'Flynn	NewAE Technology Inc., Canada
Daniel Page	University of Bristol, UK
Stjepan Picek	Technische Universität Delft, The Netherlands
Chester Rebeiro	Indian Institute of Technology Madras, India
Georg Sigl	Technische Universität München, Germany
François-Xavier Standaert	Université Catholique de Louvain, Belgium
Marc Stöttinger	Hessen3C, Germany
Ruggero Susella	STMicroelectronics, Italy
Wen Wang	Yale University, USA
Vittorio Zaccaria	Politecnico di Milano, Italy
Fan Zhang	Zhejiang University, China

Additional Reviewers

Anubhab Baksi
Debapriya Basu Roy
Anirban Chakraborty
Durba Chatterjee
Christoph Dobraunig
Zheng Gong
Mathieu Gross
Michael Gruber
Loïc Masure
Michael Meyer
Florian Mendel

Marcel Müller
Robert Primas
Martin Rehberg
Thomas Schamberger
Florian Sieck
Nikhilesh Singh
Sujoy Sinha Roy
Lars Tebelmann
Jean-Pierre Thibault
Jo Vliegen
Lennert Wouters

Presentation Abstracts

Introduction to OpenTitan – An Open-Source Silicon Root of Trust Project

Michael Tempelmeier(iD)

G+D Mobile Security GmbH, Prinzregentenstraße 159, 81677 München,
Germany
michael.tempelmeier@gi-de.com, mtemp@opentitan.org

Abstract. RISC-V architectures are gaining more and more attention in both academia and industry. Security tokens also gain more and more attention. While they make authentication more secure, some concerns about their trustworthiness and their secure implementation remain [1].

OpenTitan is the first open-source project that provides a free, open-source hardware reference implementation and guidelines to create silicon root of trust (RoT) chips. It is stewarded by lowRISC and the main contributing partners are: ETH Zürich, G+D Mobile Security, Google, Nuvoton, Western Digital and Seagate [2]. OpenTitan brings the well-known concepts of open source (cryptographic) software to hardware. It enables security through transparency as the cryptographic primitives can be audited by the public [3]. Thus, the cryptographic (hardware) strength is not based on security-by-obscurity.

OpenTitan can be used for various security applications, like an universal 2nd factor (U2F) authentication key, or a platform integrity module. Its security model ensures the trustworthy state of the chip throughout its complete life cycle. Changes in the state of the chip are configured via one time programmable (OTP) memory. Devices can be personalized with a cryptographic identity. It is ensured that changes in the ownership do not allow to read out the previous owner's credentials.

The standard hardware toplevel of OpenTitan features a RISC-V Ibex core, hardened against fault attacks; 512 kB eFlash, 64 kB SRAM, and 16 kB ROM; an AES and Keccak module, protected by first order domain-oriented masking and hardened against fault attacks; the OpenTitan big-number accelerator (OTBN) for asymmetric cryptography; and various other (security) components which enable OpenTitan to be a full self-sustainable security IC. On the software side, OpenTitan features a reference implementation of the secure boot system, software that runs on the OTBN, as well as host software to communicate with the OpenTitan chip.

The cryptographic research community is encouraged to contribute to OpenTitan by analyzing the design early in its design stages. The industry can built their own chips based on OpenTitan, but also contributing hardware IPs to the project. FPGA prototyping can be done on a Xilinx Kintex 7 XC7K410T FPGA like provided by the ChipWhisperer CW310 board, as well as on a Xilinx Artix 7 XC7A200T FPGA like provided by the Nexys Video board. However the latter requires a reduced flash size. Dedicate build scripts for both target boards are provided. Software debugging can be done in a verilator simulation or on the FPGA using openocd and gdb.

Keywords: OpenTitan · RISC-V · open-source hardware · RoT

References

1. Schink, M., Wagner, A., Unterstein, F., Heyszl, J.: Security and trust in open source security tokens. IACR Trans. Cryptogr. Hardw. Embedd. Syst. (3), 176–201 (2021). https://doi.org/10.46586/tches.v2021.i3.176-201
2. OpenTitan project page. https://opentitan.org/
3. OpenTitan Source Code. https://github.com/lowRISC/opentitan

Is Revolutionary Hardware for Fully Homomorphic Encryption Important? What Else is Needed?

Charlotte Bonte[1], Rosario Cammarota[1], Wei Dai[5], Joshua Fryman[1],
Huijing Gong[1], Duhyeong Kim[1], Raghavan Kumar[1], Kim Laine[5],
Poornima Lalwaney[1], Sanu Mathew[1], Nojan Sheybani[1,3],
Anand Rajan[1], Andrew Reinders[1], Michael Steiner[1], Vikram Suresh[1],
Sachin Taneja[1], Marc Trifan[1,2], Alexander Viand[1,4], Wei Wang[5],
Wen Wang[1], Chris Wilkerson[1], Jin Yang[1]

[1] Intel Corp, USA
[2] University of California, Irvine, USA
[3] University of California, San Diego, USA
[4] ETH Zurich, Switzerland
[5] Microsoft, USA
rosario.cammarota@intel.com

Abstract. In spite of strong advances in confidential computing technologies, critical information is encrypted only temporarily – while not in use – and remains unencrypted during computation in most present-day computing infrastructures. The inability to keep critical information encrypted during computation can hinder the ability to fully share data and extract its maximum value.

Fully Homomorphic Encryption (FHE) is a cryptographic method to protect information confidentiality by enabling the processing of encrypted data without decrypting. However, the application of FHE carries a severe "performance tax" that is difficult to overcome with existing hardware.

The need for revolutionary hardware to enable FHE applications was identified by DARPA in the context of the DPRIVE program. As part of the DPRIVE program execution, Intel and Microsoft are realizing a platform to make FHE technologies more accessible by developing revolutionary hardware and software stack. Furthermore, the team is committed to the development of international standards and best practices. Overall, the initiative can enable unprecedented, cost-effective FHE performance, and pave the path for industrial deployment.

Keywords: Cryptographic hardware · Fully homomorphic encryption · Standards

Fully Homomorphic Encryption for all

Protecting the confidentiality of critical information—whether personal data or corporate intellectual property—is of strategic importance to businesses. In spite of the strong advances in trusted execution environments and other confidential computing technologies to protect data while at rest and in transit, data is unencrypted during computation. It is during this decrypted state that data can become more vulnerable to misuse, and third-party data leakage can incur severe fines for data handlers.

Fully Homomorphic Encryption (FHE) enables users to delegate computation to the cloud by enabling the cloud to process users' inputs while they remain encrypted and return encrypted output to the intended recipients. However, the adoption of FHE by industry has been slow. First, in spite of the tremendous advances in FHE, processing encrypted data still incurs a significant "performance tax" even for simple operations (ciphertext operations can be several orders of magnitude slower than clear text operations on existing hardware). Second, there is lack of automation tools for translating data and applications to enable FHE [1]. Third, the absence of international standards and best practices (including risk management tools) for secure and correct FHE deployment complicates the endorsement of FHE-based solutions [2].

The DARPA DPRIVE program [3] is the first publicly visible program that aims to build a hardware platform to enable continuous data protection with FHE, and to forge a path to commercialization intercepting segments such as healthcare, finance, communication (5G to XG), and cloud computing. Under the DPRIVE program, Intel is designing an application-specific integrated circuit (ASIC) accelerator to reduce the "performance tax" currently associated with FHE. Intel is collaborating with Microsoft to deliver a complete solution [4]. The design includes flexible arithmetic circuits for algebraic lattices with unprecedented vector parallelism capacity, to dramatically improve ciphertext computation speed, coupled with near-memory computation, to reduce data movement. The software stack will leverage the Microsoft SEAL library augmented with bootstrapping [5], and automatic translation tools to explore trade-offs in algorithmic optimization and data encoding to fit the performance requirements [6].

When fully realized, the accelerator can deliver a massive improvement in executing FHE workloads over existing CPU-driven systems, potentially reducing ciphertext processing time by five orders of magnitude. But the development of technology alone is not nearly enough to enable FHE for all. The team works with international standards bodies to develop standards and best practices for FHE usage. It continues to engage in academic research world-wide [7], including FHE cryptography, automation and risk management tools, next generation computer architecture such as in-memory compute.

References

1. Agrawal, et al.: Exploring Design and Governance Challenges in the Development of Privacy-Preserving Computation. arXiv:2101.08048
2. Cammarota, et al.: Trustworthy AI Inference Systems: An Industry Research View. arXiv:2008.04449

3. Building Hardware to Enable Continuous Data Protection. https://www.darpa.mil/news-events/2020-03-02)
4. Intel to Collaborate with Microsoft on DARPA program. https://www.intel.com/content/www/us/en/newsroom/news/intel-collaborate-microsoft-darpa-program.html
5. Microsoft SEAL. https://github.com/microsoft/SEAL
6. Viand, et al.: Fully Homomorphic Encryption Compilers. arXiv:2101.07078
7. Private AI Collaborative Research Institute. https://www.private-ai.org/

Post-quantum Cryptography
with Contemporary Co-processors

Kronecker, Schönhage-Strassen, Nussbaumer and Beyond

Joppe W. Bos, Joost Renes and Christine van Vredendaal
NXP Semiconductors
{joppe.bos,joost.renes,christine.cloostermans}@nxp.com

Abstract. There are currently over 30 billion IoT (Internet of Things) devices installed worldwide. To secure these devices from various threats one usually relies on public-key cryptographic primitives whose operations can be costly to compute on resource-constrained IoT devices. To support such operations these devices often include a dedicated co-processor for cryptographic procedures, typically in the form of a big integer arithmetic unit. Such existing arithmetic co-processors do not offer the functionality that is expected by upcoming post-quantum cryptographic primitives. Regardless, contemporary systems may exist in the field for many years to come. We discuss how to re-use existing hardware for post-quantum cryptography, and in particular how this applies to the various finalists in the post-quantum standardization effort led by NIST.

Analyzing the Harmfulness of Glitches in the Context of Side-Channel Analysis

Sylvain Guilley[ID] and Sofiane Takarabt

[1] Secure-IC S.A.S., 104 Boulevard du Montparnasse (7th floor), 75014 Paris, France
{sylvain.guilley,sofiane.takarabt}@secure-ic.com

1 Introduction

Hiding and masking are two countermeasure strategies to protect hardware circuits against power and electromagnetic analyses. However, those protections are complex to implement correctly. Hiding requires perfect balancing, and masking shall take into consideration glitches.

In this presentation, we present a tool which allows to detect harmful glitches in a combinational netlist.

2 Analyzing Glitches

Glitches are transient transitions occurring in netlists owing to the property of combinational netlist to evaluate the output as soon as any input arrives. It is known that glitches can occur upon non-linear conditions on the inputs hence can demask otherwise perfectly masked netlists. Therefore, glitches can induce a first-order leakage despite all nets are (statically) perfectly masked, as it has already been demonstrated several times (e.g., on Canright masked S-Box [1] or on ISW scheme [3]).

Managing glitches has been the topic of many researches. For instance, "threshold implementation" and "domain-oriented masking" aim at making glitches harmless by design. Combinational logic "pipelining" or implementation in "look-up-tables" allows to remove glitches.

But to the best of our knowledge, no tool to diagnose glitches has been demonstrated. Still, it is possible to classify glitches as either harmless or harmful, typically using leakage spectral decomposition [2].

The theoretical tool is the mutation of the netlist, which consists in inserting an artificial edge (modeling a delay in a wire/gate). This modified netlist is analyzed in terms of sensitivity with respect to the unmasked variable. The detection of glitches yielding a leakage can be speeded-up with adequate Walsh-transform spectral computations [5].

3   Automated Analysis with Catalyzr Tool

In this talk, we recall such analyses, and show how it is implemented in a tool, namely Catalyzr [1]. We also validate this static analysis with real simulations, which attest of the concordance in the detection.

Let us recall that the methodology leveraged in the tool does not require timing assumptions (like the exact gate or interconnect delays), since it performs an exhaustive search amongst all possible glitching situations. In this respect, this approach allows for a constructive repair of netlists to remove harmful glitches (through iterative detection-repair cycles).

References

1. Canright, D.: A very compact S-box for AES. In: Rao, J.R., Sunar, B., (eds.) CHES 2005. LNCS, vol. 3659, pp. 441–455. Springer, Heidelberg (2005). https://doi.org/10.1007/11545262_32

2. Guilley, S., Heuser, A., Ming, T., Rioul, O.: Stochastic side-channel leakage analysis via orthonormal decomposition. In: Farshim, P., Simion, E., (eds.) SecITC 2017. LNCS, vol. 10543, pp. 12–27. Springer, Cham (2017). https://doi.org/10.1007/978-3-319-69284-5_2

3. Roy, D.B., Bhasin, S., Guilley, S., Danger, J.-L., Mukhopadhyay, D.: From theory to practice of private circuit: A cautionary note. In: 33rd IEEE International Conference on Computer Design, ICCD 2015, New York City, NY, USA, October 18-21, 2015, pp. 296–303. IEEE Computer Society (2015)

4. Secure-IC. Catalyzr tool, 2021. https://cadforassurance.org/tools/software-assurance/catalyzr/, https://www.secure-ic.com/solutions/catalyzr/. Accessed 2 July 2021

5. Takarabt, S., Guilley, S., Souissi, Y., Sauvage, L., Mathieu, Y., Karray, K.: Formal evaluation and construction of glitch-resistant masked functions. In: 2021 IEEE International Symposium on Hardware Oriented Security and Trust, HOST 2021, Washington DC, USA, 12–15 December 2021. IEEE (2021)

Keynotes

Securing the Next Trillion of Chips via In-Memory and Immersed-in-Logic Design – Beyond Traditional Design Boundaries

Massimo Alioto

ECE - National University of Singapore
massimo.alioto@nus.edu.sg, malioto@ieee.org

Abstract. Divide-and-conquer design methodologies facilitate building block design, but conflict with basic security requirements, while also precluding opportunities for efficient system integration and inexpensive embedment of security features. Indeed, conventional design partitioning vastly facilitates the identification of attack targets, and reduces the related effort by focusing on specific areas of the overall attack surface. At the same time, the insertion of security primitives as standalone blocks is inherently additive in terms of area, power, design effort and integration effort, limiting their embeddability in low-cost devices (i.e., the vast majority of the upcoming trillion chips for the Internet of Things).

In this keynote, the road towards ubiquitous hardware security is pursued from a primitive design perspective, designing PUFs and TRNGs that are inherently immersed in existing memory arrays and logic fabrics, and breaking the boundaries of traditional system partitioning. From a non-recurring engineering cost viewpoint, design and system integration entail lower effort and very low silicon area thanks to extensive circuit reuse, while also facilitating technology and design portability. At the same time, their immersed and distributed nature offers inherent physical-level obfuscation against several physical attacks targeting specific primitive instances with well-defined boundaries and ports, while also allowing full reuse of conventional techniques to protect memories and logic. Stricter data locality also facilitates architecture-level security, confining secure keys within the same logic module that they are used in (e.g., within the same cryptographic engine, or within the same memory encrypting its own data). Several silicon demonstrations are illustrated to quantify the benefits and the limits of existing techniques, and identify opportunities and challenges for the decade ahead. At the end of the keynote, fundamental directions on how to make hardware security more pervasive and unceasing are discussed.

Biography: Massimo Alioto (M'01–SM'07–F'16) received the MSc degree in Electronics Engineering and the Ph.D. degree in Electrical Engineering from the University of Catania (Italy) in 1997 and 2001. He is currently a Professor at the Department of Electrical and Computer Engineering, National University of Singapore, where he leads the Green IC group, and is the Director of the Integrated Circuits and Embedded Systems area, and the FD-FAbrICS research center at NUS. Previously, he held positions at the University of Siena, Intel Labs – CRL (2013), University of Michigan Ann Arbor (2011–2012), BWRC – University of California, Berkeley (2009–2011), and EPFL (Switzerland, 2007).

He has authored or co-authored more than 300 publications on journals and conference proceedings. He is author of four books, including Enabling the Internet of Things - from Circuits to Systems (Springer, 2017), and the latest on Adaptive Digital Circuits for Power-Performance Range beyond Wide Voltage Scaling (Springer, 2020). His primary research interests include self-powered wireless integrated systems, near-threshold circuits for green computing, widely energy-scalable integrated systems, data-driven integrated systems, hardware security, and emerging technologies, among the others.

He is the Editor in Chief of the IEEE Transactions on VLSI Systems (2019–2020), and was the Deputy Editor in Chief of the IEEE Journal on Emerging and Selected Topics in Circuits and Systems (2018). In 2020–2022 he is Distinguished Lecturer of the IEEE Solid-State Circuits Society. In 2009–2010 he was Distinguished Lecturer of the IEEE Circuits and Systems Society, for which he is/was also member of the Board of Governors (2015–2020), and Chair of the "VLSI Systems and Applications" Technical Committee (2010–2012). He served as Guest Editor of several IEEE journal special issues, and Associate Editor of a number of IEEE and ACM journals. He is/was Technical Program Chair and Track Chair in a number of IEEE conferences (e.g., ISCAS 2023, SOCC, ICECS), and is currently in the IEEE "Digital architectures and systems" ISSCC subcommittee, and the ASSCC TPC. Prof. Alioto is an IEEE Fellow.

Defending CyberPhysical Systems and Infrastructures from Cyber Attacks

Alberto Sangiovanni-Vincentelli

University of California Berkeley
alberto@berkeley.edu

Abstract. Attacks against critical infrastructure such gas pipelines, power generation and water treatment plants, as well as against cars and airplanes are very possible and may create disruptions that we can only start imagining. The talk frames the problem and describes the industrial landscape in this domain.

Short Bio

Alberto Sangiovanni Vincentelli is the Edgar L. and Harold H. Buttner Chair of Electrical Engineering and Computer Sciences at the University of California, Berkeley. In 2001, he received the Kaufman Award for his pioneering contributions to EDA from the Electronic Design Automation Consortium. In 2011, he was awarded the IEEE/RSE Maxwell Medal "for groundbreaking contributions that have had an exceptional impact on the development of electronics and electrical engineering or related fields". He co-founded Cadence and Synopsys, listed in NASDAQ with market cap of over 90 Billion USD. He presently serves on the Board of Directors of Cadence Design Systems Inc., KPIT Technologies, Expert.ai, Cy4Gate (Public companies), and is the Chair of the Board of Quantum Motion, Phoelex, Innatera, and Phononic Vibes. He consulted for Intel, HP, TI, ST Microelectronics, Mercedes, BMW, Magneti Marelli, Telecom Italia, United Technologies, Camozzi Group, Pirelli, General Motors, UniCredit, and UnipolSAI. He is also serving as member of the Advisory Board of the Politecnico di Milano, and as Chairman of the International Advisory Council and of the Strategy Board of MIND (Milano Innovation District). He is a member of the United States National Academy of Engineering, an IEEE and ACM Fellow. He received an honorary Doctorate from Aalborg University (Denmark) and one from KTH (Sweden). He has published more than 1000 papers and 19 books.

Contents

Post-quantum Cryptography

Physical Unclonable Functions

Side-Channel Analysis

SideLine: How Delay-Lines (May) Leak Secrets from Your SoC

Joseph Gravellier[1]([✉]), Jean-Max Dutertre[1], Yannick Teglia[2],
and Philippe Loubet Moundi[2]

[1] Mines Saint-Etienne, CEA-Tech, Centre CMP, Gardanne, France
{joseph.gravellier,dutertre}@emse.fr
[2] Thales, La Ciotat, France
{yannick.teglia,philippe.loubet-moundi}@thalesgroup.com

Abstract. To meet the ever-growing need for performance in silicon devices, SoC providers have been increasingly relying on software-hardware cooperation. By controlling hardware resources such as power or clock management from the software, developers earn the possibility to build more flexible and power efficient applications. Despite the benefits, these hardware components are now exposed to software code and can potentially be misused as open-doors to new kind of attacks. In this work, we introduce *SideLine*, a novel side-channel vector based on delay-line components widely implemented in high-end SoCs. We demonstrate that these entities can be used to perform remote power side-channel attacks and we detail several attack scenarios in which an adversary process located in one processor core aims at eavesdropping the activity of a victim process located in another core. For each scenario, we demonstrate the adversary ability to fully recover the secret key of an AES algorithm running in the victim core. Even more detrimental, we show that these attacks are still practicable when a rich operating system is used.

1 Introduction

The need for direct physical access to a target to perform a hardware attack was recently proved obsolete. Software-exposed hardware mechanisms implemented to improve SoC performance or power consumption were shown to be susceptible to remote hijacking by attackers seeking to perform fault injection or Side-Channel Attacks (SCAs).

Since 2014, and the *Rowhammer* vulnerability's disclosure [14], the remote attack threat has become prevalent in hardware security researches. As a matter of fact, the influx of connected devices associated with the multiplication of cloud services offers a new playing field for attackers. Moreover, despite the appearance of trusted entities (ARM TrustZone, Intel SGX) that testify a growing need for SoC security, the hardware threat remains underestimated.

Between 2014 and today, *Rowhammer* capability evolved from random bit flips generation to privilege escalation on remote devices [12,17,32].

© Springer Nature Switzerland AG 2021
S. Bhasin and F. De Santis (Eds.): COSADE 2021, LNCS 12910, pp. 3–30, 2021.
https://doi.org/10.1007/978-3-030-89915-8_1

Meanwhile, the *CLKSCREW* exploit demonstrated that power and clock glitch attacks can be launched from within an ARM SoC using software programmable voltage-frequency regulators [28]. Recently, this attack was improved [24] and deployed on Intel SGX devices [13,21]. From a side-channel point of view, two novel families of remote attacks have been introduced. On the one hand, micro-architectural timing attacks with *Meltdown-Spectre* [15,19], *Foreshadow* (SGX) [29] and more recently *MDS* exploits [5,30]. These attacks leverage speculative and out-of-order execution in modern processors to steal secret data from victim processes. On the other hand, remote power SCAs have been introduced through several works on FPGA devices. Through the implementation of sensors inside a multi-user FPGA fabric, it was demonstrated that an adversary can eavesdrop the activity of the other users [26]. More recently, remote power SCAs have been extended to microcontroller devices using the ADCs they embed [10,22] and to Intel devices using the RAPL interface [18]. This spreads further the threats posed by remote SCAs from FPGA fabrics to general purpose microcontrollers as those found in usual connected devices.

In this paper we introduce *SideLine*, a novel side-channel vector based on the intentional misuse of hardware resources available in high-end SoC devices. *SideLine* leverages delay-lines components embedded in SoCs that use external memory; it neither requires embedded reconfigurable logic (FPGA) nor analog circuitry (ADC). Two delay-line blocks namely *delay-locked-loop* and programmable *delay-block* are hijacked to perform voltage measurements and maliciously used to conduct power SCAs on application processors (AP) and micro-controllers units (MCU). *SideLine* makes it possible for an attacker to perform software-induced hardware attacks without direct physical access to the target. Our contributions are listed below:

- We reveal that delay-line-based components available in a broad range of SoCs that employ external memories can be turned into power consumption measurement units.
- We describe three attacker-victim (core-vs-core) delay-line-based SCA scenarios over two SoC devices: **AP-vs-AP** attack (on a Xilinx Zynq 7000 SoC), **AP-vs-MCU** attack and **MCU-vs-AP** attack (on a STMicroelectronics STM32MP1 SoC) where AP and MCU respectively denote the application processor and the microcontroller.
- For each scenario a correlation power analysis attack is conducted against the publicly available OpenSSL AES encryption algorithm and the full secret key is successfully recovered. The attack feasibility is demonstrated on bare metal and Linux OS-based applications.

Responsible Disclosure: We responsibly disclosed our findings to Xilinx on September 22th, 2020 and STMicroelectronics on November 2nd, 2020. Both acknowledged and agreed on the publication of these results. Moreover, this disclosure led to a close collaboration with these companies to find and build efficient countermeasures against *SideLine* and similar attacks. Please keep in mind that

SideLine has been performed on these two processors for demonstration purposes but the concept is generic and any devices that embed delay-lines can be affected.

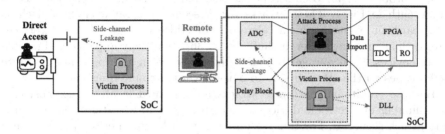

Fig. 1. On the left, local power SCA uses voltage probes to eavesdrop a leakage from a victim process. On the right, remote power SCA leverages the target's resources to monitor the victim process leakage without requiring physical access.

Outline: The remainder of this paper is organized as follows. In Sect. 2, we provide background information on power SCAs and describe the state-of-the-art. In Sect. 3, we introduce delay-lines and their applications in SoC devices. Then, we present the tested products and the associated threat model in Sect. 4. Sections 5 and 6 are dedicated to the deployment of the three attack scenarios. Finally, we discuss performance, limitations, countermeasures in Sect. 7 and conclude in Sect. 8.

2 Background

This section reminds the general side-channel background, the techniques recently introduced to monitor on-chip voltage fluctuations and the related works.

2.1 Power Side-Channel Attacks

A power SCA makes use of transistors switching activity leakage through power consumption variations to collect information about the processes running inside a device. Thanks to the correlation that exists between this leakage and the processed data, an attacker may try to launch an SCA to recover secret data or cryptographic keys from a target. Traditional power SCAs monitor the voltage variations induced by a device through a resistor attached to its power pads [16]. Simply by analysing the collected traces, an attacker can visually speculate on the different instructions executed by the target using a so-called Simple Power Analysis (SPA [16]) attack. Such SPA was proved effective to recover the private key used by asymmetric encryption algorithms like RSA or ECC [31]. Differential Power Analysis [16] and Correlation Power Analysis (CPA) [3] use statistical tools to infer secret keys by correlating guessed leakage hypotheses with a set of experimental traces.

Traditionally, power SCAs are carried out locally, in laboratories, using a voltage probe and an oscilloscope as depicted by the direct physical access attack path in Fig. 1. These attacks target secure integrated circuits, such as smart cards or cryptographic accelerators embedded in SoCs. SCA countermeasures such as masking, jitter or shuffling [34, 36] are usually implemented in such secure devices. It encourages the use of high resolution and high sampling rate oscilloscopes on the attacker side to outperform the countermeasures.

Because traditional hardware attacks are assumed local and expensive, a large number of electronic devices are not prepared to withstand remote hardware attack scenarios. For this reason, even with limited performances, digital and analog integrated sensors may manage to jeopardize the security of devices ranging from IoT components to cloud servers (remote access in Fig. 1). With the advent of these software-induced hardware attacks that do not require either direct physical access to the target or specific equipment, the alleged hardware attack limitations are called into question or even removed.

2.2 On-Chip Voltage Sensing

Two families of sensors enable malicious on-chip voltage sensing: either delay sensors built with digital logic gates which aim at measuring fluctuations in the power consumption through delay variations [37, 38], or analog sensors using ADCs usually embedded in MCUs [10, 22]. Until this work, digital sensors dedicated to SCAs have been exclusively implemented in FPGAs. Their available programmable logic makes it possible to design and tune such delay sensors in order to measure the power consumption of a device. We describe hereafter the principles of these delay sensors as their working principle is similar to the delay-line components we used.

Delay-based voltage sensors leverage a side-effect of voltage fluctuations over digital logic behavior, which is the relationship between the time taken by a signal to propagate through a digital logic gate and the on-chip voltage level. An increase of the gate's power supply translates into a shortening of its propagation delay, and respectively a reduction of the voltage induces its increase [9]. As a result, measuring the variations of the logic gates propagation delay provides an image of their voltage supply variations. Temperature and capacitive effects also play a significant part in its equation [9]. Unlike voltage, the propagation delay can be directly measured using digital logic. Commonly used FPGA-based sensors are the Ring-Oscillator (RO [37]) and the Time-to-Digital Converters (TDC [26]).

2.3 Related Works

In 2018, Schellenberg et al. demonstrated that FPGA-based sensors were precise enough to be used for SCAs on public and secret cryptographic algorithms [26]. To enable this attack, the adversary (a TDC-based delay sensor and its

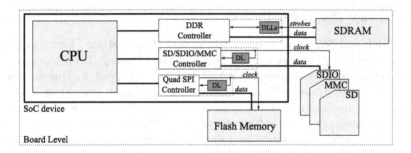

Fig. 2. Typical SoC connectivity with external memories. Delay-lines are implemented to synchronize clock and data signals arrival in the memory controllers.

control logic for power supply measurement) and the victim (an AES hardware encryption block) needed to be located within the same FPGA. We define it as an **FPGA-to-FPGA** attack. The associated threat model targets multi-user FPGA cloud services that may appear over the next few years [6]. The same year, Zhao et al. disclosed that power SCAs can be conducted on heterogeneous platforms that include both an application processor and an FPGA fabric on the same silicon die. As a proof of concept, they were able to successfully retrieve the secret key of a custom RSA implementation running within a CPU core [35]. To do so, they carried out an SPA attack using RO-based voltage sensors implemented in the FPGA fabric.

Until 2019, remote power SCA remained bounded to FPGA devices or heterogeneous SoCs embedding an FPGA fabric as its flexibility allowed the implementation of powerful sensors. Two works went beyond the FPGA by proving that on-chip power SCAs can be carried out in microcontroller devices [10,22]. These attacks use ADCs as a straightforward way to measure on-chip power supply level. Thanks to a leakage of the chip power consumption into this analog block, the ADC can substitute the voltage probe role. Even with an extremely limited sampling rate, this noise sampling method was successful in retrieving the secret keys used by real world software and hardware AES cryptographic libraries.

3 Delay-Lines in High-End SoC Devices

Delay-line-based sensors were previously used in FPGA devices as a way to monitor chip power consumption (TDC sensor). Despite offering great performance, these sensors were limited to configurable logic which is rarely integrated in SoC devices. In this section, we disclose that digital and analog delay-lines are widely implemented in SoC memory controllers. We present them and discuss their potential use as voltage sensors (delay sensors).

3.1   Memory Controller Basics

Because high-end SoCs are designed to run operating systems (Linux, Android, etc.), they require a large amount of Non-Volatile Memory (NVM) to store the OS and Random-Access-Memory (RAM) to efficiently load it. Due to technological constraints, these SoCs do not embed a significant amount of RAM nor NVM memory but are rather interconnected with external memories (memory cards, Flash memory, SDRAM memory, etc.). Thus, depending on the form-factor, speed and memory size constraints, designers can choose between a wide range of external memory devices. A typical scenario of a SoC using external memories is depicted in Fig. 2.

Several memory controllers are required to interface the SoC with its external memories. Each memory controller acts as a request arbiter, a transaction scheduler and as a physical interface to manage data flowing from the SoC to the memory, and vice-versa. In embedded systems, for cost and efficiency reasons, the memory controller is more likely to be directly integrated as a part of the SoC. At the edge of the memory controller, a physical controller (dotted lines in Fig. 2) outputs and captures the signals that will flow between the SoC I/Os and the memory device I/Os (clock, data, configuration signals, etc.). The physical controller also ensures that these signals arrive on time regardless of the interconnection tracks length on the PCB, the voltage and the temperature variations. To better understand the extent of memory signal propagation timings, we draw a simple example of SoC/Synchronous Dynamic-RAM (SDRAM) association. When a read operation is initiated by the SoC, the external SDRAM memory outputs the requested data edge-aligned with a clock signal (strobe) later dedicated to data sampling. Depending on the PCB tracks length, the clock signal is likely to shift ahead of the data signals, leading then to a sampling error. To mitigate this effect, the SoC physical controller implements delay-line-based components (delay-locked-loop *DLL* and programmable delay-block *DL* in Fig. 2) to calibrate the phase alignment between the sampling clock and the data signals. This calibration can be manual and made once and for all after testing at manufacturing or performed at each chip power-up. It can also be adjusted dynamically to counterbalance any misalignment due to power supply or temperature fluctuations.

The relationship between the delay applied and the SoC voltage fluctuations drew our interest. In the following paragraphs, we present two different delay-line-based mechanisms that can be used to generate these delays for low and high-bandwidth external memory applications.

3.2   Delay-Blocks in Low-Bandwidth Memory Controllers

In relatively low-bandwidth external memories such as Flash memories, SD cards and multimedia cards, the impact of voltage and temperature fluctuations is considered not significant enough to jeopardize the communication integrity: dynamic calibration is not required. Delay-lines are nonetheless used to mitigate the impact of the PCB track length on the data and clock signals propagation

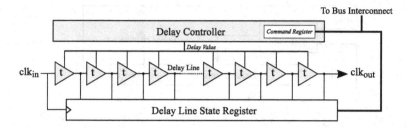

Fig. 3. An example of delay-block used in low-bandwidth memory controllers.

timings (these delays are not predictable by SoC designers, they are set only at board design time). As track lengths are fixed, a static delay is sufficient to ensure good operation. For a read transaction, the delay-line is typically calibrated in order to add a phase shift of 90° to the clock signal. Thus, it ensures that data signals are in place when sampling occurs. The delay-line calibration is carried out through a series of training steps. These training steps modify the delay of the elements forming the chain and, for each configuration, verify if the external memory has been properly read. If the training is successful, the delay-line configuration is saved in a dedicated register and remains unchanged until the next test.

Several SoC vendors provide user programmable delay-blocks as a way for developers to be able to use a wide range of memory chips or cards with different bus speeds. Unlike traditional static delay-lines, these delay-blocks come with both a complete calibration toolkit and a detailed documentation. Figure 3 illustrates the delay-block structure that was observed in one of the SoC we benchmarked. Its purpose is to delay the clock signal with respect to the data signals when a read operation is conducted. The block consists in a simple delay-line associated with a set of control and status registers. A *Command Register* controls the delay t of all the delay-line elements and thus the phase shift added to the clk signal. To ensure that the phase shift obtained is conform to the applied command, a *state register* captures the output of each element forming the delay-line every time a clk_{in} rising edge event occurs. Then, a specific training is performed to verify whether the captured pattern matches the command or not.

Despite some missing parts, this structure is reminiscent of that of a TDC as the delay-line state is continuously captured and stored in an accessible register. In Sect. 6, we demonstrate that this delay-block can be turned into a voltage sensor and hijacked to perform a power SCA.

3.3 DLLs in High-Bandwidth Memory Controllers

Because of the continuous increasing in memory bus speeds, the available slack time for data sampling is gradually shrinking. Double data rate memories (DDR) such as SDRAM memory perform one data transfer per clock edge (both rising and falling) while reaching gigahertz frequencies [25]. On these devices, the data

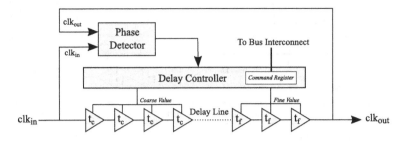

Fig. 4. An example of delay-locked-loop used in DDR memory controllers.

sampling is very likely to get corrupted by temperature and voltage variations. This time, a static delay source is not suitable to ensure correct operations. To effectively cancel voltage and temperature noise side-effects, a dynamic way to adapt the clock delay has to be considered.

Delay Locked Loops (DLLs) are generally used in recent DDR memory controllers to dynamically track and control the phase shift applied between the sampling clock and the external memory (e.g. SDRAM) data signals [2,7]. As illustrated in Fig. 4, a DLL has two main blocks: a delay-line, and a feedback circuit. The delay-line is calibrated to provide a phase shift to a *clk* signal using both *coarse* and *fine* delay elements. However, the propagation delay jitter associated with on-chip voltage and temperature fluctuations is likely to skew the applied phase. This is why a DLL includes a feedback circuit to tune the delay-line in order to provide a dynamic control of the phase shift and thus, counterbalance voltage and temperature variations. The feedback circuit comes with a phase detector that compares the phase shift between the clock signal at the input of the delay-line, clk_{in}, and its phase-shifted clock output, clk_{out}. Then, according to the measured error, a delay controller applies a correction in order to "deskew" the result, that is, to get back to the initial delay. The applied correction modifies the delay of the elements forming the delay-line and can be either analog or digital-controlled depending on the delay-line type [1].

A *command register* stores the delay settings, it is memory-mapped and hence can be read from the SoC AP or MCU cores. The DLL operates autonomously, this means that through a simple access to this register, a process can retrieve the state of the DLL, which shall be correlated to on-chip voltage and temperature variations. As a result, tracking the *command register* content shall provide an image of the SoC power consumption that may be used to carry out SCAs. Note that this measurement methodology (tracking the command of a feedback dynamically controlled system) differs from that described in Sect. 3.2 for delay-blocks (sampling a clock signal propagating inside a fixed delay-line). If this unusual measurement medium provides enough resolution and sampling rate to eavesdrop power consumption of secure applications running on a processor, this could represent an important backdoor for computer security. This hypothetical vulnerability is strengthened by the fact that this attack only requires a read access to the command register, no configuration steps are required. This attack scenario is developed in Sect. 5.

4   Experimental Setup

4.1   Tested Devices

Two devices from two different SoC providers have been studied in our experiments. The first target considered in this work is a Xilinx Zynq-7000 SoC [33] that comes with a dual-core Cortex-A9 application processor (AP). It is a typical multi-purpose SoC providing many additional resources: FPGA, I/O, ADCs, bus controllers, etc. It supports DDR2-DDR3, Flash and SD/MMC external memories and provides several DLL blocks to interface properly with DDR external memories. The experiments made on this target have been conducted without using an OS: we denote it as a **bare metal attack**. This configuration makes SCA easier as there are fewer interruptions (with respect to the case in which an OS is used) that may disturb the attack and victim processes and cause synchronization issues. The entire Zynq-based *SideLine* attack code can be cloned from GitHub: https://github.com/Remote-HWA/SideLine_Zynq.

The second target is a STMicroelectronics STM32MP157C-DK2 development board [20] that embeds a dual-core Cortex-A7 AP associated with a Cortex-M processor (MCU). It also supports DDR2-DDR3, Flash and SD/MMC external memories and embeds several DLL blocks. Additionally, it provides user programmable delay-blocks (DLYB [20]) that can be employed for interfacing low bandwidth memory (e.g. an SD card). These programmable delay-blocks are the second case we studied. The experiments done on this SoC have been carried out with a Linux OS running on its AP (i.e. the Cortex-A7 processor). The results are those of a **Linux OS attack**. The entire STM32MP1-based *SideLine* attack code can be cloned from GitHub: https://github.com/Remote-HWA/SideLine_STM32MP1.

4.2   OpenSSL AES Architecture

The OpenSSL library [23] provides several cryptographic algorithms used for securing channels over computer networks. In this work, we focus on the OpenSSL AES-128 (version 1.1.1) that implements a 32-bit tabulated version of the textbook AES encryption algorithm [8]. This variant merges the `Mixcolumn` and `SubBytes` transformations into 4 pre-computed look-up tables known as T-tables (256×32-bit) as a way to optimize the computations on 32-bit processors.

4.3   Threat Model

In this work, we introduce three core-vs-core attack scenarios in order to assess the SCA capabilities of the delay-line-based sensors. For each scenario depicted in Fig. 5, we first deploy a cryptographic application (in green) within a processor

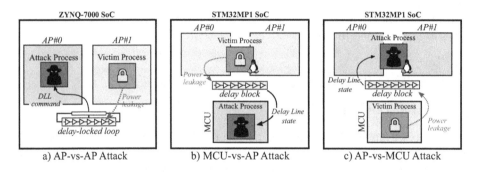

a) AP-vs-AP Attack   b) MCU-vs-AP Attack   c) AP-vs-MCU Attack

Fig. 5. Basic principle of the three core-vs-core attack variants proposed in this work. It shows the leakage path from the victim process to the delay sensor and the sensor data flow retrieved by the attack process. (Color figure online)

core. This application located either in the AP or in the MCU allows the end-user to launch AES encryptions/decryptions, with the plaintexts/ciphertexts that he provides. Secondly, we introduce a malicious user (in red) that has the privilege level necessary to access the delay-line blocks presented in Sect. 3 and that uses them to retrieve the leakage induced by the AES application.

Although not used in this research work, Trusted Execution Environment (TEE) and TrustZone [2] architecture stand as potential realistic targets for the delay-lines. TrustZone attacks from the normal-world to the secure-world have been widely covered in recent remote attack works [4,22,24,28]. However, from a side-channel point of view, the current TrustZone does not provide any countermeasures. Thus, the ability of an attacker to turn our feasibility attack into an end-to-end TrustZone attack is reasonably expected.

In the remainder of the paper, the three scenarios presented are referred to as:

1. A **DLL-based attack** (Fig. 5a), or AP-vs-AP attack, that demonstrates the ability of a DLL to serve as a power supply sensor suitable for a CPA attack against the AES algorithm. In this scenario, one core of the Zynq processor runs the AES victim application, while the second core executes the attack process (both victim and aggressor processes are C programs, in bare metal mode). The attacker code is in charge of collecting the leakage data of the AES. It does so by configuring the access to the DLL command register that makes it possible to sample its values during AES encryptions performed by the first core. The attacker core is also in charge of providing the plaintext to be ciphered by the victim process and to trigger both the encryption and readback of DLL states. This AP-vs-AP attack scenario is described in details in Sect. 5.
2. A first **Delay-Block-based attack** (Fig. 5b), or MCU-vs-AP attack, where the victim process is ran on the STM32MP1 AP (a C code AES running on top of a Linux OS) and the attack process is executed by the Cortex-M MCU (a C program, in bare metal mode). In this scenario the MCU is in charge of

calibrating and using a delay-block to eavesdrop the activity of the AP. This MCU-vs-AP attack scenario is addressed in Sect. 6.

3. A second **Delay-Block-based attack** (Fig. 5c), or AP-vs-MCU attack, that matches a typical state-of-the-art industrial case where the cryptographic and security operations of a SoC embedding AP cores are delegated to a less complex MCU core. In this scenario the AP core (Cortex-A7) runs the attack process while the MCU core (Cortex-M) runs the AES victim process. This AP-vs-MCU attack scenario is reported in Sect. 6.

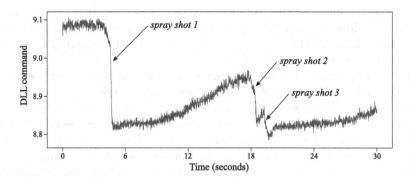

Fig. 6. DLL response to sudden temperature drops induced by three successive exposition of the SoC to a cooling spray.

5   DLL-Based Power Side-Channel Attack

This section presents a novel way to monitor on-chip voltage fluctuations and conduct power SCAs using the DLLs embedded in SoC memory controllers.

5.1   Validating DLL Effectiveness: *Monitoring Temperature*

As a proof of concept, a simple experiment was carried-out on the Zynq SoC to confirm that the DLL command is actually tracking the SoC package temperature variations. The test uses a C program designed to continuously read and store the DLL command register content into an acquisition array for a period of 30 s. Simultaneously, a cooling spray was used at specific moments to cool down the SoC package. To limit the acquisition size, each array index contains the average of 1,000 successive DLL readings. Figure 6 reports the evolution of the measured DLL command (y-axis) as a function of time (x-axis). Each spray shot induces a temperature drop (translated into a DLL command drop in Fig. 6) that progressively recovers until the next one. This simple experiment confirms that a DLL is suitable to dynamically track the SoC temperature variations. As the temperature decreases, the propagation speed of the *clk* signal through the delay-line increases [9]. Thus, the phase-shift between clk_{in} and clk_{out} progressively drifts. To counterbalance this effect, the DLL dynamically adapts its command in order to maintain a constant phase shift. Because package temperature evolves relatively slowly, the sampling frequency for this experiment was limited to 300 kHz. However, as this paper focuses on power side-channel, which itself depends on transient voltage drops measurements, a higher sampling rate needs to be achieved: it is the subject of the next Subsect. 5.2.

5.2   Improving Sampling Rate and Synchronisation Using DMA

As mentioned before, the DLL command value can be directly accessed through its memory address. Then, a loop associated with an array can be added to collect more samples. This CPU-based sampling method works in principle but has several drawbacks:

First, it requires a constant time between each acquisition. If this constant time is not achieved, the samples won't be correctly aligned. Consequently, statistical attacks will be less accurate as the averaging of several acquisitions will suffer from de-synchronisation. Achieving constant time is feasible in bare metal applications because they rarely suffer from interruptions. However, if the application runs over an OS, interrupts will dramatically affect the timing of acquisitions and make their averaging impossible. The second limitation is related to the achievable sampling rate. Indeed, the delay induced by CPU memory access plus the storage of the acquired data into an array is not optimal. Using this method on the Zynq SoC, the sampling frequency was limited to 2.2 MHz.

To solve these issues, we choose to use Direct Memory Access (DMA) in order to improve the sampling rate as well as the synchronisation of our samples (as proposed in [10]). A DMA is a hardware module able to transfer data from a peripheral to another without processor intervention. For this reason, it is faster in transmitting data, but also not affected by OS interrupts. The source address (address from which the DMA should sample the data) is the register containing the DLL command. The destination address (destination of the DMA transfer) is the base address of an array whose size depends on the number of samples required. At the end of the DMA transfer, an interrupt flag is set and ends the sampling process. With DMA up and running, we improved the DLL sampling frequency from 2.2 MHz to 16 MHz.

5.3   Bare Metal OpenSSL AES Attack Setup

According to the threat model we consider (see Subsect. 4.3), the attack process shall be able (1) to trigger the start of an AES encryption by the victim process, and (2) to control the gathering of the leakage from the AES through a DLL-based voltage sensor. Our test bench includes two processes (their pseudo codes are given in Appendix 1 and 2) executed by the two application cores of our target in bare metal mode: the attack process on AP#0 and the victim process on AP#1.

In addition to this attack setup, we used embedded hardware performance counters to precisely measure the duration of an AES encryption. On average, an encryption took 837 AP clock cycles or 1,25 μs at a frequency of 667 MHz (both attack and victim programs were compiled with the optimization parameter set to -O2). The DMA transfer method we used provides a constant 62.5 ns sampling period (i.e. a 16 MHz sampling frequency). As a result, 21 samples of the DLL command are gathered per AES encryption.

5.4   DLL-Based SCA Attack on Zynq SoC

The bottom part of Fig. 7 illustrates the results of two experiments conducted to assess the AES encryption impact on the DLL command value and precisely detect its encryption time window. The two traces depicted in black (1st case) and red (2nd case) represent the averaged DLL command value (y-axis) obtained for 1,000 acquisitions as a function of time (expressed in DMA samples). For the first experiment (in black), the victim program was kept idle during the entirety of the DMA sampling operations. The DLL command drop visible between sample 0 and 1,000 was induced by the extra power consumption linked to the DMA module activation. The DLL applied a strong correction to maintain a constant phase shift, that was finally relaxed as the power consumption returned to normal (sample 2,000 to the end of sampling). The second case (in red) reports

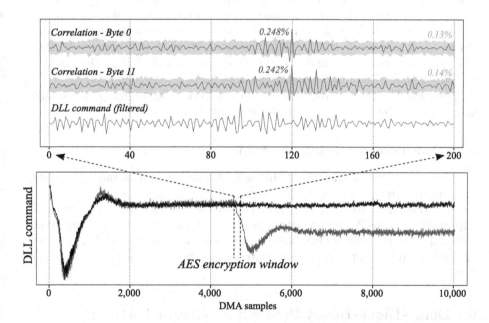

Fig. 7. DLL-based attack results: the bottom part represents the impact of an AES encryption on the DLL command value. The top part zooms on the AES encryption windows and provides the temporal correlation rate for two key bytes. (Color figure online)

an actual iteration of the attack and victim processes when an AES encryption is done. The red trace experienced the same DLL command undershoot due to DMA module activation (sample 0 to 1,000) but also a second undershoot corresponding to the AES encryption (starting at sample 4,500). It is finally restored to a steady value lower than the initial one (sample 6,000 to the end of sampling). The AES encryption window was deduced from the position of the second DLL command drop. Based on this information the CPA attack could be conducted on a smaller amount of samples.

We launched a total number of 20 million AES encryptions and acquired 200 DLL command samples per encryption. Samples and plaintexts extraction through UART took around 8 h at 921,600 bauds. Then, an external computer was used to apply post-processing to the traces and conduct the CPA attack. The top part of Fig. 7 depicts a filtered and averaged trace of the DLL command (in red). High-pass filtering was used as a way to reduce the impact of low frequency variations (induced for instance by temperature fluctuations) on the acquired traces and thus to reduce the number of traces required for the attack. Then, we performed a plaintext-based CPA attack on the first round of the AES. As we mentioned earlier the OpenSSL AES uses T-tables to upgrade its performances on 32-bit processors. This allows us to leverage a 32-bit T-tables output prediction: $HW[T_{table}(key \oplus plaintext)]$. The obtained correlation results versus the time are represented above the averaged trace in Fig. 7 (for two key bytes). The correct key hypotheses are depicted in red and emerge from the incorrect hypotheses (in grey) at sample 120. Based on 20 million encryptions, we achieved a full AES key recovery. 3 bytes were retrieved in the range 0–5M traces, 2 between 5–10M million, 5 between 10–15M an 4 between 15–20M. The key bytes number 7 and 9 never completely emerged from the incorrect candidates, but we assume that a simple brute force can be conducted to retrieve their values. The progressive correlation of the first 8 key bytes plus the failed byte #9 are depicted in Fig. 12 in the appendix.

5.5   Conclusion on DLL-Based SCA

In this section, we demonstrated that a DLL can be used to monitor on-chip temperature and power supply fluctuations. This unconventional voltage sensor was then used to conduct a power SCA on an OpenSSL AES algorithm implemented in the Zynq application processor and a full AES key recovery was achieved (with the help of brute force for the two remaining bytes). Performance, limitations and potential countermeasures regarding this attack are discussed in Sect. 7.

6   Delay-Block-Based Power Side-Channel Attack

The DLL-based attack presented in Sect. 5 was associated with the use of DDR external memories such as SDRAM in AP-based SoC. This section discloses a second attack path that allows the hijacking of a programmable delay-block and its malicious use to perform core-vs-core power SCAs. These experiments are conducted on the STM32MP1 SoC.

6.1 From Delay-Block to TDC Sensor

The STM32MP1 SoC comes with three programmable delay-blocks IPs (DLYB [20]) capable of working with different types of external memories (QSPI, SD, MMC). Their settings can be adjusted depending on the bus speeds of the external memories used. Their initial purpose is to adjust the phase of the clock signal in order to ensure a reliable exchange of data by tuning the clock delay.

The left part of Fig. 8 depicts the 12 elements delay-line provided by the STM32MP1 delay-block and the capture register designed to monitor the state of the output nodes of every delay element. When a clk_{in} rising edge occurs, the capture register takes a snapshot of the delay-line. This snapshot contains an image (represented as a waveform in Fig. 8) of the clock propagation through the delay-line. The propagation delay t of the elementary delay elements can be set using a dedicated register. If this delay is set to its minimum the delay-line width (acquisition window) is small. Thus, only a part of the clock signal can be captured. By gradually increasing t, the clock signal observation can be extended, possibly to several periods.

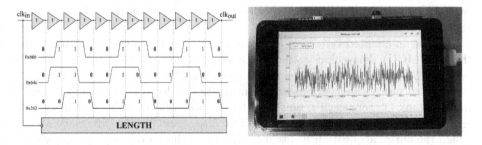

Fig. 8. Effect of on-chip voltage variations on the sampled delay values.

We leveraged this t parameter to make the delay-block sensitive to on-chip voltage fluctuations. To that end, we took a significant number of delay-line snapshots for each of the 128 possible t delay values. A vast majority of them gave stable results; which means that the captured image remained stable between successive register readings. For a few however, delay variations arose between subsequent captures. This interesting behavior can be explained by (1) on-chip voltage fluctuations that affect the clock propagation time through the delay elements, and (2) by the fact that several delay values t naturally position the clock edges in unstable places within the delay line (i.e. in between two delay elements). The left part of Fig. 8 displays three waveforms (delay-line snapshots) obtained with such a t setting. In this configuration, three clock periods stand in the entire delay line. From top to bottom we have: (1) the steady state register waveform which stands as our reference (it outputs a 0×666 reference value), (2) a slowed down waveform that can be obtained due to a supply voltage decrease (it outputs a $0 \times 64c$), and (3) an accelerated waveform that can be obtained due to a supply voltage increase (it outputs a 0×262). In our experiments, the three obtained hexadecimal digits are weighted and added to translate into an image of the voltage supply.

On the right part of Fig. 8, a program displays as an oscilloscope the actual delay-line state on the STM32MP1 touchscreen. This way, the actual power consumption noise impact on the delay-block state can be directly observed. To make it possible, the implemented program automatically calibrates the delay-block by testing various delay parameters. For each delay value, it collects multiple delay-line state samples, computes their variance and adopts the calibration that provided the highest variance. Indeed, a higher variance indicates an important delay instability and thus a stronger relationship with voltage fluctuations.

6.2   Linux-Based OpenSSL AES Attack Setup

Similarly to the attack setup described in Subsect. 5.3, we used the OpenSSL AES implementation to evaluate the threat posed by delay-block-based SCAs. The STM32MP1 embeds both a dual core AP and a MCU that makes it possible to test the MCU-vs-AP and AP-vs-MCU attack scenarios introduced in Subsect. 4.3. Depending on the scenario, the attack and victim processes were ran either on the AP core or on the MCU core. Here, we consider the MCU-vs-AP attack to describe our attack setup.

We use an adapted version of the Zynq-based attack. On the adversary's side (here the MCU), delay-block calibration and use of Hardware Performance Counters (HPCs) were added to the initial algorithm. HPCs are used to accurately time the successive encryptions and to mitigate the de-synchronisation brought by the Linux OS. For each acquisition, the number of cycles elapsed during the encryption is compared to a maximal limit Nb_{cycle} set by the adversary above which the entire acquisition is discarded. Prior to the attack, a preliminary test was conducted in order to identify the optimal value for Nb_{cycle} (assuming that a lower number of clock cycles corresponds to a lower number of interrupts). Hence, by launching thousands of AES encryptions, we were able to find a reference number of clock cycles for almost interrupt-free encryptions. Then, based on this reference, we set a maximal limit Nb_{cycle} beyond which we decided to discard the acquisitions. By doing so, at least half of the total acquisitions were retained and used for the subsequent CPA calculations.

Regarding the CPA, we embedded it directly within the STM32MP1. This way, we drastically limited the amount of data exported. Moreover, this allowed us to directly plot the results on screen as illustrated in appendix Fig. 11.

6.3   Delay-Block-Based SCA Attacks on STM32MP1 SoC

In the AP-vs-MCU Attack Scenario, the OpenSSL AES program runs within the STM32MP1 Cortex-M MCU. Using compiler optimization set to -

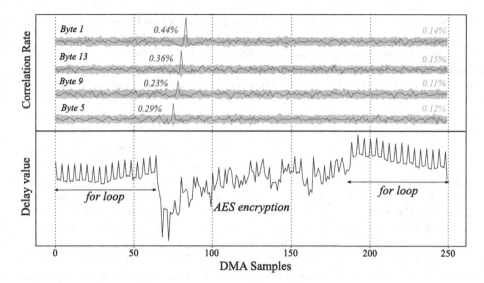

Fig. 9. AP-vs-MCU attack results: the bottom part represents the averaged AES power consumption, the top part provides the correlation rates as a function of time for four AES key bytes. (Color figure online)

O0, 1,460 clock cycles are required to perform a single AES encryption, that is 7.3 μs at the MCU operating frequency (200 MHz). Figure 9 displays in its bottom part the averaged delay values obtained for a time window of 250 DMA samples (or 16.4 μs) over 10 million acquisitions. The AES encryption, which approximately covers 110 DMA samples, is surrounded by two empty for loops added for visualisation ease. The top part of Fig. 9 provides the CPA correlation rates of four key bytes (of index #1, #13, #9, and #5) as a function of time. The correct key hypotheses are depicted in red and emerge from the incorrect hypotheses (in grey) between samples 70 and 80. We chose to represent these key bytes because they are equally distant regarding the OpenSSL byte computation order: *0 5 10 15 - 4 9 14 3 - 8 13 2 7 - 12 1 6 11*. This explains the regular temporal offset observed between them. Based on 10 million encryptions, we achieved a full AES key recovery. 6 bytes were retrieved in the range 0-2M traces, 4 between 2-6M and 6 between 6-10M. The progressive correlation of the eight last AES key bytes (#8 to #15) are depicted in Fig. 13 in the appendix.

In the MCU-vs-AP Attack Scenario, the OpenSSL AES program runs in the STM32MP1 Cortex-A7 AP. Using compiler optimization set to -O2, 865 clock cycles are required to perform a single AES encryption, that is 1.33 μs at the AP operating frequency (650 MHz). Figure 10 displays in its bottom part the averaged delay value obtained for a time window of 100 DMA samples (or 6,6 μs) over 40 million acquisitions. The AES encryption, which approximately covers 20 DMA samples, is surrounded by two empty for loops added for visu-alisation ease. The top part of Fig. 10 provides the temporal correlation rate of four key bytes as a function of time. The correct key hypotheses are depicted in red and emerge from the incorrect hypotheses (in grey) between samples 30 and 40. Again, we chose to represent these specific key bytes because they are equally distant in the OpenSSL byte computation order. However, the AES encryption in the AP is faster than that of the MCU (1.33 μs vs. 7.3 μs) and the DMA sampling frequency that remained fixed between the two experiments is no longer sufficient to let the temporal offsets appear. This limited sampling frequency partly explains the higher number of acquisitions required to retrieve some key bytes. For instance, byte #12 in Fig. 10, seems to suffer from the under sampling and gave poorer correlation results (0,07%) than byte #4 (0,32%) or byte #0 (0,29%). We were able to confirm this assumption through a second experiment where the AES encryption temporal window had been slightly shifted regarding the DMA: the AES leakage was thus sampled at different timings. This experiment gave better results on several key bytes that struggled to emerge in the previous attack. Based on 40 million encryptions, we achieved a full AES key recovery. 3 bytes were retrieved in the range 0–10M traces, 6 between 10–20M, 2 between 40–30M, 4 between 30–40M. The 13th key byte never completely emerged from the incorrect candidates, but we assume that a simple brute force can be conducted to retrieve its value. The progressive correlation of the first key bytes (0 to 7) are depicted in Fig. 14 in the appendix.

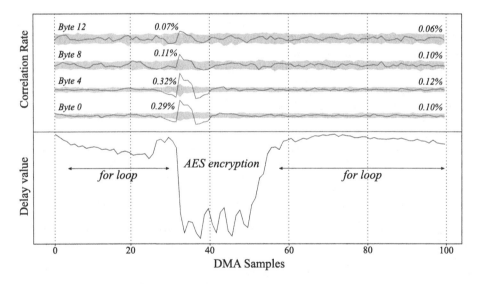

Fig. 10. MCU-vs-AP attack results: the bottom part represents the averaged AES power consumption. The top part provides the correlation over the time results over four AES key bytes. (Color figure online)

7 Discussion

Two delay-line-based power measurement techniques, using a DLL or a delay-block were introduced and studied in this research work. Because such delay-line-based components are embedded in almost every high-end digital SoC that uses external memories, the threat model we introduced is serious and shall be considered feasible for a large number of complex SoCs. In this section, we discuss performance, additional attack scenarios and potential countermeasures regarding the *SideLine* attack.

7.1 Performance and Limitations of *SideLine*

Table 1 summarizes the results obtained for the three attack scenarios considered in this paper. First, an AP-vs-AP attack was performed on a Zynq SoC using DLL-based sensors. As DLLs provide a limited resolution, a large amount of acquisitions were required to integrate enough information for the CPA to succeed (20 million traces required for full AES key recovery). It took around 12 h to extract the traces, apply post-processing (filtering) and conduct the CPA attack. The lack of resolution also made post-synchronization nearly impossible and thus implied the collection of leakage traces with a constant synchronization. Apart from performances, the DLL was by far the simplest sensor to implement in our experiments, as it only required the reading of a memory-mapped register. However, care must be taken as in certain cases, DLLs may require additional calibration. For instance, some DLLs can either perform delay calibration continuously or at a set of intervals [2]. Such parameters should be taken into account by the attacker and calibrated if needed.

Table 1. Overall delay-line-based power SCA results.

Scenario	Sensor	Nb_{Acq}	$freq_{DMA}$	$freq_{Target}$	Duration
Zynq AP-vs-AP	DLL	20M	16 MHz	667 MHz	~12 h
STM32 AP-vs-MCU	DL	10M	15.2 MHz	200 MHz	~9 h
STM32 MCU-vs-AP	DL	40M	15.2 MHz	650 MHz	~24 h

The second attack proposed in this paper required a preliminary work to properly turn the delay-block into a custom TDC. Then, two delay-block-based power SCAs were conducted on a STM32MP1 SoC. The AP-vs-MCU AES attack took around 10 million traces for a full key recovery (trace acquisition and CPA took approximately 9 h) while the MCU-vs-AP AES attack required 40 million traces (24 h). We can compare these results to the attack reported in [11] against an OpenSSL AES implementation in an FPGA-based heterogeneous SoC. In this work, FPGA-based TDCs were able to perform a similar attack using only 90,000 traces (FPGA-to-CPU attack). FPGAs indeed offer the possibility to design high resolution and high sampling rate sensors which explain the higher efficiency of their attack. Such a flexibility is obviously not available in ASICs. For instance, even using DMA in our experiments, the maximum sampling rate achieved (16 MHz) was still way under the FPGA-based TDC sampling rate given in [11] (200 MHz). Additionally delay-blocks also suffer from a poor resolution as evidenced in Fig. 15 in the appendix. Despite these limitations, we demonstrated that such an attack is still feasible without using FPGAs and within a reasonable time and number of traces.

The presence of DLLs and programmable delay-blocks is already mandatory in high-end SoC devices and should become even more prevalent in the future with the constant increase of memory bus speeds. At the same time, their voltage sensing capability will be progressively enhanced as they will need to meet higher performances requirements. This should make *SideLine* even easier to conduct and detrimental for hardware security in the future.

7.2 Hardware and Software Mitigations

This section provides some countermeasure guidelines mitigating *SideLine*:

Adding SCA Countermeasures: A simple way to make the victim process more resilient to power SCAs is the addition of software or hardware SCA countermeasures [34, 36]. As mentioned above, one of the main limitations of *SideLine* comes from the low resolution provided by DLL and delay-blocks. This forces the attacker to acquire a huge number of traces (several million in our case) and makes it nearly impossible to re-synchronize SCA traces. On the victim side, software randomization could be a good candidate to efficiently de-synchronize computations and hence to increase significantly the attack difficulty (e.g. adding random delays in T-Table computations for OpenSSL AES). On the monitoring side (delay-line), a straightforward way to mitigate the attack could rely on the addition of phase and frequency jitter to the clock signal used for sampling the delay-line registers.

Preventing Delay-Line Access: Another countermeasure would act at system level by preventing the access to the delay-line registers by unauthorized software entities. Hence, only the OS for instance would have access to this resource. TrustZone could also be used to place DLLs and Delay-blocks in the secure world and make their use by non-secure world impossible in practice. Locking the access to the DMA module or the hardware performance counters would also represent a significant limitation for the attack setup.

Reducing Delay-Line Sampling Rate: Preventing delay-line access through privilege rights seems insufficient as a malicious attacker or a compromised OS could overpass it (privileges escalation). A hardware way to mitigate the threat would be to limit the delay-block access to a lower sampling rate (e.g. 10 KHz). This could be simply achieved by limiting the access rate to the register that stores delay-line information. This way, even if the power consumption monitoring would remain feasible, it will highly affect the delay sensor performances.

With such a limited sampling rate it would be probably very challenging for an attacker to conduct SCAs on fast encryption algorithms such as AES.

Abandoning Delay-Lines in SoCs: As *SideLine* revealed their potential misuse as power consumption sensors, the delay-line-based components could be removed from SoC devices and instead, be placed directly within the external memory devices. This drastic choice would require the addition of configuration I/Os in external memories to efficiently calibrate the delay-lines but will almost entirely remove the delay-line threat from the SoC die. However, even outside the SoC, the delay-line threat may remain problematic as inter-chip power SCAs have already been shown feasible [27].

8   Conclusion

Previous works demonstrated that remote power SCAs were feasible using FPGA-based delay sensors and microcontroller ADC-based sensors. *SideLine* goes further by proving that unsuspected hardware components available in a broad range of high-end SoC devices, can be turned into power consumption measurement units. In this work, we studied two common SoC resources known as delay-locked-loops and delay-blocks and proved their capability to eavesdrop the voltage activity of cryptographic programs running in different processors. Several core-vs-core attack scenarios on application processors and microcontroller units were conducted. For each scenario, we achieved a full key recovery side-channel attack on the publicly available OpenSSL AES implementation. We believe that these findings open a new era for remote power side-channel attacks. *SideLine* has the advantage of being portable on a wide range of devices as it does not requires the presence of specific circuitry (e.g. FPGA). Because *SideLine* feeds upon SoC complexity, we also believe that it represents a major threat for actual high-end SoC security. More importantly this threat is likely to scale up in line with the constant performance improvements in SoCs and memory devices.

Appendix

Algorithm 1. Zynq processor attack, AP#0 attack pseudo-algorithm

---

Input: Nb_{acq}, Nb_{sample}

$DMA_{init}()$;

$UART_{init}()$;

while Nb_{acq} has not been reached **do**

    Send AES plaintext to AP#1;

    Launch DMA transfer(Nb_{sample});

    Send $Start_{AES}$ to AP#1;

    Wait for End_{AES} flag();

    Wait for End_{DMA} flag();

    Export samples through UART;

end while

Algorithm 2. Zynq processor attack, AP#1 victim pseudo-algorithm

---

Input: $AES_{key}, AES_{plaintext}$
$\text{AES}_{init}()$;
while infinity **do**
    Wait for $Start_{AES}$ flag();
    Get AP#0 plaintext;
    OpenSSL AES encrypt();
    Send End_{AES} flag to AP#0;
    Send AES ciphertext to AP#0;
end while

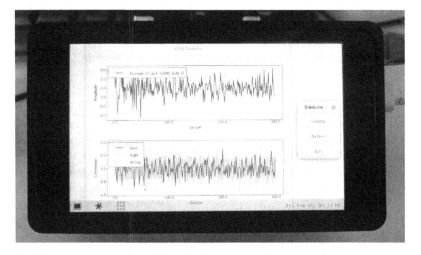

Fig. 11. AES traces acquisition, CPA computation and GTK display (implemented for demonstration) are all embedded in the same application running within the STM32MP157-DK2 board.

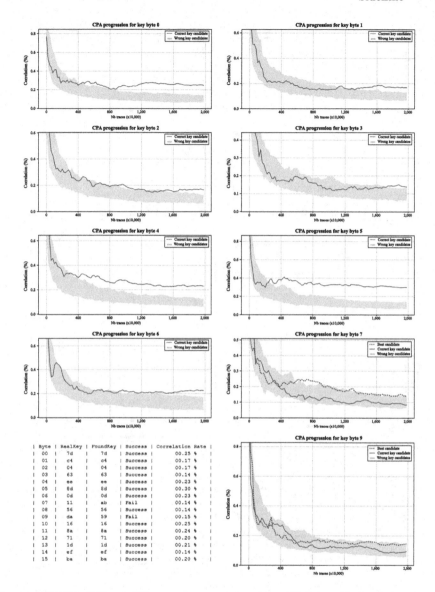

Fig. 12. ZYNQ AP-vs-AP attack scenario - The CPA progression (y-axis) over the number of traces (x-axis) is represented for the first 8 AES key bytes. Bytes 7th and 9th which never emerged from the incorrect key candidates are also represented. These CPA results were obtained over 20 million AES encryptions, the correlation rates are provided in the summary table.

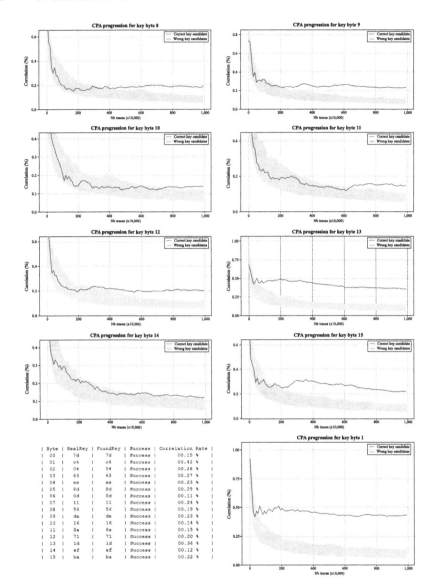

Fig. 13. STM32MP1 AP-vs-MCU attack scenario - The CPA progression (y-axis) over the number of traces (x-axis) is represented for the last 8 AES key bytes. The 1st AES key byte is also represented as it provided the best correlation rate. These CPA results were obtained over 10 million AES encryptions, the correlation rates are provided in the summary table.

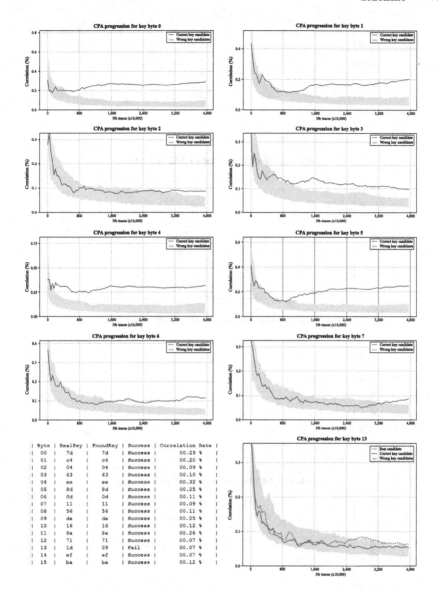

Fig. 14. STM32MP1 MCU-vs-AP attack scenario - The CPA progression (y-axis) over the number of traces (x-axis) is represented for the first 8 AES key bytes. Bytes 13th which never emerged from the incorrect key candidates is also represented. These CPA results were obtained over 40 million AES encryptions, the correlation rates are provided in the summary table.

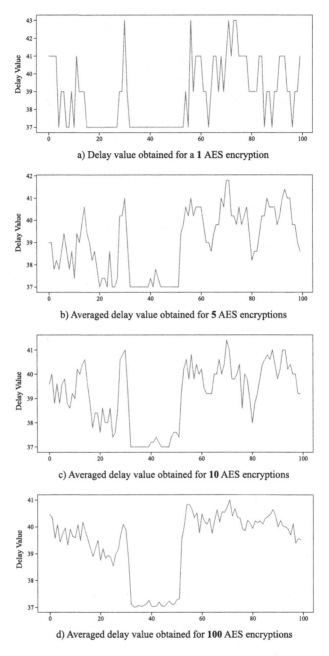

a) Delay value obtained for a **1** AES encryption

b) Averaged delay value obtained for **5** AES encryptions

c) Averaged delay value obtained for **10** AES encryptions

d) Averaged delay value obtained for **100** AES encryptions

Fig. 15. STM32MP1 MCU-vs-AP attack scenario: This figure illustrates the delay-block resolution limitation when a single AES encryption is acquired (a). This resolution can be virtually increased by averaging a higher number of traces: 5 (b), 10 (c) and 100 (d) traces.

References

1. Abdulrazzaq, B.I., Halin, I.A., Kawahito, S., Sidek, R.M., Shafie, S., Yunus, N.A.M.: A review on high-resolution CMOS delay lines towards sub-picosecond jitter performance. SpringerPlus, **5**, 434 (2016). https://doi.org/10.1186/s40064-016-2090-z
2. Limited ARM. ARM PrimeCell MultiPort Memory Controller (PL176) Technical Reference Manual. Technical report (2003)
3. Brier, E., Clavier, C., Olivier, F.: Correlation power analysis with a leakage model. In: Joye, M., Quisquater, J.J. (eds) CHES 2004. LNCS, vol. 3156, pp. 16–29. Springer, Heidelberg (2004). https://doi.org/10.1007/978-3-540-28632-5_2
4. Bukasa, S.K., Lashermes, R., Le Bouder, H., Lanet, J.L., Legay, A.: How TrustZone could be bypassed: side-channel attacks on a modern system-on-chip. In: Hancke, G., Damiani, E. (eds.) WISTP 2017. LNCS, vol. 10741, pp. 93–109. Springer, Cham (2018). https://doi.org/10.1007/978-3-319-93524-9_6
5. Canella, C., et al.: Fallout: leaking data on meltdown-resistant CPUs. In: Proceedings of the ACM Conference on Computer and Communications Security (2019)
6. Chen, F., et al.: Enabling FPGAs in the cloud. In: ACM Computing Frontiers (2014)
7. Chung, C.C., Chen, P.L., Lee, C.Y.: An all-digital delay-locked loop for DDR SDRAM controller applications. In: International Symposium on VLSI Design, Automation and Test (2007)
8. Daemen, J., Rijmen, V.: The Rijndael Block Cipher (1999)
9. Dutertre, J.-M., Robisson, B., Tria, A., Zussa, L.: Investigation of timing constraints violation as a fault injection means. In: Design of Circuits and Integrated Systems (2012)
10. Gnad, D.R., Krautter, J., Tahoori, M.B.: Leaky noise : new side-channel attack vectors in mixed-signal IoT devices. In: IACR Transactions on Cryptographic Hardware and Embedded Systems (2019)
11. Gravellier, J., Dutertre, J.-M., Teglia, Y., Moundi, P.L., Olivier, F.: Remote side-channel attacks on heterogeneous SoC. In: 18th Smart Card Research and Advanced Application Conference (2019)
12. Gruss, D., Maurice, C., Mangard, S.: Rowhammer.js: a remote software-induced fault attack in Javascript. In: Caballero, J., Zurutuza, U., Rodríguez, R. (eds.) DIMVA 2016. LNCS, vol. 9721, pp. 300–321. Springer, Cham (2016). https://doi.org/10.1007/978-3-319-40667-1_15
13. Kenjar, Z., Frassetto, T., Gens, D., Franz, M., Sadeghi, A.R.: V0LTpwn: Attacking x86 Processor Integrity from Software. CoRR (2019)
14. Kim, Y., et al.: Flipping bits in memory without accessing them: an experimental study of DRAM disturbance errors. In: 2014 ACM/IEEE 41st International Symposium on Computer Architecture (ISCA), pp. 361–372, June 2014
15. Kocher, P., et al.: Spectre attacks: exploiting speculative execution. In: 2019 IEEE Symposium on Security and Privacy (SP), May 2019
16. Kocher, P., Jaffe, J., Jun, B.: Differential power analysis. In: Wiener, M. (eds.) CRYPTO 1999. LNCS, vol. 1666, pp. 388–397. Springer, Heidelberg (1999). https://doi.org/10.1007/3-540-48405-1_25
17. Kurmus, A., Ioannou, N., Neugschwandtner, M., Papandreou, N., Parnell, T.: From random block corruption to privilege escalation: a filesystem attack vector for Rowhammer-like attacks. In: 11th USENIX Workshop on Offensive Technologies (2017)

18. Lipp, M., et al.: PLATYPUS: software-based power side-channel attacks on x86. In: 2021 IEEE Symposium on Security and Privacy (SP). IEEE (2021)
19. Lipp, M., et al.: Meltdown. CoRR, January 2018
20. ST Microelectronics. STM32MP1 Reference manual (2019)
21. Murdock, K., Oswald, D., Garcia, F.D., Van Bulck, J., Gruss, D., Piessens, F.: Plundervolt: software-based fault injection attacks against Intel SGX. In: 41st IEEE Symposium on Security and Privacy (2020)
22. O'Flynn, C., Dewar, A.: On-device power analysis across hardware security domains: stop hitting yourself. In: IACR Transactions on Cryptographic Hardware and Embedded Systems (2019)
23. OpenSSL Software Foundation (2002). https://www.openssl.org/
24. Qiu, P., Wang, D., Lyu, Y., Qu, G.: VoltJockey: breaching trustzone by software-controlled voltage manipulation over multi-core frequencies. In: Proceedings of the ACM Conference on Computer and Communications Security (2019)
25. Romo, J.: DDR Memories Comparison and overview
26. Schellenberg, F., Gnad, D.R., Moradi, A., Tahoori, M.B.: An inside job: remote power analysis attacks on FPGAs. In: Design, Automation & Test in Europe Conference & Exhibition (2018)
27. Schellenberg, F., Gnad, D.R., Moradi, A., Tahoori, M.B.: Remote inter-chip power analysis side-channel attacks at board-level. In: Proceedings of the International Conference on Computer-Aided Design, New York, NY, USA. ACM, November 2018
28. Tang, A., Sethumadhavan, S., Stolfo, S.: CLKSCREW: exposing the perils of security-oblivious energy management. In: 26th USENIX Security Symposium (USENIX Security 2017) (2017)
29. Van Bulck, J., et al.: Foreshadow: extracting the keys to the Intel SGX kingdom with transient out-of-order execution. In: Proceedings of the 27th USENIX Conference on Security Symposium, SEC 2018, USA. USENIX Association (2018)
30. van Schaik, S., et al.: RIDL: rogue in-flight data load. In: 2019 IEEE Symposium on Security and Privacy (SP) (2019)
31. Walter, C.D.: Simple power analysis of unified code for ECC double and add. In: Joye, M., Quisquater, J.J. (eds) CHES 2004. LNCS, vol. 3156, pp. 191–204. Springer, Heidelberg (2004). https://doi.org/10.1007/978-3-540-28632-5_14
32. Weissman, Z., Tiemann, T., Moghimi, D., Custodio, E., Eisenbarth, T., Sunar, B.: JackHammer: efficient Rowhammer on heterogeneous FPGA-CPU platforms. In: IACR Transactions on Cryptographic Hardware and Embedded Systems, December 2020
33. Xilinx: Zynq-7000 SoC Data Sheet 190, 1–25 (2012)
34. Zhang, L., Gutierrez, L.Z., Taylor, M.B.: Power Side Channels in Security ICs: Hardware Countermeasures. CoRR (2016)
35. Zhao, M., Edward Suh, G.: FPGA-based remote power side-channel attacks. In: IEEE Symposium on Security and Privacy (2018)
36. Zhou, Y., Feng, D.G.: Side-channel attacks: ten years after its publication and the impacts on cryptographic module security testing. IACR Cryptology ePrint Archive (2005)
37. Zick, K.M., Hayes, J.P.: Low-cost sensing with ring oscillator arrays for healthier reconfigurable systems. ACM Trans. Reconfigurable Technol. Syst. 5, 1–26 (2012)
38. Zick, K.M., Srivastav, M., Zhang, W., French, M.: Sensing nanosecond-scale voltage attacks and natural transients in FPGAs. In: ACM/SIGDA (2013)

First Full-Fledged Side Channel Attack on HMAC-SHA-2

Yaacov Belenky$^{(\boxtimes)}$ (iD), Ira Dushar(iD), Valery Teper(iD),
Hennadii Chernyshchyk(iD), Leonid Azriel(iD), and Yury Kreimer(iD)

FortifyIQ, Inc., 300 Washington Street, Suite 850, Newton, MA 02458, USA
{belenky,dushar,teper,chernyshchyk,azriel,kreimer}@fortifyiq.com
https://www.fortifyiq.com/

Abstract. Side-channel attacks pose a threat to cryptographic algorithms. Hash functions, in particular those from the SHA-2 family, can
also be an interesting target if some of their inputs are secret. HMAC is
an important use case of a hash function, in which the input is partially
secret and thus unknown to the attacker. Despite a few publications that
discuss applications of power analysis techniques to attack HMAC-SHA-
2, no generic method that shows a full attack on its hardware implementation has been proposed so far. In this article, we present a novel
practical template attack on HMAC-SHA-2 intended primarily against
its implementations in hardware. To the best of our knowledge, it is the
first practical attack on a true hardware implementation. We detail all
the stages of the attack and validate it experimentally. Our experiments
are based on an open-source hardware SHA-256 implementation that
was implemented on two targets: (1) a pre-silicon side-channel leakage
simulator and (2) an FPGA. In both cases, we show a full attack implementation up to the discovery of the key derivatives that allow for forging
HMAC signatures. The setup used to attack the FPGA implementation
cost less than $3K. The entire attack (the trace acquisition and the anal-
ysis) on the FPGA took about two hours including the profiling stage,
and about half an hour excluding the profiling stage.

Keywords: Side-channel analysis · Cryptographic hardware · DPA ·
HMAC · SHA-2 · SHA-256

1 Introduction

More than 20 years ago, Kocher *et al.* in his seminal work [15,16] discovered side
channel attacks, a new class of attacks capable of exposing secrets by observing
the side effects of the algorithm execution. This discovery laid the ground for
vast research that continues to reveal new channels that leak secret information,
starting from timing, electromagnetic emanation and cache miss patterns and
including exotic channels such as acoustics [12,16,30]. Yet, power side-channel
attacks of different types, such as simple power analysis (SPA), differential power
analysis (DPA) and correlation power analysis (CPA) remain the most popular.

© Springer Nature Switzerland AG 2021
S. Bhasin and F. De Santis (Eds.): COSADE 2021, LNCS 12910, pp. 31–52, 2021.
https://doi.org/10.1007/978-3-030-89915-8_2

Naturally, cryptographic algorithms are the main targets of side-channel attacks, and in particular of power analysis attacks. Numerous side-channel attacks on virtually all the popular cryptographic algorithms, including AES, RSA, ECC and Diffie-Hellman have been published. However, the cryptographic hash functions such as SHA-1 and SHA-2 stand out in this list with very few known attacks. While hash algorithms themselves do not involve secrets, the hash-based message authentication code (HMAC) uses a secret key to generate a keyed digest of a message [7]. HMAC is as widely used as AES or RSA, and thus must be adequately protected. Nevertheless, HMAC is given less attention in the system vulnerability analysis due to the general belief that no practical attacks on it exist [4].

The difficulty of attacking HMAC starts from its structure [6] which involves two invocations of its underlying hash function on the secret key K (1).

$$HMAC_{Hash}(K,M) = Hash\left(\overbrace{(K_0 \oplus opad)\|Hash\overbrace{\left((K_0 \oplus ipad)\|M\right)}^{\text{inner hash}}}^{\text{outer hash}}\right) \quad (1)$$

where K_0 is a known function of the secret key K, M is the input message, and *ipad* and *opad* are known constants. The two invocations are called inner and outer hashes, and the variable part of the input to the outer hash is the output of the inner hash. Even if the adversary has full control over the input data and manages to break the inner hash, the input to the outer hash becomes known, yet not chosen, which limits the possibilities of the adversary.

Susceptibility of the HMAC construction to side-channel attacks has been addressed by several researchers. Okeya *et al.* [22] showed that block cipher based HMAC schemes may be vulnerable to power attacks even if the underlying compression function is secure against them. This vulnerability was demonstrated on a simple software based experiment. Their work was further expanded in [10]. Both publications discussed block cipher based compression functions. Although the SHA-1 addition function was mentioned as an operation similar to XOR, no analysis or evaluation of hash function based constructions have been performed. Similarly, Lemke *et al.* [17] presented a method to perform DPA on SHA-1 based HMAC by applying the Hamming weight model on linear operations, such as XOR and modulo addition. No experimental data with HMAC was provided. Fouque *et al.* [9] proposed a template attack on a software implementation of HMAC-SHA-1. Here, the adversary obtains the key from electromagnetic emanations during the loading of each of the 32-bit key segments from the memory to a CPU register. Oswald [23] published a successful grey-box CPA attack on SHA-1 in a real-life authentication IC with a SHA-1 accelerator. Rather than targeting weaknesses of the hash function, he exploited an ill-constructed challenge-response protocol used for authentication.

HMAC-SHA-2 introduces additional complexity. Although the compression functions of both SHA-1 and SHA-2 comprise mainly arithmetic operations, there is a substantial difference between the two hash functions. The SHA-1 round function contains a single addition operation which involves the input word. The result of this addition is stored in a state register, which can be used as a target for a correlation attack. In contrast, the round function of SHA-2 contains two additions involving the input word, and the results are sampled in two different sub-words (A and E) of the state register. It is difficult to separate between the side channel leakages from the two additions executed in parallel; thus, a naïve attack on one of them is not likely to succeed. McEvoy *et al.* [18] suggested attacking an intermediate result (T_1) shared between A and E, using the Hamming distance model and focusing on the inner hash. McEvoy *et al.* note that the attack does not reveal the key, but allows forging HMAC signatures by extension. However, in a typical hardware implementation of SHA-2, T_1 is hidden in the combinational logic, where different operations with mutually correlated side channel leakages are executed in parallel, and therefore are very difficult to isolate. In the experimental part of the article, an FPGA implementation is used to show the correlation between the measured power and the Hamming distance between A and E. However, due to the linear nature of the compression function, correlation alone is a necessary, but not a sufficient condition for mounting an attack. Rohatgi *et al.* [25] presented the general lines for a possible attack on SHA-256, but no details were provided. Rohatgi mentions that the outer hash can only be attacked with a known message model that makes the DPA/CPA attack extremely difficult. Belaïd *et al.* [3] proposed an attack somewhat similar to the attack by McEvoy *et al.* [18], while switching to the Hamming weight model. The Hamming weight model is appropriate for attacking software realizations of cryptographic algorithms, but is generally less effective for hardware. No experimental data was provided. In a more recent article Kannwischer *et al.* [14] used this approach for attacking the HMAC-SHA-256 block of the XMSS hash-based signature algorithm, and presented the results of a simulation based on the Hamming weight leakage model. This article also assumes sequential execution of different parts of the SHA-256 round function, while in a hardware implementation parallel execution is typically used. Gebotys *et al.* [11] suggested an attack on hardware implementations of SHA-2. This attack relies on chosen input data. Therefore, it cannot be applied to the outer hash of HMAC, which takes the inner hash as its input, and it is computationally infeasible to find the input data with a chosen inner hash. In the article [1] Archambeau *et al.* present different attacks on the open-source and open-hardware project WooKey, and in particular (in Section 13) on the HMAC-SHA-256 part of WooKey. However, the WooKey protocol uses HMAC in a non-standard way, namely the key is known and the message is secret. Attacking such a setting is a different, and much easier, task.

To the best of our knowledge, no attack on a real parallel hardware implementation of HMAC-SHA-2 that shows a full path up to the key extraction has been proposed so far. In general, it is very difficult (if at all possible) to apply a DPA/CPA attack on this function without a profiling stage. The reason is the combination of two facts: (1) attacking the inner hash produces a derivative of the key rather than the key itself [18], therefore the outer hash must be attacked as well, however using known messages only (as opposed to chosen messages); and (2) attacking SHA-2 using DPA with a known message is difficult due to its linear nature [26]. To understand the intuition of fact (1), recall that a correlation-based attack model assumes control/knowledge of the data and a constant key. Since the first invocation of the SHA-2 compression function works with a constant string ($K_0 \oplus ipad$), it cannot be attacked using DPA. The second invocation mixes the result of the first invocation with the message (or with its initial part). A successful attack on the second invocation will reveal $Hash(K_0 \oplus ipad)$, but not the key itself. Hence, $Hash(K_0 \oplus opad)$ must be derived separately. The input to the outer hash is an output of the inner hash, therefore the adversary possesses the knowledge, but not the control of the inner hash result. As for fact (2), known-message attacks work well on non-linear functions for which even a 1-bit change in the input completely changes the output, e.g., the AES S-box. In contrast, due to the linearity and large word sizes of the SHA-2's algebraic constructions, DPA may choose a related, but wrong key hypotheses. Therefore, power analysis of SHA-2 requires a divide and conquer strategy that gradually reveals the internal bits with carefully crafted input text [28], a strategy that is only possible with a chosen message. Since a DPA-type analysis is difficult as explained, the alternative direction to obtain the secrets from HMAC-SHA-2 using power analysis is by profiling the underlying hash function, i.e., mounting a template attack.

The template attack [2,5,24] is the most powerful power analysis attack from the information theoretic perspective. In order to mount the template attack, the attacker must have access to an experimental device, identical or very similar to the target device, that he can program to his choosing. Thus, the main effort is applied during the profiling stage, but only once. The following extraction stage can use a smaller number of traces. Chari *et al.* [5] were the first to describe a template attack that uses the Multivariate Gaussian Model to build a template, and uses the maximum likelihood approach to match the power traces, collected during the attack phase, to the template.

In this paper, we introduce a template attack on HMAC-SHA-2 based on template tables and Euclidean distance for matching. During the profiling stage, the addition operation is split into 2-bit slices that include carry-in and carry-out, and for each slice a power profile is built. The attack works in successive iterations, matching the slices starting from the least significant and, for each iteration going to the following slice using the calculated carry-in from the previous iteration.

We provide a detailed attack algorithm for SHA-256, but the extension to the other members of the SHA-2 family is straightforward. Furthermore, we demonstrate how the attack can be applied to multiple rounds per cycle implementations. In the experimental part, we demonstrate a successful attack using a power leakage simulator and an FPGA platform. For the latter, the trace acquisition was implemented using equipment costing less than $3,000, and the analysis was performed on a regular laptop. To mount the proposed template attack, the adversary needs direct access to the SHA-2 function without the HMAC wrapper. This is a reasonable assumption for many products that provide both HMAC and pure cryptographic hash functionality to the user. Moreover, our experiments show that the attack works even when the profile traces were acquired from a different FPGA board. This setting is important, because even if the target device using plain SHA-2 is disabled by factory settings, the attacker may use a different device with enabled plain SHA-2 for profiling, and then attack the device with disabled plain SHA-2.

To summarize, we make the following contributions in this paper:

1. To the best of our knowledge, we are the first to publish a side-channel attack on a real parallel hardware implementation of HMAC-SHA-2.
2. With the proposed attack, we demonstrate a complete process of forging an HMAC-SHA-256 signature in simulation and on an FPGA platform.
3. We present a generic attack that does not make assumptions on implementation, such as the pipeline structure and the sequence of operations.
4. We demonstrate an extension of the proposed attack that can be applied to two and three rounds per clock implementation as well.
5. We demonstrate that the attack may work even when the profiling was done on a different device of the same type.

The remainder of this article is organized as follows: Sect. 2 briefly describes the SHA-2 family and HMAC and introduces some notation used in the next sections. Section 3 describes the attack stage by stage. Section 4 describes our experiments, which validate the attack. Section 5 suggests possible countermeasures against the attack. Finally, in Sect. 6 we draw our conclusions.

2 Preliminaries

2.1 SHA-2

The SHA-2 family of hash algorithms, standardized by NIST [7], utilizes the Merkle-Dåmgard construction, in which the input (properly padded) is represented as a sequence of blocks $Bl_0, Bl_1, \ldots, Bl_{n-1}$, and the hash function is iteratively calculated as $S_{j+1} = CF(S_j, Bl_j)$ for $j \in [0, 1, \ldots, n-1]$ where CF is the compression function, S_0 is a predefined constant, and S_n is the final output (hash value).

The compression function $CF(S_j, Bl_j)$ is calculated in the following steps (see SHA-256 example in Fig. 1):

1. The message schedule expands the input block Bl_j to a sequence of $s \times t$-bit "words" $W_0, W_1, \ldots, W_{s-1}$, where $s = 64$, $t = 32$ for SHA-224 and SHA-256, and $s = 80, t = 64$ for SHA-512/224, SHA-512/256, SHA-384 and SHA-512. The details of the expansion algorithm are omitted since they are irrelevant to our attack.
2. The round function RF is applied s times so that $R_i = RF(R_{i-1}, W_i, K_i)$ for $i \in [0, 1, \ldots, s-1]$, where K_i are predefined "round constants", and $R_{-1} = S_j$.

3. Finally, the output of the compression function CF is calculated as a word-wise sum modulo 2^t of $R_{-1} = S_j$ and R_{s-1}.

For the round function RF, the state R_{i-1} is split into eight t-bit words $A_{i-1}, B_{i-1}, C_{i-1}, D_{i-1}, E_{i-1}, F_{i-1}, G_{i-1}, H_{i-1}$. R_i is calculated from R_{i-1} as follows:

$$T_1 = H_{i-1} \boxplus \Sigma_1(E_{i-1}) \boxplus Ch(E_{i-1}, F_{i-1}, G_{i-1}) \boxplus K_i \boxplus W_i \tag{2}$$

$$T_2 = \Sigma_0(A_{i-1}) \boxplus Maj(A_{i-1}, B_{i-1}, C_{i-1}) \tag{3}$$

$$A_i = T_1 \boxplus T_2 \tag{4}$$

$$E_i = D_{i-1} \boxplus T_1 \tag{5}$$

$$B_i = A_{i-1}, \ C_i = B_{i-1}, \ D_i = C_{i-1}, \ F_i = E_{i-1}, \ G_i = F_{i-1}, \ H_i = G_{i-1} \tag{6}$$

where "$\boxplus$" stands for addition modulo 2^t, Σ_0 and Σ_1 are rotation functions, Ch is the bit-wise choice function

$$Ch(x, y, z) = (x \wedge y) \oplus (\neg x \wedge z) \tag{7}$$

and Maj is the bit-wise majority function

$$Maj(x, y, z) = (x \wedge y) \oplus (x \wedge z) \oplus (y \wedge z) \tag{8}$$

Notably, in every round, only two words of the state are calculated; the remaining six words are copied from the previous state under a different name. Thus, for convenience, we introduce a different notation, in which every word receives its unique name that does not change from round to round. First, we

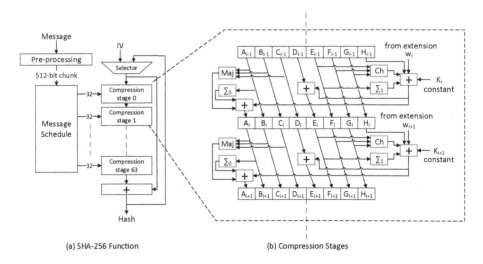

(a) SHA-256 Function   (b) Compression Stages

Fig. 1. SHA-256 algorithm block diagram. (a) SHA-256 execution flow, including pre-processing stage, message schedule, which outputs 64×32-bit words, and 64 compression stages. (b) Detailed diagram of two 256-bit wide compression stages.

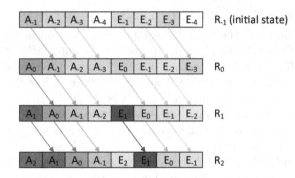

Fig. 2. Illustration of the notation used in the paper in the first three rounds. Arrows show copy operations. All the tiles that have incoming edges, receive an exact copy of a word in the previous round. The remaining tiles receive results of manipulated data from the previous round.

denote the words of the initial state R_{-1} as $A_{-1}, A_{-2}, A_{-3}, A_{-4}, E_{-1}, E_{-2}, E_{-3}, E_{-4}$. The state R_i after round i will be $A_i, A_{i-1}, A_{i-2}, A_{i-3}, E_i, E_{i-1}, E_{i-2}, E_{i-3}$. The motivation for this indexing is assigning the index 0 to the result of the first calculation and negative indices to the words that are merely copies of the initial state (Fig. 2). The only two words newly created at every round are A_i and E_i, and they are calculated using the following formulas:

$$\epsilon_i = E_{i-4} \boxplus \Sigma_1(E_{i-1}) \boxplus Ch(E_{i-1}, E_{i-2}, E_{i-3}) \boxplus K_i \tag{9}$$

$$\alpha_i = \Sigma_0(A_{i-1}) \boxplus Maj(A_{i-1}, A_{i-2}, A_{i-3}) \tag{10}$$

$$\Delta E_i = A_{i-4} \boxplus \epsilon_i \tag{11}$$

$$\Delta A_i = \epsilon_i \boxplus \alpha_i \tag{12}$$

$$E_i = \Delta E_i \boxplus W_i \tag{13}$$

$$A_i = \Delta A_i \boxplus W_i \tag{14}$$

Note that ϵ_i is different from T_1 in that it does not include W_i as an addend. Therefore ΔA_i and ΔE_i depend on the previous state but not on W_i. In particular, ΔA_0 and ΔE_0 depend only on the initial state R_{-1}.

2.2 HMAC

HMAC is a Message Authentication Code (MAC) algorithm based on a hash function, standardized by NIST in [6]. It is defined by (1). The details of the derivation of K_0 from K are irrelevant to our article, but it is important that, regardless of the size of K, the size of K_0 is equal to the block size of the function $Hash$. The two applications of the function $Hash$ during the HMAC calculation are called the "inner" application and the "outer" application.

If $Hash$ is a function from the SHA-2 family, e.g. SHA-256, then for a fixed K the first application of the SHA-256 compression function in the inner SHA-256 calculates $S^{in} = CF(S_0, K_0 \oplus ipad)$, and in the outer SHA-256 calculates $S^{out} = CF(S_0, K_0 \oplus opad)$. Note that both S^{in} and S^{out} depend only on K. The goal of the attack is to find S^{in} and S^{out}. Since it is difficult to invert the compression function, it is difficult to derive K or K_0 from S^{in} and S^{out}. However it is not necessary, since an attacker who knows S^{in} and S^{out} can forge $HMAC_{SHA256}(K, M)$ for any message M, which is the ultimate goal of an attack on a MAC algorithm.

In order to find S^{in} and S^{out}, both the inner and outer SHA-256 must be attacked. There is a subtle difference between the two attacks. While when attacking the inner SHA-256 the attacker may choose the message M as he wishes, this is not the situation with the outer SHA-256, because the variable part of the input to it is the output of the inner SHA-256—which is known to the attacker, but cannot be chosen arbitrarily. This makes designing an attack on the outer SHA-256 more difficult. The attack described below works for both.

2.3   Additional Notation

Everything, in particular traces and input words, is numbered starting from 0, the only exception being the initial words A and E of the SHA-256 internal state which are numbered starting from -4 as described in Sect. 2.1. The bits in each word are also numbered starting from 0, where index 0 corresponds to the least significant bit.

- $X[i:j]$ stands for bits $j \ldots i$ of the word X ($32 > i \geq j \geq 0$).
- $Carry(x, y, i)$ stands for the carry bit into the bit position i when adding x and y.
- W_i^t stands for the ith input word corresponding to the trace with index t in both the profiling set and the attack set.
- A_i^t and E_i^t stand for the words A_i and E_i respectively in the calculation corresponding to the trace with index t. Note that for negative lower indices i, words A_i^t, E_i^t do not depend on t: for the first (profiling) attack stage they are the words of the standard initial state S_0, and for the second and third attack stages they are the secret words of S^{in} or S^{out}, respectively. For this reason we will omit the upper index when the lower index is negative.

3   Description of the Attack

3.1   The Aim and the Strategy

The classical objective of a side channel attack is to obtain the secret key K. However, as outlined in Sect. 2.2, K does not interact directly with data that the adversary can know, hence it cannot be obtained by statistical analysis. Nevertheless, since the ultimate goal of the adversary is to be able to forge signatures, it is sufficient to obtain the two values $S^{in} = CF(S_0, K_0 \oplus ipad)$ and $S^{out} = CF(S_0, K_0 \oplus opad)$.

The profiling stage of our template attack assumes that the adversary has access to the pure SHA-256 invocation. In this stage, $CF(M)$ is calculated using the SHA-256 engine on a variety of one-block messages M, and the profiling set of power traces is acquired. These traces are processed to generate the template tables described in Sect. 3.2; these tables are further used for matching in the attack stage.

In the attack stage, the key K is unknown, and the input message M is known, but not necessarily controlled by the adversary. This stage is applied twice, first on the inner and then on the outer hash calculation. In the attack stage, a set of power traces (the attack set) is acquired for the calculation of $HMAC_{SHA256}(K, M)$ for a variety of messages M. It suffices here to record only certain parts of every trace, corresponding to the first two rounds of the second block calculation in both the inner and outer SHA-256. The first block of both the inner and outer SHA-256 is constant, being dependent only on the key, so the side channel data corresponding to the first block bears no useful information.

First, we find S^{in} using the template table and the parts of the traces corresponding to the inner SHA-256. Knowing S^{in}, it is possible to calculate $SHA256((K_0 \oplus ipad)\|M)$ for every trace, thus obtaining the input message to the outer SHA-256. Next, we find S^{out} using the same template table and the parts of the traces corresponding to the outer SHA-256.

In Sects. 3.2–3.3, we describe the attack under the assumption that the implementation of the SHA-256 compression function calculates one round in one clock cycle. Section 3.4 outlines an expansion of the proposed method to the two and three rounds-per-cycle implementations.

3.2 Profiling Stage—Building the Template Tables

In the profiling stage, we collect a set of traces and build a fixed-size set of template tables. Different template tables correspond to different rounds and different bit positions. In every table, the set of all the traces is split into a set of disjoint sets. Every line in the table corresponds to one of these sets, and contains the traces averaged over that set. These disjoint sets are characterized by the values of specific bits in the SHA-256 round function calculation, as described below (see Fig. 3).

In the SHA-256 calculation, in round i, two new values are calculated: $A_i = \Delta A_i \boxplus W_i$ and $E_i = \Delta E_i \boxplus W_i$. If one round is calculated in one cycle, these values overwrite A_{i-1} and E_{i-1}, respectively.

During the attack we are going to find the vectors $A_{i-1}, \Delta A_i, E_{i-1}, \Delta E_i$ split into windows of size J for different values of i. The value of J determines the size of the template tables, so it should be kept reasonably small. Already for $J = 3$, the traces will be divided into $2^{5J+2} \geq 2^{17}$ groups (see below). On the other hand, for $J = 1$, a one-bit addition with carry is a linear operation, and in general it is more difficult to mount side-channel attacks on linear functions.

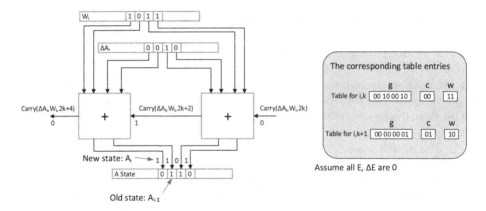

Fig. 3. Illustration of the virtual 2-bit adder units that form the basis for the template table. A separate table is built for each unit, where the entries in the table are indexed by the 12-bit vector, comprising the adder inputs, including carry and the previous state of the corresponding bits of the state register. Only the calculation of A_i is shown.

Therefore, we chose $J = 2$ as a best trade-off between accuracy and complexity, and the following description assumes $J = 2$.

The aim of the profiling set is to characterize the part of the side channel information corresponding to the overwriting of A_{i-1} and E_{i-1} with the new values $A_i = \Delta A_i \boxplus W_i$ and $E_i = \Delta E_i \boxplus W_i$. For that purpose, the calculation is split into two-bit units, indexed by k. For this purpose, for every $k < 16$ and for some value(s) of the round index i (see more below) the traces are split into 2^{12} groups, according to the values of the following bits:

1. $A_{i-1}[2k + 1 : 2k]$ (2 bits)
2. $E_{i-1}[2k + 1 : 2k]$ (2 bits)
3. $\Delta A_i[2k + 1 : 2k]$ (2 bits)
4. $\Delta E_i[2k + 1 : 2k]$ (2 bits)
5. $Carry(\Delta A_i, W_i, 2k)$ (1 bit)
6. $Carry(\Delta E_i, W_i, 2k)$ (1 bit)
7. $W_i[2k + 1 : 2k]$ (2 bits)

We split the 12-bit vector above into three groups and denote the 8 unknown bits of data items (1–4 in the list above) as g, the two carry bits obtained from iteration $k - 1$ (5–6) as c, and the two known message bits $W_i[2k + 1 : 2k]$ (7) as w. We will denote the average value of a sample number s over all traces with specific values g, c, w at the round number i at the bit position k as $\overline{M_{g,c,w,s}^{i,k}}$.

Finding Points of Interest (POIs). Note that both indices i and s correspond to the time offset in the calculation. If the points on the time axis corresponding to these two indices are far apart, no dependency of $\overline{M_{g,c,w,s}^{i,k}}$ on w should be expected—a sample taken in round j should not depend on the bits of the input in round i if i and j are sufficiently spread apart. The correspondence between the two indices is not necessarily known a priori, so a technique to find out which pairs (i,s) bear relevant information and to drop all other pairs is required. For example, one of the two following techniques can be used:

1. For every round i and for every trace index t, calculate

$$hd_i^t = HD(A_{i-1}^t, A_{i-1}^t) + HD(E_{i-1}^t, E_{i-1}^t) \tag{15}$$

   where HD stands for Hamming distance.
   Then for every s, calculate the correlation coefficient between the vectors hd_i^t and T_s^t (the sample with index s of the trace with index t). Drop the pairs (i,s) with low correlations.

2. For every round i and for every s, calculate the standard deviation of $\overline{M_{g,c,w,s}^{i,k}}$ over all values of k,g,c,w. Drop the pairs (i,s) with low standard deviations.

We observed in our experiments that the two techniques yield similar results. We chose the second technique to calculate the points of interest. As a result, from every entry (an averaged trace) in the table, only several points of interest remained. We denote the number of the points of interest as p.

Normalization. The average level of the signal is likely to be different between the profiling set and the attack set, because all the calculations in the first round of the second block of the attack set start from the same (unknown) internal state, while in the profiling set, the internal state before a round is distributed uniformly. To accommodate for this difference, we normalize every value $\overline{M_{g,c,w,s}^{i,k}}$ by subtracting the average over four values $\overline{M_{g,c,w',s}^{i,k}}$ with the same i,k,g,c,s and all possible values of w'.

While using normalization the attack succeeds (provided enough traces have been acquired), all our experiments without normalization with similar amounts of traces, both on FPGA and in simulation, have blatantly failed. See more details in Sect. 4.

Reuse of the Profiling Traces. Since every round of the calculation is executed on the same hardware, it is expected that the points of interest at different rounds will have the same distribution regardless of the round index, assuming that the initial internal state in the profiling set is chosen randomly, the only difference in the distribution being that the sample indices of the points of interest are shifted according to the round index. For example, if n samples are taken at every round, then the distribution of $\overline{M_{g,c,w,ni+p}^{i,k}}$ does not depend on the value of i. For this reason we use an optimization which enables us to extract more information from the same number of traces. Namely, we merge together data corresponding to different rounds i, so that two traces, one with specific values of g,c,w at the bit position k at round i_1 and the other with the same values of g,c,w at the same bit position at round i_2 are classified to the same group, while shifting them so that the sample number $ni_1 + s$ of the first trace corresponds to the sample number $ni_2 + s$ of the second trace. The result is a set of averaged samples at POIs, every averaged sample characterized by the values of g, c, w, the bit position k, and the POI index s. We organize these averaged samples into 16 tables T^k. The table T^k has 2^{10} rows $T^k_{g,c}$ corresponding to all possible values of g, c, and $4p$ columns corresponding to 4 values of w and p POIs. Every row is seen as a $4p$-dimensional vector.

3.3   Attack Stage

Both the inner and the outer SHA-256 are attacked in the same manner. The attack comprises several steps as described below.

Step 1: Finding A_{-1}, E_{-1}. In order to find a group of bits of A_{-1}, E_{-1}, based on the set of traces acquired during the attack stage for every $k < 16$ we build vectors of dimension $4p$ (where p is the number of the points of interest) and search for the closest vectors in the table T^k. This is done iteratively from the least significant ($k = 0$) to the most significant ($k = 15$) bits, as described below. In parallel to the discovery of bits of A_{-1}, E_{-1}, we find the corresponding bits of ΔA_0 and ΔE_0. It is done in parallel for all four words, finding two bits in every iteration, starting from the least significant bits.

In iteration k, we attempt to find the pair of bits $2k + 1 : 2k$ of these four words, assuming that the bits $2k - 1 : 0$ of all four words are already known. This allows for calculating $Carry(\Delta A_0, W_0^t, 2k)$ and $Carry(\Delta E_0, W_0^t, 2k)$ for every trace t. With these calculated carry values, we split all the traces into several subsets U_c according to the two carry bits c. Although there exist four possible values for c, the actual number of non-empty subsets is always strictly less than 4. For $k = 0$ there is only one possible combination $(0, 0)$ because $Carry(x, y, 0) \equiv 0$. For $k > 0$ and $A_0[2k - 1 : 0] = E_0[2k - 1 : 0]$ clearly $Carry(A_0, W_0^t, 2k) = Carry(E_0, W_0^t, 2k)$, and only two combinations $(0, 0)$ and $(1, 1)$ are possible. Finally, if $A_0[2k - 1 : 0] \neq E_0[2k - 1 : 0]$, e.g. $A_0[2k - 1 : 0] > E_0[2k - 1 : 0]$, then $Carry(A_0, W_0^t, 2k) \geq Carry(E_0, W_0^t, 2k)$, so one of the four combinations is excluded, and only three remain.

Every non-empty set U_c is then subdivided into four subsets $U_{c,w}$ according to $w = W_0^t[2k + 1 : 2k]$. Finally, the samples at the p points of interest are averaged over $U_{c,w}$ for all four values of w, resulting in a vector of dimension $4p$ for every non-empty subset U_c.

It is expected that for every c, for which U_c is not empty, V_c is close to the vector $T^k_{g,c}$, where g represents bits $2k + 1 : 2k$ of the four words. To guess the correct g, for every g, a sum $\sigma_g = \sum_{c|U_c! = \emptyset}(L^2(V_c, T^k_{g,c}))$ is calculated. Here, L^2 stands for the Euclidean metric. The value of g, for which σ_g has the minimal value, is taken. Then, we proceed to iteration $k + 1$.

Step 2: Finding $A_{-2}, A_{-3}, E_{-2}, E_{-3}$. In this stage, we make all possible hypotheses about the bits of $A_{-2}, A_{-3}, E_{-2}, E_{-3}$, for each hypothesis calculate the corresponding measured vectors and corresponding vectors from the template table, and choose the hypothesis with the lowest Euclidean distances. Similarly to the first step, we will find $A_{-2}, A_{-3}, E_{-2}, E_{-3}$ iteratively, finding two bits of every word in every iteration.

In iteration k, we attempt to find the pair of bits $2k + 1 : 2k$ of these four words, assuming that bits $2k - 1 : 0$ of all four words are already known. In addition, the words $\Delta A_0, \Delta E_0, A_{-1}, E_{-1}$ are known from the first step. This allows for calculating the following values for every trace t (note that functions Maj and Ch are bit-wise):

- $A_0^t = \Delta A_0 \boxplus W_0^t$
- $E_0^t = \Delta E_0 \boxplus W_0^t$
- $\Sigma_0(A_0^t)$
- $\Sigma_1(E_0^t)$
- $Maj(A_0^t, A_{-1}, A_{-2})[2k - 1 : 0] =$
  $Maj(A_0^t[2k - 1 : 0], A_{-1}[2k - 1 : 0], A_{-2}[2k - 1 : 0])$
- $Ch(E_0^t, E_{-1}, E_{-2})[2k - 1 : 0] =$
  $Ch(E_0^t[2k - 1 : 0], E_{-1}[2k - 1 : 0], E_{-2}[2k - 1 : 0])$
- $\epsilon_1^t[2k - 1 : 0] =$
  $E_{-3}[2k-1 : 0]\boxplus\Sigma_1(E_0^t)[2k-1 : 0]\boxplus Ch(E_0^t, E_{-1}, E_{-2})[2k-1 : 0]\boxplus K_1[2k-1 : 0]$
- $\alpha_1^t[2k - 1 : 0] = \Sigma_0(A_0^t)[2k - 1 : 0] \boxplus Maj(A_0^t, A_{-1}, A_{-2})[2k - 1 : 0]$
- $\Delta E_1^t[2k - 1 : 0] = A_{-3}[2k - 1 : 0] \boxplus \epsilon_1^t[2k - 1 : 0]$
- $\Delta A_1^t[2k - 1 : 0] = \epsilon_1^t[2k - 1 : 0] \boxplus \alpha_1^t[2k - 1 : 0]$
- $Carry(\Delta A_1^t, W_1^t, 2k)$
- $Carry(\Delta E_1^t, W_1^t, 2k)$

We classify the traces into 2^8 groups U^σ, where σ represents a quadruple $A_0^t[2k + 1 : 2k], E_0^t[2k + 1 : 2k], \Sigma_0(A_0^t)[2k + 1 : 2k], \Sigma_1(E_0^t)[2k + 1 : 2k])$. Note that for any σ all traces from U^σ have the same (presently unknown) values of $\Delta A_1^t[2k + 1 : 2k]$ and $\Delta E_1^t[2k + 1 : 2k]$. Every set U^σ is then subdivided, similarly to what was done at the first step, into subsets U_c^σ according to $Carry(\Delta A_1^t, W_1^t, 2k)$ and $Carry(\Delta E_1^t, W_1^t, 2k)$, and then every U_c^σ into subsets $U_{c,w}^\sigma$ according to $W_1^t[2k + 1 : 2k]$. However, unlike the first step, all four subsets U_c^σ are typically non-empty, except for the case $k = 0$ where only the combination $(0, 0)$ of the carry bits is possible.

Similarly to the first step, for every subset U_c^σ a vector V_c^σ is built. Now for every one of the 2^8 possible values of $A_{-2}[2k + 1 : 2k], A_{-3}[2k + 1 : 2k], E_{-2}[2k + 1 : 2k], E_{-3}[2k + 1 : 2k]$ and for every U^σ we find $\Delta A_1^t[2k + 1 : 2k]$ and $\Delta E_1^t[2k + 1 : 2k]$. Along with already known $A_0^t[2k + 1 : 2k]$ and $E_0^t[2k + 1 : 2k]$, they define a value g and a vector $T_{g,c}^k$ from the template table; summing up the Euclidean distances between V_c^σ and the vector from the template table corresponding to U_c^σ over all the pairs σ, c, we obtain a number (the sum of the distances) corresponding to the combination of $A_{-2}[2k+1 : 2k], A_{-3}[2k+1 : 2k], E_{-2}[2k+1:2k], E_{-3}[2k + 1 : 2k]$. The combination with the lowest sum of the distances is assumed to be the correct combination.

Step 3: Finding A_{-4}, E_{-4}. When $\Delta A_0, A_{-1}, A_{-2}, A_{-3}, \Delta E_0, E_{-1},$ E_{-2}, E_{-3} are already known, a simple linear calculation suffices to find A_{-4}, E_{-4}.

Rewriting Eqs. 9–12 for $i = 0$ we have

$$\epsilon_0 = E_{-4} \boxplus \Sigma_1(E_{-1}) \boxplus Ch(E_{-1}, E_{-2}, E_{-3}) \boxplus K_0 \tag{16}$$

$$\alpha_0 = \Sigma_0(A_{-1}) \boxplus Maj(A_{-1}, A_{-2}, A_{-3}) \tag{17}$$

$$\Delta E_0 = A_{-4} \boxplus \epsilon_0 \tag{18}$$

$$\Delta A_0 = \epsilon_0 \boxplus \alpha_0 \tag{19}$$

A_{-4} and E_{-4} now remain the only unknowns in these expressions, and they can be found as follows:

$$\epsilon_0^* = \Sigma_1(E_{-1}) \boxplus Ch(E_{-1}, E_{-2}, E_{-3}) \boxplus K_0 \tag{20}$$

$$E_{-4} = \Delta A_0 \boxminus \epsilon_0^* \boxminus \alpha_0 \tag{21}$$

$$A_{-4} = \Delta E_0 \boxminus \Delta A_0 \boxplus \alpha_0 \tag{22}$$

where "$\boxminus$" stands for subtraction modulo 2^{32}.

3.4 Extension of the Attack to the Multiple Rounds per Clock Implementation

If more than one round is performed per clock cycle (up to three rounds), the attack still applies, with some modifications. In this section we briefly describe the modifications for the two rounds per clock cycle case. We will denote the number of rounds per clock (2 or 3) as d.

Template Tables Calculation. Since in this mode A_i and E_i overwrite A_{i-d} and E_{i-d}, respectively, rather than A_{i-1} and E_{i-1}, the classification of the traces for building the table $\overline{M_{g,c,w,s}^{i,k}}$ is based on the following values:

1. $A_{i-d}[2k+1 : 2k]$ (two bits)
2. $E_{i-d}[2k+1 : 2k]$ (two bits)
3. $\Delta A_i[2k+1 : 2k]$ (two bits)
4. $\Delta E_i[2k+1 : 2k]$ (two bits)
5. $Carry(\Delta A_i, W_i, 2k)$ (one bit)
6. $Carry(\Delta E_i, W_i, 2k)$ (one bit)
7. $W_i[2k+1 : 2k]$ (two bits)

Note the change of the indices of A and E in the first two lines, compared to the case of one round per clock cycle.

Separation of Template Tables Based on the Round Index Modulo d. Since in every clock cycle d rounds are calculated, if any two round numbers are different modulo d, then they use different physical gates. Therefore, different template tables should be built based on the the round number modulo d. (In experiments that we do not present in this article we managed to find the secret even without distinction between the rounds. However, we believe it is more accurate to differentiate between them.)

Changes to Step 1. In the first clock cycle, the calculated values of A_0^t and E_0^t overwrite A_{-d} and E_{-d}, rather than A_{-1} and E_{-1}. For this reason, the four words found in the first step, are $A_{-d}, E_{-d}, \Delta A_0, \Delta E_0$, rather than $A_{-1}, E_{-1}, \Delta A_0, \Delta E_0$. Excepting this, the first step is performed in exactly the same manner as in the case of one round per clock cycle.

Changes to Step 2. After the first step, A_{-d} and E_{-d} are already known, while $A_{-1}, E_{-1}, A_{5-d}, E_{5-d}$ are still unknown. So the hypotheses in this case are on $A_{-1}, E_{-1}, A_{5-d}, E_{5-d}$.

4 Experimental Results

Both the profiling and the attack stages of the presented template attack run at the scope of a single SHA-2 invocation. Therefore, a successful recovery of the SHA-2 output from power traces is a sufficient condition for forging an HMAC-SHA-2 signature.

4.1 Setup

To evaluate the proposed method we took a low-area SHA-256 realization from [27]. We synthesized the RTL for the following two target platforms:

1. ASIC netlist using the Yosys synthesizer [29] and the NanGate FreePDK45 Open Cell Library [19]. The netlist was then simulated using the SideChannel Studio, a pre-silicon side channel leakage simulator by FortifyIQ [8]. The simulator comprises two stages: the first (ScopeIQ) performs a power-aware functional simulation of the netlist and generates power traces and the second stage (ScoreIQ) runs the analysis.
2. Two CW305 Artix FPGA target boards by NewAE Technology [21] with the Keysight E36100B Series DC Power Supply for power stabilization. The traces were collected using the NewAE Technology ChipWhisperer-Lite kit and, after extracting the points of interest as described in Sect. 3.2, the traces were analyzed using ScoreIQ, similarly to the simulation-based traces. The power signal was obtained by measuring current via a shunt resistor connected serially to the FPGA supply line.

The power traces acquisition by the ScopeIQ simulator for the first platform was performed in Amazon cloud in 64 parallel threads. The trace analysis by ScoreIQ for both platforms ran on a local macOS machine.

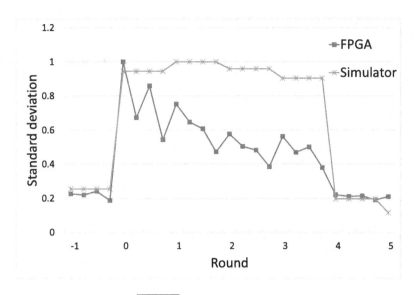

Fig. 4. Standard deviation of $\overline{M_{g,c,w,s}^{i,k}}$ over time for some constant i from the simulation and the FPGA-based measurements.

4.2 Choosing the Points of Interest

The points of interest were chosen in a way that maximizes the standard deviation of the trace samples. Namely, we calculated the standard deviation for each sample in the averaged power trace $\overline{M_{g,c,w,s}^{i,k}}$ for a fixed i over all possible values of the vector (g, c, w, k). Figure 4 shows the normalized standard deviation of $\overline{M_{g,c,w,s}^{i,k}}$ over time in the first five rounds for the traces taken from the simulation and from the FPGA. Note that the simulator is cycle-based, and therefore it produces a single power sample per cycle. In the FPGA-based setup, four samples per cycle were taken.

Both the FPGA and the simulator-based graphs clearly show that the first 4 rounds (0 to 3) provide the most information about the data. There is a slight difference between the two graphs which results from the noisy FPGA environment in contrast to the simulator that assumed no noise.

4.3 Working with Multiple Hypotheses

Our experiments with a known key showed that the required number of traces both for the attack stage and for the profiling stage can be significantly reduced by considering a few finalists rather that taking only the winner hypothesis. Hence, we followed the strategy described below.

Recall (Sect. 3.3) that the attack stage comprises three steps, where steps 1 and 2 produce a prioritized list of hypotheses and step 3 is a simple calculation. At step 1 (finding A_{-1}, E_{-1}), we start by choosing q_1 best hypotheses for bits

$0, 1$, where q_1 is a parameter. For the subsequent bit windows, $(k > 0)$ we start from the q_1 best hypotheses for bits $2k - 1 : 0$, and combine them with 256 hypotheses for bits $2k + 1 : 2k$, thus obtaining a total of $256q_1$ hypotheses for bits $2k + 1 : 0$. From these we choose the best q_1 hypotheses for the next step. Finally, we obtain q_1 hypotheses for the full values of $A_{-1}, \Delta A_0, E_{-1}, \Delta E_0$.

Step 2 (finding $A_{-2}, A_{-3}, E_{-2}, E_{-3}$) is performed for each one of these q_1 hypotheses separately. It is performed in a similar way to step 1 by 2-bit windows, this time choosing the best q_2 at each iteration. At the end of this step, we obtain q_2 hypotheses for each of the q_1 hypotheses from step 1, giving us a total of $q_1 q_2$ hypotheses for the full initial internal state of the inner SHA-256.

After obtaining $q_1 q_2$ hypotheses for the inner SHA, the outer SHA should be attacked in the same way, repeating the attack for each of them, resulting in a total of $(q_1 q_2)^2$ iterations. However, we observed the following phenomenon that helped us accelerate this process significantly. Using the technique for finding POIs from Sect. 3.2, it is possible to find the correct hypothesis by correlation. Namely, for each of the $q_1 q_2$ hypotheses for the inner SHA initial state, and for every trace from a subset of the attack traces we calculate the Hamming distance hd_δ^t according to (15), and calculate its correlation with samples at the points of interest at round δ. Only if the hypothesis is correct, the correlations are expected to be significantly above the noise level. Experimentally we found that in both our setups—FPGA and simulation—this test always works with an arbitrary subset of 7K traces, $\delta = 6$ and the threshold value of 5% to distinguish between significant correlations and noise. For a different setup, these parameters may need adjustment.

If one of the hypotheses has passed the test, we can attack the outer SHA-256 assuming it is correct. Namely, for every trace, we can calculate the output from the inner SHA-256 and in the same way attack the outer SHA-256, obtaining a total of $q_1 q_2$ hypotheses for the full initial internal state of the outer SHA-256. The correct hypothesis can then be found by a brute-force attack.

In our setup we used the values $q_1 = 15, q_2 = 10$. For a different setup, different values of q_1, q_2 may work better.

4.4   Trace Acquisition and Analysis

For the trace acquisition setup we used a simulator and two FPGA devices: FPGA1 and FPGA2. First, we acquired pools of profiling traces from FPGA1 and from the synthesized ASIC netlist in simulation. After that, we acquired attack traces from FPGA2, using a key $key0$ and in the simulation using three keys $key0, key1, key2$. The traces have been analyzed as follows:

1. We chose several subset sizes for the profiling and several subset sizes for the attack (the set of sizes depends on the setup).
2. From every pool and for every subset size we randomly picked several subsets of that size out of the pool (the number of subsets differed between the profiling and the attack trace pools, and between the setups).

48   Y. Belenky et al.

Table 1. Summary of the experiments

Setup		FPGA	Simulator		
Key		key0	key0	key1	key2
Profile	Pool size	8.4M	6M		
	Subset sizes (x1000)	1500, 2000, 3000	200, 300, 750		
	# of subsets of each size	14	13		
	Needed for 100% success	3M	750K	750K	750K
Attack	Pool size	1.5M	1M		
	Subset sizes (x1000)	100, 200, 300, 400, 500, 600, 700			
	# of subsets of each size	10			
	Needed for 100% success	400K	200K	300K	600K
Approximate time (min)	Acquisition of profile traces	90	75	75	75
	Acquisition of attack traces	12	20	30	60
	Attack	16	3	4	8
	Total (without profiling)	28	23	34	68
	Total (with profiling)	118	98	109	143

3. We mounted the attack for every combination of a subset of profile traces and a subset of attack traces.
4. We built graphs of the success rate as a function of the setup, the key and the subset sizes (see Fig. 5).

Table 1 summarizes the details of each setup, the amounts of traces for which we received 100% success, and the corresponding time by stage.

From the graphs we can see that:

1. For every key used in our experiments, with sufficient profiling traces and attack traces we reached 100% success, while there is a substantial difference in the required amounts of attack traces for different keys.
2. It is possible to attack one device using profiling data from another device of the same type.

In all these experiments we normalized the profiling tables as described in Sect. 3.2. We also performed experiments without normalization. For both the FPGA and the simulator, using each of the keys, we used the entire pool of traces (8.4M for the profile and 1.5M for the attack on the FPGA, 6M for the profile and 1M for the attack on the simulator). In all cases the attack failed already at step 1. Moreover, the number of incorrect bits in the best hypothesis after step 1 was 63 out of 128 for FPGA and 49 out of 128 for the simulator. Clearly, the attack does not work without the normalization, at least without significantly increasing the amounts of traces.

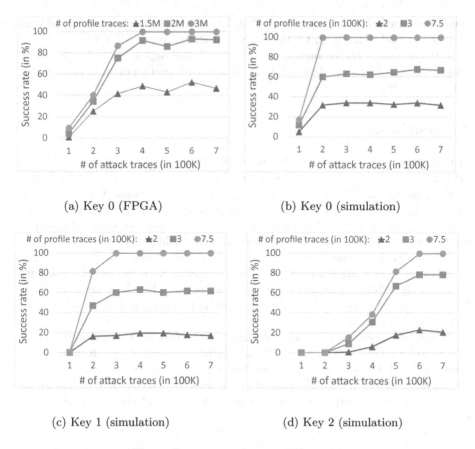

(a) Key 0 (FPGA)   (b) Key 0 (simulation)

(c) Key 1 (simulation)   (d) Key 2 (simulation)

Fig. 5. Percentage of successful attacks.

5 Suggested Mitigation

The template attack in general and the attack described in this article in particular both require a profiling stage. If a hardware unit is dedicated solely to calculating HMAC with a fixed key, and does not permit an arbitrary SHA-2 calculation, then this attack cannot be mounted. However, two points must be taken into account:

1. Access to pure SHA-2 units must be blocked in all units of the IC in the market, otherwise the attacker may exploit the unit with the plain SHA-2 enabled for profiling.
2. If somewhere in the chip there is a hardware unit which provides the plain SHA-2 functionality, it must be based on a different architecture, otherwise it is possible to use this hardware unit on the same chip for the profiling.

A similar but softer approach is to define a policy which will prevent massive invocations of a pure SHA-2 function; for example, by enforcing time intervals between the invocations. Thus, the HMAC calculation for each message will start from the second block both for the inner and for the outer SHA-2.

Alternatively, a power analysis resistant SHA-256 engine can be implemented using an adapted version of one of the methods developed for other cryptographic modules [13, 20].

6 Conclusions

In this article we have presented a novel practical template attack on HMAC-SHA-2 and have demonstrated its successful application to two HMAC implementations: on an FPGA and on a side channel leakage simulator. We showed that the profile built from the traces collected on one device can be used for attacking another device of the same type. To the best of our knowledge, this is the first time a full attack has been demonstrated which recovers a key derivative that allows for the forging of signatures. The attack was presented and demonstrated on a single round per cycle implementation of the SHA-256 hash function. Its extension to the other members of the SHA-2 family is straightforward. Furthermore, we have shown a method to generalize this attack to a higher number of rounds per cycle.

A notable outcome of this publication is the fact that power analysis on hardware-based HMAC-SHA-2 works in practice. This should result in increased attention to HMAC-SHA-2 during product vulnerability assessment.

We also suggested possible ways of mitigation. We believe there is a place for further academic research to come up with effective and efficient countermeasures.

References

1. ANSSI, Amossys, EDSI, LETI, Lexfo, Oppida, Quarkslab, SERMA, Synacktiv, Thales, Trusted Labs: Inter-CESTI: Methodological and Technical Feedbacks on Hardware Devices Evaluations. Technical report (2020). https://www.sstic. org/2020/presentation/inter-cesti_methodological_and_technical_feedbacks_on_ hardware_devices_evaluations/
2. Archambeau, C., Peeters, E., Standaert, F.X., Quisquater, J.J.: Template attacks in principal subspaces. In: Goubin, L., Matsui, M. (eds.) CHES 2006. LNCS, vol. 4249, pp. 1–14. Springer, Heidelberg (2006). https://doi.org/10.1007/11894063_1
3. Belaïd, S., Bettale, L., Dottax, E., Genelle, L., Rondepierre, F.: Differential power analysis of HMAC SHA-1 and HMAC SHA-2 in the hamming weight model. In: Obaidat, M., Holzinger, A., Filipe, J. (eds.) ICETE 2014. CCIS, vol. 554, pp. 363–379. Springer, Cham (2015). https://doi.org/10.1007/978-3-319-25915-4_19
4. BSI: Anwendungshinweise und Interpretationen zum Schema (AIS) 46. Technical report, BSI (2013). https://www.bsi.bund.de/SharedDocs/Downloads/DE/BSI/ Zertifizierung/Interpretationen/AIS_46_pdf.pdf?__blob=publicationFile&v=1
5. Chari, S., Rao, J.R., Rohatgi, P.: Template attacks. In: Kaliski, B.S., Koç, K., Paar, C. (eds.) CHES 2002. LNCS, vol. 2523, pp. 13–28. Springer, Heidelberg (2002). https://doi.org/10.1007/3-540-36400-5_3

6. FIPS: PUB 198-1, The Keyed-Hash Message Authentication Code (HMAC). Technical report, National Institute of Standards and Technology, Gaithersburg, MD, July 2008. https://doi.org/10.6028/NIST.FIPS.198-1. https://nvlpubs.nist.gov/nistpubs/FIPS/NIST.FIPS.198-1.pdf
7. FIPS: PUB 180-4, Secure Hash Standard (SHS). Technical report, National Institute of Standards and Technology (NIST) (2012)
8. FortifyIQ Inc.: SideChannel Studio. https://www.fortifyiq.com/sidechannel-studio.html
9. Fouque, P.A., Leurent, G., Réal, D., Valette, F.: Practical electromagnetic template attack on HMAC. In: Clavier, C., Gaj, K. (eds.) CHES 2009. LNCS, vol. 5747, pp. 66–80. Springer, Heidelberg (2009). https://doi.org/10.1007/978-3-642-04138-9_6
10. Gauravaram, P., Okeya, K.: An update on the side channel cryptanalysis of MACs based on cryptographic hash functions. In: Srinathan, K., Rangan, C.P., Yung, M. (eds.) INDOCRYPT 2007. LNCS, vol. 4859, pp. 393–403. Springer, Heidelberg (2007). https://doi.org/10.1007/978-3-540-77026-8_31
11. Gebotys, C.H., White, B.A., Mateos, E.: Preaveraging and carry propagate approaches to side-channel analysis of HMAC-SHA256. ACM Trans. Embed. Comput. Syst. **15**(1), 1–19 (2016). https://doi.org/10.1145/2794093. https://dl.acm.org/doi/10.1145/2794093
12. Genkin, D., Shamir, A., Tromer, E.: RSA key extraction via low-bandwidth acoustic cryptanalysis. In: Garay, J.A., Gennaro, R. (eds.) CRYPTO 2014. LNCS, vol. 8616, pp. 444–461. Springer, Heidelberg (2014). https://doi.org/10.1007/978-3-662-44371-2_25
13. Gross, H., Mangard, S., Korak, T.: Domain-oriented masking: compact masked hardware implementations with arbitrary protection order. In: TIS@ CCS, p. 3 (2016). https://doi.org/10.1145/2996366.2996426
14. Kannwischer, M.J., Genêt, A., Butin, D., Krämer, J., Buchmann, J.: Differential power analysis of XMSS and SPHINCS. In: Fan, J., Gierlichs, B. (eds.) COSADE 2018. LNCS, vol. 10815, pp. 168–188. Springer, Cham (2018). https://doi.org/10.1007/978-3-319-89641-0_10
15. Kocher, P., Jaffe, J., Jun, B.: Differential power analysis. In: Wiener, M. (eds.) CRYPTO 1999. LNCS, vol. 1666, pp. 388–397. Springer, Heidelberg (1999). https://doi.org/10.1007/3-540-48405-1_25
16. Kocher, P.C.: Timing attacks on implementations of Diffie-Hellman, RSA, DSS, and other systems. In: Koblitz, N. (eds.) CRYPTO 1996. LNCS, vol. 1109, pp. 104–113. Springer, Heidelberg (1996). https://doi.org/10.1007/3-540-68697-5_9
17. Lemke, K., Schramm, K., Paar, C.: DPA on n-bit sized Boolean and arithmetic operations and its application to IDEA, RC6, and the HMAC-construction. In: Joye, M., Quisquater, J.J. (eds.) CHES 2004. LNCS, vol. 3156, pp. 205–219. Springer, Heidelberg (2004). https://doi.org/10.1007/978-3-540-28632-5_15
18. McEvoy, R., Tunstall, M., Murphy, C.C., Marnane, W.P.: Differential power analysis of HMAC based on SHA-2, and countermeasures. In: Kim, S., Yung, M., Lee, H.W. (eds.) WISA 2007. LNCS, vol. 4867, pp. 317–332. Springer, Heidelberg (2007). https://doi.org/10.1007/978-3-540-77535-5_23
19. NanGate Inc.: NanGate FreePDK45 Open Cell Library (2008). http://www.nangate.com/?page_id=2325
20. Nikova, S., Rechberger, C., Rijmen, V.: Threshold implementations against side-channel attacks and glitches. In: Ning, P., Qing, S., Li, N. (eds.) ICICS 2006. LNCS, vol. 4307, pp. 529–545. Springer, Heidelberg (2006). https://doi.org/10.1007/11935308_38

21. O'Flynn, C., Chen, Z.D.: ChipWhisperer: an open-source platform for hardware embedded security research. In: Prouff, E. (eds.) COSADE 2014. LNCS, vol. 8622, pp. 243–260. Springer, Cham (2014). https://doi.org/10.1007/978-3-319-10175-0_17

22. Okeya, K.: Side channel attacks against HMACs based on block-cipher based hash functions. In: Batten, L.M., Safavi-Naini, R. (eds.) ACISP 2006. LNCS, vol. 4058, pp. 432–443. Springer, Heidelberg (2006). https://doi.org/10.1007/11780656_36

23. Oswald, D.: Side-channel attacks on SHA-1-based product authentication ICs. In: Homma, N., Medwed, M. (eds.) CARDIS 2015. LNCS, vol. 9514, pp. 3–14. Springer, Cham (2016). https://doi.org/10.1007/978-3-319-31271-2_1

24. Rechberger, C., Oswald, E.: Practical template attacks. In: Lim, C.H., Yung, M. (eds.) WISA 2004. LNCS, vol. 3325, pp. 440–456. Springer, Heidelberg (2005). https://doi.org/10.1007/978-3-540-31815-6_35

25. Rohatgi, P., Marson, M.: NSA Suite B Crypto, Keys, and Side Channel Attacks (2013). https://www.rambus.com/nsa-suite-b-crypto-keys-and-side-channel-attacks-2013-rsa-conference/

26. Schindler, W., Lemke, K., Paar, C.: A stochastic model for differential side channel cryptanalysis. In: Rao, J.R., Sunar, B. (eds.) CHES 2005. LNCS, vol. 3659, pp. 30–46. Springer, Heidelberg (2005). https://doi.org/10.1007/11545262_3

27. Strömbergson, J.: secworks/sha256: Hardware implementation of the SHA-256 cryptographic hash function. https://github.com/secworks/sha256

28. Tunstall, M., Hanley, N., McEvoy, R.P., Whelan, C., Murphy, C.C., Marnane, W.P.: Correlation power analysis of large word sizes. In: IET Irish Signals and Systems Conference (ISSC), pp. 145–150 (2007)

29. Wolf, C.: Yosys open synthesis suite (2016)

30. Yarom, Y., Genkin, D., Heninger, N.: CacheBleed: a timing attack on OpenSSL constant time RSA. In: Gierlichs, B., Poschmann, A.Y. (eds.) CHES 2016. LNCS, vol. 9813, pp. 346–367. Springer, Heidelberg (2016). https://doi.org/10.1007/978-3-662-53140-2_17

Learning When to Stop: A Mutual Information Approach to Prevent Overfitting in Profiled Side-Channel Analysis

Guilherme Perin[1], Ileana Buhan[2], and Stjepan Picek[1(✉)]

[1] Delft University of Technology, Delft, The Netherlands
{g.perin,s.picek}@tudelft.nl
[2] Radboud University, Nijmegen, The Netherlands
ileana.buhan@ru.nl

Abstract. Today, deep neural networks are a common choice for conducting the profiled side-channel analysis. Unfortunately, it is not trivial to find neural network hyperparameters that would result in top-performing attacks. The hyperparameter leading the training process is the number of epochs during which the training happens. If the training is too short, the network does not reach its full capacity, while if the training is too long, the network overfits and cannot generalize to unseen examples.

In this paper, we tackle the problem of determining the correct epoch to stop the training in the deep learning-based side-channel analysis. We demonstrate that the amount of information, or, more precisely, mutual information transferred to the output layer, can be measured and used as a reference metric to determine the epoch at which the network offers optimal generalization. To validate the proposed methodology, we provide extensive experimental results.

Keywords: Side-channel analysis · Neural networks · Overfitting · Mutual information · Information bottleneck

1 Introduction

Recently, deep learning techniques proved to be a powerful option for profiled side-channel analysis (SCA) as they 1) do not need the pre-processing phase to select the points of interest, and 2) perform well even in the presence of noise and countermeasures [3,8]. Although the application of deep learning for profiled SCA became popular, there are many open questions like the selection of hyperparameters for successful side-channel attacks. For hyperparameters like architectural details (e.g., number of layers, neurons), recent works provided

This work was supported by the European Union's H2020 Programme under grant agreement number ICT-731591 (REASSURE).

directions to follow [16,29,30]. At the same time, the ability to select the right moment to stop the training phase is left to instinct (and sometimes luck) as there does not seem to be a direct connection between the machine learning metrics and the performance of a side-channel attack, as discussed later [14]. While the lack of a clear connection may not be deemed crucial, the training phase's end depends on metrics like accuracy, loss, recall, and performance on a validation set. If the training phase finishes too late, the machine learning model overfits. As a consequence of overfitting, the model will not generalize to unseen data, and the attack phase will fail.[1]

One way to analyze the generalization of a deep neural network is through the lens of information theory. In [19], the authors proposed a new methodology to interpret the training of a multilayer perceptron (MLP) through a theory called the *Information Bottleneck* (IB) [25]. They demonstrated that the training of an MLP provides two distinct phases - *fitting* and *compression*. These phases are determined by computing the mutual information between the intermediate representations (activations from hidden layers) and input (raw data) or output (labels). The output of a hidden layer can be seen as a summary of statistics containing information about the input and output. The fitting phase is usually very fast, requiring only a few epochs, while the compression phase lasts longer. The compression phase is also responsible for the neural network's generalization, i.e., its ability to perform on unseen data. We consider the mutual information between output layer activation's and the data labels (as given by the leakage model) as a metric to identify the epoch when the neural network achieves its optimal generalization capacity. Our results show that training a network for too many epochs harms generalization, and early stopping based on the mutual information metric is a reliable technique to avoid this scenario. We test our metric against three masked AES implementations and show that our metric provides superior results than the typical metrics like accuracy, recall, or loss.

To the best of our knowledge, this is the first result providing a reliable attack performance metric different from conducting an actual attack (key ranking). While key ranking is a reliable validation metric to optimize the generalization of a deep neural network for side-channel attacks [3], it brings significant computational overhead when using large validation sets. On the other hand, mutual information offers remarkable performance at a fraction of the computational cost as it does not have to be computed for all key hypotheses. To facilitate reproducible research, we will make the source code publicly available.

1.1   Related Works

From the first paper considering convolutional neural networks for SCA [10], deep learning gained significant recognition in the SCA community as an important

---

[1] It is also possible for a machine learning model to underfit if the training stopped too early. Still, this is usually of less concern as the resulting machine learning model would generalize to unseen data but not use its full potential, i.e., the attack would not be as powerful as possible.

direction to follow for profiled SCA. Despite good results, even when considering protected targets [3,8,13,30], there are open questions. For instance, progress on topics like interpretability and explainability of neural networks is difficult in general, and as such, there are not many results for SCA [11,26,27].

A second important research direction explored by the SCA community is how to find optimal architectures, i.e., tune hyperparameters [28–30]. Common options for hyperparameter exploration are number/types of layers/neurons, activation functions, and the number of epochs. Determining the number of training epochs is relevant for any application domain but is a particularly challenging problem in SCA since machine learning metrics are known not to indicate well the SCA performance [14]. Indeed, during the machine learning training process, we aim to minimize loss, which often appears to be inversely proportional to accuracy, but there is no mathematical relationship between those two metrics. What is more, in side-channel analysis, the goal is to break the target with as few as possible attack traces, which again does not seem to have direct mathematical relationships with accuracy (or other common machine learning metrics like precision and recall). This gap comes as a consequence of the context of the problem more than the profiling method. Indeed, it is common in machine learning applications to discuss the classification or prediction of single observations for which accuracy, precision and recall are natural metrics. By contrast, the most standard (and powerful) SCAs are the continuous DPAs for which information theoretic metrics are more reflective since they are correlated with the complexity of these attacks (in the number of traces). Common options are the use of early stopping or a predetermined number of epochs for training [7,8,15,30]. In both cases, as the performance is observed through machine learning metrics, it is difficult to know if the training stopped at the right moment.

To evaluate the resilience against side-channel attacks, two different types of metrics are required. Mutual information has been long established in the context of side-channel evaluations as the metric of choice for evaluating the quality of an implementation [21]. Mutual information has two interesting properties: first, it is independent of the adversary, and second, it has the same meaning for any implementation or countermeasure. It is, however, advisable to complement an information-theoretic metric with a security metric (success rate or guessing entropy) that captures the success of an adversary in exploiting such information [23]. Conditional entropy has also been used to compare the strength of profiled attacks [22]. One limitation for applying information-theoretical metrics is the computation of metrics on real measurements due to statistical sampling, making the estimation of the true statistical distribution impossible. As a solution, [2] proposed easy-to-compute bounds Perceived Information (lower bound) and Hypothetical Information (upper bound). These metrics have been shown to work well under the assumption that the target variable has a uniform probability distribution. Perceived Information has also been shown to be asymptotically equivalent to the Negative Log-Likelihood when used as a loss function during the training of a neural network [12]. Although the maximization of perceived information from [12] is a consistent objective in deep learning-based profiled side-channel analysis, the usage of PI value to estimate, e.g., the best epoch to stop the training directly implicates that the loss function value is an adequate metric for this task, which unfortunately is not a general observation in deep learning-based profiled SCA. As observed in [14], inconsistency between loss function and SCA metrics might occur very often for several deep learning models, especially in the presence of the class imbalance problem. Still, as long as a metric embeds a sum of log probabilities, the intuition that it represents a good predictor of continuous attacks (and, therefore, good for model comparisons) should hold to a good extent. To circumvent this problem, Robissout et al. [17] conducted a success rate evaluation for every epoch of training and validation. This solution leads to a significant time overhead for large number of attack traces. More importantly, there is no consensus on calculating the key rank for training sets with random keys, as best practice recommends.

1.2 Contributions

This work provides two main contributions as follows:

1. A new application for the use of mutual information as a metric to select the epoch where a deep network achieves its best performance for profiled side-channel analysis. We show that the information about the labels transferred to the output layer can be measured and used as a reliable metric to determine when to stop the training phase. Our approach offers four distinct improvements compared to existing results. First, the mutual information metric is precise and can accurately predict the epoch at which the network achieves its best performance, while the alternative, validation key ranking, will give a range of values for the best epoch. Second, the computational overhead for computing the information transferred to the output layer is much smaller than performing a full attack to obtain the key ranking at each epoch's end. Third, mutual information is suitable for training sets with randomized keys, as recommended by best practices, while there is no consensus on calculating the key ranking for this type of training sets, as far as the authors are aware. Forth, we extend [19], where the authors show how to calculate the information path for MLP architectures to CNN architectures.
2. The use of mutual information consistently offers good performance. We test it on three publicly available datasets, using two leakage models and two different architectures. In the experimental section, we thoroughly compare its performance to the four conventional metrics: validation loss, validation accuracy, validation recall, and validation key rank. We conclude that in all cases, the use of mutual information will lead to better generalization.

2   Background

2.1   Deep Learning in the Context of Side-Channel Analysis

In the profiled scenario, we assume the adversary has full control of a device identical to the targeted one. Thus, we consider the supervised learning task, i.e., learning a function f mapping an input to the output $(f : \mathcal{X} \rightarrow Y)$ based on examples of input-output pairs. The examples come from a dataset divided into three parts: profiling set consisting of N traces, validation set consisting of V traces, and attack set consisting of Q traces.

Once we learn the function f, the goal of the attack phase is to make predictions about the classes

$$y(x_1, k^*), \ldots, y(x_Q, k^*),$$

where k^* represents the secret (unknown) key of the device under the attack.

In the profiled SCA, the trained neural network is tested against a Q side-channel traces, in which the secret key is unknown, and the key recovery methodology assumes that the correct key is the one that maximizes the summation probabilities S_k for each key byte candidate:

$$S_k = \sum_{i=1}^{Q} \log(p_{i,j}). \tag{1}$$

The value (i.e., the probability) $p_{i,j}$ is an element of a matrix P with size *number of traces* × *number of classes*. This matrix gives the output class probabilities obtained by using the model f on a test or validation set. Thus, $p_{i,j}$ is the probability element obtained as a function of the attack trace x_i, leakage model l, and input data p_{k_i} for every possible key guess k: $f_k(x_i, p_{k_i}, l)$. In the context of neural networks, $p_{i,j}$ represents the neuron's activation value for trace i from the *Softmax* output layer.

A usual approach to assess the attacker's performance is to use metrics that denote the number of measurements required to obtain the secret key k^*. Common examples of such metrics are guessing entropy (GE) and success rate (SR) [23]. *Guessing entropy* represents the average number of key candidates an adversary needs to test to determine the correct key, denoted with k^*, after conducting a side-channel analysis. More specifically, given Q traces in the attack phase, an attack outputs a vector $g = [g_1, g_2, ..., g_{|K|}]$ in decreasing order of probability. The guessing entropy is the average position of k^* in g over several experiments (commonly 50 or 100). The *success rate* is defined as the average empirical probability that g_1 equals the secret key k^*.

For a deep learning-based SCA to be successful, the trained model must generalize well, which means as small as a possible error on the test set. Next, we define the generalization interval in SCA.

Definition 1. *Generalization Interval in SCA. Given (X_{train}, Y_{train}) where X_{train} represents the input training data and Y_{train} represents a set of training labels, the generalization interval defines the epochs where a successful key recovery can be obtained using Eq. (1).*

Techniques used to reduce test errors are commonly known as regularization techniques, among which *early-stopping* is one of the best-known techniques [6]. Early stopping works under the assumption that the neural network achieved the best generalization and will start overfitting and deteriorate the generalization after this point (of best generalization), which is an undesired behavior. Consequently, determining the pre-specified number of iterations (epochs) is a hyperparameter selection process.

2.2 Datasets

We consider three publicly available datasets, instances of software AES implementations protected with the first-order Boolean masking. The first one is the ASCAD database [15]. We use the trace set where the plaintext and key are **randomly** defined for each separate encryption. This trace set is used as a training set. A second fixed-key trace set is split into validation and test sets. We attack the third key byte. In this dataset, each trace contains 1 400 features. This dataset is available at https://github.com/ANSSI-FR/ASCAD/tree/master/ATMEGA_AES_v1/ATM_AES_v1_variable_key.

The second dataset is the DPA Contest v4 (DPAv4) [24]. DPAv4 dataset provides traces collected from an AES-256 RSM (rotate shift masking) implementation. This dataset has a **fixed key**, and we attack the first key byte. Each trace consists of 2 000 features. This dataset is available at http://www.dpacontest.org/v4/.

The third dataset refers to the CHES Capture-the-flag (CTF) masked AES-128 encryption trace set, released in 2018 for the Conference on Cryptographic Hardware and Embedded Systems (CHES). In our experiments, the training set has a **fixed key** that is different from the key configured for the validation and test sets. Each trace consists of 2 200 features. We attack the first key byte. This dataset is available at https://chesctf.riscure.com/2018/news.

2.3 Information Theory

In information theory, the (marginal) entropy $H(X)$ of a random variable X is defined as the average information obtained by observing X, and it can be quantitatively defined as:

$$H(X) = - \sum_{x \in X} p(x) \log_2 p(x), \tag{2}$$

where $p(x)$ represents the probability of variable X taking value x. The *conditional entropy* of X given Y, which represents the entropy of X when Y is known, is defined as:

$$H(X|Y) = - \sum_{x \in X} p(x) \sum_{y \in Y} p(x|y) \log_2 p(x|y). \tag{3}$$

Finally, *mutual information* defines the dependence between variables X and Y, and it can be defined using entropy and conditional entropy values as:

$$I(X;Y) = H(X) - H(X|Y). \tag{4}$$

An important property of mutual information in this context is the Data Processing Inequality (DPI), which states that for any three variables X, Y, Z, forming a Markov chain, $X \to Y \to Z$, the mutual information between the variables can only decrease and $I(X; Y) \geq I(X; Z)$.

3   Information Theory of Deep Neural Networks

Shwartz-Ziv and Tishby [19] showed that information theory could be used to visualize the training phase of a deep network to compare the performance of different network architectures. Intuitively, when training a network, each layer gets its information from the layer before and transforms it using matrix multiplication of nonlinear functions. Their insight was to treat each layer (the hidden activation functions) in the deep network as a random variable fully described by the information captured about the input data and the labels. Modeling each layer in the deep network as a random variable gives an alternative view of a deep network as a Markov chain. Each variable represents the nonlinear activation function, which successively transforms the input data into the label space. Using the mutual information between the layers, the input data, and the labels, we can visualize the input data's transformation into the label space.

Definition 2. *Information Path. Given a tuple* (X, Y, T_i) *where* X *represents the input data,* Y *represents a set of labels and* T_i *is a hidden layer in an n-layered network, described as* $X, Y \to T_1 \to ... \to T_n$, *the information path is defined as the set of points* $\{[I(X; T_i), I(T_i; Y)] | i \in \{1, n\}\}$.

The *information path* is a record of the information each hidden layer preserves about the input data X and the output variables Y. It is typically computed for each epoch during the training phase. The information is plotted in a two-dimensional coordinate system referred to as the *information plane*. The coordinates of the information plane quantify the bits of information layer T_i has about the input data X as $I(X; T_i)$, and the bits of information layer T_i has about the labels Y as $I(T_i; Y)$. We can view the variable T_i as a compressed representation of the input X, and $I(X; T_i)$ calculated based on the value $p(x)p(t_i|x)$, which measures how compact the representation of X is. The maximum value for $I(X; T_i)$ is $H(X)$, which is the Shannon entropy corresponding to the case where T_i copies X and there is no compression. The minimal value for $I(T_i; X)$ is 0 and corresponds to the case where T has one value.

Lemma 1. *Information Path Uniqueness. For each tuple* (X, Y, T_i), *where* X *represents the input data,* Y *represents a set of labels, and* T_i *is a layer in an n-layered network described as* $X, Y \to T_1 \to ... \to T_n$ *there exists a unique information path that satisfies the following two inequalities:*

$$H(X) \geq I(X; T_1) \geq ... \geq I(X; T_n) \geq I(X; \hat{Y}), \tag{5}$$

where $\hat{Y}$ *are the labels predicted by the network, and*

$$I(X; Y) \geq I(T_1; Y) \geq ... \geq I(T_n; Y) \geq I(\hat{Y}; Y). \tag{6}$$

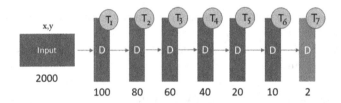

Fig. 1. MLP with five hidden layers ($T_{2:6}$). The letter "D" denotes the dense (fully-connected) layer while the labels T_1 and T_7 corresponds input and output layers, respectively, with the *Tanh* activation function. The output layer T_7 has the *Softmax* activation function. The numbers under the layers indicate the number of neurons.

Proof. The proof for this lemma follows immediately by applying the DPI principle. □

3.1 Information Bottleneck Principle

Shwartz-Ziv and Tishby observed that stochastic gradient descent (SGD) optimization defines two distinct phases during training [19]. The first one is the *fitting* phase, where both $I(X;T_i)$ and $I(T_i;Y)$ increase fast as the training progresses. During the fitting phase, the deep network layers increase information about the input data and the labels. The second phase is the *compression* phase, where the network starts to compress or forget information about the input data and slowly increases its generalization capacity by retaining more information about the labels.

The network's behavior during the compression phase has been linked to the form of the activation functions [4]. This happens due to a random diffusion-like behavior of the SGD algorithm if double-sided saturating[2] nonlinear activation function such as *Tanh* is employed. More precisely, Shwartz-Ziv and Tishby provided results for *Tanh* and showed how information about the labels increases in the compression phase [19]. On the other hand, Saxe et al. demonstrated that the non-saturating activation functions like *ReLU* provide a different behavior in the compression phase as there is no causal connection between generalization and compression [18].

Figure 2 gives an overview of the information path of the deep network architecture described in Fig. 1 at epochs: 1, 20, 100, and 200 during the training process. Each figure contains the coordinates of the information $[I(X;T_i),I(T_i;Y)]$ where i represents the i-th layer. The information is captured from the five hidden layers ($T_{2:6}$) plus an input layer (T_1) and an output layer (T_7).

For the above example, we see that information changes only for the last two hidden layers T_5 and T_6, and the output layer T_7. The plot contains mutual information results for twenty training experiments (i.e., twenty dots for each layer). These results demonstrate that at the beginning of the training phase, the mutual

---

[2] A saturating activation function squeezes the input data, i.e., the output is bounded to a certain range.

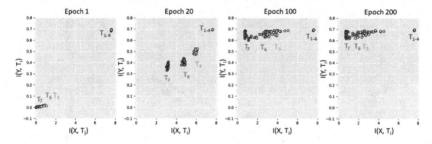

Fig. 2. The information flow captured at epoch 1, 20, 100, and 200 for the network architecture depicted in Fig. 1 when using the DPAv4 dataset (training set).

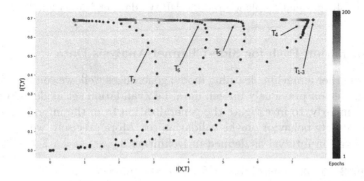

Fig. 3. Information plane for the DPAv4 dataset (training set).

information quantities $[I(X;T_i), I(T_i;Y)]$ are at a minimum level for hidden layers T_5 and T_6, and for the output layer T_7. As the training progresses (epochs 20 and 100), the mutual information values increase until the $[I(X;T_i), I(T_i;Y)]$ reaches its maximum for all layers, including the output layer. If we continue the training process, the compression phase starts to happen as $I(X;T_i)$ starts to decrease and $I(T_i;Y)$ stays at a maximum level. In Fig. 2, this information path is clearly observed for hidden layers T_5 and T_6, and the output layer T_7. The values obtained for layers T_1 to T_4 provide very small changes during training, which are difficult to visualize due to the scale of Fig. 1.

Figure 3 shows the evolution of the information path for all training epochs for the DPAv4 dataset for the same architecture given in Fig. 1. The training evolution provides two distinct phases (fitting and compression), as discussed in [19]. In the first phase, the layers (mostly visible for hidden layers $T_{4:6}$ and output layer T_7) are fitting the training data. The information of an inner state T_i or layer increases for the input X and output Y^3. In the second phase, the output information stays high, but the input information starts to decrease. From the figure, it is clear that the second phase starts before epoch 100.

---

3 Note, information plane figures show different layers, but it is not possible to recognize a specific layer by just "observing" the graph, i.e., there is no pre-specified behavior for a specific layer. We store and plot data for each layer separately.

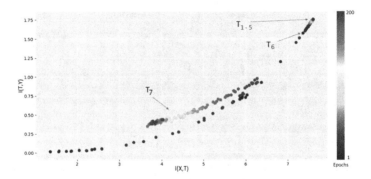

Fig. 4. Information plane from the DPAv4 dataset (validation set).

3.2   Information Path for Side-Channel Analysis Data

To assess whether a machine learning model generalizes well, we commonly check its performance on previously unseen data, i.e., validation set as defined in Definition 1. Similarly, to investigate the generalization from the information path, we must assess its behavior on the validation set. More precisely, we aim to find the generalization interval as defined in Definition 3.

Definition 3. *SCA Generalization Interval via Information Path.*
Given a tuple $(X_{train}, Y_{train}, T_i)$ where X_{train} represents the input training data, Y_{train} represents a set of training labels, and T_i is a hidden layer in an n-layered neural network, the generalization interval for SCA defines the interval of training epochs where the quantities $[I(X;T_i), I(T_i;Y)]$ reach the maximal values and we can obtain successful key recovery with Eq. (1) by predicting on the dataset X_{test} with the trained neural network.

The results in Fig. 4 show it is possible to observe a different "movement" of the points $[I(X;T_i), I(T_i;Y)]$ in the information path when using the validation set. The fitting phase is clearly seen, as $I(X;T_i)$ and $I(T_i;Y)$ increase with the processing of first epochs (for the validation set, this movement is observable for hidden layer T_6 and output layer T_7).

The compression phase is different from the information plane observed in Fig. 3. Now, the points $[I(X;T_i), I(T_i;Y)]$ reach the maximum value for each hidden layer, and, later, both quantities decrease with the processing of more epochs. This indicates the overfitting scenario for the given trained machine learning model. More specifically, this happens because the generalization in difficult SCA settings (i.e., masked or protected AES) is minimal when given in terms of deep learning metrics (accuracy, loss, recall). At the same time, we aim to capture the machine learning model at an epoch when the best possible generalization occurs. From our observations, the epoch at which the generalization is optimal is given by the moment when $I(T_n;Y)$ reaches a maximum value.

3.3   Improving the Generalization in Deep Learning-Based SCA

Recall, for a deep learning-based side-channel analysis to be successful, the trained model must generalize well to previously unseen data (validation/test set). Given a deep neural network defined by a set of hyperparameters θ, the internal representations T_i, $i \in \{1, n\}$, (where T_1 and T_n are the input and output layers, respectively) should inform about the labels Y and input X [1].

As observed from Figs. 3 and 4, we stop the training when we reach the maximum value for $I(T_n; Y)$. As such, we assume:

1. During the training, the intermediate representation T_i will be compressed to estimate Y correctly.
2. The intermediate representation T_i should be robust such that small addition of noise should not affect this compressed internal representation.
3. Only the information transferred to the output network layer is important for measuring the generalization [4].

Our investigation suggests that the maximum value for $I(T_n; Y)$ for the output layer happens when the fitting phase is finished, and the compression started. This means that the training does not need to go through the full compression phase to achieve the best generalization. This is also in line with findings from Shwartz-Ziv and Tishby as they observed that the beginning of the compression phase coincides with the best generalization [19], and Saxe et al., who showed empirical results demonstrating that the compression phase does not necessarily improve generalization [18].

In essence, the value for $I(T; Y)$ should increase for all hidden layers as the training progresses and reach a maximum value at the end of the fitting phase. This directly means that the information path helps to indicate the optimal number of training epochs for all hidden layers, especially the outer layers. As the experiments in the Sect. 4 suggest, taking the maximum value for $I(T_n; Y)$ from the output layer (where T_n are the output class probabilities after *Softmax*) provides an efficient early stopping metric for profiled side-channel analysis.

The calculation of $I(T_n; Y)$ gives minimal overhead during the training process since we need to make the computation for a small fraction of the validation set. We estimate that the time overhead to compute $I(T_n; Y)$ at the end of each epoch is less than 2%.

4   Experimental Validation

4.1   Estimating Mutual Information

The first step of calculating mutual information, Eq. (4), is *density estimation* [9], aiming to construct an approximation of the density function (denoted with p in Eqs. (2) and (3)) using observed data. There are two main approaches to density estimation. The first approach is *parametric*, where we assume the observed data to be drawn from a known family of distributions (e.g., normal distribution), while the second approach, *non-parametric*, does not assume the distribution of the observed data. We consider the non-parametric approach more suitable for our setting as we have little information about the underlying data distribution.

Common approaches for non-parametric estimation are simple discretization methods such as *equal interval binning*, (or histogram estimator), which divides the observed data into equal-sized bins, or *equal frequency intervals*, which divides the observed data into bins with an equal number of samples [5]. The generic approach's price is a user-supplied parameter such as the bin width in the case of equal-sized bins or the number of samples in each bin for the frequency-based binning. A variation of the discretization techniques described above is the *kernel density estimator*, where a kernel function replaces the "box" of the bin estimators. The user-supplied parameter is the kernel bandwidth, and its choice will significantly impact its performance.

Finding the optimal value for the user-supplied parameter is nontrivial but important as its value could directly affect the estimator error. The quality of an estimator is evaluated by its bias and variance, and generic expressions for all estimators mentioned above are known [20]. However, such expressions require as input the value of the distribution from which the data is observed, which in our case is not known.

Adaptive estimators use a recursive algorithm to determine the optimal bin width [4]. Such methods use entropy to measure disorder in the observed data and determine the bin width that minimizes the entropy function over all possible thresholds. Although they offer good performance, we found this last method lacking for our purpose as it is very time-consuming. Our investigation showed that it would be faster to calculate the key rank for every epoch than to use entropy-based binning.

As there is no optimal solution for the non-parametric estimation and low computational overhead is an important requirement in our case, we decided to use the histogram estimator. We thoroughly tested its reliability by running two types of experiments. In the first, we simply considered all possible values for the bin widths. In the second, we considered the different known rules for determining the bin widths. For both experiments, we consider all three datasets, described in Sect. 2.2 and provide detailed results in Appendix A.

We conclude from the first experiment that although the histogram estimator's bin width impacts the achieved performance, the mutual information metric is stable, and we observe the same behavior for several values of this parameter. More precisely, any value between 25 and 170 will give similar results. Therefore, we selected the value of 100 for the number of bins as it is in the middle of the interval. This observation holds for both the Hamming weight and the identity leakage models.

In the second experiment, we use plug-in estimates to determine the value for the bin-width. These estimates work by making assumptions on the distribution of the observed data and are known as empirical rules for determining the bin width. The results are depicted in Appendix A, where we can observe that the bin width obtained with different rules result in very similar attack performance. Our experiments confirm that the mutual information metric is not very sensitive to the histogram bin size, making it a robust procedure for practical applications where one needs to consider different datasets, leakage models, and neural network architectures. Our strategy is to choose the bin value as the average value with good performance for all tested scenarios based on this observation.

Additionally, we consider how long the generalization interval lasts, as longer intervals mean it will be easier to stop the training while in the generalization. The analysis for the length of the generalization interval is given in Appendix C, and it shows that using a regularization technique prolongs the interval.

4.2   Results for the Publicly Available Datasets

In this section, we compare the performance of five metrics (validation loss, validation accuracy, validation recall, key rank for the validation set, and $I(T_n; Y)$) to select the epoch t at which the machine learning model achieves the best performance. Besides these five metrics, we depict the results when we do not use an early stopping regime but rather allow the full number of training epochs. Those results are denoted as "GE all epochs" and "SR all epochs" for guessing entropy and success rate, respectively. Note, when giving results for guessing entropy and success rate, we conduct 100 key rank executions by randomly selecting attack traces from a larger set. The best success rate value equals 100%, and the best guessing entropy value is 1. When giving results with distributions (e.g., Fig. 6), we repeat experiments 100 times, i.e., there are 100 training phases to be able to build distributions.

For the three tested datasets (ASCAD, DPAv4, and CHES CTF), the results are obtained by attacking one key byte in the first AES encryption round. For ASCAD, we give results for the HW and identity leakage models. For DPAv4, we give results in Appendix D, and we consider only the HW leakage model as the identity leakage model allows an easy attack where there are no significant differences among neural network architectures or validation metrics. We note that the results for DPAv4 are in line with the results for the other datasets. For CHES CTF, we consider only the Hamming weight leakage model as the available dataset contains only 43 000 traces, which is not enough to break the target in the identity leakage model.

We first conduct a tuning phase where we experiment with varying CNN and MLP architectures. We emphasize that we do not claim that the obtained architectures are optimal, as finding optimal architectures was not the goal of this work. The final neural network configurations use the *Adam* optimizer, and the learning rate is set to 0.001. Initial weights are initialized at random using *random uniform* method. The selected loss function is the categorical cross-entropy provided by the *Keras* library. All the experiments were performed on a computer equipped with a GPU Nvidia RTX 2060. The details about selected convolutional neural networks hyperparameters are listed in Table 1. For MLP, we use an architecture with five dense layers containing 600 neurons each. We verified that the selected MLP provides good results for the ASCAD dataset, and the selected CNNs provide strong results for all three considered datasets.

Table 1. Hyperparameters for CNNs.

Dataset	DPAv4	ASCAD	CHES CTF
Learning rate	0.001	0.001	0.001
Optimizer	Adam	Adam	Adam
Batch-size	400	400	400
Convolution layers	1	1	1
Filters, Kernel Size, Stride	16, 10, 10	16, 10, 10	16, 4, 4
Dense (fully-connected) layers	4	3	2
Neurons (for dense or fully-connected layers)	400	200	100
Activation function (all layers)	*ReLU*	*ReLU*	*ReLU*

ASCAD Random Keys Results. The empirical validation on the ASCAD dataset (key byte 3) considers 200 000 traces for training, 500 traces for validation, and 500 traces for the test. Both validation and test sets have a fixed key. The selected CNN architecture is trained for 50 epochs. After identifying the best epoch for each of the five metrics, the corresponding machine learning models are applied to the test set. Note we provide additional results about the best epoch based on the information path in Appendix B.

Figure 5 shows GE and SR for the test set obtained for each validation metric for the HW leakage model. From Fig. 5b, the best success rate is achieved when the machine learning model is selected from the epoch when the metric is the maximum value of $I(T_n; Y)$. More precisely, around the processing of 460 traces, the success rate reaches 100% if the model is selected from the epoch determined by the maximum $I(T_n; Y)$ value. The lines "GE all epochs" and "SR all epochs" correspond to the results when evaluating GE and SR after processing 50 epochs. We can see that those lines also depict the worst attack performance as in those cases, due to too many training epochs, the machine learning models overfit and do not generalize for the test set. Figure 5a shows no significant differences among most of the metrics (except the scenario where we do not use early stopping), and for both SCA metrics, we see that mutual information works well and gives consistently strong attack performance.

Figure 6 shows the results for 100 experiments with the same CNN architecture. Figure 6a gives the $I(T_n; Y)$ evolution for the processed epochs. On average, the highest $I(T_n; Y)$ values are achieved between epochs 20 and 30 (the highest for epoch 24), as indicated by the plot distribution in Fig. 6b. Figure 6c shows the test and validation GE results for the number of epochs (training phase) and $I(T_n; Y)$ metric. We see an interval (epochs between 8 and 26) when the key rank is low and, consequently, generalization is satisfactory. This indicates that GE reaches good values even before $I(T_n; Y)$ becomes maximal. Still, allowing more epochs does increase $I(T_n; Y)$ while keeping GE minimal. Figure 6d shows the distribution of the best epochs based on the validation key rank metric. This histogram contains the results of 100 experiments (unchanged hyperparameters)

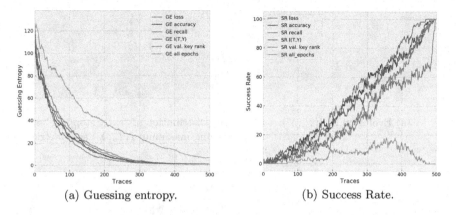

(a) Guessing entropy.   (b) Success Rate.

Fig. 5. Results on ASCAD for the HW leakage model, CNN architecture.

and indicates that the best validation key rank may happen at different epochs. More precisely, we see the highest value already around epoch 12, which explains why the validation key rank is among the worst-performing metrics for both SR and GE. While this could sound counter-intuitive, there is a simple explanation for such behavior. As we use a validation set often (whenever evaluating whether to stop training), the validation set indirectly influences the trained model. Consequently, it is possible to observe some differences when applying trained models to the test set, which was never evaluated before. As we can observe, $I(T_n; Y)$ metric seems to be less sensitive to this issue, and as such, it represents a more suitable choice for an early stopping metric.

Next, we repeat the ASCAD dataset experiments in the HW leakage model, but with an MLP architecture. From Figs. 7a and 7b, $I(T_n; Y)$ is the most successful metric, followed closely by loss. Again, if there is no early stopping, neural network overfits, resulting in poor attack performance. Figure 8a indicates that $I(T_n; Y)$ reaches the best performance for epochs 25 to 35. This is confirmed in Fig. 8b where we observe the highest frequency for epoch 31. Considering the validation and test set behavior when using $I(T_n; Y)$ to indicate stopping, several epochs give good behavior (from 10 to 35). This is in line with CNN's behavior, as GE can indicate a successful attack even before $I(T_n; Y)$ reaches the maximal value. Finally, Fig. 8b gives insight into the performance of the validation key rank, where several epochs have high frequency, but the highest value happens around epoch 5, which is too early as confirmed when evaluating the attack performance (Fig. 7 where the validation key rank performs significantly worse than $I(T_n; Y)$).

Next, we consider the identity leakage model for the ASCAD dataset. First, in Fig. 9, we depict the results for guessing entropy and success rate. The differences among attack performances are very small, but the mutual information metric gives good results for both guessing entropy and success rate. Here, not having the early stopping mechanism does not affect attack performance. This behavior

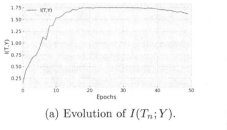

(a) Evolution of $I(T_n; Y)$.

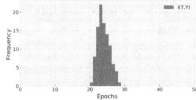
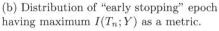

(b) Distribution of "early stopping" epoch having maximum $I(T_n; Y)$ as a metric.

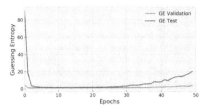

(c) Guessing entropy w.r.t. number of training epochs for validation and test sets.

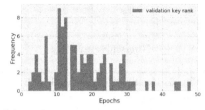

(d) Distribution of "early stopping" epoch having validation key rank as metric.

Fig. 6. Results on ASCAD for the HW leakage model, CNN architecture.

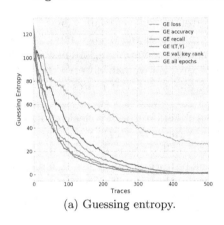

(a) Guessing entropy.

(b) Success Rate.

Fig. 7. Results on ASCAD for the HW leakage model, MLP architecture.

is expected, as due to more classes, neural networks need more epochs to fit the data into the model (and naturally, to overfit).

Figure 10a displays the $I(T_n; Y)$ evolution over 50 epochs. The mutual information increases with the number of epochs and reaches a steady level around epoch 47. This is confirmed in Fig. 10b, where we can indeed observe that epochs 47 to 49 give the best results. Considering GE, both validation and test set values indicate strong performance when having more than 15 epochs. Using the validation key rank as the early stopping metric shows several epochs as suitable to stop the training process (Fig. 10d). Still, the two highest peaks are observed

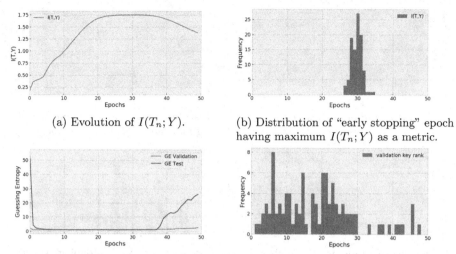

(a) Evolution of $I(T_n; Y)$.

(b) Distribution of "early stopping" epoch having maximum $I(T_n; Y)$ as a metric.

(c) Guessing entropy w.r.t. number of training epochs for validation and test sets.

(d) Distribution of "early stopping" epoch having validation key rank as metric.

Fig. 8. Results on ASCAD for the HW leakage model, MLP architecture.

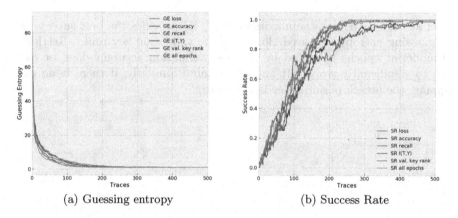

(a) Guessing entropy

(b) Success Rate

Fig. 9. Results on ASCAD for the identity leakage model, CNN architecture.

around epochs 32 and 48. As the validation key rank and $I(T_n; Y)$ point to similar epochs to stop the training, the results in Fig. 9 are as expected – no significant difference in the attack performance.

CHES CTF Results. We consider 43 000 traces in the training set and 1 000 traces in the validation set. Additional 1 000 traces are used as a test set. These results were obtained from the 100 training runs on CNN configured with the unchanged hyperparameters. Figure 11 shows the guessing entropy and success rate for the five considered metrics. We can observe that using the training

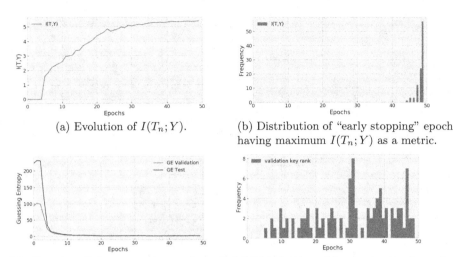

(a) Evolution of $I(T_n; Y)$.

(b) Distribution of "early stopping" epoch having maximum $I(T_n; Y)$ as a metric.

(c) Guessing Entropy w.r.t. number of training epochs for validation and test sets.

(d) Distribution of "early stopping" epoch having validation key rank as metric.

Fig. 10. Results on ASCAD for the identity leakage model, CNN architecture.

model at the epoch with the maximum $I(T_n; Y)$ provides the best success rate and guessing entropy (followed closely by the validation key rank). Retrieving the model at epochs indicated by the best validation accuracy, loss, or recall leads to significantly worse SR and GE results. Similarly, if there is no early stopping, the attack performance is also poor.

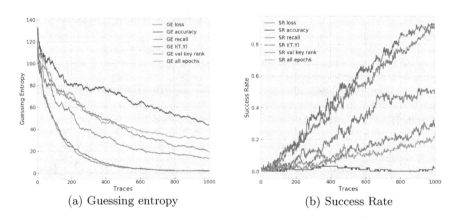

(a) Guessing entropy

(b) Success Rate

Fig. 11. Results on CHES CTF for the HW leakage model, CNN architecture.

Figure 12a provides the mutual information value $I(T_n; Y)$ for training phase and every epoch. The maximum $I(T_n; Y)$ is reached between epochs 10 and 18. Figure 12b gives similar indication with epoch 14 having the highest frequency. Those results are confirmed in Fig. 12c, where epochs 10 to 15 have the lowest guessing entropy. After epoch 18, the neural network starts to degrade its generalization capacity as it starts to overfit on the training set. On the other hand, the generalization capacity before epoch seven also provides, on average, poor generalization since the network is inside the fitting phase, where satisfactory generalization is not achieved yet (i.e., the network underfits). Finally, in Fig. 12d, the validation key rank gives similar results (there are similar SCA metrics results in Fig. 11). Still, again the validation key rank indicates to stop the training a little bit earlier than $I(T_n; Y)$.

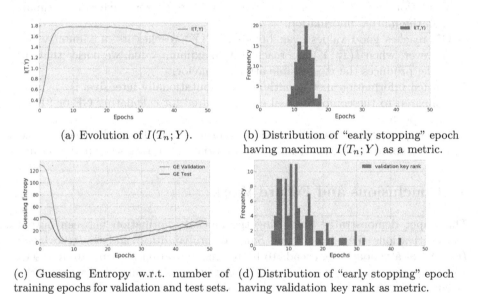

(a) Evolution of $I(T_n; Y)$.

(b) Distribution of "early stopping" epoch having maximum $I(T_n; Y)$ as a metric.

(c) Guessing Entropy w.r.t. number of training epochs for validation and test sets.

(d) Distribution of "early stopping" epoch having validation key rank as metric.

Fig. 12. Results on CHES CTF for the HW leakage model, CNN architecture.

4.3 Discussion

When attacking a protected target, like the public databases consisting of the first-order masked AES implementations, model generalization is very limited, and validation or test metrics are close to random guessing. For side-channel analysis, a sufficient generalization is given by a low guessing entropy or high success rate. As we can observe from the results given in Sect. 4, the trained model at each epoch provides different key rank results, and the over-training easily leads to deterioration of the model's generalization. This problem can be addressed by using an appropriate metric to save the trained model at the epoch that provides the best SR or GE. Our experimental analysis shows that having the maximum value of $I(T_n; Y)$ as a metric to select the model at the best epoch provides a better success rate and guessing entropy results when compared to machine learning metrics like loss, recall, or accuracy. Our results show that $I(T_n; Y)$ works especially well in settings where other metrics could have problems, as is the Hamming weight leakage model, which suffers from data imbalance. The $I(T_n; Y)$ metric works even better than the validation key rank, where we notice that the key rank validation indicates somewhat earlier to stop the training. Based on the obtained results, we give several observations for deep learning-based SCA:

1. It is necessary to implement early stopping regularization.
2. Early stopping based on mutual information consistently gives the best results.
3. Validation key rank seems to be somewhat more conservative in its estimate than the mutual information.
4. GE reaches good values even before $I(T_n; Y)$ reaches its maximum value. However, when $I(T_n; Y)$ has reached its maximum value, we notice that the model produces the most stable attack behavior.
5. Mutual information metric, although computationally intensive, is "lighter" compared to the computational effort required for calculating GE or SR for each epoch.
6. For simple datasets, various metrics will provide "good enough" results. However, for complex datasets, the mutual information metric gives superior results.

5   Conclusions and Future Work

This paper demonstrates that using the mutual information between output layer activations (i.e., the output *Softmax* probabilities) and the true labels $I(T_n; Y)$ of a validation set leads to better generalization for separate test sets. We compared $I(T_n; Y)$ metric against conventional machine learning metrics (accuracy, recall, and loss), and we verified that mutual information could be a more reliable metric to detect an epoch at which the trained neural network is inside a generalization interval.

In future work, we plan to investigate the mutual information metric as a reference for selecting other hyperparameters. Additionally, we would like to investigate this metric's behavior when the traces contain misalignment, and consequently, the generalization is more difficult. Such analysis is also essential to improve the portability capabilities of trained deep neural networks for side-channel attacks.

A   Bin Size Estimators

To estimate the probability density, a critical step is to determine the bin width, which is the user-supplied parameter for the histogram estimator. The results of our experiments are shown in Figs. 13, 14, and 15. As shown in the figures on the right, any bin width larger than 15 leads to a final key rank lower than 4 (key rank equal to 1 indicates the successful key recovery). The key rank is computed for a separate test set and is obtained by selecting the machine learning model at the epoch that gives the highest $I(T_n; Y)$ for each tested bin width. The plots on the left side of Figs. 13, 14, and 15 show the value of $I(T_n; Y)$ w.r.t. the number of epochs for all tested bin sizes. As we can see, if the bin size is too small, the mutual information $I(T_n; Y)$ barely changes.

Figure 16 shows results for eight different well-known estimators, vs. the choice of fixing the number of bins to 100. We tested Freedman Diaconis ('fd'), 'sturges', 'auto' (which is the maximum of 'fd' and 'sturges' estimators), 'rice', 'scott', square-root estimator ('sqrt'), and 'doane' estimators. The results show the guessing entropy resulting from early stopping by having $I(T_n; Y)$ as a metric by testing different bin size estimators. Notice they all lead to successful key recovery with similar guessing entropy convergence for all tested datasets and leakage models.

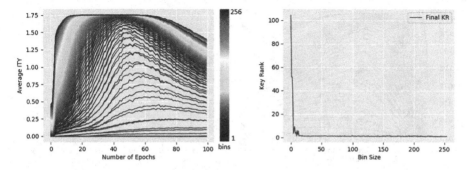

Fig. 13. (to be viewed in colors) The influence of the number of bins in the calculation of $I(T_n; Y)$ for the ASCAD dataset. Average $I(T_n; Y)$ w.r.t. the number of epochs for different bin sizes (left). The final key ranking having the maximum value of $I(T_n; Y)$ as a reference metric for different bin sizes (1 to 256) (right).

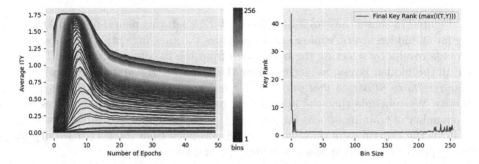

Fig. 14. (to be viewed in colors) The influence of the number of bins in the calculation of $I(T_n; Y)$ for the DPAv4 dataset. Average $I(T_n; Y)$ w.r.t. the number of epochs for different bin sizes (left). The final key ranking having the maximum value of $I(T_n; Y)$ as a reference metric for different bin sizes (1 to 256) (right).

B   From Information Path to the Best Epoch to Stop the Training

We use the information path for visualizing how much information each hidden layer has learned about the true labels (Y). The amount of information learned is an estimation of how well each hidden layer fits the distribution of Y, which is directly derived from the selected leakage model.

We repeat the experiment for the ASCAD random key dataset (Fig. 17, MLP architecture). Using the visualization provided by the information path, we confirm that all hidden layers are a transformed representation of the input traces and contain information about Y. However, the estimate of the mutual information between Y and the output layer probabilities (after the Softmax activation layer) captures best the prediction capability of the network. In our experiments *the best epoch to stop the training is the epoch where the value of $I(T_n; Y)$ reaches its maximum value.*

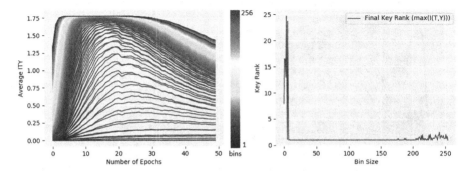

Fig. 15. (to be viewed in colors) The influence of the number of bins in the calculation of $I(T_i, Y)$ for the CHES CTF dataset. Average $I(T_i, Y)$ w.r.t. the number of epochs for different bin sizes (left). The final key ranking having the maximum value of $I(T_i, Y)$ as a reference metric for different bin sizes (1 to 256) (right).

Figure 17a shows the evolution value for $I(T_i; Y)$ during neural network training for all hidden layers, while Fig. 17b provides the guessing entropy results. We provide results by selecting the best epoch from the maximum value of $I(T_i; Y)$ for all the hidden layers, as suggested by the reviewer. *We provide these particular results to illustrate that only the last layer is indicative for early stopping results.* We conclude that the information path can lead to optimal choices for the number of training epochs for profiling side-channel analysis. Note, however, that for the general solution selection, the best epoch from the $I(T_n; Y)$ (output layer) provided better results across multiple datasets.

C   On the Length of the Generalization Interval

As stated, we aim to reach the generalization interval and then stop the training. By doing so, we ensure that the trained machine learning model will generalize to unseen data. The question remains how difficult it is to stop at the generalization interval. Intuitively, the shorter the interval, the easier it would be to miss it. Ideally, we aim to have a neural network that reaches the generalization interval relatively fast and stays in that interval for a longer period. Before discussing how to obtain a long generalization interval, we must ensure it happens and that we do not go to the overfitting phase from the underfitting phase.

Regularization techniques can help prevent a deep neural network from overfitting during the training process. To check the impact of the regularization on the neural network and its generalization interval, we use the information

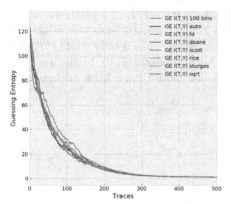

(a) Guessing entropy results for the ASCAD dataset on the Hamming weight leakage model.

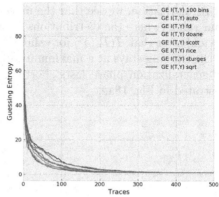

(b) Guessing entropy results for the ASCAD dataset on the identity leakage model.

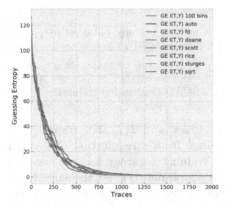

(c) Guessing entropy results for the CHES CTF dataset on the Hamming weight leakage model.

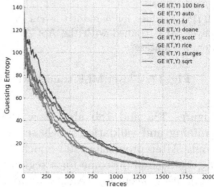

(d) Guessing entropy results for the DPAv4 dataset on the Hamming weight leakage model.

Fig. 16. Guessing entropy results when early stopping is conducted with mutual information as a metric for different binning size estimators.

plane as it provides a visual indication for the relationship between $I(X;T_n)$ and $I(T_n;Y)$. The maximum value of $I(T_n;Y)$ during training indicates an epoch at which the neural network should be inside the generalization interval for the training process, as defined in Definition 3. When the network does not implement any regularization technique in its hyperparameter configuration, the trained model has a higher chance of overfitting the training data.

Figure 18 depicts results for a CNN with and without regularization (dropout). This experiment is conducted on a proprietary unprotected software AES implementation (STM32 microcontroller). For that, we considered 6 000 traces for the training set and 1 000 traces for the validation set, both having fixed keys. The traces contain 400 features. Observing Fig. 18b, for the case without regularization, we see that the mutual information $I(T_n;Y)$ reaches a maximum value (where the distributions T_n and Y are obtained from the validation set) and after that, $I(T_n;Y)$ for validation decreases continuously while $I(T_n;Y)$ for the training stays at a maximum value. Additionally, $I(T_n;Y)$ indicates that the generalization phase lasts shorter than one would infer from accuracy, as illustrated in Fig. 18a.

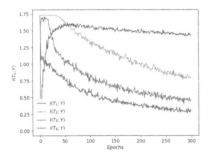 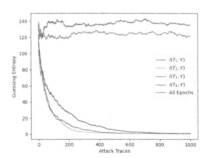

(a) $I(T_i;Y)$ values for 4 hidden layers in a 4-layer MLP trained with the ASCAD random key dataset.

(b) Guessing entropy obtained at epoch with maximum $I(T_i;Y)$.

Fig. 17. 4-layer MLP trained with the ASCAD random key dataset.

Figures 18a and 18b also show the accuracy and $I(T_n;Y)$, respectively, for training and validation labels sets obtained from a regularized CNN with dropout. After processing 200 epochs, the training accuracy has not reached 100%, the desired outcome for a regularized neural network. At the same time, the validation accuracy reaches approximately 56%, which is a significantly higher value compared to 51% without regularization, as shown in Fig. 18a. The mutual information $I(T_n;Y)$ for the validation set (see Fig. 18b) reaches its maximum value and stays longer at this level. This indicates that the same generalization level is kept until at least epoch 100. Consequently, as the value of $I(T_n;Y)$ stays high for more training epochs, the neural network provides better generalization for those epochs. Again, accuracy cannot indicate the same

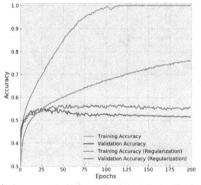
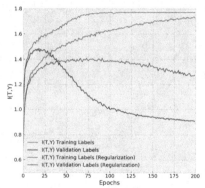

(a) Accuracy with and without regulariza-   (b) $I(T_n, Y)$ with and without regularization (dropout).   tion (dropout).

Fig. 18. Convolutional neural network configurations (learning rate = 0.001, *Adam* optimizer, batch size = 400, randomly uniform initialized weights).

phenomenon, as its value remains stable (albeit of different magnitude for the validation set) for regularized and non-regularized networks.

The neural network configurations (with and without dropout) are illustrated in Fig. 19. The "R" and "S" labels refer to *ReLU* and *Softmax*, respectively. The number under the layer block indicates the number of neurons in dense layers ("D") and the dropout rate for dropout layers.

(a) CNN   (b) CNN with dropout

Fig. 19. Convolutional neural network configurations (learning rate = 0.001, *Adam* optimizer, batch size = 400, randomly uniform initialized weights).

D   DPAv4 Results

For the DPAv4 dataset, we consider 34 000 traces in the training set and 2 000 traces in the validation set. An additional 2 000 traces are used as a test set. These results were obtained from the 100 training runs on CNN configured with unchanged hyperparameters. Fig. 20 shows guessing entropy and success rate obtained from the selected metrics (accuracy, recall, loss, key rank, and maximum $I(T_n; Y)$) from the validation set. Selecting the model at an epoch with the maximum $I(T_n, Y)$ for the validation set provides the best results for both SR and GE. Like the ASCAD dataset in the HW leakage model, $I(T_n; Y)$ gives better results than the validation key rank for a small number of attack traces.

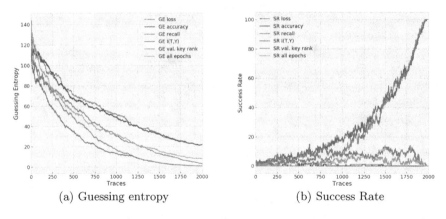

(a) Guessing entropy　　　　　　　(b) Success Rate

Fig. 20. Results on DPAv4 for the Hamming weight leakage model, CNN architecture.

Again, this happens due to the influence of the validation set on the trained model. Interestingly, allowing training for all 50 epochs leads to overfitting, but the same behavior happens if we stop training based on loss, recall, and accuracy.

Observe from Figs. 21a and 21b that the network achieves its maximum $I(T_n; Y)$ value between epochs 10 and 16. Figure 21c confirms that we require around 10 epochs to reach guessing entropy of 1. Additionally, the behavior stays relatively stable up to epoch 38 (where there is no deterioration up to epoch 15, and afterward, there are slight changes in GE). Finally, in Fig. 21d, the validation key rank agrees with $I(T_n; Y)$ by reaching the maximal frequency values for epochs 11 to 15 (cf. Fig. 21b).

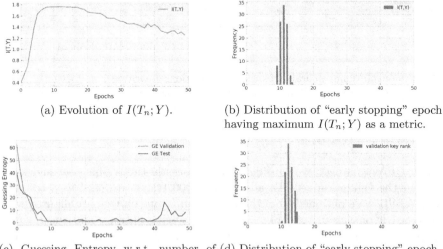

(a) Evolution of $I(T_n; Y)$.　　　　(b) Distribution of "early stopping" epoch having maximum $I(T_n; Y)$ as a metric.

(c) Guessing Entropy w.r.t. number of (d) Distribution of "early stopping" epoch training epochs for validation and test sets. having validation key rank as metric.

Fig. 21. Results on DPAv4 for the Hamming weight leakage model, CNN architecture.

References

1. Amjad, R.A., Geiger, B.C.: How (not) to train your neural network using the information bottleneck principle. CoRR abs/1802.09766 (2018). http://arxiv.org/abs/1802.09766
2. Bronchain, O., Hendrickx, J.M., Massart, C., Olshevsky, A., Standaert, F.-X.: Leakage certification revisited: bounding model errors in side-channel security evaluations. In: Boldyreva, A., Micciancio, D. (eds.) CRYPTO 2019. LNCS, vol. 11692, pp. 713–737. Springer, Cham (2019). https://doi.org/10.1007/978-3-030-26948-7_25
3. Cagli, E., Dumas, C., Prouff, E.: Convolutional neural networks with data augmentation against jitter-based countermeasures. In: Fischer, W., Homma, N. (eds.) CHES 2017. LNCS, vol. 10529, pp. 45–68. Springer, Cham (2017). https://doi.org/10.1007/978-3-319-66787-4_3
4. Chelombiev, I., Houghton, C., O'Donnell, C.: Adaptive estimators show information compression in deep neural networks. In: International Conference on Learning Representations (2019). https://openreview.net/forum?id=SkeZisA5t7
5. Dougherty, J., Kohavi, R., Sahami, M.: Supervised and unsupervised discretization of continuous features. In: Prieditis, A., Russell, S.J. (eds.) Machine Learning, Proceedings of the Twelfth International Conference on Machine Learning, Tahoe City, California, USA, 9–12 July 1995, pp. 194–202. Morgan Kaufmann (1995). https://doi.org/10.1016/b978-1-55860-377-6.50032-3
6. Goodfellow, I., Bengio, Y., Courville, A.: Deep Learning. MIT Press (2016). http://www.deeplearningbook.org
7. Hettwer, B., Gehrer, S., Güneysu, T.: Profiled power analysis attacks using convolutional neural networks with domain knowledge. In: Cid, C., Jacobson, M.J., Jr. (eds.) Selected Areas in Cryptography - SAC 2018, pp. 479–498. Springer, Cham (2019). https://doi.org/10.1007/978-3-030-10970-7_22
8. Kim, J., Picek, S., Heuser, A., Bhasin, S., Hanjalic, A.: Make some noise. unleashing the power of convolutional neural networks for profiled side-channel analysis. IACR Trans. Cryptogr. Hardw. Embed. Syst. **2019**(3), 148–179 (2019). https://doi.org/10.13154/tches.v2019.i3.148-179
9. Kraskov, A., Stögbauer, H., Grassberger, P.: Estimating mutual information. Phys. Rev. E **69**(6) (2004). https://doi.org/10.1103/physreve.69.066138
10. Maghrebi, H., Portigliatti, T., Prouff, E.: Breaking cryptographic implementations using deep learning techniques. In: Carlet, C., Hasan, M.A., Saraswat, V. (eds.) SPACE 2016. LNCS, vol. 10076, pp. 3–26. Springer, Cham (2016). https://doi.org/10.1007/978-3-319-49445-6_1
11. Masure, L., Dumas, C., Prouff, E.: Gradient visualization for general characterization in profiling attacks. In: Polian, I., Stöttinger, M. (eds.) COSADE 2019. LNCS, vol. 11421, pp. 145–167. Springer, Cham (2019). https://doi.org/10.1007/978-3-030-16350-1_9
12. Masure, L., Dumas, C., Prouff, E.: A comprehensive study of deep learning for side-channel analysis. IACR Trans. Cryptogr. Hardw. Embed. Syst. **2020**(1), 348–375 (2020). https://doi.org/10.13154/tches.v2020.i1.348-375
13. Perin, G., Chmielewski, L., Picek, S.: Strength in numbers: improving generalization with ensembles in machine learning-based profiled side-channel analysis. IACR Trans. Cryptogr. Hardware Embed. Syst. **2020**(4), 337–364 (2020). https://doi.org/10.13154/tches.v2020.i4.337-364. https://tches.iacr.org/index.php/TCHES/article/view/8686

14. Picek, S., Heuser, A., Jovic, A., Bhasin, S., Regazzoni, F.: The curse of class imbalance and conflicting metrics with machine learning for side-channel evaluations. IACR Trans. Cryptogr. Hardw. Embed. Syst. **2019**(1), 209–237 (2019). https://doi.org/10.13154/tches.v2019.i1.209-237

15. Prouff, E., Strullu, R., Benadjila, R., Cagli, E., Dumas, C.: Study of deep learning techniques for side-channel analysis and introduction to ASCAD database. IACR Cryptology ePrint Archive 2018, 53 (2018). http://eprint.iacr.org/2018/053

16. Rijsdijk, J., Wu, L., Perin, G., Picek, S.: Reinforcement learning for hyperparameter tuning in deep learning-based side-channel analysis. Cryptology ePrint Archive, Report 2021/071 (2021). https://eprint.iacr.org/2021/071

17. Robissout, D., Zaid, G., Colombier, B., Bossuet, L., Habrard, A.: Online performance evaluation of deep learning networks for profiled side-channel analysis. In: Bertoni, G.M., Regazzoni, F. (eds.) COSADE 2020. LNCS, vol. 12244, pp. 200–218. Springer, Cham (2021). https://doi.org/10.1007/978-3-030-68773-1_10

18. Saxe, A.M., Bansal, Y., Dapello, J., Advani, M., Kolchinsky, A., Tracey, B.D., Cox, D.D.: On the information bottleneck theory of deep learning. In: 6th International Conference on Learning Representations, ICLR 2018, Vancouver, BC, Canada, 30 April–3 May 2018, Conference Track Proceedings. OpenReview.net (2018). https://openreview.net/forum?id=ry_WPG-A-

19. Shwartz-Ziv, R., Tishby, N.: Opening the black box of deep neural networks via information. CoRR abs/1703.00810 (2017). http://arxiv.org/abs/1703.00810

20. Silverman, B.W.: Density Estimation for Statistics and Data Analysis. Chapman and Hall (1998). https://doi.org/10.1201/9781315140919

21. Standaert, F.-X., Peeters, E., Archambeau, C., Quisquater, J.-J.: Towards security limits in side-channel attacks. In: Goubin, L., Matsui, M. (eds.) CHES 2006. LNCS, vol. 4249, pp. 30–45. Springer, Heidelberg (2006). https://doi.org/10.1007/11894063_3

22. Standaert, F.-X., Koeune, F., Schindler, W.: How to compare profiled side-channel attacks? In: Abdalla, M., Pointcheval, D., Fouque, P.-A., Vergnaud, D. (eds.) ACNS 2009. LNCS, vol. 5536, pp. 485–498. Springer, Heidelberg (2009). https://doi.org/10.1007/978-3-642-01957-9_30

23. Standaert, F.-X., Malkin, T.G., Yung, M.: A unified framework for the analysis of side-channel key recovery attacks. In: Joux, A. (ed.) EUROCRYPT 2009. LNCS, vol. 5479, pp. 443–461. Springer, Heidelberg (2009). https://doi.org/10.1007/978-3-642-01001-9_26

24. TELECOM ParisTech SEN research group: DPA Contest (4th edition) (2013–2014). http://www.DPAcontest.org/v4/

25. Tishby, N., Zaslavsky, N.: Deep learning and the information bottleneck principle (2015)

26. van der Valk, D., Picek, S.: Bias-variance decomposition in machine learning-based side-channel analysis. Cryptology ePrint Archive, Report 2019/570 (2019). https://eprint.iacr.org/2019/570

27. van der Valk, D., Picek, S., Bhasin, S.: Kilroy was here: the first step towards explainability of neural networks in profiled side-channel analysis. Cryptology ePrint Archive, Report 2019/1477 (2019). https://eprint.iacr.org/2019/1477

28. Wouters, L., Arribas, V., Gierlichs, B., Preneel, B.: Revisiting a methodology for efficient CNN architectures in profiling attacks. IACR Trans. Cryptogr. Hardware Embed. Syst. **2020**(3), 147–168 (2020). https://doi.org/10.13154/tches.v2020.i3.147-168. https://tches.iacr.org/index.php/TCHES/article/view/8586

29. Wu, L., Perin, G., Picek, S.: I choose you: automated hyperparameter tuning for deep learning-based side-channel analysis. Cryptology ePrint Archive, Report 2020/1293 (2020). https://eprint.iacr.org/2020/1293
30. Zaid, G., Bossuet, L., Habrard, A., Venelli, A.: Methodology for efficient CNN architectures in profiling attacks. IACR Trans. Cryptogr. Hardw. Embed. Syst. **2020**(1), 1–36 (2019). https://doi.org/10.13154/tches.v2020.i1.1-36. https://tches.iacr.org/index.php/TCHES/article/view/8391

Fault Attacks

Transform Without Encode is not Sufficient for SIFA and FTA Security: A Case Study

Sayandeep Saha$^{(\boxtimes)}$ and Debdeep Mukhopadhyay

Indian Institute of Technology Kharagpur, Kharagpur, India

Abstract. Statistical Ineffective Fault Analysis (SIFA) and Fault Template Attack (FTA) are two recently proposed classes of Fault Attacks (FA), which evade almost all existing FA countermeasures, even while they are combined with Side-Channel Analysis (SCA) countermeasures such as masking. Protecting against these attacks requires an entirely new class of mechanisms, and only a handful of suggestions have been made in the context of SIFA so far. Recently, a countermeasure targeting both of these attack classes has been proposed in DATE 2021 [1], claiming security for single-bit faults. In this paper, we present successful SIFA and FTA attacks against this countermeasure using single-bit faults only. Considering the fact that the target countermeasure is a partial instantiation of one of the earliest SIFA countermeasures proposed in [2] (which, on the contrary, is secure against SIFA), this attack establishes that any unproven modification to a countermeasure can be fatal. The proposed attacks were validated in simulation considering state-of-the-art fault models.

Keywords: Fault attack · Fault propagation · Countermeasure

1 Introduction

Fault Attack (FA) is a class of active implementation-based attacks on cryptosystems, where an adversary deliberately perturbs a cryptographic computation and extracts the secret by analyzing the faulty system responses. Initially proposed by Boneh et al. [3] for public-key crypto-systems and extended by Biham et al. [4] for symmetric-key ciphers, FAs proved themselves as one of the most potent threats to modern cryptography. Especially with the continuous improvement in fault injection mechanisms, several FA variants have become practical, which can easily bypass countermeasures based on classical fault tolerance. Therefore, in the last few years, there has been a continuous effort from the cryptographic community in developing robust countermeasures as well as new attack vectors in the context of FA.

FAs rely on the fact that an adversary is able to inject faults with at least some control during the computation. Such fault injection can be achieved in several ways – using low-precision mechanisms like clock/voltage-glitching [5,6], to sophisticated setups like electromagnetic (EM) pulses [7,8] and laser beams [9,10].

© Springer Nature Switzerland AG 2021
S. Bhasin and F. De Santis (Eds.): COSADE 2021, LNCS 12910, pp. 85–104, 2021.
https://doi.org/10.1007/978-3-030-89915-8_4

The nature of the injected fault (i.e., the randomness, precision, repeatability etc.) depends on the injection mechanism. In general, laser and EM pulses can be tailored to create highly repeatable and precise single-bit faults for software and hardware implementations. While most of these abovementioned techniques target embedded platforms, there also exist mechanisms for remote software-controlled fault injections. Examples include the Row-Hammer DRAM bug [11], and dynamic voltage frequency scaling [12–14] features in modern CPUs and GPUs.

In this paper, we focus on FA for symmetric-key cryptosystems, which is, in fact, the most widely explored area in FA research so far. Differential Fault Analysis (DFA) is the most prominent FA class in a symmetric-key context. DFAs encrypt each plaintext two times – once with and once without fault and exploit the differential between the correct and the faulty ciphertext to reduce the size of the keyspace to some practically searchable value. The required number of fault injections is small, and the fault model is highly relaxed – often, a random single/multiple-byte fault can practically break ciphers like AES [15,16]. However, the analysis mechanism is complex and cipher-specific[1]. While DFAs require minimum assumptions over the nature of the faults (also called *fault model*), in practice, the faults in practical devices are never uniformly random but highly biased and repeatable. Exploiting this biased and repeatable nature of faults, one may devise FAs, which are able to bypass many state-of-the-art FA countermeasures based on classical fault tolerance principles. Examples of FAs with biased faults include Statistical Fault Analysis (SFA) [18], Fault Sensitivity Analysis (FSA) [19], Differential Fault Intensity Analysis (DFIA) [20] etc. Some of these attacks do not require access to any correct ciphertext and can work with faulty ciphertexts only. There also exists FAs which does not explicitly require ciphertext accesses, such as Safe Error Attacks (SEA) [21] and Blind Fault Attacks (BFA) [22].

Traditionally, FA countermeasures incorporate some form of redundancy in the computation to detect the presence of faults and either mute or randomize the output upon detecting the fault. Early proposals suggest performing the same computation multiple times (at least twice) and check the ciphertexts or round outputs to detect the presence of error in computation (we call it simple redundancy, for convenience). A relatively lightweight approach is to use some form of error-detection/correction (ECC) instead of multiple cipher computations. Countermeasures using simple redundancy or ECC are collectively called *detection-based countermeasures* [23]. ECCs do not guarantee 100% error-detection, and a biased fault adversary can bypass them easily by generating

---

[1] Recently, automated tools have been proposed to figure out DFAs in block ciphers [17].

an undetectable fault [24][2]. Detection based on simple redundancy can also be bypassed potentially by corrupting the check block with another fault, which is often a single-bit signal. Also, a biased fault adversary can inject the same fault in all computational branches with a reasonably high probability to make the check operation fail and output a faulty ciphertext [25]. The *infection counter-measures* were proposed to prevent such attacks on simple redundancy. Infection countermeasures avoid an explicit check operation and tailor the countermeasure algorithm in a way that provides a random outcome in the presence of a fault and a correct outcome, otherwise [26].

Statistical Ineffective Fault Analysis (SIFA) [27,28] and Fault Template Attack (FTA) [8] are two recently proposed FA classes, which can bypass most of such detection and infection-based FA countermeasures with single fault injections per encryption. SIFA exploits the fact that depending on the intermediate state values of a cipher, some fault may remain *ineffective* and correct ciphertexts will be obtained. Such correct ciphertexts can reveal the secret key as it has been shown in SIFA. FTA attacks, on the other hand, go one step further and exploit the information from both correct and faulty computations. The advantage over SIFA is that it does not require any access to the ciphertexts and can work only with the information whether they are faulty or not. This feature is important in several practical contexts such as secure-boot, authenticated encryption (AE), etc. In many cases, SIFA and FTA also work even if Side-Channel (SCA) countermeasures such as shuffling and masking are in place along with FA countermeasures[3]. In essence, most of the existing FA countermeasures can be bypassed with these two formidable attack classes.

Recently, a number of proposals have been made to prevent SIFA attacks [29–32]. In [29], an in-depth analysis of SIFA attacks have been performed. Eventually, the work presents a framework called Transform-and-Encode for constructing SIFA-protected block ciphers. More precisely, [29] proposes two models for SIFA faults, namely SIFA-1 and SIFA-2. The SIFA-1 model only considers biased faults injected at the state registers (e.g. at the beginning or end of S-Box or the linear layer) of a cipher. On the other hand, SIFA-2 model considers biased and unbiased faults during the computation of non-linear sub-operations such as S-Boxes. For the SIFA-1, they showed that a randomized transform (called Transform) of the state to some encoded domain is a good approach for preventing attacks. One general and practical example of such domain-transforms is a masking scheme. However, as pointed out in [29], masking cannot provide security for SIFA-2 faults. A potential solution for SIFA-2 faults is to apply a share-level error-correction, which is called Encode [29]. A concrete example called AntiSIFA has been provided on

---

[2] Biased faults can bypass many code-based error-detection because code-based fault-tolerance techniques always assume that faults are random, and the probability of fault bypassing the detection code is very low. This assumption is not true for biased repeatable faults as the fault bypassing the protection can be created with probability close to one.

[3] Note that, the potency against SCA countermeasures is important even in the fault context because masking can prevent a certain class of FAs (such as BFA, SEA, etc.), especially those which does not require ciphertext access.

PRESENT block cipher with Threshold Implementation (TI) for first-order masking and bit-level triplication for single-bit error-correction (extendable to multi-bit faults with higher overhead). Among other proposals for countering SIFA, the other notable one is due to [31], which also proposes gate-level error correction, but does not take the good impact of masking into account. The presence of masking is advantageous, as it inherently brings the SCA security into the context. The third proposal for SIFA countermeasure is due to [30], which prevents single-bit SIFA by changing the sequence of gate operations performed in masked S-Boxes. This technique ensures that an injected fault can never remain ineffective. It does not require error-correction to be performed and works by detecting the errors only. Finally, the work in [32] presents a SIFA countermeasure solely based on efficient error-correcting codes (ECC).

To the best of the authors' knowledge, no countermeasure has been proposed so far in the context of FTA. However, some of the existing SIFA countermeasures (including AntiSIFA) can be successful to some extent. A recent work sheds some light on the FTA security of certain SIFA countermeasures in the presence of an SCA-FA combined adversary [33]. In this regard, the DATE 2021 [1] is the first proposal explicitly considering these two attacks. The goal of this work is to analyze the true security of this countermeasure.

Our Contributions: The proposal in [1] (and its predecessor in [34] claiming only SIFA security) adopts a state-randomization technique providing single-bit SIFA security, which was also reported as a potential Transform in [29]. While the SIFA-1 security for this construction can be proven and also verified in [1] and [29], the security against SIFA-2 faults were never analyzed. We note that such verification is important, both from the perspective of an attacker and a countermeasure designer. While the proposal in [29] suggests using Encode for preventing SIFA-2 faults, no such suggestion was made in [1]. This raises a question whether the SIFA-2 security of [29] is explicitly needed or it is subsumed by the Transform operation as mentioned in [1]. In this work, we found that the randomization in [1] does not protect against SIFA-2 faults. Such a result re-establishes the necessity of the Encode operation. Broadly, it raises a cautionary note regarding any unproven partial instantiation/optimization of a countermeasure. As shown in this work, in many cases, such partial instantiations may turn out to be fatal. Following the success of the SIFA-2 attacks, we revisit the FTA security of [1]. As it is found, the scheme also falls prey to FTA.

For both SIFA-2 and FTA attacks, we slightly modify the attack strategies as mentioned in their respective original papers. In particular, both SIFA-2 and FTA consider fault injections at the input of non-linear gates. While this is suitable for targeting masked implementations, in this particular case, we observed that faulting the output of a non-linear gate is also exploitable for the attack. The attacks described in this paper mostly follow this injection strategy.

The rest of the paper is organized as follows. In Sect. 2, we briefly recall the SIFA and FTA attacks, followed by a description of the DATE 2021 countermeasure in Sect. 3. The attacks are outlined in Sect. 4 for PRESENT block cipher. Section 5 presents a comprehensive discussion on the impact of our attack on DATE 2021 countermeasure for different implementation styles. Finally, we conclude in Sect. 6.

2 Recapitulating SIFA and FTA

2.1 SIFA Attacks

The main crux of SIFA attacks is in exploiting the statistical bias (at some intermediate state of an encryption operation) introduced by ineffective faults. In this paper, we follow the same nomenclature introduced in [29], where the biased faults in state registers (i.e. input/output of a round or a sub-operation, such as S-Box or bit-permutation) are denoted as SIFA-1 faults. On the other hand, faults (biased/unbiased) in S-Box intermediates are denoted as SIFA-2 faults. Both of these faults can be represented as *ineffective transition probability* of a value $x \in \mathscr{X}$ denoted as $p_x^*(x)$, which is nothing but the probability of x remaining unaltered even after the injection of a fault. The prime condition for SIFA is that $p_x^*(x)$ must be varying for different valuations of x. In case of biased state faults, this is ensured by the bias present in the fault itself. For example, let us consider a bit stuck-at-0 fault (a transient fault equivalent to the transient bit-reset) at the LSB of a 4-bit state (i.e. $x \in \{0, 1, 2, \cdots 15\}$). Clearly, $p_x^*(x) = 1$ for all the even valuations of the state, and for the rest of the cases $p_x^*(x) = 0$. This indeed creates a statistical bias within the state for correct ciphertexts, which can be distinguished by statistical tests such as Squared Euclidean Imbalance (SEI).

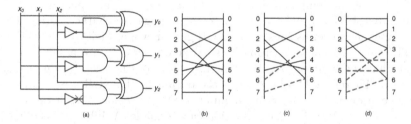

Fig. 1. Fault in χ_3 S-Box: a) Fault location; b) Correct S-Box mapping; c) Mapping for stuck-at-1 fault; d) Mapping for bit-flip fault.

For SIFA-2 faults, the desired statistical bias is generated by faulting the mapping realized by a sub-operation. The non-linear sub-operations, such as the S-Boxes, are the best candidates for this purpose. The faults are injected at the intermediates of an S-Box, preferably corrupting the inputs of a non-linear gate computation. To illustrate this further, we consider the following 3-bit S-Box called χ_3 from [35]. The Boolean equations are given as follows:

$$y_0 = x_0 + x_1\overline{x_2}$$
$$y_1 = x_1 + x_2\overline{x_0}$$
$$y_2 = x_2 + x_0\overline{x_1} \qquad (1)$$

In these equations x_0, x_1, x_2 denote the input bits of the S-Box and y_0, y_1, y_2 represent the output bits. x_0 and y_0 denote the Most Significant Bits (MSB) of the input and output, respectively. The corresponding circuit diagram, along with the fault location, is also displayed in Fig. 1 (a). For a bit stuck-at-1 fault, the original mapping (ref. Fig. 1 (b)) changes to the one displayed in Fig. 1 (c). One may observe that the bijectivity of the mapping is not maintained anymore. Moreover, the mapping remains non-uniform even if only the correct outputs are considered (i.e. the cases when the fault remains ineffective). More precisely, the outcome is correct when $x = (x_0, x_1, x_2) \in \{0, 1, 2, 3, 4, 5\}$ and faulty for the rest, which establishes that $p_x^*(x)$ is not same for all valuations of x. A similar situation happens if the fault is a bit-flip. The faulted mapping, in this case, is displayed in Fig. 1 (d). Finally, as shown in [28], the creation of such bias is also feasible for masked implementations.

2.2 FTA Attacks

FTA exploits fault propagation patterns through logic circuits for constructing fault templates over an implementation for which the secrets are known. In the online phase of the attack, a similar implementation with unknown keys is targeted with the fault template. The template construction and matching take place without any knowledge of ciphertexts. In some variants of the attack targeting middle rounds, the plaintext is kept fixed. However, the plaintext can be different for the template-building and template matching phases.

The crux of FTA attacks lies in the fault propagation characteristics of logic gates. For example, let us consider an XOR gate shown in Fig. 2 (a). A stuck-at-0 fault at input a of this gate propagates to the output only if a assumes a value 1. Note that the fault propagation, in this case, does not depend on the value at input b. Therefore, by observing if the output of the XOR gate is faulty or not, one can determine the value at input a. One may note that if the fault at a is bit-flip, no such value determination can be made. A different phenomenon happens in the case of an AND gate (ref. Fig. 2 (b)). Any fault at a (stuck-at or

Table 1. Fault Template for the χ_3 S-Box. Variables (in the table headers) marked in bold or inside enclosures are fault injection points.

$f_0 = x_1\overline{\boldsymbol{x_2}}$	$f_1 = x_2(\overline{x_0})$	$f_2 = x_0\overline{\overline{x_1}}$	State
			0
			1
			2
			3
			4
			5
			6
			7

bit-flip), in this case, propagates to the output only if the other input b assumes a value 1. In other words, by observing the output is faulty or not, one can determine the value of b in this case. Moreover, if the fault is a stuck-at-0, the value of a can also be determined simultaneously (as the fault *activates* only if the original value at a is 1). A similar observation can be made for the stuck-at-1 case.

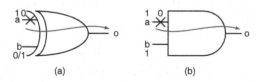

(a)   (b)

Fig. 2. Fault propagation in logic gates: a) Stuck-at-0 fault in XOR gate; c) Stuck-at-0 fault in AND gate.

The fault propagation through basic gates also extends for larger combinational circuits. To illustrate, once again, we consider the S-Box presented in Eq. (1). We also utilize the same fault location we considered for SIFA attacks. Considering the bit-flip case, the outputs are correct for inputs $\{0, 1, 2, 3\}$ and faulty for inputs $\{4, 5, 6, 7\}$. A closer investigation reveals that the outputs are correct when $x_0 = 0$ and faulty when $x_0 = 1$. This is because the computation of $x_0\overline{x_1}$ propagates the fault to the AND output only when $x_0 = 1$. No fault propagation happens for the other case. The XOR computation following the AND operation unconditionally propagates the fault to the output. Therefore, the output of the S-Box becomes faulted only when $x_0 = 1$ in this case. The observation can also be extended for the stuck-at cases.

It is clear from the above discussion that the bit x_0 is revealed by this fault injection. In order to recover other bits, two other fault locations are utilized in this case. A fault injection in $x_2\overline{x_0}$ (at the x_0 input) reveals the value of x_2, and an injection in $x_1\overline{x_2}$ reveals x_1. Note that these injections happen at independent fault campaigns, and FTA does not need to inject more than one fault per encryption in this case. Combining the outcomes of all fault campaigns, one can construct templates that map the faulty or correct observables to the intermediate values. An example fault template for this S-Box is presented in Table 1, where the black cells represent faulty outcomes and the grey cells represent correct outcomes. For example, if none of the outcomes for the three chosen fault locations are faulty, then the associated intermediate value is 0. One may note that the exploitable fault locations are not limited to the one we utilized in this example. In practice, there can be several other fault locations, and the template will change depending on them. Also, the choice of fault locations largely depends upon the implementation under consideration and the precision of the injection setup.

3 The DATE 2021 Countermeasure

The DATE 2021 countermeasure aims to prevent DFA, SIFA, and FTA simultaneously with a single solution. The main idea is to utilize one random bit for randomizing the entire state, which can be related to an instantiation of Transform operation defined in [29] (Sect. 5.2.1). Following the terminology from [29], we denote this randomization strategy as Randomized Reverse Encoding (RRT). Given a state register S of length n, and a 1-bit random coin r_{RRT}, the RRT transform $\mathscr{C}_{RRT}(S)$ of S is defined as:

$$\mathscr{C}_{RRT}(S) = \begin{cases} S, & \text{if } r_{RRT} = 0. \\ \overline{S}, & \text{otherwise.} \end{cases} \tag{2}$$

In other words, depending on a random coin toss, either S or its reverse will be processed. This scheme provides protection against single-bit SIFA-1 faults (biased faults in the state register but not inside the sub-operation computations) according to [29]. The following theorem establishes this claim:

Theorem 1. *If the fault influences one bit within S then RRT ensures SIFA-1 protection.*

Proof. Without loss of generality, we assume that the i-th bit in a w-bit state S is influenced by the fault. We also assume that the fault is biased. Let $p_=(x)$ denote the probability of a fault being ineffective on a state value x, with the probability defined over a state-space $\mathscr{X}_{red}$ (i.e. $x \in \mathscr{X}_{red}$). Now, we know

$$p_=(x) = p_x^*(x) / \sum_{x \in \mathscr{X}_{red}} p_x^*(x)$$

(ref. Theorem-1 in [29]). Note that $p_x^*(x) = \prod_{i=0}^{w} p_{x_i}^i = \prod_{i=0}^{w} p_{x_i \to x_i}^i$ in this case, as we have one bit fault. Also, since the fault is single bit $|\mathscr{X}_{red}| = 2$. Let, b_i^* be the ith bit of $\mathscr{C}_{RRT}(S)$. Now, with RRT transform we have $b_i^* = b_i + r_{RRT}$ and,

$$p_{x_i}^i = \sum_{x \in \{x_i, \overline{x_i}\}} \mathbb{P}[b_i^* = x] \cdot p_x^{'i}$$

$$= \mathbb{P}[r_{RRT} = 0] \cdot p_{x_i}^{'i} + \mathbb{P}[r_{RRT} = 1] \cdot p_{\overline{x_i}}^{'i} = \frac{p_{x_i}^{'i} + p_{\overline{x_i}}^{'i}}{2} \tag{3}$$

Here $p_{x_i}^{'i}$ is the ineffective transition probability of the i-th bit in the transformed domain. One may easily observe that $p_{x_i}^i = p_{\overline{x_i}}^i$ after this transform. Further,

$$p_=(x) = p_{x_i}^i / (p_{x_i}^i + p_{\overline{x_i}}^i) = \frac{1}{2}, \tag{4}$$

which indicate that the distribution is uniform. The security against 1-bit SIFA-1 fault injections is thus established.   □

It is worth mentioning that, RRT cannot provide security if the fault affect w' ($w' > 1$) bits of S. We elaborate this by a counterexample as follows:

Example: Consider two consecutive bits b_i and b_{i+1} of S influenced with the biased ineffective faults. Without loss of generality, let us consider two values of S as x and x' where for x, $(x_i, x_{i+1}) = (0,0)$ and for x', $(x'_i, x'_{i+1}) = (1,0)$. Rest of the bit positions of x and x' assume same values. With the RRT transform (x_i, x_{i+1}) will be in two possible states $(0,0)$ and $(1,1)$ in x. Likewise, it will be in two possible states $(0,1)$ and $(1,0)$ in x'. Clearly, transition probabilities for x and x' will be different while (b_i, b_{i+1}) will be influenced by ineffective faults. More precisely, for the first case, the ineffective transition probability will be $p_x^*(x) = \frac{p_0^i p_0^{i+1} + p_1^i p_1^{i+1}}{2}$, whereas for the second case it will be $p_{x'}^*(x') = \frac{p_0^i p_1^{i+1} + p_1^i p_0^{i+1}}{2}$. Clearly, the distribution $p_=(x)$ will not be uniform.

The DATE 2021 [1] countermeasure proposes the abovementioned approach for combined SIFA and FTA protection. However, the SIFA-2 security of this approach was not verified. The FTA security claim follows from the fact that *due to the randomized reversal of bits in each execution, none of the nonlinear gates ever have inputs which remains unchanged even if the same plaintext is processed multiple times. As a result, no information can be leaked about the gate inputs from the fault propagation patterns.* Later in this paper, we show why such protection is inadequate. In order to enable DFA protection, [1] proposes to create two redundant branches, one computing on S and the other on $\overline{S}$ depending on the outcome of r_{RRT}. The end results are compared at the end, and the output is muted or randomized upon the detection of a fault. The exact algorithm proposed in [1] is outlined in Algorithm 1, where $E_K^1()$ and $E_K^2()$ denote the actual and redundant computations, respectively. The security claim against the DFA adversary is that, *it is infeasible to inject two identical fault masks in the main and redundant computation branches as they are computing on different (reversed) data.*

Algorithm 1. *DATE 2021 COUNTERMEASURE*

Input: P, K, $r_{RRT} \xleftarrow{\$} \{0,1\}$
Output: C if no fault, garbage otherwise.
1: **if** ($r_{RRT} = 0$) **then**   ▷ Actual Computation
2:     $C' = E_K^1(P)$
3: **else**
4:     $C' = \overline{E_K^1(\overline{P})}$
5: **end if**
6: **if** ($\overline{r_{RRT}} = 0$) **then**   ▷ Redundant Computation
7:     $C'' = E_K^2(P)$
8: **else**
9:     $C'' = \overline{E_K^2(\overline{P})}$
10: **end if**
11: **if** ($C' \oplus C'' = 0$) **then**   ▷ Check
12:     **Return** C'
13: **else**
14:     **Return** Garbage
15: **end if**

---

4   Attacks on DATE 2021 Countermeasure

In this section, we outline several attacks on the countermeasure outlined in the previous section. One should note that we have already shown one vulnerability against 2-bit SIFA-1 faults in the counterexample stated in the previous section. In this section, we mainly explore the vulnerabilities with respect to single-bit SIFA and FTA using the following fault models. Additionally, we use one case of double faults to break the DFA security of the scheme.

– **Single-bit SIFA-2 Faults:** In this case, the faults are single-bit, but instead of corrupting the state-registers, they corrupt the intermediate computation of non-linear sub-operations (such as S-Boxes). For hardware implementations, precise gate-level faults are feasible with sophisticated laser equipment. However, in most of the practical cases, such as for masked implementations, they are easily achievable with state-of-the-art equipment with a medium precision, as often register stages are put in between the non-linear function computation to get rid of glitches. On the other hand, gate-faults are straightforward to achieve for software (especially bit-sliced) implementations, as most of the time, they are computed gate-by-gate in each clock cycle.
– **FTA Faults:** FTA faults are also single-bit faults targeting the gate computations within non-linear sub-operations. They are physically similar to the SIFA-2 faults.
– **Bit-flip State Faults in Two Redundant Branches:** In this case, the faults are paired, with each fault in the pair targeting different branches of redundancy. We consider both faults to be bit-flip faults. This case is considered to show the vulnerability of the target countermeasure against standard DFA attacks.

4.1 The Target Implementation

The implementation under consideration plays a significant role while choosing suitable fault locations and fault types in SIFA and FTA. For realizing the attacks we are going to describe next, we consider bit-sliced software implementations. The main idea of a bit-sliced implementation is to compute the cipher in a gate-by-gate manner. Given each instruction computes a unary or binary gate operation, it is straightforward to target an individual gate with a fault. For example, one might fault the computation of an AND gate simulating a stuck-at-0 fault at the output register of the AND computation. One should note that this is just one example of how our target faults can be created, and in practice, such faults can be generated in many other ways. To create a stuck-at-0 situation at the input of a gate, one may fault a load instruction. With laser beams, one may also selectively fault a bit in memory (or register).

The most complex part of the DATE 2021 countermeasure is its S-Box which is also our main surface of attack. Following the original proposal in [1], we realize the countermeasure for PRESENT [36]. According to [1], the 4×4 S-Box is converted to a 5×4 version by incorporating the r_{RRT} bit. We follow the same procedure and derive the following S-box equations (Eq. (5); note that r stands for r_{RRT}):

$$
\begin{aligned}
y_0 = {} & rx_0x_1 + rx_0x_2 + rx_1x_2 + rx_1 + rx_2 + rx_3 + (x_0x_1x_3 + x_0x_2x_3 + x_0 + x_1x_2x_3 + x_1x_2 \\
& + x_2 + x_3 + 1) \\
y_1 = {} & rx_0x_1 + rx_0x_2 + rx_1x_3 + rx_1 + rx_2x_3 + rx_2 + (x_0x_1x_3 + x_0x_2x_3 + x_0x_2 + x_0x_3 \\
& + x_0 + x_1 + x_2x_3 + 1) \\
y_2 = {} & rx_0x_1 + rx_0x_2 + rx_1x_2 + rx_1 + rx_2 + rx_3 + (x_0x_1x_3 + x_0x_1 + x_0x_2x_3 + x_0x_2 + x_0 \\
& + x_1x_2x_3 + x_2) \\
y_3 = {} & rx_1 + rx_2 + r + (x_0 + x_1x_2 + x_1 + x_3)
\end{aligned}
\tag{5}
$$

Listing 1.1. Representation of the S-Box

```
t_1 = r   & x_0
t_2 = t_1 & x_1
t_3 = t_1 & x_2
t_4 = t_2 ^ t_3
t_5 = r   & x_1
t_6 = t_5 & x_2
         . . .

         . . .
```

In our prototype, each Boolean expression is represented as a series of assignment statements, with each statement implementing a one/two-input gate operation (ref. Listing 1.1). One notable fact in this implementation is that while representing a three-input AND with two 2-input AND expressions, it always combines the first two variables in the first AND and then performs the second AND on the partial product and the remaining variable. For example, the expression rx_0x_1 is expressed as $t_1 = rx_0$ and $t_2 = t_1x_1$. Another fact is that after computing an AND expression (two/three input) and assigning it to a variable, we keep it stored and use it later in expressions where it is required. A concrete illustration of this can be seen in the first three lines of Listing 1.1.

One must note that this is not the only possible way for implementing these Boolean expressions, and there may exist other (perhaps more optimized) similar implementations. However, our attacks are not limited to a specific implementation style, as they are founded on the basic properties of the logic gates.

4.2   The Fault Locations

Classically, SIFA-2 and FTA attacks consider faults at gate inputs. While this consideration is necessary in many cases, especially for masked implementations, there can be other feasible options too. As an example, let us consider a stuck-at-0 fault at the output of an AND gate. The actual outcome will become faulted only if the inputs are $a = 1$ and $b = 1$. For the rest of the cases, the fault will not be manifested, as the correct outputs are also 0. Now, this can be used as a potential source of information leakage. Observing the outcome is faulty or not, one can reduce the entropy of the inputs to the AND gate. Moreover, if this AND gate is a part of a larger circuit, it will create a statistical bias in the correct value space, which is essential for SIFA.

In the rest of the paper, we shall use such gate output faults for realizing our attacks. We acknowledge the fact that attacks are also feasible with faults injected at gate inputs. However, the security claim of [1] against FTA strongly depends upon the concept that FTA faults are always injected at inputs of non-linear gates and due to the state randomization imposed, all the gate inputs in their hardened implementation would become randomized, hindering the FTA. In order to make the attacks still viable, we adopt them with fault locations at the gate outputs. Also, one should observe that a stuck-at-0 fault at the AND gate output is equivalent (in terms of fault propagation) to a stuck-at-0 fault at one of the AND gate inputs, provided the input does not fan out to any other gate.

4.3   The SIFA Attack

In order to realize the SIFA attack, we have to target one non-linear operation within the S-Box equations. Without loss of generality, we choose the one marked in bold in the given equation system (Eq. (5)). The output of this gate is corrupted with a stuck-at-0 fault. We note that the same gate output is re-used for other expressions of the S-Box, and as a result, several other expressions get corrupted due to fault propagation. All these expressions are shown in bold in Eq. 6 (which is nothing but the protected PRESENT S-Box with fault locations marked).

$$y_0 = rx_0x_1 + rx_0x_2 + rx_1x_2 + rx_1 + rx_2 + rx_3 + (\mathbf{x_0x_1}x_3 + x_0x_2x_3 + x_0 + x_1x_2x_3 + x_1x_2 \\ + x_2 + x_3 + 1)$$

$$y_1 = rx_0x_1 + rx_0x_2 + rx_1x_3 + rx_1 + rx_2x_3 + rx_2 + (\mathbf{x_0x_1}x_3 + x_0x_2x_3 + x_0x_2 + x_0x_3 \\ + x_0 + x_1 + x_2x_3 + 1)$$

$$y_2 = rx_0x_1 + rx_0x_2 + rx_1x_2 + rx_1 + rx_2 + rx_3 + (\mathbf{x_0x_1}x_3 + \mathbf{x_0x_1} + x_0x_2x_3 + x_0x_2 + x_0 \\ + x_1x_2x_3 + x_2)$$

$$y_3 = rx_1 + rx_2 + r + (x_0 + x_1x_2 + x_1 + x_3) \tag{6}$$

Table 2. Faulted S-Box truth-table for protected PRESENT S-Box. The rows for which the S-Box outputs are faulty are shown in gray.

r	x0	x1	x2	x3	y0	y1	y2	y3	r	x0	x1	x2	x3	y0	y1	y2	y3
0	0	0	0	0	1	1	0	0	1	0	0	0	0	1	1	0	1
0	0	0	0	1	0	1	0	1	1	0	0	0	1	1	1	1	0
0	0	0	1	0	0	1	1	0	1	0	0	1	0	1	0	0	0
0	0	0	1	1	1	0	1	1	1	0	0	1	1	1	0	1	1
0	0	1	0	0	1	0	0	1	1	0	1	0	0	0	1	1	1
0	0	1	0	1	0	0	0	0	1	0	1	0	1	0	0	0	0
0	0	1	1	0	1	0	1	0	1	0	1	1	0	0	0	0	1
0	0	1	1	1	1	1	0	1	1	0	1	1	1	1	1	0	0
0	1	0	0	0	0	0	1	1	1	1	0	0	0	0	0	1	0
0	1	0	0	1	1	1	1	0	1	1	0	0	1	0	1	0	1
0	1	0	1	0	1	1	1	1	1	1	0	1	0	1	1	1	1
0	1	0	1	1	1	0	0	0	1	1	0	1	1	0	0	1	0
0	1	1	0	0	0	1	1	0	1	1	1	0	0	0	1	1	0
0	1	1	0	1	1	0	1	1	1	1	1	0	1	0	1	0	1
0	1	1	1	0	0	0	1	1	1	1	1	1	0	1	0		0
0	1	1	1	1	1	1	1	0	1	1	1	1	1	1	1	1	1

The results of this attack are depicted in Fig. 3. One may clearly observe that the SIFA attack is successful in this case. To further explain why the attack is successful, we present the S-Box mapping in Table 2 (with the r_{RRT} represented as r) by pointing out the faulty outputs with gray. One may observe that the S-Box output is correct only for a subset of S-Box inputs under the influence of fault, which clearly indicates a value-based statistical bias[4]. Putting it differently, the S-Box output is correct for inputs $(0, 1, 2, 3, 4, 5, 6, 7, 8, 9, 10, 11)$ irrespective of the value of r (i.e. r_{RRT}), and faulty for the rest of the cases. In essence, even with single-bit faults, the DATE 2021 countermeasure can be bypassed. This re-establishes the essentiality of the Encode step for protecting against SIFA-2, as proposed in [29].

One might wonder what happens if any other non-linear gate is chosen for the attack. It can be shown that the impact is very similar to the present case, with only a slight change in the statistical bias. Also, if the fault is injected at the input of a specific gate, the results remain consistent. The only requirement is that the fault must not fan out to a linear gate[5]. The required number of

---

[4] One may wonder how the bias from the S-Box output gets transferred to the input. This is straightforward as the S-Box is bijective.

[5] The net where the fault is injected should not be an input of an XOR gate. In such a case, conditional propagation of the fault due to non-linear gates would not hold.

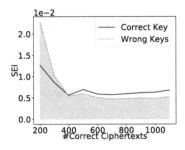

Fig. 3. SIFA Attack on protected PRESENT. The black line represents the SEI for the correct key, and the shaded region represents SEI values for the wrong key guesses.

ciphertexts may vary depending on the change in bias, but the attack remains feasible for every case. Changing the type of the fault to stuck-at-1 would have a similar impact. In summary, the attack described here is highly flexible in terms of fault injection location and thus remains practical for a large class of implementations.

4.4 The FTA Attack

The FTA attack begins by analyzing the underlying circuit of the target implementation. Fault injections at suitable locations help to construct fault templates that allow the recovery of intermediate states. Throughout the attack, the original plaintext is kept fixed, but the r varies randomly. Although fault-induced information leakage is possible through both non-linear and linear gates, non-linear gates are preferred as fault injection points, in general, as fault propagation through them depends upon more bits than the linear gates.

The number of different fault locations required for state-recovery strongly depends on the choice of each individual location. After analyzing the protected S-Box, we find total 5 locations for constructing the fault templates. The locations are indicated with different enclosing shapes or in bold in the S-Box equations shown in Eq. 7. The template corresponding to the attack is shown in Table 3. The fault locations in this template are $f_0 = rx_0$, $f_1 = rx_1$, $f_2 = rx_2$, $f_3 = rx_3$ and $f_4 = x_0x_1$.

$$y_0 = \boxed{rx_0}x_1 + \boxed{rx_0}x_2 + \boxed{rx_1}x_2 + \boxed{rx_1} + (\overline{rx_2}) + \boxed{rx_3} + (\mathbf{x_0x_1x_3} + x_0x_2x_3 + x_0 + x_1x_2x_3$$
$$+ x_1x_2 + x_2 + x_3 + 1)$$

$$y_1 = \boxed{rx_0}x_1 + \boxed{rx_0}x_2 + \boxed{rx_1}x_3 + \boxed{rx_1} + (\overline{rx_2})x_3 + (\overline{rx_2}) + (\mathbf{x_0x_1x_3} + x_0x_2x_3 + x_0x_2 + x_0x_3$$
$$+ x_0 + x_1 + x_2x_3 + 1)$$

$$y_2 = \boxed{rx_0}x_1 + \boxed{rx_0}x_2 + \boxed{rx_1}x_2 + \boxed{rx_1} + (\overline{rx_2}) + \boxed{rx_3} + (\mathbf{x_0x_1x_3} + \mathbf{x_0x_1} + x_0x_2x_3 + x_0x_2$$
$$+ x_0 + x_1x_2x_3 + x_2)$$

$$y_3 = \boxed{rx_1} + (\overline{rx_2}) + r + (x_0 + x_1x_2 + x_1 + x_3) \tag{7}$$

There are several interesting points associated with the templates in Table 3. Let us first provide the mathematical explanation of the fault patterns. Without loss of generality, we consider the first pattern from the template, which occurs if the S-Box input is $(0, 8)$. None of the faults propagate to the output in this case. Considering the first fault location $f_0 = rx_0$, we can observe that propagation of this fault to the S-Box output requires $rx_0(x_1 + x_2) = 1$, which is only feasible if $(r = 1, x_0 = 1, x_1 = 0, x_2 = 1)$, or $(r = 1, x_0 = 1, x_1 = 1, x_2 = 0)$. For the rest of the cases, there is no fault propagation to the output. Considering the second fault location $f_1 = rx_1$, fault propagation requires $(r = 1, x_1 = 1)$. Similarly fault propagation for other three fault locations require $(r = 1, x_2 = 1)$, $(r = 1, x_3 = 1)$ and $(x_0 = 1, x_1 = 1)$, respectively. Now, a critical observation here is that r is an independent uniformly distributed random bit which does not depend upon any other bit and assumes value 1 with probability 0.5. Therefore, repeated injections at each fault location will encounter events with $r = 1$ with probability 0.5. Therefore, no fault propagation even after repeated injections at f_1, f_2 and f_3 clearly indicates that $(x_1 = 0, x_2 = 0, x_3 = 0)$ for $r = 1$. However, the value of x_0 cannot be determined uniquely even while $r = 1$. This is because $x_1 + x_2 = 0$ hinders the fault propagation in this case irrespective of the value of x_0. One interesting outcome of this explanation is that, any information leakage from f_0, f_1, f_2 requires r to assume value 1. Therefore, while recovering the actual S-Box inputs, it is mandatory to complement the values suggested by the template. For example, the actual state values corresponding to the first fault pattern in the template is either 15 or 7. One may further wonder why such information leakages are feasible in this countermeasure even while each bit toggles with a probability 0.5. The reason is that, although the probability of toggling for an individual bit is 0.5, the bits within a nibble are not independent for a fixed plaintext. For this same reason, the countermeasure only provides single-bit security against SIFA-1 faults. In our attack, the faults are carefully placed at the gate outputs, which always makes the fault propagation dependent on both the gate inputs. These gate inputs, in turn, are dependent on each other, as shown in the counterexample of Sect. 3. This is the underlying cause for the FTA being successful in this case. But we achieve this with single-bit faults.

As already pointed out in the previous paragraph, each fault location requires several faults to be injected for template building and matching. For template matching, we follow the same technique mentioned in the original FTA paper. More precisely, we estimate two distributions for each x_i − 1) with $x_i = 0$ and with $x_i = 1$ (note that, here we talk about the actual value of x_i, not the one XOR-ed with random r_{RRT}) during the template building phase. In the template matching phase, we try to figure out which of these two distributions has occurred. In our simulations with stuck-at-0 faults, each fault location requires roughly 30 injections. Overall, 140 injections were sufficient for recovering a nibble of the intermediate state. Recovering a complete state requires approximately 2200 faults, and a complete round key recovery needs roughly 3800 faults.

4.5   Fault Injection on Redundant Branches

The DATE 2021 countermeasure also claims to provide security against the same faults on two redundant branches, which may result in successful DFAs in many cases. However, this claim cannot hold in the presence of single bit-flip faults, which is a very common and easily realizable fault model. We explain this by means of a simple counterexample.

Let us consider a cipher state S and a redundant state RS. According to the DATE 2021 countermeasure, $RS = \overline{S}$. This relation between the actual and redundant computation states remains invariant till the ciphertext. Any fault (in two branches) that does not disturb this invariant would bypass the final check easily. Now, without loss of generality, let us consider a single-bit flip fault at the i-th bit of S and a single-bit flip at the same location in RS. Such fault injection does not disturb the invariant. To see why let us consider the faulty valuation of S denoted as S_f and the faulty valuation of RS denoted as RS_f. According to our injection pattern $S_f = S + M_i$, where M_i is a fault mask with all bits at 0, except the i-th bit, set to 1. Similarly $RS_f = RS + M_i$. Hence, $\overline{S_f} = \overline{(S + M_i)} = (\overline{S} + M_i) = (RS + M_i) = RS_f$, which maintains the invariant. In other words, such a fault pair in two redundant branches can easily bypass the DFA protection of the target countermeasure. Therefore, the risk of bypassing the countermeasure with double faults still remains.

Table 3. Template for attacking protected PRESENT (middle round). The black cells indicate a faulty outcome and gray cells represent correct outcome.

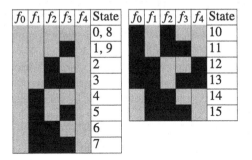

5   The Impact on Different Implementations

The previous section has elaborated on the theoretical aspects of the SIFA and FTA attacks on the DATE 2021 countermeasure. Although the attacks have been described largely in the light of bit-sliced software implementations, their applicability towards certain other implementations cannot be ruled out. In this section, we present a general discussion on the practicality of such attacks on different implementation classes.

5.1   Software Implementations

Software implementations of block ciphers are largely classified into table-based implementations and bit-sliced implementations. While bit-sliced implementations have already been shown vulnerable against SIFA and FTA, table-based implementations are not easy to corrupt gate-wise. However, table-based implementations are already found vulnerable against Persistent Fault Attacks (PFA) [37,38], which limits its direct usage. Overall, it can be concluded that security against SIFA, FTA, DFA, and PFA attacks cannot be ensured by the DATE 2021 countermeasure for the software implementations, in general.

5.2   Hardware Implementations

Similar to software implementation, one may choose to implement the hardware circuits using gates or memory elements such as BRAMs. In the case of a gate-level implementation, the attacker needs to target an individual gate computation, which is feasible with highly precise laser beams. For BRAM-based implementations, individual gates are not accessible. However, just like table-based implementations, BRAM-based implementations are also supposed to be vulnerable against PFA.

In summary, the attacks proposed by us in this paper are applicable to many of the existing implementation paradigms. For some hardware implementations, it might require a relatively sophisticated injection setup. In case such setups are not available, one may take advantage of injecting two faults at the input and output of the S-Box to make the attacks happen. This attack model has already been reported in [39], as FTA*. Interestingly, this attacker model is weaker than the identical fault models in two redundant branches (considered in the DATE 2021 paper), as it requires the faults to be injected in two different clock cycles (therefore, one fault per clock cycle, which is highly practical in modern laser stations which mount two laser beams) even in the case of hardware implementation.

6   Conclusion

SIFA and FTA are the two most formidable classes of FA, which have bypassed most of the existing countermeasures. Protecting against these two attacks is tricky, as we have established in this work by showing the vulnerabilities of a recently proposed SIFA+FTA countermeasure. One important lesson from this work is that countermeasures should never be optimized without proof of security for the optimized version. The target countermeasure here can be interpreted as an instantiation of the Transform-and-Encode framework, without the Encode part. Such partial instantiation is eventually found to be fatal. A potential future work in this direction is to find a lightweight Encode step for this countermeasure as a fix.

References

1. Baksi, A., Bhasin, S., Breier, J., Chattopadhyay, A., Kumar, V.B.Y.: Feeding three birds with one scone: a generic duplication based countermeasure to fault attacks (extended version). Cryptology ePrint Archive, Report 2020/1542 (2020). https://eprint.iacr.org/2020/1542

2. Saha, S., et al.: A framework to counter statistical ineffective fault analysis of block ciphers using domain transformation and error correction. IEEE Trans. Inf. Forensics Secur. **15**, 1905–1919 (2019)

3. Boneh, D., DeMillo, R.A., Lipton, R.J.: On the importance of checking cryptographic protocols for faults. In: Fumy, W. (eds.) EUROCRYPT 1997. LNCS, vol. 1233, pp. 37–51. Springer, Heidelberg (1997). https://doi.org/10.1007/3-540-69053-0_4

4. Biham, E., Shamir, A.: Differential fault analysis of secret key cryptosystems. In: Kaliski, B.S. (eds.) CRYPTO 1997. LNCS, vol. 1294, pp. 513–525. Springer, Heidelberg (1997). https://doi.org/10.1007/BFb0052259

5. Selmane, N., Guilley, S., Danger, J.L.: Practical setup time violation attacks on AES. In: 2008 Seventh European Dependable Computing Conference, pp. 91–96. IEEE (2008)

6. Barenghi, A., Bertoni, G.M., Breveglieri, L., Pellicioli, M., Pelosi, G.: Low voltage fault attacks to AES. In: 2010 IEEE International Symposium on Hardware-Oriented Security and Trust (HOST), pp. 7–12. IEEE (2010)

7. Schmidt, J.M.: Optical and EM fault-attacks on CRT-based RSA: concrete results. In: Austrochip 2007, pp. 61–67 (2007)

8. Saha, S., Bag, A., Basu Roy, D., Patranabis, S., Mukhopadhyay, D.: Fault template attacks on block ciphers exploiting fault propagation. In: Canteaut, A., Ishai, Y. (eds.) EUROCRYPT 2020. LNCS, vol. 12105, pp. 612–643. Springer, Cham (2020). https://doi.org/10.1007/978-3-030-45721-1_22

9. Selmke, B., Brummer, S., Heyszl, J., Sigl, G.: Precise laser fault injections into 90 nm and 45 nm SRAM-cells. In: Homma, N., Medwed, M. (eds.) CARDIS 2015. LNCS, vol. 9514, pp. 193–205. Springer, Cham (2015). https://doi.org/10.1007/978-3-319-31271-2_12

10. Selmke, B., Heyszl, J., Sigl, G.: Attack on a DFA protected AES by simultaneous laser fault injections. In: 2016 Workshop on Fault Diagnosis and Tolerance in Cryptography (FDTC), pp. 36–46. IEEE (2016)

11. Bhattacharya, S., Mukhopadhyay, D.: Curious case of Rowhammer: flipping secret exponent bits using timing analysis. In: Gierlichs, B., Poschmann, A. (eds.) CHES 2016. LNCS, vol. 9813, pp. 602–624. Springer, Heidelberg (2016). https://doi.org/10.1007/978-3-662-53140-2_29

12. Murdock, K., Oswald, D., Garcia, F.D., Van Bulck, J., Gruss, D., Piessens, F.: Plundervolt: software-based fault injection attacks against Intel SGX. In: Proceedings of 41st IEEE Symposium on Security and Privacy (S&P), pp. 1466–1482. IEEE, San Francisco, May 2020

13. Chen, Z., Vasilakis, G., Murdock, K., Dean, E., Oswald, D., Garcia, F.D.: VoltPillager: hardware-based fault injection attacks against Intel SGX enclaves using the SVID voltage scaling interface. In: 29th USENIX Security Symposium. USENIX (2020)

14. Sabbagh, M., Fei, Y., Kaeli, D.: A novel GPU overdrive fault attack. In: 2020 57th ACM/IEEE Design Automation Conference (DAC), pp. 1–6. IEEE (2020)

15. Tunstall, M., Mukhopadhyay, D., Ali, S.: Differential fault analysis of the advanced encryption standard using a single fault. In: Ardagna, C.A., Zhou, J. (eds.) WISTP 2011. LNCS, vol. 6633, pp. 224–233. Springer, Heidelberg (2011). https://doi.org/10.1007/978-3-642-21040-2_15

16. Saha, D., Mukhopadhyay, D., Chowdhury, D.R.: A diagonal fault attack on the advanced encryption standard. IACR Cryptol. ePrint Arch. 2009(581) (2009)

17. Saha, S., Mukhopadhyay, D., Dasgupta, P.: ExpFault: an automated framework for exploitable fault characterization in block ciphers. IACR Trans. Crypt. Hardw. Embed. Syst. 242–276 (2018)

18. Fuhr, T., Jaulmes, E., Lomné, V., Thillard, A.: Fault attacks on AES with faulty ciphertexts only. In: Proceedings of the 10th IEEE Workshop Fault Diagnosis Tolerance Cryptography (FDTC), pp. 108–118. IEEE, Santa Barbara, August 2013

19. Li, Y., Sakiyama, K., Gomisawa, S., Fukunaga, T., Takahashi, J., Ohta, K.: Fault sensitivity analysis. In: Mangard, S., Standaert, F.X. (eds.) CHES 2010, vol. 6225, pp. 320–334. Springer, Heidelberg (2010). https://doi.org/10.1007/978-3-642-15031-9_22

20. Ghalaty, N.F., Yuce, B., Taha, M., Schaumont, P.: Differential fault intensity analysis. In: Proceedings of the 11th Workshop Fault Diagnosis Tolerance Cryptography (FDTC), pp. 49–58. IEEE, Busan, September 2014

21. Yen, S.M., Joye, M.: Checking before output may not be enough against fault-based cryptanalysis. IEEE Trans. Comput. 49(9), 967–970 (2000)

22. Korkikian, R., Pelissier, S., Naccache, D.: Blind fault attack against SPN ciphers. In: FDTC, pp. 94–103. IEEE (2014)

23. Guo, X., Mukhopadhyay, D., Jin, C., Karri, R.: Security analysis of concurrent error detection against differential fault analysis. J. Cryptogr. Eng. 5(3), 153–169 (2015). https://doi.org/10.1007/s13389-014-0092-8

24. Breier, J., He, W., Jap, D., Bhasin, S., Chattopadhyay, A.: Attacks in reality: the limits of concurrent error detection codes against laser fault injection. J. Hardw. Syst. Secur. 1(4), 298–310 (2017). https://doi.org/10.1007/s41635-017-0020-3

25. Patranabis, S., Chakraborty, A., Nguyen, P.H., Mukhopadhyay, D.: A biased fault attack on the time redundancy countermeasure for AES. In: Mangard, S., Poschmann, A. (eds.) COSADE 2015. LNCS, vol. 9604, pp. 189–203. Springer, Cham (2015). https://doi.org/10.1007/978-3-319-21476-4_13

26. Tupsamudre, H., Bisht, S., Mukhopadhyay, D.: Destroying fault invariant with randomization. In: Batina, L., Robshaw, M. (eds) CHES 2014, vol. 8731, pp. 93–111. Springer, Heidelberg (2014). https://doi.org/10.1007/978-3-662-44709-3_6

27. Dobraunig, C., Eichlseder, M., Korak, T., Mangard, S., Mendel, F., Primas, R.: SIFA: exploiting ineffective fault inductions on symmetric cryptography. IACR Trans. Cryptogr. Hardw. Embed. Syst. 2018(3), 547–572 (2018)

28. Dobraunig, C., Eichlseder, M., Gross, H., Mangard, S., Mendel, F., Primas, R.: Statistical ineffective fault attacks on masked AES with fault countermeasures. In: Peyrin, T., Galbraith, S. (eds.) ASIACRYPT 2018. LNCS, vol. 11273, pp. 315–342. Springer, Cham (2018). https://doi.org/10.1007/978-3-030-03329-3_11

29. Saha, S., Jap, D., Roy, D.B., Chakraborty, A., Bhasin, S., Mukhopadhyay, D.: A framework to counter statistical ineffective fault analysis of block ciphers using domain transformation and error correction. IEEE Trans. Inf. Forensics Secur. 15, 1905–1919 (2020)

30. Daemen, J., Dobraunig, C., Eichlseder, M., Gross, H., Mendel, F., Primas, R.: Protecting against statistical ineffective fault attacks. Cryptology ePrint Archive, Report 2019/536 (2019). https://eprint.iacr.org/2019/536

31. Breier, J., Khairallah, M., Hou, X., Liu, Y.: A countermeasure against statistical ineffective fault analysis. Cryptology ePrint Archive, Report 2019/515 (2019). http://eprint.iacr.org/2019/515

32. Shahmirzadi, A.R., Rasoolzadeh, S., Moradi, A.: Impeccable circuits II. In: Proceedings of 57th ACM/IEEE Design Automation Conference, (DAC), pp. 1–6. IEEE, San Francisco, July 2020

33. Saha, S., Bag, A., Mukhopadhyay, D.: Pushing the limits of fault template attacks: the role of side-channels. Cryptology ePrint Archive, Report 2020/892 (2020)

34. Baksi, A., Kumar, V.B.Y., Karmakar, B., Bhasin, S., Saha, D., Chattopadhyay, A.: A novel duplication based countermeasure to statistical ineffective fault analysis. In: Liu, J.K., Cui, H. (eds.) ACISP 2020. LNCS, vol. 12248, pp. 525–542. Springer, Cham (2020). https://doi.org/10.1007/978-3-030-55304-3_27

35. Daemen, J., Hoffert, S., Assche, G.V., Keer, R.V.: The design of Xoodoo and Xoofff. IACR Trans. Symmetric Cryptol. **2018**(4), 1–38 (2018)

36. Bogdanov, A., et al.: PRESENT: An ultra-lightweight block cipher. In: Paillier, P., Verbauwhede, I. (eds.) CHES 2007. LNCS, vol. 4727, pp. 450–466. Springer, Heidelberg (2007). https://doi.org/10.1007/978-3-540-74735-2_31

37. Zhang, F., et al.: Persistent fault analysis on block ciphers. IACR Trans. Cryptogr. Hardw. Embed. Syst. 150–172 (2018)

38. Pan, J., Zhang, F., Ren, K., Bhasin, S.: One fault is all it needs: breaking higher-order masking with persistent fault analysis. In: 2019 Design, Automation & Test in Europe Conference & Exhibition (DATE), pp. 1–6. IEEE (2019)

39. Mukhopadhyay, D.: Faultless to a fault? The case of threshold implementations of crypto-systems vs fault template attacks. In: IEEE/ACM International Conference on Computer Aided Design, ICCAD 2020, San Diego, CA, USA, 2–5 November 2020, pp. 66:1–66:9. IEEE (2020)

Generalizing Statistical Ineffective Fault Attacks in the Spirit of Side-Channel Attacks

Guillaume Barbu$^{(\boxtimes)}$, Laurent Castelnovi, and Thomas Chabrier

IDEMIA, Cryptography and Security Labs, Pessac, France
{guillaume.barbu,laurent.castelnovi,thomas.chabrier}@idemia.com

Abstract. At CHES 2018, Statistical Ineffective Fault Attacks were introduced to apply Differential Fault Analysis techniques on AES implementations protected against faults by detective or infective countermeasures. Soon after, other works have adapted SIFA to a couple of authenticated encryptions and a lightweight cipher. In this paper, we introduce the idea that SIFA is actually closer to Side-Channel Attacks than it is to DFA. We show how SIFA can actually target all selection functions known to be sensitive to SCA for any kind of algorithm. In particular, we apply for the first time SIFA in the context of asymmetric cryptography, reviving the threat of fault attacks on RSA even when faulty ciphertexts are not released to the adversary. Besides, with the results obtained by SIFA against proven side-channel countermeasures, this work opens new questions regarding established masking schemes.

Keywords: SIFA · Fault attacks · Side-channel attacks

1 Introduction

Side-Channel attacks (SCA) and Fault Attacks have been evolving quite independently since the late 90s and the seminal works respectively by Kocher *et al.* [23] and Boneh *et al.* [4]. The intersection of these two fields mainly consists in SCA targeting FA countermeasures or vice-versa [2,3,9,17,33,35,38]. Some publications, such as [8,18,25], have however considered some FA results from a statistical point of view, thus leaning towards the spirit of SCA. In particular, Dobraunig *et al.* proposed in [15] a new approach to take advantage of fault attacks. Statistical Ineffective Fault Attacks (SIFA) intend to take advantage of the fact that a successful fault injection may or may not alter an intermediate result, depending on its value. The authors analysed an AES implementation in their seminal work and soon after, SIFA has also been applied to some authenticated and lightweight ciphers [16,21,31]. By analysing only non-faulted outputs, one can observe the bias induced by the so-called ineffective fault on the intermediate result, which eventually gives information on a secret value. Consequently, SIFA naturally withstands usual fault countermeasures such as

© Springer Nature Switzerland AG 2021
S. Bhasin and F. De Santis (Eds.): COSADE 2021, LNCS 12910, pp. 105–125, 2021.
https://doi.org/10.1007/978-3-030-89915-8_5

detection or infection. The authors showed in a follow-up publication [14] that it can also defeat some state-of-the-art masking schemes. These works triggered a new interest in a statistical (or even *side-channel*) approach of fault attacks. Indeed several publications tackling fault injection results from a side-channel perspective followed [34,36,37].

In this article we pursue this line of work and propose a generalization of SIFA to all kind of cryptosystems, including asymmetric ones which were previously thought safe as long as faulty ciphertexts were not output.

Previous publications have mainly considered SIFA from a *fault-attack* perspective and have conservatively targeted intermediate results that were known to open the path for a classical Differential Fault Analysis (DFA), such as introduced in [29]. We extend SIFA, building on top of the tremendous work done within the side-channel community to identify the relevant selection functions allowing to recover the secrets manipulated by cryptographic algorithms. Using this *side-channel* approach to apply SIFA against AES, we can target classical side-channel selection functions and divide the secret in 8-bit words instead of 32-bit words in previous works. This can give a crucial advantage when applying the attacks in complex practical set-ups where the combinatorial of fault parameters is already high[1]. Pushing our analysis, we show that the SIFA approach can be the fault *alter ego* to the well-known Differential Power Analysis [24] or Correlation Power Analysis [6], the measure of the fault-induced bias depending on key guesses which takes the part of the *difference of mean* or *correlation* with the observed side-channel traces.

We also show that following this approach, SIFA can be applied to recover private keys in asymmetric contexts such as RSA or ECC schemes. This supports our claim that SIFA can actually threaten all targets of side-channel attacks.

This paper is organized as follows. Section 2 introduces SIFA and the related works. Afterwards, Sect. 3 presents our improvement of SIFA and apply it to AES. In Sect. 4, we show how SIFA can be generalized and applied on any SCA selection functions, with an example targeting RSA implementations. Finally, Sect. 5 discusses the possible applications of SIFA, future works and concludes this article.

2   Related Works

2.1   Statistical Ineffective Fault Attacks

While most fault attacks require faulty ciphertexts to proceed, SIFA is only interested in ineffective faults, *i.e.* when the injected fault has no effect during the cryptographic operation. SIFA combines both principles of Statistical Fault Attacks (SFA) [18] and Ineffective Fault Attacks (IFA) [8]. In SIFA, the attacker targets a precise intermediate value during the cipher execution. Then for each ineffective fault, he computes the state where the fault was injected from a

---

[1] For a laser pulse for instance, one should consider multiple parameters such as the spot location and width, the delay, as well as the pulse power and duration.

key hypothesis and the ciphertext. Comparing the expected distribution to the observed one for each key hypothesis, he can determine the secret key by choosing the key guess that leads to the furthest distribution from the expected one.

The initial step leading to the concept of SIFA is the analysis of the fault effect depending on the considered fault model. Table 1 shows the transition probability from a 2-bit state x to the state $\tilde{x}$ after a bitwise AND with a 2-bit random defining our fault model. For example, when $x = 0$, $\tilde{x}$ will be zero, whatever the value of the random. We can notice that the distribution of the faulty output is not uniform when we consider ineffective faults, that is to say that the probability that $\tilde{x} = b$ given $x = b$ (given on the diagonal of Table 1) is not the same for all $b \in \{0, 1, 2, 3\}$.

Table 1. Transition probabilities from x to $\tilde{x}$ when applying a random-AND on 2 bits.

x	$\tilde{x}$			
	0	1	2	3
0	1	0	0	0
1	$\frac{1}{2}$	$\frac{1}{2}$	0	0
2	$\frac{1}{2}$	0	$\frac{1}{2}$	0
3	$\frac{1}{4}$	$\frac{1}{4}$	$\frac{1}{4}$	$\frac{1}{4}$

Based on this observation, one can mount attacks on block ciphers in a usual DFA spirit like in [29]. For example, if we consider the AES encryption, the attack is based on a fault before the last *MixColumns*, as illustrated in Fig. 1. This is precisely the attack that was demonstrated in the seminal work in [15].

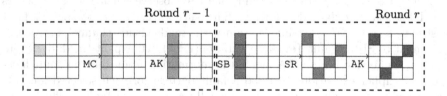

Fig. 1. Fault propagation from a faulted byte before the last *MixColumns*.

In a nutshell, the original SIFA from [15] works in 3 steps:

1. **Collecting ciphertexts** The fault injection target is one byte, before the last application of *MixColumns* (see Fig. 1). N encryptions (with different plaintexts) are faulted. The fault model must induce a non-uniform distribution when only ineffective faults are considered; they used the random-AND introduced above.

2. **Key guessing** The attacker guesses 4 bytes $\hat{k}$ of the last round key K_{10}, denoted $\hat{k}$, and partially decrypts the last operations for all ineffectively faulted ciphertexts $C^{(i)}$

$$S_{9,\hat{k}}^{(i)} = MC^{-1} \circ SB^{-1} \circ SR^{-1} \circ AK^{-1}(\hat{k}, C^{(i)}).$$

No information on K_9 is needed as AK does not alter the distribution of the state.

3. **Determining the correct key** For each key candidate, the bias induced in the targeted byte is estimated, for instance with the Square Euclidean Imbalance (SEI). Here, due to the effect of the fault, the correct hypothesis should lead to the most biased distribution:

$$k = \underset{\hat{k} \in \mathbb{F}_{2^{32}}}{\operatorname{argmax}} \left(\operatorname{SEI}(S_{9,\hat{k}}^{(i)}) \right).$$

In this attack, the knowledge of the bias in the fault distribution is not required. It is sufficient to have a non-uniform distribution of the faulted values (*e.g.* random-AND), and a metric (*e.g.* SEI) to compare the observed distribution with an expected one. By exploiting the dependency between the ineffectiveness of the faults and the processed data, we can see a link between SIFA and side-channel attacks.

2.2 Other Works Linking Faults and Side-Channel Analysis

Several attacks have shown a relationship between side-channel and fault injection attacks.

Fault Sensitivity Analysis (FSA) [25] exhibits sensitivity-data dependency between transitions of signals in a device and fault injection. By increasing the intensity of a fault injection medium, one can observe when the fault occurs to exhibit sensitive-data dependency. The authors used this leakage of fault sensitivity to retrieve secret information with standard side-channel analysis.

Similar to SIFA, Fault Template Attacks (FTA) [34] exploit the data dependency of ineffective fault. FTA combines information from different fault locations and cipher executions to build a fault pattern for each selected location depending on a so-called *observable*, typically whether the fault is effective or not. This attack takes root in the notions of activation and propagation of faults in a combinational circuits. Similar to side-channel template attacks, the attack is composed of an offline building phase (template construction for circuit characterization) and an online matching phase.

Automatic Leakage Assessment for Fault Attacks (ALAFA) [36] provides a statistical framework to detect information leakage from the correct and faulty ciphertexts differential. In particular, authors use the Welch's t-test to reveal side-channel information leakage.

For Fault Correlation Analysis (FCA) [37], the authors inject faults at each clock cycle for different inputs, repeating the operations several times for each input. They can then establish a probability of fault for each clock cycle and input to create traces of fault probability. These traces are then exploited with a standard side-channel analysis to recover the secret key. To some extent this can be seen as adding a temporal dimension to SIFA, however we will see that these two attacks differ in a couple of ways.

Together with SIFA, these attacks contribute in building a link between side-channel analysis and fault attacks. These attacks are all based on the observation of whether or not the fault injection did affect the algorithm execution and require a very good precision on the targeted step to exploit this observation. Consequently, they differ only in some prerequisites or particular properties. A quite unique property of SIFA is that it does not require the attacker to be able to replay several times the same input, which can turn out as a strong advantage when the input cannot be controlled by the attacker. Also, unlike FSA and FCA, SIFA does not require the knowledge of the legitimate ciphertext when a fault does alter the output. FTA requires the ability to build the templates on a fully controlled device, but offers some unique properties if this requirement is met since it allows to attack middle rounds of block ciphers even without ciphertext knowledge. We can also note that ALAFA fails when strong detection countermeasures are implemented, unlike the other presented attacks. Finally, SIFA requires a more modest number of fault injections than the other thanks to the absence of characterization or trace building process. However, one of its drawbacks is that it requires bruteforcing 32-bit subkeys, which can turn out problematic in some settings. Moreover, SIFA has been successfully applied only on a couple of ciphers, contrary to the other works that can potentially target any algorithm. This work intends to solve those two limitations.

3 Improving SIFA Against AES

In [15], the authors derived their attack from classical DFA on AES. Consequently, they restricted themselves to faults on the penultimate round and needed to work on 32-bit subkey hypothesis. In this section, we show that it is possible to take advantage of the SIFA approach on various intermediate values of the AES encryption, hence a lighter bruteforce requirement. In addition, we show that this approach preserves the ability to defeat masked implementations, as already observed in [14].

3.1 Enabling 8-Bit SIFA

A classical side-channel target is the input of the S-box layer of the last round of AES. In this setting, each S-box input is attacked separately. Let us denote by S the AES S-box and by $(m_i)_{i=1,\ldots,N}$ the sequence of the input bytes of the jth S-box when the attacker feeds the AES with N uniformly random plaintexts, for an arbitrary $1 \leqslant j \leqslant 16$. The fault the attacker induces during the evaluation of the AES is modelled by a function $F_i : \mathbb{F}_{256} \to F_i(\mathbb{F}_{256})$ such that, if X is a uniformly distributed random variable over $\mathbb{F}_{256}$, then $F_i(X)$ does not follow a uniform distribution – for instance, F_i can be a logical AND with a random byte. At the end of the faulted AES, the attacker gets, omitting the ShiftRows transformation, $S(F_i(m_i)) \oplus k_j$, where k_j is the 8-bit subkey he aims at recovering.

In order to guess k_j, the attacker then applies SIFA principles: making a hypothesis $\hat{k}$ on k_j, he reverts the AES until he reaches the input of the S-box, that is to say, he computes $\hat{Y}_i = S^{-1}(S(F_i(m_i)) \oplus k_j \oplus \hat{k})$ for all i. Let $f_{\hat{k}}$ be the distribution of the $(\hat{Y}_i)_{i=1,...,N}$, he expects that $f_{\hat{k}}$, with $\hat{k} \neq k_j$, is closer to the uniform distribution than f_{k_j}. But this is actually not true. It is quite easy to see that for any guess $\hat{k}$, the Euclidean distance between $f_{\hat{k}}$ and the uniform distribution – that is to say, the SEI of $f_{\hat{k}}$ – is the same. By definition, $f_{\hat{k}}(x) = 1/N \cdot \mathrm{card}(\{F_i(m_i) \,|\, Y_i^H = x\})$; then for any $a \in \mathbb{F}_{256}$:

$$
f_{\hat{k} \oplus a}(x) = \frac{1}{N} \mathrm{card}(\{F_i(m_i) \,|\, S^{-1}(S(F_i(m_i)) \oplus k \oplus \hat{k} \oplus a) = x\})
$$
$$
= \frac{1}{N} \mathrm{card}(\{F_i(m_i) \,|\, S^{-1}(S(F_i(m_i)) \oplus k \oplus \hat{k}) = S^{-1}(S(x) \oplus a)\})
$$
$$
= f_{\hat{k}}(g_a(x)),
$$

where $g_a : x \mapsto S^{-1}(S(x) \oplus a)$. Thus:

$$
\mathrm{SEI}(f_{\hat{k} \oplus a}) = \sum_{x \in \mathbb{F}_{256}} \left(f_{\hat{k} \oplus a}(x) - \frac{1}{256} \right)^2
$$
$$
= \sum_{x \in \mathbb{F}_{256}} \left(f_{\hat{k}}(g_a(x)) - \frac{1}{256} \right)^2
$$
$$
= \sum_{y \in \mathbb{F}_{256}} \left(f_{\hat{k}}(y) - \frac{1}{256} \right)^2
$$
$$
= \mathrm{SEI}(f_{\hat{k}}).
$$

The problem here is that, denoting by U the distribution of the $(\hat{Y}_i)_i$ when no fault occurs (*i.e.* when F_i is the identity for all i), for two different key guesses $\hat{k}$ and $\hat{k}'$, there exists a bijection g defined on the domain of the $(f_i)_{i=0,...,255}$ such that $(f_{\hat{k}} - U)^2 = ((f_{\hat{k}'} - U) \circ g)^2$. This can be circumvented by applying a non-bijective $\mathcal{L}$ to the $\hat{Y}_i$'s to break this link between U and the f_i's. In the following we give two examples of such a $\mathcal{L}$ inspired from classical side-channel leakage functions: the Hamming weight (HW) and a single bit of the targeted value, connected respectively to the Correlation Power Analysis introduced in [6] and the Differential Power Analysis from [24].

3.2   Results on an Unprotected Implementation

To verify this result, we have implemented an AES without side-channel countermeasure. Our goal is to recover k_0 the first byte of the last round key. We draw $N = 2\,500$ plaintexts uniformly at random and we run this AES twice on each of them: the first time we let the algorithm run normally, the second time we apply a logical AND with a random value on the first byte of the input state of the last round S-box layer. We only keep the ciphertexts that are equal on both executions[2]. Let $(c_i)_{i=1,\dots,N}$ be the sequence of the first byte of the gathered ciphertexts; then for each key guess $\hat{k}$ we compute twice the sequence $(\hat{Y}_i)_{i=1,\dots,N}$ of the $\hat{Y}_i = \mathcal{L}(S^{-1}(c_i \oplus \hat{k}))$: once with $\mathcal{L}$ as the Hamming weight, a second time with $\mathcal{L}$ as a logical AND with 1.

In the case where $\mathcal{L} = \text{HW}$, the expected distribution U when no fault occurs is a binomial distribution with parameters $(n,p) = (8, 1/2)$. Since we apply a random-AND fault model, the Hamming weight of the targeted variable can only decrease after the fault, thus we expect to observe a distribution f_{k_0} for the correct key guess k_0 that provides much greater probabilities than U that values strictly lower than 4 happen, whereas $f_{\hat{k}}$ should be close to U if $\hat{k} \neq k_0$. This expectation is confirmed by our experiment as shown on Fig. 2a on which are plotted the 256 distributions $(f_i)_i$. Figure 2b moreover shows that only a small number of ciphertexts – around 30 – is necessary to estimate the f_i's accurately enough to use the SEI to recover the correct subkey.

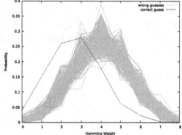

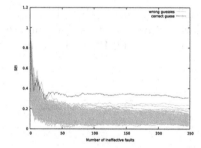

(a) Distribution of the Hamming weight of the intermediate result for all key hypotheses (correct one in dashed red).

(b) Evolution of the SEI for the different key hypotheses (correct one in dashed red) with an increasing number of ineffective faults.

Fig. 2. Result of the SIFA targeting the HW of byte 0 of the last round S-box input (unprotected AES). (Color figure online)

In the case where $\mathcal{L}$ is a logical AND with 1, the expected distribution U when no fault occurs is the uniform distribution over $\{0, 1\}$. Since we apply a random-AND fault model, we expect to observe a distribution f_{k_0} such that $f_{k_0}(0) \approx 3/4$ and $f_{k_0}(1) \approx 1/4$, whereas $f_{\hat{k}}$ should be closer to U if $\hat{k} \neq k_0$. Figure 3 confirms this intuition by showing that the attack is successful. Interestingly, more ciphertexts are necessary to find the key – around 180 – compared to

---

[2] This is equivalent to the filter we would have if a detection countermeasure were implemented.

the choice $\mathcal{L} = \text{HW}$, like what happens in the side-channel context where CPA usually requires less traces than DPA to succeed.

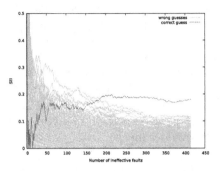

Fig. 3. Evolution of the SEI for the different key hypotheses (correct one in dashed red) with an increasing number of ineffective faults. The SIFA targets the least significant bit of byte 0 (unprotected AES). (Color figure online)

Similar experiments have been led on the first round S-box input and output as selection function, with the Hamming weight leakage model. Figure 4 has been obtained simulating 10,000 fault injections, resulting in around 1,000 ineffective faults.

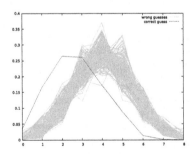
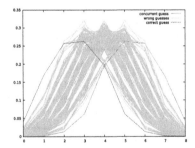

(a) Distribution of the Hamming weight of the first round SubBytes output for all key hypotheses (correct one in dashed red).

(b) Distribution of the Hamming weight of the first round SubBytes input for all key hypotheses (correct one in dashed red).

Fig. 4. Result of the SIFA targeting the HW of byte 0 of the first round S-box output (left) and input (right) (unprotected AES). (Color figure online)

As expected, the distributions obtained targeting the first round S-box output (Fig. 4a) are very similar to the distributions obtained targeting the last round S-box input (Fig. 2a). Regarding the distributions of the first round S-box input, the symmetry with respect to the axis $x = 4$ that we can observe in Fig. 4b is easily explained: the two complementary key hypotheses $\hat{k}$ and $\hat{k} \oplus \texttt{0xFF}$ respectively result in a sequence $(\hat{Y}_i)_{i=1,...,N}$ and $(8 - \hat{Y}_i)_{i=1,...,N}$. This means that each key hypothesis – and in particular the correct one – has a concurrent hypothesis which is at the same distance from U, and that the attacker remains with two key candidates after the attack. Moreover, estimating the $f_{\hat{k}}$'s accurately enough to succeed in attacking the first round S-box input requires a significant amount of extra ineffective faults compared to the same round S-box output: Fig. 2a was obtained using 250 ineffective faults and the correct key guess already clearly stands out, whereas Fig. 4b was obtained with 1,000 ineffective faults and the correct key guess still timidly appears.

Let us now see what happens when we deal with SCA-protected implementations.

3.3   Results on a Protected Implementation

In [14], Dobraunig et al. show that the classical Boolean masking used to protect sensitive implementations from arbitrary-order side-channel attacks does not prevent SIFA, whatever the order of protection. We show in this section that our improved SIFA still has this property.

As in [14], we attack the open-source Rivain-Prouff [32] protected AES implementation provided by Coron [12]. Since we expect from [14] to get similar results whatever the order of protection we choose, we arbitrarily decide to protect AES against 3rd-order SCA to save experimentation time. The sensitive intermediate value we target is the first byte of the input state of the last round S-box layer. We set $\mathcal{L} = \text{HW}$, thus the expected distribution U when no fault is injected is the binomial distribution with parameters $(n, p) = (8, 1/2)$.

To evaluate the S-box, Rivain-Prouff algorithm inverts $x \in \mathbb{F}_{256}$ (with the convention $0^{-1} = 0$) by computing $z = x^{254}$ through the following sequence of operations, where $\cdot$ denotes the multiplication in $\mathbb{F}_{256}$:

$$z \leftarrow x \cdot x^2$$
$$y \leftarrow z^4$$
$$z \leftarrow (z \cdot y)^{16} \cdot y$$
$$z \leftarrow z \cdot x^2$$

When x is masked, i.e. when $x = x_1 \oplus \cdots \oplus x_n$ for a given integer n (in our experiment then $n = 4$), the sensitive operation is the multiplication – a squaring in $\mathbb{F}_{256}$ is linear and thus easily protected. In the Rivain-Prouff secure inversion, the multiplication is performed according to Algorithm 1.

We injected a fault during one of the first three calls to Algorithm 1, sticking at zero one of its $2n$ inputs. This results in an ineffective fault at the end of the full inversion essentially in two cases:

– either if the corrupted input was already equal to zero, and the fault actually had no effect,

---

Algorithm 1: Secure multiplication in the Rivain-Prouff inversion [32]

Input: $(a_i)_{i=1,...,n}$ such that $\bigoplus_i a_i = a$, $(b_i)_{i=1,...,n}$ such that $\bigoplus_i b_i = b$
Result: $(c_i)_{i=1,...,n}$ such that $\bigoplus_i c_i = a \cdot b$
for i *from* 1 *to* n **do**
  | $c_i \leftarrow a_i \cdot b_i$;
end
for i *from* 1 *to* n **do**
  | **for** j *from* $i+1$ *to* n **do**
  | | draw r uniformly at random from $\mathbb{F}_{256}$;
  | | $c_i \leftarrow c_i \oplus r$;
  | | $c_j \leftarrow c_j \oplus ((r \oplus a_i \cdot b_j) \oplus a_j \cdot b_i)$;
  | **end**
end

- or if the value to invert x equalled zero: then the final multiplication by x^2 in the inversion algorithm set z to the expected result 0 since neither this multiplication nor the squaring of x was corrupted.

The second point implies that a great number of the received c_i's are equal to $S(0) \oplus k_0$, then 0 should be overrepresented in the sequence $(\hat{Y}_i)_i$ under the correct key guess. This is confirmed by our experiment, as shown by Fig. 5a on which are plotted the 256 distributions $(f_i)_i$.

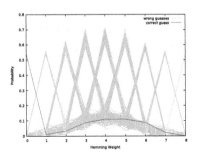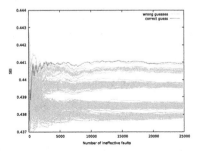

(a) Distribution of the Hamming weight of the intermediate result for all key hypotheses (correct one in dashed red).

(b) Convergence of the SEI for the different key hypotheses (correct one in dashed red).

Fig. 5. Result of the SIFA targeting the HW of byte 0 (protected AES). (Color figure online)

It is interesting to notice that this figure is almost symmetric with respect to the line HW = 4 and thus that f_{k_0} has a symmetric distribution that reaches its maximum in HW = 8 and that could compete with f_{k_0} to realise the maximum of the SEI – leading then to a wrong key guess. It can be shown however that this concurrent distribution f_{k^*} leads to the correct key guess too. When we revert the AES from $c_i = S(0) \oplus k_0$ under the hypothesis k^*, we compute $S^{-1}(c_i \oplus k^*)$, which is equal to 0xff by assumption on f_{k^*}. Therefore, $k^* = S(0) \oplus S(0\text{xff}) \oplus k_0 = k_0 \oplus 0\text{x}75$.

Regarding the number of ciphertexts required to approximate the f_i's accurately enough to recover the key, it is sensibly higher – around 4,000 – than in the case of an unprotected implementation (Fig. 5b).

Remark. Dealing with SIFA it is usually assumed that the attacker does not know the effect of the fault he injects. This is why we used the SEI to guess k_0 instead of a much simpler distinguisher: if the attacker knew the fault model to be a "stuck-at-zero", he would simply have to count the number of occurrences of each integer among the c_i's and xor the most frequent with $S(0)$ to get k_0.

4   SIFA as Another Side-Channel Attack

Our previous experiments on the AES let us think that all known targets of classical SCA can also be attacked through SIFA. We explore this track in this section and expose some new results on RSA cryptosystems even when no faulty output is released. To highlight the versatility of SIFA, we expose both results on RSA implementations with and without the CRT parameters.

4.1   A Side-Channel Attack

Let us consider the different steps used to set-up a SIFA and explain how they map to the traditional SCA context.

Our proposition for applying the SIFA strategy will go through the following steps:

1. A device performs some cryptographic computations E on plaintexts P_i given a key $K : E_K(P_i)$
   For an SCA, there is no difference.
2. To recover the key, an attacker would first determine the targeted intermediate value t_i. This value should depend on a portion of the key that the attacker can brute-force. We call this portion the *subkey*, denoted k.
   For an SCA, there is no difference.
3. During each computation, the device handles some intermediate values $v_{i,j}$ at each given moment in time j. The attacker injects a fault at the precise moment j_0 when the targeted intermediate value v_{i,j_0} is manipulated, changing it to $\tilde{v}_{i,j_0}$ which may or may not be equal to v_{i,j_0}.
   For an SCA, the attacker would be interested in the physical leakage $\mathcal{L}(v_{i,j_0})$ that is produced when the device handles v_{i,j_0}.
4. Considering only the ineffective faults (*i.e.* $\tilde{v}_{i,j_0} = v_{i,j_0}$), the attacker can then evaluate the intermediate values for all possible *subkeys* $\hat{k}$, resulting in $\hat{v}_{i,j_0}$. For each *subkey*, the attacker shall then evaluate the distribution of $f(\hat{v}_{i,j_0})$ for a given function f and confront it to the expected distribution of $f(v_{i,j_0})$,

say by computing the SEI if the expected distribution is uniform.

For an SCA, he would apply the $\hat{v}_{i,j_0}$ a physical leakage model L and confront $L(\hat{v}_{i,j_0})$ to $\mathcal{L}(v_{i,j_0})$ thanks to a side-channel distinguisher, say Pearson's correlation coefficient for instance.

5. The key guess that maximizes the distinguisher should be the correct one.
   For an SCA, there is no difference.

The similarity between SIFA and classical SCA appears then quite straightforward. In a sense, one can consider the evaluation of the bias of an intermediate value in ineffectively faulted operations as a side-channel distinguisher. The side-channel leakage resides here in the effectiveness (or ineffectiveness) of the fault injection.

To illustrate this, the next sections will present the adaptation of some well-known SCAs on the RSA cryptosystem, either in its straightforward form or using the CRT.

4.2 Application to RSA-STD's Modular Exponentiation

In [27], the authors propose a DPA on the modular exponentiation performed during a straightforward (*i.e.* not using CRT) RSA signature generation. More clearly, the target is the operation $m^d \bmod n$, where m is the message to be signed, n is the RSA modulus, product of two secret primes, and d is the RSA private key. This idea has been further extended by Amiel *et al.* [1] to target exponent l-bit words ($d_i \in \mathbb{F}_2^l$, for $d = (d_0, d_1, \cdots, d_{k-1})$) with a CPA. These attacks consist in correlating some hypothetical values $m^{\hat{d}} \bmod n$ against multiple side-channel traces observed during the exponentiation $m^d \bmod N$.

Our proposal is very similar to these attacks except that the leakage observed in our case is the effectiveness of the fault injection, and a distribution difference is used to identify the correct key guess. In particular, we adapt the attack of Amiel *et al.* on l-bit words of d, denoted d_i, with $l = 8$.

We simulated the results of the attack on an RSA-1024 by faulting the least significant byte of the intermediate result $m^{d_i} \bmod n$. We use the random-AND fault model defined previously and used in [15]. We performed the operations for 1,600 random messages m and kept only the $N = 164$ messages resulting in a correct signature (when the fault has been ineffective).

Once the faults injected, the attack consists in searching for a bias in the least significant byte of hypothetical values $m^{\hat{d}_i} \bmod n$. Let $(m_j)_{j=1,\ldots,N}$ be the gathered messages; then for each guess on a key word $\hat{d}_i$, we compute the sequence $(Y_j)_{j=1,\ldots,N}$ of the $Y_j = \mathcal{L}(m_j^{\hat{d}_i} \bmod n)$, with $\mathcal{L}$ defined as the Hamming weight of the least significant byte. The attack process can be found in Algorithm 2 and allows to reconstruct the k words of d, one word after the other. Algorithm 2 considers the attacker targets a left-to-right exponentiation method but it can also be adapted for the right-to-left case.

Algorithm 2: SIFA on RSA modular exponentiation

Input: N messages (m_j) corresponding to ineffective faults
Result: i^{th} secret exponent l-bit word of d
initialize table $sei[256]$;
for $\hat{d}_i \in \mathbb{F}_{2^l}$ **do**
> initialize histogram h;
> $\hat{d} \leftarrow \hat{d}_i 2^{l(i-1)} + \sum_{j=i+1}^{k-1} d_j 2^{l(j-1)}$;
> **for** $j = 0 \to N - 1$ **do**
> > $\hat{s} \leftarrow m_j^{\hat{d}} \bmod n$;
> > increment $h(\mathcal{L}(\hat{s}))$;
>
> **end**
> $sei[\hat{d}_i] \leftarrow \text{SEI}(h)$;

end
$d_i \leftarrow \underset{\hat{d}_i \in \mathbb{F}_{2^l}}{\operatorname{argmax}} sei[\hat{d}_i]$;

Since the fault model we consider here can only decrease the Hamming weight of the targeted variable, we expect to observe a distribution f_{d_i} that is biased, compared to the binomial distribution expected for $f_{\hat{d}_i \neq d_i}$. This expectation is confirmed by our experiments, as shown on Fig. 6a showing the 256 distributions $(f_i)_i$.

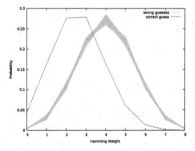
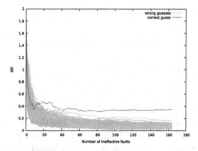

(a) Distribution of the Hamming weight of the intermediate result for all key hypotheses (correct one in dashed red).

(b) Convergence of the SEI for the different key hypotheses (correct one in dashed red).

Fig. 6. Result of the SIFA targeting the most significant byte of the secret exponent. (Color figure online)

Figure 6b shows that less than 20 ineffective faults are sufficient to let the SEI discriminate the correct key-word guess. Here we considered 8-bit words, so the total number[3] of ineffective faults necessary to recover the whole secret exponent should be close to $128 \times 20 = 2{,}560$.

We can note that, in the context of Elliptic Curve Cryptography (ECC), similar side-channel attacks exists, targeting the scalar multiplication. These attacks can be straightforwardly adapted with a SIFA approach.

Effects of Side-Channel Countermeasures. We focused on a selected subset of the countermeasure usually considered in the literature [7,10,11], namely:

- Blinding of the message and modulus: $m' = m + r_1 \cdot n \bmod r_2 \cdot n$, with r_1 and r_2 being λ-bit values drawn at random each time the computation is executed.
- Euclidean splitting: $d = \delta_0 \cdot r + \delta_1$, with r a λ-bit random and δ_0 and δ_1 respectively the quotient and remainder of the euclidean division of d by r. Then $m^d = (m^{\delta_0})^r \cdot m^{\delta_1}$.

Unsurprisingly, both message/modulus blinding and euclidean splitting are efficient countermeasures against our attack. Indeed, in such a case, the least significant byte of the value $m^{d_i} \bmod n$ we construct during our attack for the correct subkey guess is no more correlated to the faulted value if λ is large enough. Consequently, no biases can be observed in the distributions, as can be observed in Fig. 7.

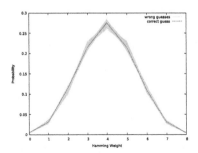 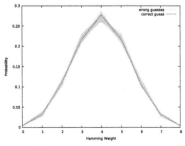

(a) Distribution of the Hamming weight of the intermediate result for all key hypotheses (correct one in dashed red) when message/modulus blinding is implemented.

(b) Distribution of the Hamming weight of the intermediate result for all key hypotheses (correct one in dashed red) when Euclidean splitting of the exponent is implemented.

Fig. 7. Observed distributions for the different key hypotheses with countermeasures. 32-bit randoms are used in both cases. (Color figure online)

---

[3] Note that this number could be halved since only half of the secret exponent should be sufficient to break the RSA modulus [5].

4.3   Application to CRT-RSA's Garner Recombination

We recall that the modular exponentiation in RSA signature generation can be made more efficiently by using the CRT [13]. Given an RSA modulus $N = p \cdot q$, the idea is to compute separately $s_p = m^{d_p} \bmod p$ and $s_q = m^{d_q} \bmod q$, with $d_p = d \bmod p - 1$ and $d_q = d \bmod q - 1$, and then to combine the results to recover the signature $s = m^d \bmod N$. In [1] the authors target one of the prime factors during the CRT recombination following Garner's formula:

$$s = s_q + q \cdot (i_q \cdot (s_p - s_q) \bmod p) \bmod n,$$

with $i_q = q^{-1} \bmod p$.

More precisely, the attack takes advantage of the following relation:

$$\left\lfloor \frac{s}{q} \right\rfloor = \left\lfloor \frac{s_q}{q} \right\rfloor + (i_q \cdot (s_p - s_q) \bmod p) = i_q \cdot (s_p - s_q) \bmod p.$$

The attack consists in correlating some hypothetical values $\left\lfloor \frac{s}{q_i{}_H} \right\rfloor$ against side-channel traces observed during the recombination.

Again, our proposal is very similar to the original attack, except that the leakage observed in our case is the ineffectiveness of the fault injection, and a distribution difference is used to highlight the correct key guess.

We simulated the attack on an RSA-1024 by inducing a bias in the targeted byte of the intermediate value $i_q \cdot (s_p - s_q) \bmod p$. The fault model is the same as the one used previously, a random-AND. We performed the operations for $1\,300$ random messages m and kept only the $N = 133$ messages resulting in a correct signature (when the fault has been ineffective). It is important to note that our fault injection should impact only the targeted byte.

The key recovery can then be achieved l-bit word by l-bit word, by searching for bias in the targeted word of hypothetical values $\left\lfloor \frac{s}{\hat{q}} \right\rfloor$. Let $(s_j)_{j=1,\dots,N}$ be the gathered signatures; then for each guess on a key word $\hat{q}_i$, we construct $\hat{q}$ and compute the sequence $(Y_j)_{j=1,\dots,N}$ of the $Y_j = \mathcal{L}\left(\left\lfloor \frac{s_j}{\hat{q}} \right\rfloor\right)$, with $\mathcal{L}$ defined as the Hamming weight of the target word. As proposed in [1], we add $2^{l(i-1)}128$ to $\hat{q}$ to take into consideration the unknown following bits of q. The attack process can be found in Algorithm 3.

Algorithm 3: SIFA on CRT-RSA Garner recombination

Input: N signatures (s_j) corresponding to ineffective faults
Result: i^{th} l-bit word of secret prime q
initialize table $sei[256]$;
for $\hat{q}_i \in \mathbb{F}_{2^l}$ **do**
  initialize histogram h;
  $\hat{q} \leftarrow \hat{q}_i 2^{l(i-1)} + \sum_{j=i+1}^{k-1} q_j 2^{l(j-1)} + 128 \times 2^{(i-2)l}$;
  for $j = 0 \rightarrow N - 1$ **do**
    $\hat{t} \leftarrow \lfloor \frac{s_j}{\hat{q}} \rfloor$;
    increment $h(\mathcal{L}(\hat{t}))$;
  end
  $sei[\hat{q}_i] \leftarrow \text{SEI}(h)$;
end
$q_i \leftarrow \underset{\hat{q}_i \in \mathbb{F}_{2^l}}{\text{argmax}} \, sei[\hat{q}_i]$;

Again, we expect to observe a distribution f_{q_i} that is biased, compared to the binomial distribution expected for $f_{\hat{q}_i \neq q_i}$. This expectation is confirmed by our experiments, as shown on Fig. 8a plotting the 256 distributions $(f_i)_i$. We can note that the effect of our fault injection does not appear as obviously as in Fig. 6a. This is due to the fact that each byte is recovered within a margin of error due to the unknown following words of the prime q. Figure 8b shows that less than 40 ineffective faults are necessary to let the SEI discriminate the correct key-word guess. Again, as we consider 8-bit words, a total number of $64 \times 40 \approx 2,500$ ineffective faults is required to recover the full 512-bit secret prime q.

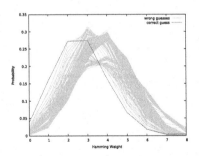

(a) Distribution of the Hamming weight of the intermediate result for all key hypotheses (correct one in dashed red).

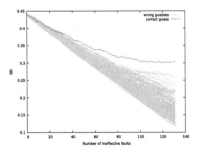

(b) Convergence of the SEI for the different key hypotheses (correct one in dashed red).

Fig. 8. Result of the SIFA targeting the most significant byte of the secret exponent. (Color figure online)

Effects of Side-Channel Countermeasures. In this case, countermeasures based on exponent splitting alone do not prevent our attack. This is expected as this countermeasure only protects the exponentiation itself, not the recombination. This can be seen in Fig. 9a, where the distribution of the correct key guess clearly stands out. On the other hand, message and modulus blinding do add some security as long as they are kept for the Garner recombination, as proposed in [19]. Indeed, the attack takes advantage of a bias induced by the fault in one byte $\left\lfloor \frac{s}{q} \right\rfloor$ but the blinding countermeasure spreads this bias across all the bits of this intermediate value because of the modular operations, thus making the attack impractical. Consequently, no biases can be observed for any key hypothesis, as can be seen in Fig. 9b.

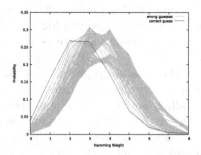 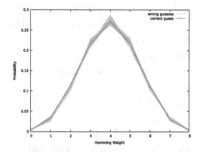

(a) Distribution of the Hamming weight of the intermediate result for all key hypotheses (correct one in dashed red) when Euclidean splitting of the exponent is implemented.

(b) Distribution of the Hamming weight of the intermediate result for all key hypotheses (correct one in dashed red) when message/modulus blinding is implemented.

Fig. 9. Observed distributions for the different key hypotheses with countermeasures. 32-bit randoms are used in both cases. (Color figure online)

5   Discussion

So far, SIFA has been mainly considered as an alternative to fault attacks when fault detection or infective countermeasures were present. As a result, it has been targeting operations and intermediate values that were known to open the path to DFA. The major outcome of our work is a tremendous increase of the scope of applicability of SIFA across the spectrum of cryptographic algorithms. Actually, this brings SIFA at the same level as FCA in terms of targetable implementations, with an important improvement on the number of fault injections required (by several orders of magnitude). Besides, SIFA has shown unexpected results on masking schemes proven secure in the probing model such as [32], whatever the masking order. However, our experiments on usual masking schemes in asymmetric cryptography did not reveal the same weaknesses that were observed on

122 G. Barbu et al.

AES. A more thorough analysis of the behaviour of side-channel countermeasures with regards to bias injections appears then as an interesting topic for future works.

Considering that side-channel countermeasures should prevent SIFA, its applicability in the wild is then restricted to contexts in which side-channel attacks have not been considered practical whereas fault injections have. Until very recently, this has been the case when remote attacks are required, for attacks targeting mobile phone's System-on-Chip for instance. Remote fault attacks have become a reality in the last couple of years [22,28,30], using some specific software capabilities or hardware bugs. Such faults might reveal a lever to activate SIFA remotely on some device that do not implement side-channel countermeasures. Very recent works [20,26] have shown that side-channel analysis can also be performed remotely, provided the attacker has (or gains) appropriate privileges. Our work adds up to these results to argue for the need of implementing countermeasures against side-channel attacks in widespread cryptographic libraries that are shipped with devices manipulating more and more sensitive assets such as mobile phones.

Finally, we did not consider in this work the possible application of SIFA against candidates to the NIST Post-Quantum Cryptography standardisation effort. However, we believe that all schemes falling prey to SCA should also be considered from the SIFA perspective, even after the addition of countermeasures. And this is backed-up by the results obtained on protected AES implementations in this work and in [14]. Still, for lack of established protected implementation, we keep this as another promising topic for future works.

Acknowledgements. We would like to thank Christophe Giraud for his help during the redaction process as well as the anonymous reviewers of COSADE for pointing out some possible improvements on the initial submission.

References

1. Amiel, F., Feix, B., Villegas, K.: Power analysis for secret recovering and reverse engineering of public key algorithms. In: Adams, C., Miri, A., Wiener, M. (eds.) SAC 2007. LNCS, vol. 4876, pp. 110–125. Springer, Heidelberg (2007). https://doi.org/10.1007/978-3-540-77360-3_8
2. Amiel, F., Villegas, K., Feix, B., Marcel, L.: Passive and active combined attacks: combining fault attacks and side channel analysis. In: International Workshop on Fault Diagnosis and Tolerance in Cryptography, FDTC 2007. IEEE Computer Society (2007)
3. Barbu, G., et al.: Combined attack on CRT-RSA. In: Kurosawa, K., Hanaoka, G. (eds.) PKC 2013. LNCS, vol. 7778, pp. 198–215. Springer, Heidelberg (2013). https://doi.org/10.1007/978-3-642-36362-7_13
4. Boneh, D., DeMillo, R.A., Lipton, R.J.: On the Importance of checking cryptographic protocols for faults (extended abstract). In: Fumy, W. (ed.) EUROCRYPT 1997. LNCS, vol. 1233, pp. 37–51. Springer, Heidelberg (1997). https://doi.org/10.1007/3-540-69053-0_4

5. Boneh, D., Durfee, G., Frankel, Y.: An attack on RSA given a small fraction of the private key bits. In: Ohta, K., Pei, D. (eds.) ASIACRYPT 1998. LNCS, vol. 1514, pp. 25–34. Springer, Heidelberg (1998). https://doi.org/10.1007/3-540-49649-1_3

6. Brier, E., Clavier, C., Olivier, F.: Correlation power analysis with a leakage model. In: Joye, M., Quisquater, J.-J. (eds.) CHES 2004. LNCS, vol. 3156, pp. 16–29. Springer, Heidelberg (2004). https://doi.org/10.1007/978-3-540-28632-5_2

7. Ciet, M., Joye, M.: (Virtually) free randomization techniques for elliptic curve cryptography. In: Qing, S., Gollmann, D., Zhou, J. (eds.) ICICS 2003. LNCS, vol. 2836, pp. 348–359. Springer, Heidelberg (2003). https://doi.org/10.1007/978-3-540-39927-8_32

8. Clavier, C.: Secret external encodings do not prevent transient fault analysis. In: Paillier, P., Verbauwhede, I. (eds.) CHES 2007. LNCS, vol. 4727, pp. 181–194. Springer, Heidelberg (2007). https://doi.org/10.1007/978-3-540-74735-2_13

9. Clavier, C., Feix, B., Gagnerot, G., Roussellet, M.: Passive and active combined attacks on AES combining fault attacks and side channel analysis. In: Workshop on Fault Diagnosis and Tolerance in Cryptography, FDTC 2010. IEEE Computer Society (2010)

10. Clavier, C., Feix, B., Gagnerot, G., Roussellet, M., Verneuil, V.: Horizontal correlation analysis on exponentiation. In: Soriano, M., Qing, S., López, J. (eds.) ICICS 2010. LNCS, vol. 6476, pp. 46–61. Springer, Heidelberg (2010). https://doi.org/10.1007/978-3-642-17650-0_5

11. Clavier, C., Joye, M.: Universal exponentiation algorithm a first step towards *provable* SPA-resistance. In: Koç, Ç.K., Naccache, D., Paar, C. (eds.) CHES 2001. LNCS, vol. 2162, pp. 300–308. Springer, Heidelberg (2001). https://doi.org/10.1007/3-540-44709-1_25

12. Coron, J.S.: Higher-Order Countermeasures for AES and DES (2017). https://github.com/coron/htable

13. Couvreur, C., Quisquater, J.J.: Fast decipherment algorithm for RSA public-key cryptosystem. Electron. Lett. **18**(21), 905–907 (1982)

14. Dobraunig, C., Eichlseder, M., Gross, H., Mangard, S., Mendel, F., Primas, R.: Statistical ineffective fault attacks on masked AES with fault countermeasures. In: Peyrin, T., Galbraith, S. (eds.) ASIACRYPT 2018. LNCS, vol. 11273, pp. 315–342. Springer, Cham (2018). https://doi.org/10.1007/978-3-030-03329-3_11

15. Dobraunig, C., Eichlseder, M., Korak, T., Mangard, S., Mendel, F., Primas, R.: SIFA: exploiting ineffective fault inductions on symmetric cryptography. IACR Trans. Cryptogr. Hardw. Embed. Syst. **2018**(3) (2018)

16. Dobraunig, C., Mangard, S., Mendel, F., Primas, R.: Fault attacks on nonce-based authenticated encryption: application to Keyak and Ketje. In: Cid, C., Jacobson Jr., M. (eds.) SAC 2018. LNCS, vol. 11349, pp. 257–277. Springer, Cham (2019). https://doi.org/10.1007/978-3-030-10970-7_12

17. Fan, J., Gierlichs, B., Vercauteren, F.: To infinity and beyond: combined attack on ECC using points of low order. In: Preneel, B., Takagi, T. (eds.) CHES 2011. LNCS, vol. 6917, pp. 143–159. Springer, Heidelberg (2011). https://doi.org/10.1007/978-3-642-23951-9_10

18. Fuhr, T., Jaulmes, É., Lomné, V., Thillard, A.: Fault attacks on AES with faulty ciphertexts only. In: Fischer, W., Schmidt, J. (eds.) 2013 Workshop on Fault Diagnosis and Tolerance in Cryptography, FDTC 2013. IEEE Computer Society (2013)

19. Giraud, C.: An RSA implementation resistant to fault attacks and to simple power analysis. IEEE Trans. Comput. **55**(9) (2006)

20. Gravellier, J., Dutertre, J., Teglia, Y., Loubet-Moundi, P.: SideLine: How Delay-Lines (May) Leak Secrets from your SoC. CoRR abs/2009.07773 (2020)

21. Gruber, M., Probst, M., Tempelmeier, M.: Statistical ineffective fault analysis of GIMLI. In: 2020 IEEE International Symposium on Hardware Oriented Security and Trust, HOST 2020. IEEE (2020)
22. Kim, Y., et al.: Flipping bits in memory without accessing them: an experimental study of DRAM disturbance errors. In: ACM/IEEE 41st International Symposium on Computer Architecture, ISCA 2014. IEEE Computer Society (2014)
23. Kocher, P.C.: Timing attacks on implementations of Diffie-Hellman, RSA, DSS, and other systems. In: Koblitz, N. (ed.) CRYPTO 1996. LNCS, vol. 1109, pp. 104–113. Springer, Heidelberg (1996). https://doi.org/10.1007/3-540-68697-5_9
24. Kocher, P., Jaffe, J., Jun, B.: Differential power analysis. In: Wiener, M. (ed.) CRYPTO 1999. LNCS, vol. 1666, pp. 388–397. Springer, Heidelberg (1999). https://doi.org/10.1007/3-540-48405-1_25
25. Li, Y., Sakiyama, K., Gomisawa, S., Fukunaga, T., Takahashi, J., Ohta, K.: Fault sensitivity analysis. In: Mangard, S., Standaert, F.-X. (eds.) CHES 2010. LNCS, vol. 6225, pp. 320–334. Springer, Heidelberg (2010). https://doi.org/10.1007/978-3-642-15031-9_22
26. Lipp, M., et al.: PLATYPUS: software-based power side-channel attacks on x86. In: 2021 IEEE Symposium on Security and Privacy (SP) (2021)
27. Messerges, T.S., Dabbish, E.A., Sloan, R.H.: Power analysis attacks of modular exponentiation in smartcards. In: Koç, Ç.K., Paar, C. (eds.) CHES 1999. LNCS, vol. 1717, pp. 144–157. Springer, Heidelberg (1999). https://doi.org/10.1007/3-540-48059-5_14
28. Murdock, K., Oswald, D.F., Garcia, F.D., Bulck, J.V., Piessens, F., Gruss, D.: Plundervolt: how a little bit of undervolting can create a lot of trouble. IEEE Secur. Priv. 18(5) (2020)
29. Piret, G., Quisquater, J.-J.: A differential fault attack technique against SPN structures, with application to the AES and KHAZAD. In: Walter, C.D., Koç, Ç.K., Paar, C. (eds.) CHES 2003. LNCS, vol. 2779, pp. 77–88. Springer, Heidelberg (2003). https://doi.org/10.1007/978-3-540-45238-6_7
30. Qiu, P., Wang, D., Lyu, Y., Qu, G.: VoltJockey: breaking SGX by software-controlled voltage-induced hardware faults. In: Asian Hardware Oriented Security and Trust Symposium, AsianHOST 2019. IEEE (2019)
31. Ramezanpour, K., Ampadu, P., Diehl, W.: A statistical fault analysis methodology for the ascon authenticated cipher. In: IEEE International Symposium on Hardware Oriented Security and Trust, HOST 2019. IEEE (2019)
32. Rivain, M., Prouff, E.: Provably secure higher-order masking of AES. In: Mangard, S., Standaert, F.-X. (eds.) CHES 2010. LNCS, vol. 6225, pp. 413–427. Springer, Heidelberg (2010). https://doi.org/10.1007/978-3-642-15031-9_28
33. Roche, T., Lomné, V., Khalfallah, K.: Combined fault and side-channel attack on protected implementations of AES. In: Prouff, E. (ed.) CARDIS 2011. LNCS, vol. 7079, pp. 65–83. Springer, Heidelberg (2011). https://doi.org/10.1007/978-3-642-27257-8_5
34. Saha, S., Bag, A., Basu Roy, D., Patranabis, S., Mukhopadhyay, D.: Fault template attacks on block ciphers exploiting fault propagation. In: Canteaut, A., Ishai, Y. (eds.) EUROCRYPT 2020. LNCS, vol. 12105, pp. 612–643. Springer, Cham (2020). https://doi.org/10.1007/978-3-030-45721-1_22
35. Saha, S., Jap, D., Breier, J., Bhasin, S., Mukhopadhyay, D., Dasgupta, P.: Breaking redundancy-based countermeasures with random faults and power side channel. In: Workshop on Fault Diagnosis and Tolerance in Cryptography, FDTC 2018. IEEE Computer Society (2018)

36. Saha, S., Kumar, S.N., Patranabis, S., Mukhopadhyay, D., Dasgupta, P.: ALAFA: automatic leakage assessment for fault attack countermeasures. In: Design Automation Conference, DAC 2019. ACM (2019)
37. Spruyt, A., Milburn, A., Chmielewski, L.: Fault injection as an oscilloscope: fault correlation analysis. IACR Trans. Cryptogr. Hardw. Embed. Syst. **2021**(1) (2021)
38. Sung-Ming, Y., Kim, S., Lim, S., Moon, S.: A countermeasure against one physical cryptanalysis may benefit another attack. In: Kim, K. (ed.) ICISC 2001. LNCS, vol. 2288, pp. 414–427. Springer, Heidelberg (2002). https://doi.org/10.1007/3-540-45861-1_31

Countermeasures

Protecting Secure ICs Against Side-Channel Attacks by Identifying and Quantifying Potential EM and Leakage Hotspots at Simulation Stage

Davide Poggi[1,2]([✉]), Philippe Maurine[2]([✉]), Thomas Ordas[1]([✉]), and Alexandre Sarafianos[1]([✉])

[1] STMicroelectronics, Rousset, France
{davide.poggi,thomas.ordas,alexandre.sarafianos}@st.com
[2] University of Montpellier, LIRMM, Montpellier, France
{davide.poggi,philippe.maurine}@lirmm.fr

Abstract. For many years EM Side-Channel Attacks, which exploit the statistical link between the magnetic field radiated by secure ICs and the data they process, are a critical threat. Indeed, attackers need to find only one hotspot (position of the EM probe over the IC surface) where there is an exploitable leakage to compromise the security of the IC and its data. As a result, designing secure ICs robust against these attacks is incredibly difficult because designers must ensure there is no exploitable hotspot over the whole IC surface. This task is all the more difficult as there is no CAD tool to compute the magnetic field radiated by ICs and hence no methodology to detect hotspots at the design stages. In addition, simulations are noise-free and that makes correlation maps useless in identifying potential hotspots. Within this context, this paper introduces a flow allowing predicting the EM radiations of ICs as well as two different methodologies to disclose coordinates of an IC where an attacker can break the security. The first one aims at identifying and quantifying the potential risks of EM hotspots at the surface of ICs, i.e. positions where to place an EM probe to capture a leakage. The second aims at locating leakage hotspots in ICs, i.e. areas in circuits from where these leakages originate.

Keywords: EM side-channel analysis · Simulation · Secure IC design

1 Introduction

Over the last decade, side-channel attacks have proven very effective in exploiting secret data from secure ICs, microcontrollers and Systems-on-Chip (SoC) [21]. The soundness of these attacks has been published in numerous publications, [3,5,6,8], and their effectiveness is increasing more and more with the development of deep learning based techniques [22]. Among the most dreaded attacks

© Springer Nature Switzerland AG 2021
S. Bhasin and F. De Santis (Eds.): COSADE 2021, LNCS 12910, pp. 129–147, 2021.
https://doi.org/10.1007/978-3-030-89915-8_6

are those that exploit the electromagnetic (EM) channel. These are performed by placing a tiny EM probe, with a diameter ranging between $50\,\mu$m and 500 μm [14], at a height h, varying between a few microns and 1 mm, above the IC surface to collect EM radiations. These traces, representing the evolution in the time domain of the magnetic field radiated by the Device Under Test (DUT), are then stored and analyzed using statistical distinguishers or related tests. Among these distinguishers, the most popular is the correlation coefficient (ρ), which is involved in the significance test for a correlation coefficient [1,2]. It was first used by E. Brier to set up the well-known correlation power analysis (CPA) [3]. CPA works very well and allows identifying with incredible ease (without exaggerated means or important skills) the encryption key or exponent manipulated by cryptographic algorithms mapped on silicon without hardware or software countermeasures. In presence of countermeasures, such as masking, higher order CPA can be used [12]. Hence the risks constituted by side-channel attacks (SCA) and the need for effective countermeasures.

Many countermeasures have been published, but few of them are focused on EM countermeasures. This is surprising especially if we consider the enormous quantity of money and time employed to apply hardware and software patches to fix EM leakages in a design. Furthermore, to the best of our knowledge today, there is no industrial CAD tool nor CAD tool based methodology to verify if a design is free of any EM leakage and checks are thus often limited to analyzing the signal switching using SystemC or HDL simulators [7,11] or the power consumption usually performed with Signoff Power Analysis tools [13,17].

Following [15,16,20] and [11], the study introduced in [10] proposes a simulation flow designed to reproduce the magnetic field radiations of a microcontroller. This flow, based on the use of a voltage drop tool (RedHawk from Ansys), simulates the evolution in the time domain of the currents flowing over IC's entire surface. By applying the Biot-Savart law on these current traces, one can reproduce maps of the EM field of the entire circuit. In [9], the authors follow a similar approach of [10] but, in addition, they provide attack results. They were in fact capable of performing correlation power analyses (CPA) [3] by simulation.

Within this context, the first contribution of this document is to introduce, through a concrete example, a complete simulation flow able to predict the EM radiations of ICs, starting from the model of a simple current-carrying wire of finite length and by applying the Biot-Savart law.

A second and even more important contribution is a methodology that can be used during the design stage to locate and quantify the potential risks of EM and leakage hotspots. An EM hotspot is a position above the IC surface at which an EM probe must be placed to exploit a leakage, while a leakage hotspot is a part of circuit where the root cause of a leakage can be found. This methodology is based on an innovative technique for interpreting simulation results. In fact, as we will show later in the paper, simulations are noise-free and this makes the correlation maps, based on the significance test for a correlation coefficient, completely ineffective in determining EM hotspots in a design. Resolving this problem led us to another interesting result; by calculating the minimal

Signal-to-Noise-Ratio (SNR) it is possible to determine, during the design and simulation stage, if a leakage is critical or not.

This paper is structured as follows: Sect. 2 starts with some useful considerations about the currents flowing in ICs and, then, continues with the description of the simulation flow. Both the mathematical computations of the EM radiations of an IC and the choice of the voltage drop analysis tool (RedHawk) are inspired from [10] and [9]. Section 3 describes a methodology to correctly identify EM and leakage hotsposts, considering the absence of noise in simulation and, thus, proposing a solution to interpret results. Section 4 covers the preliminary validation of the EM simulation flow and introduces the testcase on which results have been obtained. Then, Sect. 5 is a final validation of the flow, showing the advantages of applying this flow during the design stage. Finally, Sect. 6 concludes the document.

2   Magnetic Field Simulation of an IC

2.1   IC Structure and Lessons From Practice

The study of dedicated publications as well as our experience acquired in performing electromagnetic analysis on secure ICs has taught us that adversaries often use EM probes made by the Langer company to carry out EM attacks. Furthermore, the observation of various IC layouts and the running of power noise simulations tell us that the strongest currents flow in the upper wires of the power (Vdd) and ground (Gnd) network supplying CMOS gates.

Following these observations, one can simplify the model of the magnetic field emitted by an IC by only studying the EM field generated by the upper wires of the power supply. (Obviously, this reasoning can be done only when EM analyses are performed with the chip front side). Normally, the width of these wires is in a range between 5 μm and 20 μm and we can thus consider them as finite length wires with a negligible width compared to the dimension of the probe diameter. So, after these simplifications, the Biot-Savart law can be used to determine the magnetic field emitted by the entire IC. To achieve better results, we can split the largest wires in n smaller and parallel wires with a n times smaller current flowing in.

2.2   Magnetic Field, Magnetic Flux and Electromotive Force

To compute the magnetic field, the magnetic flux and the electromotive force, we consider a surface parallel to the IC surface at a height h from it. This surface is split into small squares to get a matrix which coefficients are either the magnetic field at the center of the squares or the magnetic flux crossing them. The computation of the vertical magnetic field, $B_z(x, y, h, t)$, at the coordinate (x, y, h) corresponding at the center of a square, is done by summing the contributions, $B_z^i(x, y, h, t)$, of the w wire segments denoted $[AB]$ of length

$l_{AB} = \sqrt{(x_A - x_B)^2 + (y_A - y_B)^2}$:

$$B_z(x, y, h, t) = \sum_{i=0}^{w} B_z^i(x, y, h, t) \tag{1}$$

These contributions are estimated using the Biot-Savart law. By manipulating this law we found the equations below, which express the vertical component of the magnetic field emanated by w, depending on whether the EM probe is parallel to the x (Eq. 2) or y (Eq. 3) axis:

$$B_z(x, y, h, t) = \frac{\mu_0 \cdot I(t)}{4\pi} \cdot \frac{x}{\sqrt{x^2 + h^2}} \cdot \left(\frac{1}{\sqrt{x^2 + (y - y_A)^2}} + \frac{1}{\sqrt{x^2 + (y - y_B)^2}} \right) \tag{2}$$

$$B_z(x, y, h, t) = \frac{\mu_0 \cdot I(t)}{4\pi} \cdot \frac{y}{\sqrt{y^2 + h^2}} \cdot \left(\frac{1}{\sqrt{y^2 + (x - x_A)^2}} + \frac{1}{\sqrt{y^2 + (x - x_B)^2}} \right) \tag{3}$$

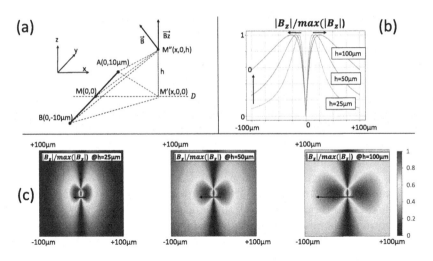

Fig. 1. (a) Illustration associated to Eq. 2 and 3. (b) Evolution of the normalized vertical magnetic field along the bisecting line D for different values of h. (c) Maps of the normalized magnetic field for different values of h.

These formulas, besides being useful to compute $B_z(x, y, h, t)$, also provide interesting information. First, the vertical magnetic field, B_z, radiated by a wire segment, at the vertical of this segment, is null. Second, when measured over a plane, it reaches its maximal value at a distance from the wire segment which directly depends on h. In the example of Fig. 1, this distance is equal to 26 μm and 4 μm for h equal to 100 μm and 25 μm respectively. Third, the greater h is, the more B_z can be perceived further from the wire segment, in relation to its maximal amplitude. These observations are illustrated in Fig. 1b and 1c that give maps of B_z at different heights (with $x_A = x_B = 0$ and $y_A = -y_B = 10\,\mu\text{m}$) and the normalized evolution of the B_z along the bisecting line D. All these observations mean that the near field scan of the vertical magnetic field can not be directly used to determine, with a high accuracy, the origin of a leakage in ICs. However, reducing h significantly reduces the localization errors.

Now, knowing the B_z matrix, we can easily compute the vertical magnetic flux $\phi_z(t)$ by integrating $B_z(t)$ over all the squares enclosed in its surface; the vertical flux through a square being given by $B_z(x, y, h, t) \cdot S_q$, assuming it uniform over the surface S_q of the squares. Then, the electromotive force $\epsilon(t)$ is simply the differentiation of $\phi_z(t)$ in time.

$$\phi_z(t) = \int_{S_q} B_z(t) \cdot dS_q \tag{4}$$

$$\epsilon(t) = -\frac{d\phi_z(t)}{dt} \tag{5}$$

2.3   Current Extraction with RedHawk

From Eq. 2 and 3, it is clear that, if one wants to compute the magnetic field radiated by an IC, they need to know the coordinates of all the wires in the IC surface. To complete this task, a dedicated CAD tool like RedHawk from Ansys is needed. RedHawk is a voltage drop tool used to, among other functions, extract the evolution in the time domain of the current flowing in each segment of wire in the circuit. Then, static and voltage drop maps can be drawn and these maps are data dependent because one must provide VCD files to RedHawk. One can extract current traces by placing virtual probes on metal layers between vias. Python scripts were written to this purpose, allowing to place regularly (every $X\,\mu m$) these probes on the entire surface of the IC. Figure 2 shows an example of probe placement on RedHawk and a trace of current extracted with a sampling rate of 200 ps, showing the ten rounds of a 128-bit AES cipher.

3   Finding EM Leakages

To validate the concepts expressed in the previous sections, we have tested the simulation flow on a 40 nm testchip integrating, among others blocks, an unprotected AES co-processor. To this purpose, experimental and simulated CPA maps of the magnetic field were drawn. The goal was to determine if we could localize, by simulation, the EM hotspots found on silicon. However, the results were disappointing: simulated and experimental maps were considerably different. In fact, simulated maps showed that we could retrieve the encryption key almost everywhere on the IC surface, whereas experimental ones showed only small parts of the IC where it was possible to find the key (with a fixed number of measurements).

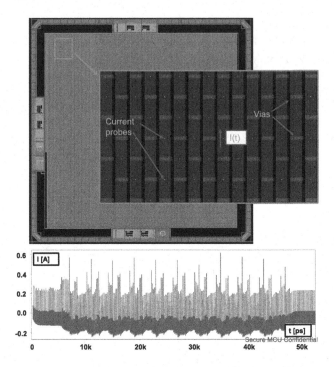

Fig. 2. Probe placement on the metal layers with RedHawk. Below, a current trace showing the ten rounds of the AES.

To identify the problem, we took a step back and simulated a simple IC integrating only a simple wire of length 20 μm at the center. Figure 3a shows the correlation map of a wire carrying a current having a high correlation compared to the Hamming Weight (HW) of the encryption key. As expected, the correlation is strong at the center, where the wire is placed, and null elsewhere. But if we perform the correlation $\rho(B_z, HW)$, between B_z and the HW (Fig. 3c), we can see that the wire leaks everywhere in its neighborhood (except along the vertical line supporting the wire). This is a direct illustration of the fact that correlation maps cannot be used to locate by simulation EM leakages in a design and, if a designer aims at locating where leakages originate, they must use a distinguisher taking into account the magnitude of signals and ideally allowing to classify leakages according to their measurability and thus dangerousness. The following paragraph introduces a solution to this problem.

3.1 Problem Statement and Noise-to-Add Concept

The first reason why simulated correlation maps performed on magnetic field traces do not correctly reproduce the experimental results is that simulations are noise-free, whereas measured traces obviously are not and, indeed, are polluted by noise (assumed normal and of zero mean: $N(0, \sqrt{V(\eta)})$ that can be considered

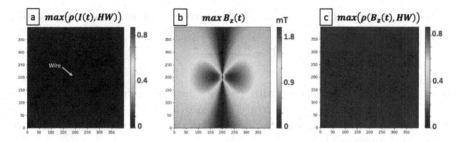

Fig. 3. (a) Map showing the correlation on the current. (b) Magnetic field radiated by a current-carrying wire. (c) Map showing the correlation on the magnetic field.

with identical characteristics over the IC surface. The second reason is that the correlation coefficient, ρ, is insensitive to the magnitude of data processed, in fact $\rho(1e9 \times X, Y) = \rho(X, Y)$. As a result of this insensitiveness and of the absence of measurement noise in simulated traces, CPA applied to the magnetic field radiated by the wire was successful everywhere in determining the correct key, even at coordinates where the signal was very weak. To resolve these problems, we analyzed the expression of the correlation coefficient, that is the base of the significance test for a correlation coefficient:

$$\rho(H, S) = \frac{cov(H, S)}{\sqrt{V(H) \cdot V(S)}} \tag{6}$$

where S and H are the simulated EM signal and the Hamming Weight of the intermediate data processed by the ICs, respectively. $V(H)$, $V(S)$ and $cov(H, S)$ are instead the variances of both variables and the covariance between them.

To thwart the problem of insensitiveness of the correlation to the magnitude of data, a direct solution is to neglect the denominator in Eq. 6 which plays a normalization role. However, in order to link the simulation results to the measurement noise (assumed normal and of zero mean: $N(0, \sqrt{V(\eta)})$ and to the quality of the adversary's equipment, the solution we propose is different while remaining simple. It takes advantage of the fact that simulated traces are noise-free to compute the variance of the Gaussian noise that must be added to the simulated traces to force the correlation to be insignificant, i.e. to fail the significance test for a correlation coefficient. The null hypothesis ($H0$) of this test being that $\rho = 0$; the composite one ($H1$) being $|\rho| > 0$.

To that end, let us consider that the measurement noise is independent of the signal. With η a sample of the noise, this leads to:

$$cov(H, S + \eta) = cov(H, S) \mid V(S + \eta) = V(S) + V(\eta) \tag{7}$$

and to express the link between the correlation, ρ, obtained with the noise-free simulated traces and the correlation, ρ_η, after introduction of the Gaussian noise in traces:

$$\rho_\eta = \sqrt{\frac{V(S)}{V(S) + V(\eta)}} \cdot \rho \tag{8}$$

Considering now the significance test of the correlation coefficient with statistic:

$$T = \frac{\rho \cdot \sqrt{n-2}}{\sqrt{1-\rho^2}} \tag{9}$$

follows a Student distribution (with $(n-2)$ degrees of freedom, n being the number of traces) to decide, with a confidence level $(1-\alpha)$, if ρ_η is null or not, we get the critical value of the correlation, ρ_{crit}, above which ρ_η must be considered significant ($H0$ rejected):

$$\rho_{crit} = \sqrt{\frac{V(S)}{V(S) + V(\eta)}} \cdot \rho \tag{10}$$

Finally, from Eq. 10, the variance $V(\eta)$ of the noise that must be added to simulated traces to render the correlation insignificant can be deduced:

$$V(\eta) = V(S) \cdot \left[\frac{\rho^2}{\rho_{crit}^2} - 1 \right] \tag{11}$$

Because ρ and $V(S)$ are known from simulations and because ρ_{crit}^2 is fixed by the choice of the confidence level $(1-\alpha)$, $V(\eta)$ can easily be computed in an automated manner. However, as shown by Eq. 11, $V(\eta)$ could be positive (if $|\rho| > |\rho_{crit}|$) or negative (if $|\rho| < |\rho_{crit}|$). A positive value defines the minimal measurement noise required to hide the leakage, a negative value is not acceptable for a variance. In that case, the obtained value means that no measurement noise is required to render the correlation insignificant and thus that there is no leakage: $V(\eta)$ must be considered equal to zero.

From Eq. 11 and as part of the continuity of [4], we can determine an important information that is the minimal Signal-to-Noise-Ratio, SNR_{min}, required to retrieve, at a given coordinate of the IC, a significant EM leakage. The computation of SNR_{min} is straightforward from Eq. 11:

$$SNR_{min} = \frac{V(S)}{V(\eta)} = \frac{\rho_{crit}^2}{\rho^2 - \rho_{crit}^2} \tag{12}$$

We believe that Eq. 12 constitutes a very useful information for secure IC designers. In fact, expert designers usually know the typical level of the signal that is sufficient to disclose a leakage in a design and thus they know if this leakage must be considered critical or not. Obviously, even knowing the SNR_{min}, is it extremely difficult to design a circuit totally leakage free!

If we now apply the approach just outlined to the example of Fig. 3, we can draw a map showing the standard deviation (i.e. the square root of the variance) of the noise, $\sqrt{V(\eta)}$, that must be added to the magnetic field radiated by the wire to render the correlation $\rho(B_z, HW)$ insignificant. The $\sqrt{V(\eta)}$ map shown in Fig. 4 is really close to the distribution of the magnetic field of Fig. 3b. This is a direct demonstration of the effectiveness of this method.

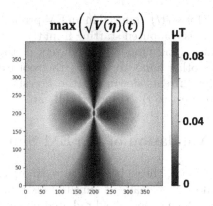

Fig. 4. Map showing the standard deviation of the noise to add (in our testcase) when analyzing the magnetic field.

3.2 Combining Key Guess Ranking and Noise-to-Add Concepts

The Noise-to-Add concept is still not enough to conclude if, at a specific coordinate of the IC, there is an exploitable leakage. In fact, Eq. 11 only gives us the information about which is the noise level that must be added to render a correlation insignificant, compared to its significance. To determine if there is an EM leakage, the absolute value of the correct key guess, $|\rho^{k^*}|$, must be higher than the other incorrect key guesses, $|\rho^k|$. However, we need to ask ourselves if the ranking of the Noise-to-Add, $\sqrt{V(\eta)}$, is the same as the ranking of the correlation, ρ. The answer is yes because, from Eq. 11, if $|\rho^i| \geq |\rho^j|$ then $\sqrt{V(\eta)^i} \geq \sqrt{V(\eta)^j}$.

3.3 EM Leakages and Their Origin

An EM leakage is a position on the surface of an IC where one can place an EM probe to retrieve secret data. EM leakages must not be confused with leakage hotspots, which are the sources (root causes) of EM leakages and which are the coordinates where there is a leaky standard cell gate. The solution we propose to locate both leakages is given in Eq. 13 and consists in drawing maps, called $\sqrt{V^*(\eta)}$, containing, at each coordinate, the value of $\sqrt{V(\eta)}$ of the correct key guess if the correlation of the latter is higher than the other key guesses, and 0 otherwise.

$$\sqrt{V^*(\eta)} = \begin{cases} \sqrt{V^{k^*}(\eta)} & if \sqrt{V^{k^*}(\eta)} \geq \sqrt{V^k(\eta)}, \quad \forall k \in \kappa \\ 0 & \text{otherwise} \end{cases} \tag{13}$$

with κ the set of all the key guesses and k^* the correct one.

Equation 13 can be thus used to identify both leakage hotspots and EM leakages. The only difference in this method is the physical data manipulated during the computations. In fact, to locate EM hotspots, Eq. 13 is applied to the simulated electromotive force $\epsilon(t)$, induced in an EM probe capturing the vertical magnetic field $B_z(t)$. $\epsilon(t)$ is computed starting from the current traces, collected using RedHawk, flowing in the upper metal layers of the power and ground network (PGN). On the other hand, to identify the root causes of EM leakages, Eq. 13 is applied to the currents flowing in the lowest metal layer (normally metal1) which are the closest to the standard cell gates.

4   Testcase and Validation of the EM Simulation Flow

This section aims to validate, through a concrete example, the EM simulation flow described above. More specifically, it aims to illustrate the soundness of our technique used to model the magnetic field radiated by an IC and the usefulness of the Noise-to-Add concept.

4.1   Testcase

The results shown below were obtained on a testchip, denoted TC from now on, designed in a 40 nm low-power CMOS technology with 5 metal layers. The thickness of the substrate is equal to 180 μm. It integrates different blocks, among which one can find an unprotected 128-bit AES co-processor operating at 50 MHz and supplied by 1.2 V. The AES, on which our experiments were focused, is placed at the center of the die whose length and width are both equal to 2.2 mm. The experimental maps showed in the next paragraphs will not cover the entire surface of TC due to the bonding wires limiting the surface we are able to scan. The entire design database was available on RedHawk, allowing to launch current consumption simulations.

4.2   Collecting Current Traces with RedHawk

1000 current traces (a sufficient number since simulations are noise-free) were collected with RedHawk by placing virtual probes every 20 μm between vias. In this way, just about 30000 wire segments of length 20 μm were obtained. Each trace corresponds to the encryption of a specific plain-text manipulated by the AES. The sampling rate of each trace was set to 200 ps. The total time spent to obtain these traces and to manipulate them was about 12 h, which is reasonable if we think about the amount of data processed (1000 current traces for about 30000 probes!). As a matter of fact, the only problem was the size of data stored. In fact, RedHawk provides current traces in txt format which takes up too much space. Therefore, Python scripts were written to convert these results into the Hierarchical Data Format version 5 (HDF5). This operation slightly extends the total processing time but has a great impact on the memory employed and on the time needed to compute the magnetic field.

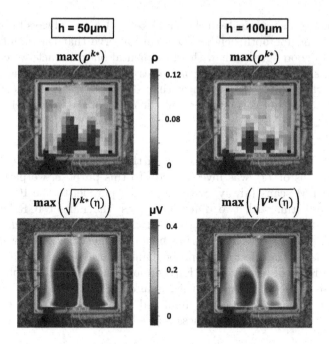

Fig. 5. Comparison between experimental correlation maps (first row) and simulated $\sqrt{V^{k*}(\eta)}$ maps (second row). Probe at a height of 50 μm and 100 μm. Diameter of the probe 100 μm.

4.3   Impact of the Probe Height on EM Analysis

In order to provide a first corroboration of the effectiveness of the entire simulation flow, we first performed two experimental EM scans on the TC surface with a Langer ICRHH100 probe (diameter equal to 100 μm) parallel to the IC surface. In the first scan, the probe was placed at a height of 50 μm, while in the second at 100 μm. The shift step of the probe was set to 100 μm and at each coordinate we collected 5000 traces, one for each plain-text processed by the AES. Then, a CPA was carried out and the corresponding map was drawn.

Afterwards, starting from the simulated current traces, $I(t)$, collected with RedHawk, we computed $B_z(t)$, $\phi_z(t)$ and $\epsilon(t)$, with the probe at a height of 50 μm and 100 μm. Finally, the correlation $\rho(H, \epsilon(t))$, between $\epsilon(t)$ and the Hamming Weight, was calculated.

Figure 5 shows the results. The first row exhibits the experimental correlation maps performed with the correct key guess, k^*, with $h = 50\,\mu m$ and $h = 100\,\mu m$ respectively. Both maps have the same color scale in order to enhance the effect of the height on results. As we can see, h has an important impact. Indeed, increasing the height decreases the number of coordinates where the ρ^{k^*} is grater than 0.12. This is in accordance with the theory since the higher h is, the lower the SNR of the collected EM traces.

The second row shows instead the simulated $\sqrt{V^{k^*}(\eta)}$, always for the correct key guess k^* and for both heights. One can observe that the simulated maps are visually in good agreement with experimental ones. In fact, we can observe that, also in simulation, increasing h causes the diminution of the number of coordinates where $\sqrt{V^{k^*}(\eta)}$ is greater than 0.4. This result demonstrates that the EM flow correctly takes into account the effect of the probe height.

4.4   Impact of the Probe Diameter on EM Analysis

Following the same procedure, the effect of the probe diameter on the electromagnetic analysis of TC was investigated. To this purpose, we performed two experimental EM scans (always with the probe parallel to the IC surface), at a height of 100 µm, with two different probes: the Langer ICRHH100 (with diameter $d = 100\,\mu m$) and the Langer ICRHH150 (with diameter $d = 150\,\mu m$). The resulting maps are given in Fig. 6, where the same color scales were taken in order to emphasise the effect of the probe diameter d. Once again, simulated and experimental results are very alike. Furthermore, increasing the probe size leads to an increase in the magnitude of the signal collected by the probe and, therefore, the experimental ρ^{k^*} and the simulated $\sqrt{V^{k^*}(\eta)}$. This is, in our opinion, further confirmation of the soundness and effectiveness of this EM simulation flow.

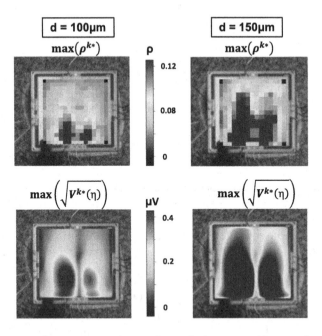

Fig. 6. Comparison between experimental correlation maps (first row) and simulated $\sqrt{V^{k^*}(\eta)}$ maps (second row). Probe at a height of 100 µm. Diameter of the probe 50 µm and 100 µm.

4.5 Comparison Between Front-Side and Back-Side EM Analysis

This section aims to demonstrate that, in order to model the magnetic field, one can actually focus on the currents flowing in the upper metal layers of the power and ground network. Comparing front-side and back-side maps is useful, because if front-side and back-side analysis gave different results, it would mean that there are some other metal layers (such as metal1 and metal4) whose contributions to the total magnetic field emitted by the IC cannot be ignored.

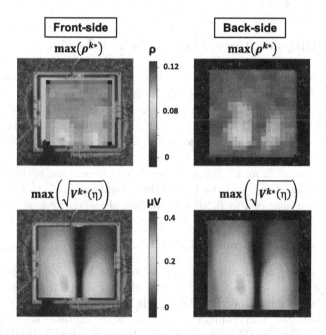

Fig. 7. Comparison between front-side and back-side configuration. Experimental correlation maps in the first row and simulated $\sqrt{V^{k*}(\eta)}$ maps in the second row.

To this purpose, we performed two EM scans with TC set in front-side and back-side respectively. Both scans were performed with the Langer ICRHH100 (diameter $d = 100\,\mu\text{m}$) parallel to the IC surface. Back-side analysis was carried out with the probe as close as possible to the IC surface, while for front-side the probe was placed at a height of $180\,\mu\text{m}$, which corresponds to the thickness of the substrate. Then, correlation maps where drawn for both experimental and simulated traces. Note that back-side scan allows to move the probe over the entire surface of the chip because we are not limited by the bonding wires, thus back-side maps are a little larger. Figure 7 shows the results. The leakage areas in simulated maps (second row) are the same because there is no difference in the traces simulated with RedHawk. On the other hand, one can observe that the leakage areas in experimental maps (first row) are pretty the same than those obtained front-side (see Fig. 7), except that the magnitude is lower as it is reported in [18]. This is because the distance between the probe and metal layers is grater: $180\,\mu$m (Fig. 7) and $100\,\mu$m (Fig. 6). This similitude between front-side and back-side maps and between simulated and experimental maps confirms that one can only consider top metal layers while modeling the magnetic field. The main reason explaining that is possible is that the upper part of the power and ground network concentrates into few metal stripes all the current flowing (spread) in the lower part of these networks. As a result, the magnitude of the currents is, for our testchip, 50 times greater in the upper metal wires than in the lower ones (metal1).

5   Evaluating the Potential Risks of a Leakage

After the experiments and results showed in the previous paragraphs, let us consider this flow valid and successful. In fact, we have proved that we can reproduce, by simulation, the EM radiations of an entire IC and the effects of the EM probe (height and diameter). As anticipated in Sect. 3, evaluating the magnitude of p^{k^*} and $\sqrt{V^{k^*}(\eta)}$ is not enough to locate a leakage and to decide if it is critical or not. Indeed, we are interested in finding out if the correct key guess, k^*, stands out from all others. Therefore, the next paragraph introduces a procedure to localize, prior to fabrication, leakage and EM hotspots. This paragraph is also intended as further validation of the entire simulation flow.

5.1   Disclosing Root Causes of EM Leakages

Section 3 introduces the method to locate leakage hotspots in a design. The idea is to apply Eq. 13 to each time sample of the current traces flowing in the lowest metal layer (metal1) of TC. The result is given in Fig. 8, where the yellow rectangles delimit the AES co-processor, placed at the center of the die. To obtain these figures, about 120000 current probes where placed with RedHawk on the power and ground grids routed in metal1, in order to have the best possible resolution. Time samples n° 1 and 7 show the apparition of a leakage and time samples n° 10 and 15 show its spreading along the power and ground network due to the propagation of the current.

Applying Eq. 13 time sample by time sample instead of considering the maximal value of Noise-to-Add over some time samples is very important. In fact, the identification of the origin of the root causes of leakages is clearer and is not blurred by the propagation of the currents along the power and ground network. The yellow area encompassing the AES allows to highlight where the leakages originate. More precisely, the wire segments enclosed in this area are close to some CMOS gates which are leaking. We believe that this type of result could be very useful for a designer because, after having identified all the leaking CMOS, he could be able to immediately fix the leakage through RTL level simulations and relaunch this analysis to check if the leakage has correctly been fixed.

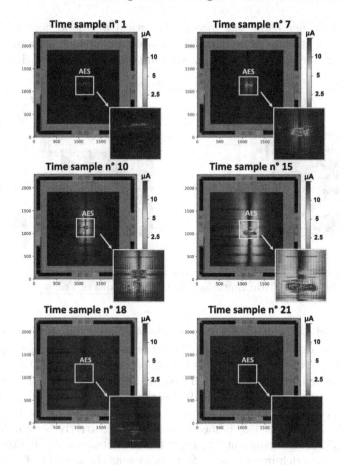

Fig. 8. Maps at different time samples disclosing leaking standard cell gates.

The same procedure is now applied to localize EM hotspots and we can now also make a comparison between experimental and simulated maps. So, we applied Eq. 13 to the simulated electromotive force generated in an EM probe with diameter $d = 100\,\mu m$ placed at a height $h = 100\,\mu m$ from the IC surface. Figure 9 illustrates the comparing map obtained on silicon by applying the following criteria:

$$|\rho^*| = \begin{cases} |\rho^{k^*}| & if\,|\rho^{k^*}| \geq |\rho^k|, \quad \forall k \in \kappa \\ 0 & \text{otherwise} \end{cases} \tag{14}$$

As Fig. 9 shows, we are unable to find the correct key guess when placing the probe just above the AES. That is not surprisingly because, as we know, the vertical magnetic field at the vertical of a wire in which flows a current is null. Since the currents flowing in the AES are strong, the EM signals collected above the AES with an EM probe measuring the vertical magnetic field are necessarily weak. On the other hand, the measured vertical magnetic field is strong on the left and right sides of it. Besides these considerations, experimental and simulated maps are in good agreement showing the effectiveness of this approach.

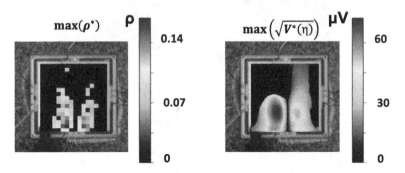

Fig. 9. Experimental ρ^* and simulated $\sqrt{V^*(\eta)}$ maps obtained with a probe at $h = 100\,\mu$m and with $d = 100\,\mu$m capturing the EM radiations of TC.

Finally, and as the final validation of the simulation flow and corroboration of the Noise-to-Add concept, we calculated the partial Guessing Entropy (pGE) on the third byte of the key, k^*, after having processed 1000, 2000 and 3000 EM radiations, measured with an ICRHH100 probe from Langer. Figure 10 shows maps representing the $(255 - pGE)$ [19], i.e. the average ranking of the third byte of the correct key after having performed a CPA 10 times for each coordinate of TC. If the ranking is 255, it means that k^* has correctly been individuated ($255 - 0 = 255$). The results of Fig. 10, which must be compared with the right figure of Fig. 9, is rich in lessons. In fact, as soon as the number of manipulated traces is sufficient (this number depends on the experimental noise and on the equipment at disposal), the $\sqrt{V^*(\eta)}$ map is very similar to the $255 - pGE$ map. This is further confirmation that $\sqrt{V^*(\eta)}$ maps can localize the position where one needs to place an EM probe to capture a leakage.

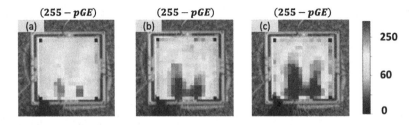

Fig. 10. $(255 - pGE)$ maps drawn after the processing of (a) 1000, (b) 2000 and (c) 3000 traces.

6   Conclusion

The first contribution of this paper is a detailed simulation methodology allowing modeling the EM radiations of an entire IC, with a simulation time absolutely acceptable for designers. This solution is fully based on commercial voltage drop analysis tools such as RedHawk from ANSYS and on Biot-Savart law. Furthermore, a second contribution is a procedure to locate, during the design stage, leakage hotspots in a circuit (part of the IC from where a leakage originates) and EM hotspots (position where a probe must be placed to measure it). In particular, the Noise-to-Add concept has been proposed, which is, in our opinion, a simple but innovative proposal, allowing to interpret simulation results which are noise-free. Starting from the Noise-to-Add concept, a direct link to the Signal-to-Noise-Ratio (SNR), so useful for designers, can be done. The effectiveness of both contributions have been demonstrated by confronting simulation results with experimental ones. This latter have been obtained on a testchip designed in 40 nm CMOS technology. Comparisons showed that the flow correctly predicts the positions of the hotspots and allows ranking them with respect to their intensity and easiness of measure by exploiting the concept of measurement Noise-to-Add for hiding the leakage.

In addition to the localization of hotspots, this simulation methodology could be useful to evaluate different floor-planning and power planing strategies at design stage, but also to verify the effectiveness of countermeasures and, finally, as an EM leakage sign-off methodology to detect design neglects or errors prior to fabrication.

A   Appendix

Equation 12 is obtained knowing that the SNR is defined as the ratio between the signal and noise variances. $V(S)$ is computed starting from simulated traces and $V(\eta)$ is given by Eq. 11. Detailed calculations below:

$$V(\eta) = V(S) \cdot \left[\frac{\rho^2}{\rho_{crit}^2} - 1 \right] \longrightarrow \frac{V(\eta)}{V(S)} = \left[\frac{\rho^2}{\rho_{crit}^2} - 1 \right]$$

$$\longrightarrow \frac{V(S)}{V(\eta)} = SNR_{min} = \frac{\rho_{crit}^2}{\rho^2 - \rho_{crit}^2} \tag{15}$$

References

1. Artusi, R., Verderio, P., Marubini, E.: Bravais-pearson and spearman correlation coefficients: meaning, test of hypothesis and confidence interval. Int. J. Biol. Mark. **17**(2), 148–151 (2002). https://doi.org/10.1177/172460080201700213. pMID: 12113584
2. Bobko, P.: Correlation and Regression: Applications for Industrial Organizational Psychology and Management, 2nd edn. Sage Publications, Thousand Oaks (2001)

3. Brier, E., Clavier, C., Olivier, F.: Correlation power analysis with a leakage model. In: Joye, M., Quisquater, J.-J. (eds.) CHES 2004. LNCS, vol. 3156, pp. 16–29. Springer, Heidelberg (2004). https://doi.org/10.1007/978-3-540-28632-5_2

4. Diop, I., Carbone, M., Ordas, S., Linge, Y., Liardet, P.Y., Maurine, P.: Collision for estimating SCA measurement quality and related applications. In: Homma, N., Medwed, M. (eds.) CARDIS 2015. LNCS, vol. 9514, pp. 143–157. Springer, Cham (2016). https://doi.org/10.1007/978-3-319-31271-2_9

5. Gandolfi, K., Mourtel, C., Olivier, F.: Electromagnetic analysis: concrete results. In: Koç, Ç.K., Naccache, D., Paar, C. (eds.) CHES 2001. LNCS, vol. 2162, pp. 251–261. Springer, Heidelberg (2001). https://doi.org/10.1007/3-540-44709-1_21

6. Gierlichs, B., Batina, L., Tuyls, P., Preneel, B.: Mutual information analysis. In: Oswald, E., Rohatgi, P. (eds.) CHES 2008. LNCS, vol. 5154, pp. 426–442. Springer, Heidelberg (2008). https://doi.org/10.1007/978-3-540-85053-3_27

7. He, M.T., Park, J., Nahiyan, A., Vassilev, A., Jin, Y., Tehranipoor, M.M.: RTL-PSC: automated power side-channel leakage assessment at register-transfer level. CoRR abs/1901.05909 (2019). arXiv:1901.05909

8. Kocher, P., Jaffe, J., Jun, B.: Differential power analysis. In: Wiener, M. (ed.) CRYPTO 1999. LNCS, vol. 1666, pp. 388–397. Springer, Heidelberg (1999). https://doi.org/10.1007/3-540-48405-1_25

9. Kumar, A., Scarborough, C., Yilmaz, A., Orshansky, M.: Efficient simulation of EM side-channel attack resilience. In: Parameswaran, S. (ed.) 2017 IEEE/ACM International Conference on Computer-Aided Design, ICCAD 2017, Irvine, CA, USA, 13–16 November 2017, pp. 123–130. IEEE (2017). https://doi.org/10.1109/ICCAD.2017.8203769

10. Lomné, V., Maurine, P., Torres, L., Ordas, T., Lisart, M., Toublanc, J.: Modeling time domain magnetic emissions of ICs. In: van Leuken, R., Sicard, G. (eds.) PATMOS 2010. LNCS, vol. 6448, pp. 238–249. Springer, Heidelberg (2011). https://doi.org/10.1007/978-3-642-17752-1_24

11. Menichelli, F., Menicocci, R., Olivieri, M., Trifiletti, A.: High-level side-channel attack modeling and simulation for security-critical systems on chips. IEEE Trans. Dependable Secur. Comput. 5(3), 164–176 (2008). https://doi.org/10.1109/TDSC.2007.70234

12. Messerges, T.S.: Using second-order power analysis to attack DPA resistant software. In: Koç, Ç.K., Paar, C. (eds.) CHES 2000. LNCS, vol. 1965, pp. 238–251. Springer, Heidelberg (2000). https://doi.org/10.1007/3-540-44499-8_19

13. Nahiyan, A., et al.: SCRIPT: a CAD framework for power side-channel vulnerability assessment using information flow tracking and pattern generation. ACM Trans. Design Autom. Electron. Syst. 25(3), 26:1–26:27 (2020). https://doi.org/10.1145/3383445

14. Ordas, T., Lisart, M., Sicard, E., Maurine, P., Torres, L.: Near-field mapping system to scan in time domain the magnetic emissions of integrated circuits. In: Svensson, L., Monteiro, J. (eds.) PATMOS 2008. LNCS, vol. 5349, pp. 229–236. Springer, Heidelberg (2009). https://doi.org/10.1007/978-3-540-95948-9_23

15. Regazzoni, F., et al.: A simulation-based methodology for evaluating the dpa-resistance of cryptographic functional units with application to CMOS and MCML technologies. In: Blume, H., Gaydadjiev, G., Glossner, C.J., Knijnenburg, P.M.W. (eds.) Proceedings of the 2007 International Conference on Embedded Computer Systems: Architectures, Modeling and Simulation (IC-SAMOS 2007), Samos, Greece, 16–19 July 2007, pp. 209–214. IEEE (2007). https://doi.org/10.1109/ICSAMOS.2007.4285753

16. Regazzoni, F., et al.: A design flow and evaluation framework for DPA-resistant instruction set extensions. In: Clavier, C., Gaj, K. (eds.) CHES 2009. LNCS, vol. 5747, pp. 205–219. Springer, Heidelberg (2009). https://doi.org/10.1007/978-3-642-04138-9_15

17. Sijacic, D., Balasch, J., Yang, B., Ghosh, S., Verbauwhede, I.: Towards efficient and automated side channel evaluations at design time. In: Batina, L., Kühne, U., Mentens, N. (eds.) PROOFS 2018, 7th International Workshop on Security Proofs for Embedded Systems, colocated with CHES 2018, Amsterdam, The Netherlands, 13 September 2018. Kalpa Publications in Computing, vol. 7, pp. 16–31. EasyChair (2018). http://www.easychair.org/publications/paper/xPnF

18. Specht, R., Heyszl, J., Sigl, G.: Investigating measurement methods for high-resolution electromagnetic field side-channel analysis. In: 2014 International Symposium on Integrated Circuits (ISIC), Singapore, 10–12 December 2014, pp. 21–24. IEEE (2014). https://doi.org/10.1109/ISICIR.2014.7029532

19. Standaert, F.-X., Malkin, T.G., Yung, M.: A unified framework for the analysis of side-channel key recovery attacks. In: Joux, A. (ed.) EUROCRYPT 2009. LNCS, vol. 5479, pp. 443–461. Springer, Heidelberg (2009). https://doi.org/10.1007/978-3-642-01001-9_26

20. Tiri, K., Verbauwhede, I.: A digital design flow for secure integrated circuits. IEEE Trans. Comput. Aided Des. Integr. Circuits Syst. **25**(7), 1197–1208 (2006). https://doi.org/10.1109/TCAD.2005.855939

21. Vasselle, A., Maurine, P., Cozzi, M.: Breaking mobile firmware encryption through near-field side-channel analysis. In: Chang, C., Rührmair, U., Holcomb, D.E., Schaumont, P. (eds.) Proceedings of the 3rd ACM Workshop on Attacks and Solutions in Hardware Security Workshop, ASHES@CCS 2019, London, UK, 15 November 2019, pp. 23–32. ACM (2019). https://doi.org/10.1145/3338508.3359571

22. Wei, L., Luo, B., Li, Y., Liu, Y., Xu, Q.: I know what you see: power side-channel attack on convolutional neural network accelerators. In: Proceedings of the 34th Annual Computer Security Applications Conference, ACSAC 2018, San Juan, PR, USA, 03–07 December 2018, pp. 393–406. ACM (2018). https://doi.org/10.1145/3274694.3274696

Low-Latency Hardware Masking of PRINCE

Nicolai Müller[✉] [iD], Thorben Moos[iD], and Amir Moradi[iD]

Horst Görtz Institute for IT Security, Ruhr University Bochum, Bochum, Germany
{nicolai.muller,thorben.moos,amir.moradi}@rub.de

Abstract. Efficient implementation of Boolean masking in terms of low latency has evolved into a hot topic due to the necessity of embedding a physically secure and at-the-same-time fast implementation of cryptographic primitives in e.g., the memory encryption of pervasive devices. Instead of fully minimizing the circuit's area and randomness requirements at the cost of latency, the focus has changed into finding optimal tradeoffs between the circuit area and the execution time. The main latency bottleneck in hardware masking lies in the need for registers to stop the propagation of glitches and maintain non-completeness. Usually, an exponentially growing number of shares (hence an extremely large circuit), as well as a high demand for fresh randomness, are the result of avoiding registers in a securely masked hardware implementation of a block cipher. In this paper, we present several first-order secure and low-latency implementations of PRINCE. In particular, we show how to realize the masked variant of round-based PRINCE with only a single register stage per cipher round. We compare the resulting architectures, based on the popular TI and GLM masking scheme based on the area, latency, and randomness requirements and point out that both designs are suited for specific use cases.

1 Introduction

Industry and academia are aware that the integration of cryptographic primitives into embedded devices is inevitable to ensure the confidentiality of processed data. From a mathematical point of view, cryptographic primitives must resist analytical attacks, for instance, linear and differential cryptanalysis. Moreover, from an economic perspective, the area overhead of the integrated cryptographic circuits forms an additional cost factor without providing new features for the user. Nevertheless, marked requirements or a security-aware target group make it impossible to avoid cryptographic protection of sensitive data. Hence, the research field of lightweight cryptography focuses on mathematically secure ciphers that result in a small circuit size when implemented in hardware. Besides cryptanalytical attacks, embedded devices are prone to side-channel analysis (SCA) attacks. The vulnerability results from the fact that embedded devices are handed over to, potentially malicious, owners. Hence, the owner can measure and manipulate the physical properties of his purchased device. In the past, attackers could recover the secret key of several commercial devices with physical attacks [10, 15].

© Springer Nature Switzerland AG 2021
S. Bhasin and F. De Santis (Eds.): COSADE 2021, LNCS 12910, pp. 148–167, 2021.
https://doi.org/10.1007/978-3-030-89915-8_7

To protect devices from SCA attacks, the integration of Boolean masking to the cryptographic algorithm is a common and well-studied countermeasure. Unfortunately, the realization of a cryptographic algorithm protected with Boolean masking requires significantly more area due to the processing of multiple shares. Hence, researchers focus on the area-efficient integration of masking to algorithms that potentially handle sensitive data. Usually, the generic approach for reducing the area is to minimize the number of processed shares which makes it necessary to integrate additional register stages into the circuit. As a result, minimizing the circuit area comes at the cost of latency.

The steadily increasing demand for embedded real-time applications, especially for fast memory encryption on smartcards and IoT microcontrollers[1] shifts the focus from the reduction of the circuit size to the minimization of latencies. The PRINCE block cipher [6] fills this gap since it is a lightweight cipher designed to perform an encryption or decryption operation within a single cycle. However, its low latency characteristic gets lost if Boolean masking is applied without considering the latency as shown in [20]. Several adaptions of the popular masking schemes show that accepting a higher circuit size reduces the latency significantly. The most prominent examples are given in [7,12]. The protection with this so-called "low-latency masking" is a special challenge since the resulting circuit must ensure low latency and has to be small enough to be practical. Hence, the main task is to find an acceptable tradeoff between latency on one side and area and randomness requirements on the other side.

Our Contribution. In this work, we show the integration of low-latency masking in PRINCE. In contrast to comparable publications [7,20], we focus on achieving as small latencies as possible whereby we allow larger, but realistic, circuit sizes. In particular, we reduce the number of register stages per round to one in order to process one cipher round per clock cycle. Hence, we achieve an up to three times lower number of clock cycles per encryption than competitive designs. We focus on first-order SCA security due to the integration of the provably secure GLM and TI masking schemes. We remark that other works also aim at SCA resistance of unrolled PRINCE but with the integration of hiding and by taking advantage of the high asynchronicity, glitch number, and parallelism of unrolled circuits [18]. While these works may achieve practical resistance against DPA and CPA, the provable security of hiding countermeasures is not given.

2   Preliminaries

2.1   PRINCE

PRINCE [6] is a 64-bit block cipher with a 128-bit secret key k and has been designed for fully-unrolled implementation. The key is composed of two

---

[1] The LPC55S series of IoT microcontrollers by NXP Semiconductors is one example where PRINCE is employed for memory encryption and where SCA resistance is relevant.

concatenated 64-bit subkeys k_0 and k_1 and extended to 192 bits by applying the following linear mapping:

$$(k_0||k_1) \rightarrow (k_0||k'_0||k_1) := (k_0||(k_0 \ggg 1) \oplus (k_0 \gg 63)||k_1)$$

To be secure against an exhaustive key search, PRINCE follows the FX construction [16] and applies k_0 and k'_0 as whitening keys. The remaining subkey k_1 is fed to the actual cipher named PRINCE_{core}.

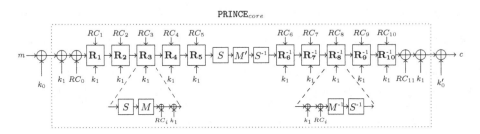

Fig. 1. Schematic description of PRINCE_{core} including the structure of a regular round R_i and an inverse round R_i^{-1}.

Each round performs a *substitution layer* which applies a 4-bit S-Box to each nibble of the state, followed by a linear *M-layer* and the XOR concatenation of k_1 and RC_i (referred to as *constant addition*) to the state. The M-layer is realized as a matrix multiplication of the state with a 64×64 matrix M followed by the *ShiftRows* operation of the AES applied to 4-bit nibbles. Note that the matrix multiplication without ShiftRows builds the *M'-layer* in the middle of PRINCE_{core}. After the middle part, all rounds are inverted.

Since M' is an involution and the round constants satisfy $RC_i \oplus RC_{11-i} = \alpha$, the whole PRINCE_{core} can be inverted by changing the underlying key k_1 to $k_1 \oplus \alpha$. If the whitening keys are swapped, PRINCE satisfies:

$$D_{(k_0||k'_0||k_1)}(\cdot) = E_{(k'_0||k_0||k_1 \oplus \alpha)}(\cdot)$$

which is named α-*reflection property*. This feature allows encryption and decryption with the same underlying circuit and consequently saves an independent decryption routine overhead.

2.2 Probing Security

The d-probing model [14] is a widely used and accepted standard attacker model. To specify an attacker's capabilities, the model depends on the *security order* d. An attacker can place up to d different probes on freely chosen spots of the chip. Since a probe measures one spotted wire or gate's power consumption, the attacker can record intermediate signals of any chosen wire or gate. If a design is d-probing secure, the attacker can not recover any sensitive information by probing d different intermediate values. Formally, this means that every possible d-tuple of intermediate values is independent of every secret value [19]. While this model allows an evaluation of a circuit, in theory, and with simulations, it does not fit for security proofs under real-world conditions. Real hardware is not idealized, so *glitches* can lead to the propagation of unexpected intermediate signals over a wire. Hence, an attacker can read the intermediate value of a probed wire and receive additional information by propagated toggles from previous parts of the circuit. The d-probing model does not reflect the unexpected additional information by propagating glitches, which cause leakage, despite the circuit's security in the d-probing model being proven.

To better match the conditions on real hardware, the d-probing model has been extended to the *glitch-extended d-probing model* [11]. This model allows the attacker to record up to d intermediate values and all possibly propagated values on the probed wires. The attacker can record every intermediate value of the connected combinatorial circuit back to the last register stage. While the glitch-extended d-probing model can simulate an attacker's information gain due to glitches, it does not reflect all other physical properties of the target architecture. Therefore, it is essential to measure each design on the real underlying hardware, even if the security in the glitch-extended d-probing model is proven.

2.3   Threshold Implementation

The concept of threshold implementation (TI) [22] is the oldest provably secure masking scheme which is also resistant to glitches. The core idea is to split any non-linear transformation with algebraic degree t, e.g. the cubic PRINCE Sbox $S(a, b, c, d) = (w, x, y, z)$ with $t = 3$, into a set of at least $t + 1$ component functions $S_{i \in 0,\ldots,t}$. The set of component functions must satisfy *correctness*. Hence, it must hold that $S(a, b, c, d) = S_0 \oplus S_1 \oplus S_2 \oplus S_3$ to ensure the correct functionality of the Sbox.

To ensure first-order security of the Sbox TI, each Sbox input, e.g. the MSB a, is given as a set of four *shares* $(a_{i \in 0,\ldots,t})$. Moreover, it holds that $a = a_0 \oplus a_1 \oplus a_2 \oplus a_3$. Each S_i can process a subset of shares that is independent of at least one share per variable. We refer to this security-critical condition as *first-order non-completeness*. Besides non-completeness, the security of the Sbox is only given if *uniformity* holds for all input sharings. Since the Sbox output builds the input of following Sboxes, the Sbox output sharing must also satisfy uniformity. Hence, we must ensure that each valid sbox output sharing occurs equally likely for all possible input sharings.

All linear functions, e.g. the PRINCE M-layer, are computed share-wise. Hence, all component functions compute the M-layer on one share independently. The area overhead of TI depends on the number of applied shares which is bounded by the algebraic degree. Since the Sbox consists of cubic coordinate functions, at least four shares are required to achieve non-completeness. To reduce t, one approach is to decompose the cubic functions into multiple chained quadratic functions ($t = 2$) and then separate them with register stages.

While several works show a significant improvement in the area due to *quadratic decomposition*, we avoid it because of two reasons:

1. It is shown in [20] that the decomposition of the cubic PRINCE Sbox into two consecutive quadratic functions is not possible. Hence, the decomposition of the PRINCE Sbox results in at least three quadratic functions.
2. The separation of the quadratic functions is necessary to stop the propagation of glitches. As a result, each subfunction requires an additional register stage which increases the latency by one clock cycle per subfunction. For the PRINCE Sbox, this means that the evaluation of a decomposed Sbox requires three clock cycles. The increment of the cycle count violates our goal of one clock cycle per round.

As a tradeoff, we accept the higher number of shares as long as the circuit size does not explode.

2.4 $d + 1$-Masking

In contrast to TI, another scheme, first published in [23] achieves the same security level as TI but with a fixed number of $d + 1$ input shares. Hence, the number of input shares no longer depends on the algebraic degree but only on the security order. This is achieved since the non-completeness also holds if each component function receives only d shares per variable. Hence, a set of component functions that achieves correctness and non-completeness with $(d + 1)$ input shares must contain at least $(d + 1)^t$ component functions. Since the number of output shares grows exponentially with the algebraic degree, only the $d + 1$-masking of low degree functions is more efficient in area than TI. For the cubic PRINCE Sbox, eight component functions per coordinate function are necessary to achieve first-order security. The output sharing is usually not uniform. Hence, fresh randomness is added to the output shares to make them uniform. Right after that, registers store the remasked shares. As the last step, the eight shares are compressed into two shares by XORing two quadruples of shares.

Similar to quadratic decomposition, the circuit size and the amount of fresh randomness is decreased if the cubic Sbox is split into quadratic functions with a register stage and share compression at the output. As for the TI, we omit the decomposition to execute one round per clock cycle.

The concept of $d + 1$-masking builds the foundation for advanced masking schemes such as *domain oriented masking (DOM)* [13]. In particular, the *generic low latency masking (GLM)* [12] offers an interesting approach for low-latency masking. For the GLM scheme, the authors implement no share compression. Hence it allows the probing-secure evaluation of every Boolean function with a combinatorial circuit. While GLM is provably secure, the evaluation of high-degree functions is not practical due to the exponentially growing number of output shares. Nevertheless, GLM allows the designer to adjust every function in terms of area and latency.

We remark that skipping the share compression does not necessarily mean that the output shares can be fed to the following modules without caution. If the shares are not compressed, the combination during the next modules can violate the non-completeness, although the non-completeness holds for each module independently. This is the case if one variable is part of two inputs of a non-linear gate. The authors of [12] refer to these flaws as *collisions*. To ensure that two inputs are independent, we must design the circuit in a way that the same intermediate value is not fed twice to a non-linear gate or that an intermediate value gets a reshared copy before the intermediate and copy are fed to a non-linear gate.

3   Low-Latency TI Architecture

The intended implementation strategy of PRINCE is an unrolled architecture. Hence, it consists of combinatorial logic only. As a first thought experiment, the whole combinatorial circuit can be shared with GLM without any register stage. As PRINCE encompasses 12 consecutive and cubic substitution layers, the overall algebraic degree for the whole encryption function is $t = 3^{12} = 531441$. Clearly, the number of $s_{out} = 2^{531441}$ output shares is not realizable. As a consequence, it is not possible with currently known methods to achieve single-cycle encryption and provable first-order security together.

Thus, we focus on the evaluation of one round per clock cycle. It is necessary to transform the unrolled design into a round-based architecture with one register stage per round. To the best of our knowledge, four round-based architectures of PRINCE exist in literature [6,7,20,24]. Following the arguments of [20], we choose their design for the following TI experiments. We visualize the unprotected circuit in Fig. 2. The authors present a design requiring only a single substitution layer and register stage if no decomposition is applied. Moreover, the authors eliminate the inverse substitution layer, so either the S-Box or its inverse is part of the circuit. Since S and S^{-1} are affine equivalent, there is a tuple of functions consisting of an affine input and output transformation. Applying affine transformations to the input and the substitution layer's output allows computing the inverse substitution layer from the regular substitution layer. In more detail, it holds that $S^{-1} = A \circ S \circ A$ with $A : 5764FDCE1320B98A$ so input and output transformation are equal. In an unmasked fashion, one complete encryption requires 12 clock cycles, e.g. one clock cycle per round.

3.1   TI Sharing of the Sbox

The Sbox of PRINCE, referred to as $S \in \mathbb{F}_2^4 \to \mathbb{F}_2^4$, consists of four coordinate functions $f_0, f_1, f_2, f_3 \in \mathbb{F}_2^4 \to \mathbb{F}_2$ which are all cubic. As discussed before, a first-order non-complete TI of S requires at least four shares per variable (for input and output sharing). While finding a correct and non-complete set of component functions is relatively easy, the uniformity is challenging. We apply the TI finder tools of Nikova et al. [5] to find a uniform sharing of S algorithmically. We find

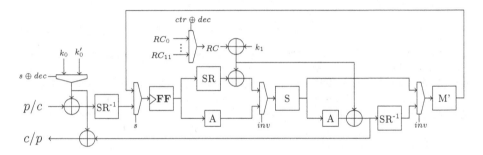

Fig. 2. The optimized round-based architecture of PRINCE with only one substitution layer and register stage.

a tuple of four-bit permutations (S', A) with $S = S' \circ A$ that builds a first-order secure TI of S if the sharing of all input and output variables encompass five shares per variable. Hence, a TI of (S', A) consists of five component functions. The corresponding lookup-tables of S' and A are given in the following:

$$S' = BF32AC918067D4E5 \quad A = 01234567AB89EFCD$$

Since A is an affine transformation on four-bit nibbles, its generated component functions compute A on all shared nibbles separately. The unmasked affine transformation $A(a, b, c, d) = (w, x, y, z) \in \mathbb{F}_2^4 \to \mathbb{F}_2^4$ is computed as:

$$w = a \quad x = b \quad y = a \oplus c \quad z = d$$

According to [5], it holds that S' is uniform if we create a non-complete sharing of S' with the concept of *direct sharing* [4]. Since the correctness is satisfied due to $S = S' \circ A$, the resulting TI is first-order secure. The full circuit, processing five shares, is given in Fig. 3.

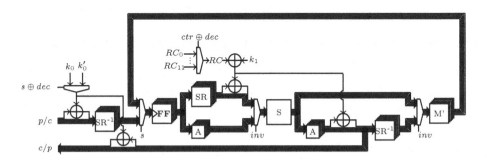

Fig. 3. Five-share uniform PRINCE TI architecture without any fresh randomness.

However a sharing with five input and output shares increases the circuit size significantly compared to a non-complete sharing with four input and output shares. To keep the circuit size as small as possible, we decide to reduce the number of input shares to four and generate a non-complete set of component functions by following direct sharing. Compared to the five-share TI, we avoid one additional component function and hence about 20% of area. We remark that this change does not influence the number of required clock cycles. Regarding the critical path, we observe that the reduction of shares leads to component functions that combine fewer monomials, so the number of consecutive XOR gates is reduced in all component functions. Moreover, we implement all component functions in a way that they are almost balanced. Hence, the critical path is almost equal-sized for all component functions resulting in a shorter critical path and higher possible clock frequencies.

Obviously, the resulting component functions S_0, S_1, S_2, S_3 are first-order non-complete but not uniform anymore. We satisfy the uniformity of the output sharing manually by adding initial randomness according to the *changing of the guards* method [9] (referred in the Fig. 4 as R). This technique guarantees uniformity at the price of a small overhead of 12 random initial bits per encryption. In particular, we require no fresh-randomness per clock cycle. This small amount of initial randomness is acceptable to reduce the number of shares by one as the five-share variant would require more area *and* a larger amount of initial randomness (due to the initial sharing into five shares instead of four).

After the remasking, all shares and the *guards* are stored in registers. All following operations, especially the M-layer, are linear and performed on each share separately. We show the resulting architecture of the full PRINCE cipher in Fig. 4.

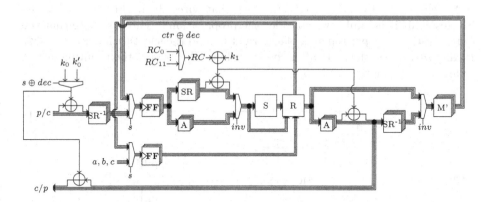

Fig. 4. Four-share uniform PRINCE TI architecture without fresh randomness.

4 Low-Latency GLM Architecture

In contrast to the TI scheme, the application of GLM is prone to the introduction of collisions during the linear layers. Hence, the underlying architecture must satisfy that the non-completeness is not violated on a path through multiple layers. Unfortunately, the previous architecture contains a collision introduced during the affine layer A and leaking during S. It holds that the outputs of $A(a, b, c, d) = (w, x, y, z)$ are not independent of each other (both w and y depend on a). Therefore, a non-linear gate with the inputs w and y violates the non-completeness.

The remaining linear layers, in particular M', are collision-free. Each output bit of M' is a linear combination of three different input bits which are forwarded from different Sboxes. Moreover, M' keeps the structure of all four-bit Sbox outputs. Each output bit of M' inside a four-bit nibble $m_{i \in 0,...,3}$ is a combination of three different Sbox output bits $s^0_{i \in 0,...,3}, s^1_{i \in 0,...,3}, s^2_{i \in 0,...,3}$ from the same position inside its computing Sbox. The resulting four-bit output nibbles encompass four bits which are all independent of each other. Hence, the output of M' can be fed as an independent input to the following Sboxes. The shifting layers operate on four-bit nibbles independently, so the structure of the M' is not changed.

The investigations above point out that we can not apply the same underlying architecture as for the TI experiments. It is inevitable to remove the affine transformations and to implement an additional circuit for S^{-1} instead. The resulting architecture is mainly influenced by the architecture applied in [24]. We only remove the second register stage and we changed the position of the SR^{-1} layer so that SR and SR^{-1} operate in parallel. Since SR^{-1} is only wiring, the additional insertions of SR^{-1} on the output path and the key path do not increase the circuit size. On the other hand, the parallel processing of SR and SR^{-1} eliminates the additional data path that wires the unshifted state to the Sboxes. This is helpful if we consider the propagation of glitches. Note that the only register stage per round is placed right behind the substitution layer so that it can synchronize the state after the remasking. We present the resulting design in an unmasked form in Fig. 5.

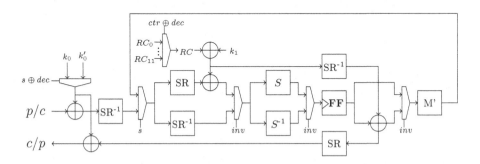

Fig. 5. The underlying target PRINCE architecture for the GLM experiments.

4.1   GLM Sharing of the Sbox

According to $d+1$ masking, we share the first-order secure Sbox input with two shares $(a_0, b_0, c_0, d_0), (a_1, b_1, c_1, d_1)$. Since all coordinate functions of S and S^{-1} are cubic, eight component functions per coordinate function are required to satisfy first-order non-completeness. We apply the sharing given in [24] to minimize the extra circuit due to an additional S^{-1} module. Hence, all component functions compute one share per coordinate function for S and S^{-1}, in total, eight output values per component function. Since we build all component functions based on the algebraic normal form (ANF), no collisions occur within the computations of the coordinate functions. To ensure the independence of the Sbox output we add fresh randomness to the shared values and store them in registers. The synchronized values are then compressed (in module C) from eight shares back to two. As all shares are refreshed, no collisions occur during the share compression. All linear components are instantiated twice to handle two shares separately. We give the full design in Fig. 6.

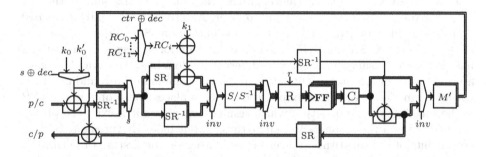

Fig. 6. The masked PRINCE GLM architecture.

Remasking and Share Compression. To ensure the independence of the following round's Sbox input, we apply a remasking to all output shares of the substitution layer. Since we integrate only one register stage, we must investigate glitches propagated through the whole circuit. Naturally, the required amount of randomness grows if the propagation of glitches stops only at a single point of the round function. We add four fresh random bits $r^{i \in 0, \dots, 3}$ to the shares $s_{i \in 0, \dots, 7}$ of each bit according to the following scheme:

$$g_0 = s_0 \oplus r^0 \quad g_1 = s_1 \oplus r^1 \quad g_2 = s_2 \oplus r^2 \quad g_3 = s_3 \oplus r^3$$
$$g_4 = s_4 \oplus r^0 \quad g_5 = s_5 \oplus r^1 \quad g_6 = s_6 \oplus r^2 \quad g_7 = s_7 \oplus r^3$$

The remasking ensures that an attacker gets no information if she probes a combination of output shares computed during the share compression. Since both compressed output shares are never combined, we can apply the same random bits to both quadruples of output shares. After the remasking, all remasked shares $g_{i \in 0,...,7}$ are synchronized in registers and the share compression XOR concatenates four shares with different randomness together. Hence, it compresses eight input shares to two output shares. Formally, the share compression is given as:

$$z_0 = g_0 \oplus g_1 \oplus g_2 \oplus g_3 \qquad z_1 = g_4 \oplus g_5 \oplus g_6 \oplus g_7$$

We remark that the remasking makes all shares independent of each other. Hence, glitches introduced within the share compression do not leak any sensitive information if we separate both additions into different modules.

Reduction of Online Randomness. As described before, we remask one shared output bit with four fresh random bits. In total, the remasking of the whole state leads to an amount of $64 \cdot 4 = 256$ random bits per clock cycle. To reduce the amount of online randomness, we refer to the structural analysis of PRINCE given in [7] and adapt it to a round circuit with a single register stage. In contrast to the architecture specified in [7], we place SR and SR^{-1} in parallel and choose the correct output via multiplexers. Moreover, we place no register stage in front of the substitution layer. Hence, glitches introduced by the multiplexers are propagated to the following substitution layer. According to the glitch-extended d-probing model, an attacker who places a probe on one Sbox input bit receives one output bit of SR and SR^{-1}. To omit information leakage, we remask all bits, wired to the same position, with different random bits. An example of such a probe propagation due to glitches through the combinatorial round circuit is visualized in Fig. 7. In this example, the attacker places one probe on the LSB of the substitution layers output which results in various glitch-extended probes on single bits in the second and fourth 16-bit input block. It turns out that all output bits of the substitution layer depend either on the first and the third or on the second and the fourth 16-bit input block. As the values from the first 16-bit block are never combined with values from the second 16-bit block during one round, we can use the same randomness to mask the first and the second block. Analogously, we use the same randomness for blocks three and four. The repeated application of the same randomness halves the number of random bits per clock cycle from 256 to 128.

5   Synthesis Results

To give comparable circuit sizes and critical path lengths of our investigated architectures, we synthesize all presented unprotected (cf. Table 1) and first-order masked (cf. Table 2) designs against a real gate library. Moreover, we implement comparable designs from literature and synthesize them against the same gate library (cf. Table 3). We apply synopsis design compiler to synthesize against Nangate 15 nm standard cell library. The synthesizer generates a gate-level netlist and the corresponding area and timing reports. As our goal is to optimize latency, we force the synthesizer to generate the fastest possible design by setting the clock period to 0.1 picoseconds. Hence, the results can never fulfill the timing requirements and the synthesizer optimizes the design's timing

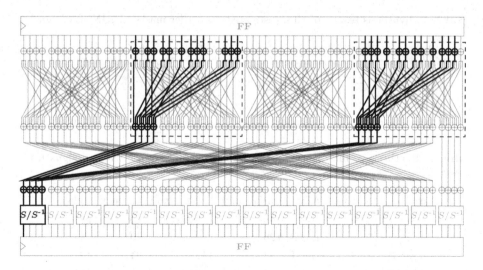

Fig. 7. Probe propagation in the glitch-extended probing model through one round of the unprotected PRINCE GLM architecture by probing the LSB of the round function output. The probed 16-bit input blocks (second and fourth) are bordered by a dashed rectangle.

as much as possible. For the area estimation, we only take the cipher core into account. Hence we ignore additional area overheads of the FSM or additional PRNGs. We give an overview of the specific requirements of each design in terms of latency, area, and randomness requirements. Note that the timing estimations are divided into the total number of clock cycles for one encryption and the critical path length. To take all design requirements into account we also show the randomness requirements, divided into initial and online randomness.

Table 1. Synthesis results of all investigated unprotected PRINCE designs.

Scheme	Area	Latency	Delay
	GE	Cycles	ps
KECCAK-PRNG [3]	4930	1	80
Unrolled (Fig. 1)	16352	1	412
Round-based (Fig. 2)	3997	12	118
Round-based (Fig. 5)	5045	12	98

We conclude that the latency improvement sourced by the application of one register stage per cipher round comes at the cost of area and randomness overheads. All investigated TI designs are at least 73% larger than the comparable TI architecture from [20] with a three-stage decomposed Sbox especially since they operate on more than the minimum number of three shares. Since fewer

Table 2. Synthesis results of all investigated first-order masked PRINCE designs.

Scheme	#Shares	Area	Initial rand	Online rand	Latency	Delay
		GE	Bits	Bits/cycle	Cycles	ps
TI (Fig. 3)	5	42158	256	0	12	153
TI (Fig. 4)	4	26158	204	0	12	145
GLM (Fig. 6)	2	20046	64	128	12	97

Table 3. Synthesis results of comparable first-order masked PRINCE designs from literature.

Scheme	#Shares	Area	Initial rand	Online rand	Latency	Delay
		GE	Bits	Bits/cycle	Cycles	ps
TI [20]	3	15063	128	0	40	85
GLM [7]	2	16951	64	112	24	101
GLM [24]	2	14235	64	0	24	85

shares are processed and combined, the circuit size and the critical path delay decrease if the number of shares is decreased. This is beneficial, for TIs with fewer shares as the changing of the guards technique allows a remasking without any online randomness. Due to these results, we recommend using the minimum number of shares and the changing of the guards technique for a low latency TI of PRINCE.

The further reduction to $d + 1$ shares makes it necessary to use either online randomness affecting the circuit size in case that additional PRNGs are required or to place another register stage in the round circuit [24] which doubles the latency. Nevertheless, we achieve the shortest critical path and the smallest cipher core area for the GLM architecture. Compared to the similar design in [24] we half the number of clock cycles at the cost of 128 bit online randomness per round and an area overhead of 41%. We sum up, that the GLM architecture is the most suited design regarding low-latency but with the restriction that a small and fast PRNG is available. We apply a PRNG based on KECCAK-f[200] [3] with parameters $r = 128$ and $c = 72$ to generate 128 bits of randomness per clock cycle. Otherwise, the TI architecture is usable in absence of a PRNG. The area requirement for the first-order masking itself grows by at least a factor of four for the GLM architecture. Nevertheless, our smallest first-order secure low-latency architecture is only 23% larger than the originally proposed unrolled architecture. We, therefore, conclude that the area requirements are still acceptable.

6 Security Analysis

We evaluate our designs' power-side-channel leakage based on physical measurements on an FPGA. We place both architectures on a SAKURA-G board [1],

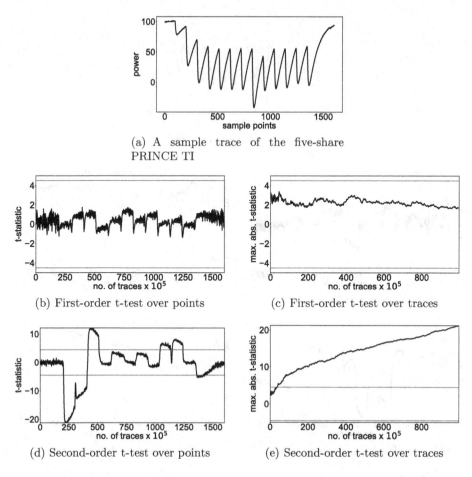

(a) A sample trace of the five-share PRINCE TI

(b) First-order t-test over points

(c) First-order t-test over traces

(d) Second-order t-test over points

(e) Second-order t-test over traces

Fig. 8. Non-specific t-test results over 100 million traces encompassing the whole encryption with the PRINCE five-share TI architecture.

specifically designed to evaluate power-analysis attacks. The board integrates two Spartan-6 FPGAs. The smaller FPGA is a controller that communicates with the target FPGA and the measurement script. Moreover, a PRNG based on the AES in counter mode is placed on the control FPGA to generate masks and additional online randomness. We measure the power consumption at a shunt resistor inserted in the target FPGA's V_{dd} path and record the traces with a digital PicoScope oscilloscope of the 6000 series. The oscilloscope operates on a sampling rate of 625 MS/s while all target designs receive a 6 MHz clock. The recorded power trace is quantized with an 8-bit resolution and stored on the host PC. A sample trace of the five-share TI architecture (cf. Fig. 8(a)), the four-share TI architecture (cf. Fig. 9(a)), and the GLM architecture (cf. Fig. 10(a)) is illustrated. We apply the non-specific t-test over 100 million traces, measured either by encrypting a fixed or a random plaintext. The t-test detects general

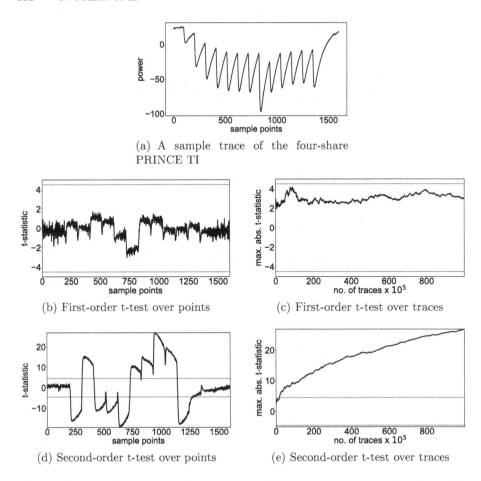

(a) A sample trace of the four-share PRINCE TI

(b) First-order t-test over points

(c) First-order t-test over traces

(d) Second-order t-test over points

(e) Second-order t-test over traces

Fig. 9. Non-specific t-test results over 100 million traces encompassing the whole encryption with the PRINCE four-share TI architecture.

information leakage by comparing the statistical properties of two groups of traces. We say that an implementation has general information leakage if an absolute t-value in a single sample point exceeds the 4.5 absolute threshold. We compute the t-values for the first and second statistical moment. The resulting plots are given in Figs. 8, 9, and 10.

Figure 8(b) indicates that the evaluated PRINCE TI architecture with five shares is first-order secure since no absolute t-value surpasses the 4.5 threshold. Moreover, Fig. 8(c) shows no growing progression of the maximum t-value. As expected, we observe strong second-order leakage after hundred thousands of traces (cf. Figs. 8(d) and 8(e)).

The same holds for the evaluated TI architecture with four-shares and remasking. Figure 9(b) shows no first-order leakage indicating that the design is first-order secure. Figure 9(c) shows no growing progression of the maximum

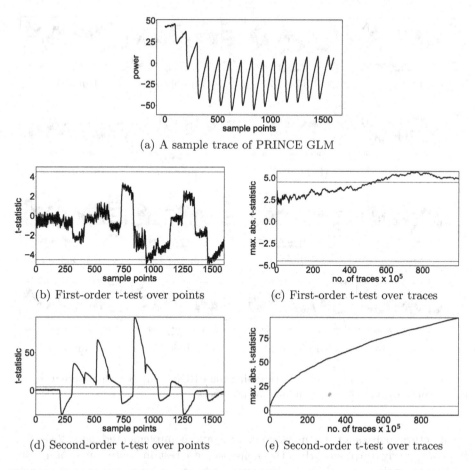

(a) A sample trace of PRINCE GLM

(b) First-order t-test over points

(c) First-order t-test over traces

(d) Second-order t-test over points

(e) Second-order t-test over traces

Fig. 10. Non-specific t-test results over 100 million traces encompassing the whole encryption with the PRINCE GLM architecture.

t-value and we observe strong second-order leakage after hundred thousands of traces (cf. Figs. 9(d) and 9(e)). Compared to the five-share TI, the maximum second-order leakage is higher than for the four-share TI architecture and the threshold is exceeded in a larger set of sample points.

For the GLM architecture, the t-test results do not indicate perfect first-order security. Figure 10(c) shows that the maximum t-statistics value exceeds the threshold after around 50 million traces. However, several previous works have observed that the t-test may indicate the presence of detectable leakage in the first order due to coupling effects, despite the implementation being glitch-extended first-order probing secure [8]. This seems to be especially relevant for $d+1$-masked implementations with $d=1$. In particular, the authors of [2] observe first-order leakage when evaluating a first-order secure DOM protected implementation of the AES with the non-specific t-test. Since the GLM

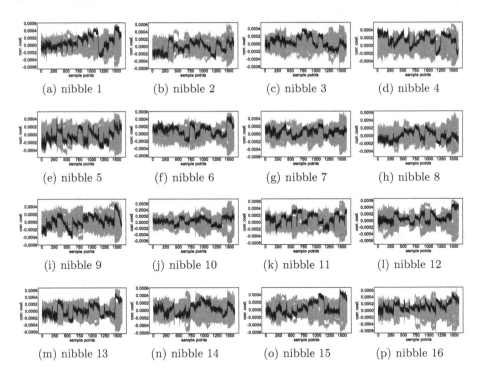

Fig. 11. 1st-order profiled MCDPA targeting the PRINCE GLM architecture using 50 million profiling traces and 50 million attack traces.

architecture utilizes a $d + 1$ masking scheme and is implemented using 2 shares, it is not overly surprising that the non-specific t-test indicates small amounts of detectable first-order leakage. However, to verify that the leakage stems from coupling effects and not from an implementation flaw we have used SILVER [17] to verify the implementation's glitch-extended probing security.

Additionally, we decided to evaluate the design with a moments-correlating DPA (MCDPA) [21]. Since the MCDPA is a collision-based attack we avoid restricting our evaluation to a specific power model. During the profiling phase, we create first and second-order models based on a set of 50 million traces for each Sbox. Another set of 50 million traces is used to perform the actual attack on each Sbox. As a result, the attack returns the correlation between the model and attack traces for all possible input differences. Since we correlate the same Sbox from the modeling set and the attack set, we expect the highest correlation for the input difference zero.

The first-order MCDPA results for each nibble are shown in Fig. 11. As the correct difference (colored black) shows no higher correlation than all other differences, we again confirm that our implementation is indeed secure against first-order attacks. The second-order MCDPA results are given in Fig. 12.

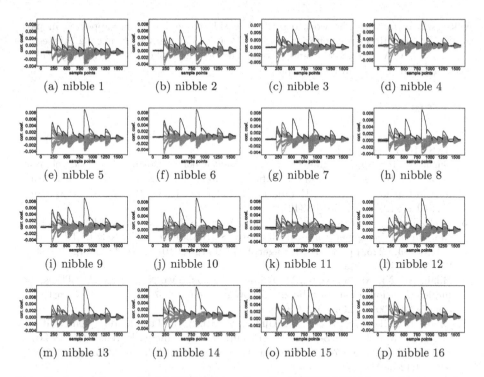

Fig. 12. 2nd-order profiled MCDPA targeting the PRINCE GLM architecture using 50 million profiling traces and 50 million attack traces.

As expected, we observe that the attack successfully recovered the key difference in the second order. In particular, the correct key difference is distinguishable from all other differences for all nibbles.

7   Conclusion

In this paper, we present several case studies on low-latency masked PRINCE architectures with the TI and GLM masking scheme. The comparison of all presented designs in Table 2 points out that every scheme comes with its characteristic requirements for area, latency, and randomness. The analyzed TI architectures offer an acceptable circuit size and require no fresh randomness. Moreover, we point out that the usage of remasking with changing of the guards is preferable compared to the usage of more shares. The reduction of shares to $d+1$ improves the circuit size significantly at the cost of online randomness. We also demonstrate all latency improvements result in at least an overhead in the area due to the processing of more shares. Hence, the lightweight property of every block cipher is decreased by applying low-latency masking to it. Nevertheless, all overheads are acceptable and applicable in practical devices.

Acknowledgments. The work described in this paper has been supported in part by the German Research Foundation (DFG) under Germany's Excellence Strategy - EXC 2092 CASA - 390781972, and through the project 435264177 'phySicAlly secUre reconfiguraBlE platfoRm (SAUBER)'.

References

1. Side-channel attack user reference architecture. http://satoh.cs.uec.ac.jp/SAKURA/index.html
2. Bache, F., Plump, C., Güneysu, T.: Confident leakage assessment — a side-channel evaluation framework based on confidence intervals. In: 2018 Design, Automation Test in Europe Conference Exhibition (DATE), pp. 1117–1122 (2018). https://doi.org/10.23919/DATE.2018.8342178
3. Bertoni, G., Daemen, J., Peeters, M., Van Assche, G.: Sponge-based pseudo-random number generators. In: Mangard, S., Standaert, F.-X. (eds.) CHES 2010. LNCS, vol. 6225, pp. 33–47. Springer, Heidelberg (2010). https://doi.org/10.1007/978-3-642-15031-9_3
4. Bilgin, B., Nikova, S., Nikov, V., Rijmen, V., Tokareva, N., Vitkup, V.: Threshold implementations of small S-boxes. Cryptogr. Commun. **7**(1), 3–33 (2014). https://doi.org/10.1007/s12095-014-0104-7
5. Bilgin, B., Nikova, S., Nikov, V., Rijmen, V., Stütz, G.: Threshold implementations of All 3 ×3 and 4 ×4 S-boxes. In: Prouff, E., Schaumont, P. (eds.) CHES 2012. LNCS, vol. 7428, pp. 76–91. Springer, Heidelberg (2012). https://doi.org/10.1007/978-3-642-33027-8_5
6. Borghoff, J., et al.: PRINCE – a low-latency block cipher for pervasive computing applications - extended abstract. In: Wang, X., Sako, K. (eds.) ASIACRYPT 2012. LNCS, vol. 7658, pp. 208–225. Springer, Heidelberg (2012). https://doi.org/10.1007/978-3-642-34961-4_14
7. Božilov, D., Knežević, M., Nikov, V.: Optimized threshold implementations: minimizing the latency of secure cryptographic accelerators. In: Belaïd, S., Güneysu, T. (eds.) CARDIS 2019. LNCS, vol. 11833, pp. 20–39. Springer, Cham (2020). https://doi.org/10.1007/978-3-030-42068-0_2
8. Cnudde, T., Ender, M., Moradi, A.: Hardware masking, revisited. IACR Trans. Cryptogr. Hardw. Embed. Syst. **2018**, 123–148 (2018)
9. Daemen, J.: Changing of the guards: a simple and efficient method for achieving uniformity in threshold sharing. Cryptology ePrint Archive, Report 2016/1061 (2016). https://eprint.iacr.org/2016/1061
10. Eisenbarth, T., Kasper, T., Moradi, A., Paar, C., Salmasizadeh, M., Shalmani, M.T.M.: On the power of power analysis in the real world: a complete break of the KEELOQ code hopping scheme. In: Wagner, D. (ed.) CRYPTO 2008. LNCS, vol. 5157, pp. 203–220. Springer, Heidelberg (2008). https://doi.org/10.1007/978-3-540-85174-5_12
11. Faust, S., Grosso, V., Merino Del Pozo, S., Paglialonga, C., Standaert, F.X.: Composable masking schemes in the presence of physical defaults & the robust probing model. IACR Trans. Cryptogr. Hardw. Embed. Syst. **2018**(3), 89–120 (2018). https://doi.org/10.13154/tches.v2018.i3.89-120. https://tches.iacr.org/index.php/TCHES/article/view/7270
12. Groß, H., Iusupov, R., Bloem, R.: Generic low-latency masking in hardware. IACR Trans. Cryptogr. Hardw. Embed. Syst. **2018**(2), 1–21 (2018). https://doi.org/10.13154/tches.v2018.i2.1-21

13. Gross, H., Mangard, S., Korak, T.: Domain-oriented masking: compact masked hardware implementations with arbitrary protection order. In: Proceedings of the 2016 ACM Workshop on Theory of Implementation Security, TIS 2016, p. 3. Association for Computing Machinery, New York (2016). https://doi.org/10.1145/2996366.2996426

14. Ishai, Y., Sahai, A., Wagner, D.: Private circuits: securing hardware against probing attacks. In: Boneh, D. (ed.) CRYPTO 2003. LNCS, vol. 2729, pp. 463–481. Springer, Heidelberg (2003). https://doi.org/10.1007/978-3-540-45146-4_27

15. Kasper, M., Kasper, T., Moradi, A., Paar, C.: Breaking KEELOQ in a flash: on extracting keys at lightning speed. In: Preneel, B. (ed.) AFRICACRYPT 2009. LNCS, vol. 5580, pp. 403–420. Springer, Heidelberg (2009). https://doi.org/10.1007/978-3-642-02384-2_25

16. Kilian, J., Rogaway, P.: How to protect DES against exhaustive key search. In: Koblitz, N. (ed.) CRYPTO 1996. LNCS, vol. 1109, pp. 252–267. Springer, Heidelberg (1996). https://doi.org/10.1007/3-540-68697-5_20

17. Knichel, D., Sasdrich, P., Moradi, A.: SILVER – statistical independence and leakage verification. In: Moriai, S., Wang, H. (eds.) ASIACRYPT 2020. LNCS, vol. 12491, pp. 787–816. Springer, Cham (2020). https://doi.org/10.1007/978-3-030-64837-4_26

18. Moos, T.: Unrolled cryptography on silicon: a physical security analysis. IACR Trans. Cryptogr. Hardw. Embed. Syst. **2020**(4), 416–442 (2020). https://doi.org/10.13154/tches.v2020.i4.416-442. https://tches.iacr.org/index.php/TCHES/article/view/8689

19. Moos, T., Moradi, A., Schneider, T., Standaert, F.X.: Glitch-resistant masking revisited: or why proofs in the robust probing model are needed. IACR Trans. Cryptogr. Hardw. Embed. Syst. **2019**(2), 256–292 (2019). https://doi.org/10.13154/tches.v2019.i2.256-292. https://tches.iacr.org/index.php/TCHES/article/view/7392

20. Moradi, A., Schneider, T.: Side-channel analysis protection and low-latency in action - case study of PRINCE and Midori. Cryptology ePrint Archive, Report 2016/481 (2016). https://eprint.iacr.org/2016/481

21. Moradi, A., Standaert, F.X.: Moments-correlating DPA. In: Proceedings of the 2016 ACM Workshop on Theory of Implementation Security, TIS 2016, pp. 5–15. Association for Computing Machinery, New York (2016). https://doi.org/10.1145/2996366.2996369

22. Nikova, S., Rechberger, C., Rijmen, V.: Threshold implementations against side-channel attacks and glitches. In: Ning, P., Qing, S., Li, N. (eds.) ICICS 2006. LNCS, vol. 4307, pp. 529–545. Springer, Heidelberg (2006). https://doi.org/10.1007/11935308_38

23. Reparaz, O., Bilgin, B., Nikova, S., Gierlichs, B., Verbauwhede, I.: Consolidating masking schemes. IACR Cryptology ePrint Archive **2015**, 719 (2015)

24. Shahmirzadi, A.R., Moradi, A.: Re-consolidating first-order masking schemes - nullifying fresh randomness. Cryptology ePrint Archive, Report 2020/890 (2020). https://eprint.iacr.org/2020/890

Security Analysis of Deterministic Re-keying with Masking and Shuffling: Application to ISAP

Balazs Udvarhelyi[(✉)], Olivier Bronchain, and François-Xavier Standaert

Crypto Group, ICTEAM Institute, UCLouvain, Louvain-la-Neuve, Belgium
{balazs.udvarhelyi,olivier.bronchain,
francois-xavier.standaert}@uclouvain.be

Abstract. Single-trace side-channel attacks are important attack vectors against the security of authenticated encryption schemes relying on an internal re-keying process, such as the NIST Lightweight Cryptography finalist ISAP. In a recent work of Kannwischer et al., it was suggested to mitigate such single-trace attacks with masking and shuffling. In this work, we first show that combining masking and re-keying is conceptually useless since this combination can always be attacked with a complexity that is just the sum of the complexities to attack a masked implementation (without re-keying) and a re-keyed implementation (without masking). We then show that combining shuffling and re-keying is theoretically founded but can be practically challenging: in low-cost embedded devices (e.g., ARM Cortex-M0) that are the typical targets of single-trace attacks, the noise level of the leakages is such that multivariate attacks can be powerful enough to recover the shuffling permutation in one trace. This second result does not prevent the shuffling + re-keying combination to be effective in more noisy contexts, but it suggests that the best use cases for leakage-resilient PRFs as used by ISAP remain the ones where no additional countermeasures are needed.

1 Introduction

ISAP [9,10] is an authenticated encryption scheme submitted to the NIST Light- weight Cryptography Standardization Process.[1] It comes with claims of improved resistance against side-channel attacks thanks to leakage-resilient features. Precisely, it embeds a re-keying process that mixes a long-term key with public data (e.g., nonces) at a low rate, which can be viewed as a permutation-based variant of the tree-based leakage-resilient PRF constructions discussed in [11,13,24]. The main underlying idea of this construction is that it allows reducing the need to resist against Differential Power Analysis (DPA) to the need to resist Simple Power Analysis (SPA).[2] Since ISAP's re-keying is quite

---

[1] https://csrc.nist.gov/projects/lightweight-cryptography.

[2] By DPA (resp., SPA), we mean side-channel attacks where the adversary can observe the leakage of many (resp., a few) different inputs of the leaking primitive.

S. Bhasin and F. De Santis (Eds.): COSADE 2021, LNCS 12910, pp. 168–183, 2021.
https://doi.org/10.1007/978-3-030-89915-8_8

expensive, this idea is then used sparsely (i.e., for initialization and finalization only), in the spirit of a leveled implementations [20]. Concretely, the relevance of this design therefore highly depends on the difficulty to prevent SPA.

In two recent and independent works, it has been demonstrated that performing SPA against a permutation-based re-keying is possible on low-end embedded devices [3,18]. In both cases, advanced analytical side-channel attacks like [27] are especially effective because the adversary can average her measurements in order to obtain a strong (noise-free) side-channel signal. In the CHES 2020 paper by Kannwischer et al., it is therefore suggested that SPA security on such low-end devices could be obtained by combining the re-keying of the ISAP design with algorithmic-level countermeasures like masking, which has been applied to the Keccak permutation in [14], or shuffling [16,28], for which the application to bitslice permutation-based designs remains to be investigated.

Combining countermeasures is a popular idea in the side-channel literature. In general, the hope is that the complexity to attack a combined countermeasure will be the product of the complexities to attack its components. For example, in case side-channel measurements are sufficiently noisy, it is known that such a multiplicative effect happens when combining masking and shuffling [21]. In this paper, we question whether the same multiplicative effect takes place when combining re-keying with masking or shuffling, as proposed in [18].

For masking, we answer the question negatively in a definitive manner by showing that a divide-and-conquer side-channel attack of its combination with re-keying is always possible. That is, the complexity to attack a masked leakage-resilient PRF is only the sum of the complexities to (1) extract the useful signal of its masked state and (2) exploit this useful signal in an analytical attack. The latter can be explained by the fact that the useful signal of a masked state is the same as the useful signal of an unprotected state since masking can only amplify the noise of an implementation.[3] In other words, and independent of the level of noise in the measurements, combining re-keying with masking will never lead to a multiplicative effect. At best, the masked implementation can become hard to attack. But in this case, the significant overheads of the re-keying scheme (which iterates the permutation n times to digest an n-bit value) becomes a waste, since this re-keying does not bring any significant additional security benefit.

For shuffling, the situation is different since it is known that its combination with a leakage-resilient PRF is at least theoretically founded [15]. Intuitively, the reason is that in case of sufficient noise, the shuffling countermeasure is modifying the shape of the signal since it emulates a parallel implementation that would combine (e.g., sum) the deterministic parts of multiple byte's leakage functions into a single leakage sample. So the security of this proposal boils down to the question whether the noise of a low-end embedded device such as considered in [3,18] is always sufficient for this emulation to take place. We

---

[3] Concretely, it could even make the situation worse since the computational overheads of some masked computations (e.g., multiplications) could even increase the signal, which we do not investigate since quite implementation-specific and leading to the same conclusion that masking and re-keying do not combine well..

answer the question negatively by describing a multivariate attack against a shuffled implementation of Keccak in an ARM Cortex M0. We show that we can recover its permutation in a single trace. It implies that a trivial side-channel dissection (in the sense of [6]) of the shuffling + re-keying combination is possible, leading to the same powerful single-trace attacks as without shuffling. So while shuffling ISAP in a more noisy device remains a good strategy in order to prevent averaging traces, it is not a sufficient one to gain high confidence in low-end embedded devices where shuffling can be the target of highly multivariate attacks that further circumvent the already low noise available on such devices.

So overall, our results mitigate the hope that countermeasures aiming to amplify the side-channel noise or to limit the side-channel signal always combine well when a leakage-resilient authenticated encryption scheme like ISAP is implemented on a low-end embedded software platform. They rather suggest that the best use cases for such schemes remain the ones where no additional countermeasures are needed, like larger parallel hardware implementations.

Besides, for designers aiming at securing low-end Cortex-like microcontrollers with a leakage-resilient primitive, relying on AES coprocessors (when available) is currently a better option. In terms of security, such coprocessors inevitably leak less than a software implementation. In terms of performances, they are faster. We refer to [5,25] for two recent examples in this direction.

Related Work. To some extent, our conclusion regarding masking and re-keying could be inferred from a previous work of Belaïd et al. [2]. It concluded that the cost vs. security trade-off of a standalone leakage-resilient primitive is better than its combination with masking when the leakage is sufficiently bounded, and that masking alone is preferable otherwise. We consolidate this conclusion by exhibiting the poor (additive) combination of complexities that such a mix implies in general. As for shuffling, it is also known that multivariate attacks can be quite damaging against them and the analysis in [15] was coming with a cautionary note in this direction. Yet, our results show the sensitivity of such security evaluations to small variations of the attack methodology. In particular, the main addition that we made compared to this previous analysis is to extract more information thanks to a dimensionality reduction step [22].

We finally note that we take the ISAP scheme as a case study, but our conclusions also apply to the application of single-trace attacks in the context of post-quantum cryptographic primitives investigated in [18].

2   Background

We next describe necessary background for the rest of the paper. We start by describing the notations, follow with reminders about template attacks (in linear subspaces) and conclude with the description of the two countermeasures we study, masking and shuffling, along with attacks against them.

2.1   Notations

A random variable is expressed with a capital letter and its realisation with a lower case letter such that x is a realisation of X. When clear from the context, we use the shortcut notation of x for $X = x$. In the context of shuffling, we denote random vectors with bold letters such that $\boldsymbol{x}$ is a realisation of the random vector $\boldsymbol{X}$. Vectors can be indexed with subscripts such that x_i is the i-th element in the vector $\boldsymbol{x}$. In the context of masking, the shares are denoted with superscripts such that x^i is the i-th share of x. The measured side-channel leakages are realisations of random vectors that we always denote $\boldsymbol{l}$. We use the subscript to distinguish the leakage source. For example, $\boldsymbol{l}_x$ is the leakage generated by the manipulation of x and $\boldsymbol{l}_{\boldsymbol{x}}$ is the leakage vector originated from the vector $\boldsymbol{x}$.

2.2   Profiled Template Attacks

A profiled template attack is performed in 2 steps. The first one is called profiling phase. There, the adversary constructs an estimation of the *Probability Density Function* (PDF) of the leakages $\boldsymbol{l}$ conditioned on a secret variable x. In this work, we will use Gaussian template attacks in a linear subspace [8,22]. It is similar to Gaussian template attacks with a preliminary linear projection of the leakage samples of length n to a n'-dimensional subspace with $n' \leq n$. Formally, the adversaries we consider build a PDF estimation of the form

$$\hat{f}(\boldsymbol{l}|x) = \frac{1}{\sqrt{(2\pi)^{n'} \cdot |\boldsymbol{\Sigma}|}} \cdot \exp^{\frac{1}{2}(\boldsymbol{W}\boldsymbol{l} - \boldsymbol{\mu}_x)\boldsymbol{\Sigma}(\boldsymbol{W}\boldsymbol{l} - \boldsymbol{\mu}_x)'}, \tag{1}$$

where $\boldsymbol{l}$ is a leakage vector of length n, $\boldsymbol{W}$ is a linear projection matrix of size $n' \times n$, $\boldsymbol{\mu}_x$ a mean vector of length n' and $\boldsymbol{\Sigma}$ a covariance matrix of size $n' \times n'$. The profiling consists in estimating a projection matrix $\boldsymbol{W}$ with Linear Discriminant Analysis (LDA), the covariance matrix $\boldsymbol{\Sigma}$ and the means $\boldsymbol{\mu}_x$ for all x.[4]

The second step in profiled attacks is to leverage the PDF estimation to recover a secret realisation x from leakage observations $\boldsymbol{l}$. Namely, based on the estimated PDFs, the adversary applies Bayes's rule such that

$$\hat{p}(x|\boldsymbol{l}) = \frac{\hat{f}(\boldsymbol{l}|x)}{\sum_{x^* \in X} \hat{f}(\boldsymbol{l}|x^*)}. \tag{2}$$

Based on the observed leakage $\boldsymbol{l}$, the adversary will guess the value of x as

$$\hat{x} = \underset{x^*}{\mathrm{argmax}} \quad \hat{p}(x^*|\boldsymbol{l}). \tag{3}$$

The adversary can optionally combine multiple leakage observations in order to recover a long-term secret such as an encryption key. To do so, she calculates

---

[4] If $\boldsymbol{W}$ is the identity, this is equivalent to standard Gaussian templates attacks [8].

172 B. Udvarhelyi et al.

the likelihoods of each possible secret by multiplying the $\hat{p}(x|l)$ obtained with Eq. (2) for multiple leakages.[5]

In order to evaluate our attacks, we will use the success rate (SR) as metric [23]. It is the probability that the adversary recovers the correct value of the secret variable, which we denote as

$$SR_x = \Pr[x = \hat{x}], \tag{4}$$

where the subscript notation defines the target variable (in this case, x).

2.3 Masking Countermeasure

Masking is a popular countermeasure against side-channel attacks. It consists in randomizing the manipulated data by replacing x by d random shares x^i. The shares are uniformly distributed and ensure that $x = \sum_{i=1}^{d} x^i$. Thus, any combination of $d - 1$ shares remains independent of x which corresponds to the so-called d-probing security [17]. In order to maintain this property during the entire computation, the linear operations can be applied straightforwardly in a share-by-share fashion, which has a cost that is linear in d. Non-linear operations (e.g., multiplications) are more challenging and require to mix shares, which implies heavier overheads and randomness. Since our following investigations hold already at the encoding level, we do not detail these multiplications.

In order to attack a masked (software) implementation, an adversary can first perform an attack on each of the shares individually as in the unprotected case from Subsect. 2.2 to obtain $\hat{p}(x^i|l)$ for all the x^i. The probability of the shared secret x is then given by

$$\hat{p}(x|l) \propto \sum_{\{x^0,\ldots,x^{d-1}\} \in \mathcal{X}^{d-1}} \prod_{i=1}^{d} \hat{p}(x^i|l). \tag{5}$$

Informally, this equation shows the interest of masking that is "multiplying" the uncertainty (or noise) of the different shares. This results in the attack complexity growing exponentially in d [7]. We note that in practice, this (exponential) guarantee only holds under the assumptions that measurements are sufficiently noisy and that leakages are a linear combination of shares [12].

2.4 Shuffling Countermeasure

Shuffling is another popular side-channel countermeasure. While masking randomizes the manipulated data, shuffling randomizes the execution flow. Namely, when an algorithm is composed of independent operations, these can be executed in a random order while maintaining correctness. One typical application

---

[5] The realisation x may not always be a long term secret. For example, when targeting a block cipher, x is usually an intermediate value that is bijectively mapped to a secret key byte k with the relation $x = \text{Sbox}(k \oplus p)$, with p a public plaintext.

of shuffling is an Sbox layer applied to an input vector x of size $|x|$ (e.g., 16 for the AES). Next we detail such an application of shuffling thanks to Algorithm 1. There, the first step is to generate a random uniform permutation π over of the set $\{0, 1, \ldots, |x| - 1\}$. This is done with gen_perm$(\cdot, \cdot)$ that takes as input the permutation size together with randomness $\mathcal{R}$.[6] The second step is to iterate over all the indexes i with $0 \leq i < |x|$. At every iteration, one value $j = \pi_i$ is fetched from the permutation π. The Sbox is then applied to j-th entry of the input vector and stored at the corresponding index of the output vector.

Algorithm 1. Shuffled Sbox layer.

Input: x and randomness $\mathcal{R}$.

Output: y such that $\forall i, 0 \leq i < |x|, y_i = \mathrm{Sbox}(x_i)$

1:   $\pi \leftarrow$ gen_perm$(\mathcal{R}, |\mathsf{x}|)$
2:   **for** i in $\{0, 1, ..., |\mathsf{x}| - 1\}$ **do**
3:     $j \leftarrow \pi_i$
4:     $y_j \leftarrow \mathrm{Sbox}(x_j)$

Informally, in order to perform a side-channel attack against a shuffled implementation, an adversary has to map the leakage of x_j to the correct x_i for every iteration. If the permutation is known by the adversary, such an implementation is equivalent to an unprotected one. If it is not, the adversary is forced to perform a so called "integration" attack which sums together every l_{x_j} (resp., l_{y_j}) [28]. This has the effect of turning the leakage of a serial implementation (e.g., software) into the leakage of a parallel one (e.g., hardware) where the adversary has only access to the sum of all leakages. In practical case studies, the permutation generally leaks partially to the adversary through l_{π_i}. These leakages can be due to the generation of the permutation π itself, to its storage and loading from memory and to the addresses used to load x_j and to store y_j. We analyse template attacks exploiting such leakages in Sect. 4.

3   Re-keying + Masking

In order to break the re-keying scheme of ISAP with an SPA, the first step is to recover a maximum of information on each of the intermediate variables. To do so, the adversary is allowed to blend measurements, meaning that she can observe multiple leakages for the same secret input. The second step is to recombine this partial information on the intermediate variable to obtain a key guess [3, 18, 27]. Next, we study the case where masking is combined with re-keying.

Since our goal is to show that re-keying and masking generically combine badly, we perform our investigations in a simulated setting where the noise level is

---

[6] In this work, we assume that gen_perm$(\cdot, \cdot)$ is pre-computed and the permutation is stored in memory. It can also be generated on-the-fly if needed.

tightly controlled. This allows us to illustrate our claims in an easily interpretable context and to show that they hold even in case masking is perfectly implemented (e.g., without independence flaws). We next present the parameters selected for our simulations and then discuss the obtained results.

3.1 Simulation Settings

For our simulations, the leakage of a given variable is its Hamming weight (HW) with additional Gaussian noise (as previously considered in the simulated setting of [18]). We consider different noise levels σ_n^2, such that the Signal to Noise Ratio (SNR) of our leakages corresponds to 0.1, 1 and 10 [19]. Our simulation settings are summarized in Fig. 1, where the sensitive variable x is an 8-bit word. For the unprotected setting (see Fig. 1a), the leakage of each variable x is written as l_x. For the first-order masking (see Fig. 1b), the leakage on both shares x^1 and x^2 are respectively denoted as l_{x^1} and l_{x^2}.

We performed our experiments 1000 times to average the results. For each experiment, we used 5000 measurements of the leakages l_x, l_{x^1} and l_{x^2}.

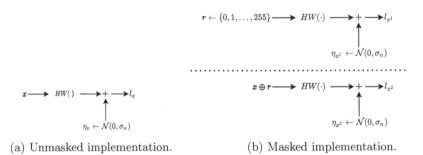

(a) Unmasked implementation.   (b) Masked implementation.

Fig. 1. Simulation settings with Hamming weight leakages and Gaussian noise.

3.2 Security Analysis

In the following, we will first detail how the adversary can blend measurements in both the masked and unmasked settings. Then, we detail what is her SR in recovering an intermediate variable x first for unmasked and then for masked implementation. We will show that their asymptotic SR are equivalent, making the effect of masking and shuffling independent for the adversary.

In order to blend independent measurements, and to exploit multiple traces that manipulate the same secret x, the adversary can use the equation

$$\hat{p}'(x|l) = \prod_{i=0}^{t-1} \hat{p}(x|l^i), \tag{6}$$

where l^i is one of the t traces to combine and l is their concatenation. In the unmasked case, the adversary can simply use Eq. (2) for $\hat{p}(x|l^i)$. In the masked case, Eq. (5) has to be used.

Unmasked Implementation. In the unmasked setting, computing Eq. (6) is equivalent to directly averaging all the l^i's. It allows recovering the mean of the leakages μ_x, which is HW(x) in our simulation since it averages the additive Gaussian noise η (see Fig. 1a). By averaging, the adversary can increase the SNR and have a tighter approximation of HW(x).

The success rate of this adversary is reported on the blue curves of Fig. 2 for different Hamming weights and SNRs. Since we focus on a SPA setting, the amount of information that can be extracted from the leakage (and therefore the SR) indeed depends on this Hamming weight. The x-axis corresponds the number of averaged traces t, the y-axis is the SR_x and the different plots are for different HW(x). We observe that: (i) the SR_x first increases with t and then saturates: this is because the noise is averaged and so the estimate of leakage mean becomes more accurate up to the point where there is no noise left; (ii) lowering the SNR (i.e., adding noise), slows down the convergence of SR_x but does not affect its asymptotic value: this is because the asymptotic value of SR_x only depends on the side-channel signal (i.e., the deterministic part of the – here Hamming weight – leakage function); (iii) this asymptotic value is larger for extreme Hamming weights (e.g., it is worth 1 for the Hamming weights 0 and 8) and lower for the intermediate Hamming weights: this is because multiple values of x then lead to the same HW, making it impossible for the adversary to recover it with probability one. More precisely, SR_x is inversely proportional to the number of values with the same HW. For example, when HW(x) = 1 (or HW(x) = 7), the asymptotic SR_x is equal to $SR_x = 1/8 = 0.125$ as we count 8 values on an 8-bit bus that have HW(x) = 1 (resp., HW(x) = 7).

Masked Implementation. We now observe that moving to a masked implementation leads to essentially similar observations. For this purpose, we first report the histograms of the two-dimensional leakages corresponding to a masked encoding with two shares in Fig. 3. The x-axis corresponds to the leakage on the first share (l_{x^1}) and the y-axis corresponds to the leakage on the second share (l_{x^2}). Each subplot is for a different Hamming weight. Clearly, we observe that just as in the unprotected case where the adversary could distinguish 9 distributions corresponding to the 9 Hamming weights, we still have 9 different distributions in the masked case. As a result, the side-channel signal that can be obtained when masking is the same as in the case of an unprotected implementation (up to the comment of Footnote 3) and this actually holds independently of the leakage function: masking amplifies the noise but does not affect the signal.

This fact is directly reflected in the orange SR_x curves of the masked implementation that are reported in Fig. 2. On the one hand, the asymptotic values are equal to the ones of the unprotected case. On the other hand, converging to this asymptotic value (i.e., extracting all the signal) will need more measurements as expected from masking security proofs [12].

As a result, attacking a combination of masking and re-keying can always proceed in two steps with additive complexities. The first one is the attack against all intermediate values x to recover partial information. The number of traces t required for each of them is impacted by masking but not the amount of sig-

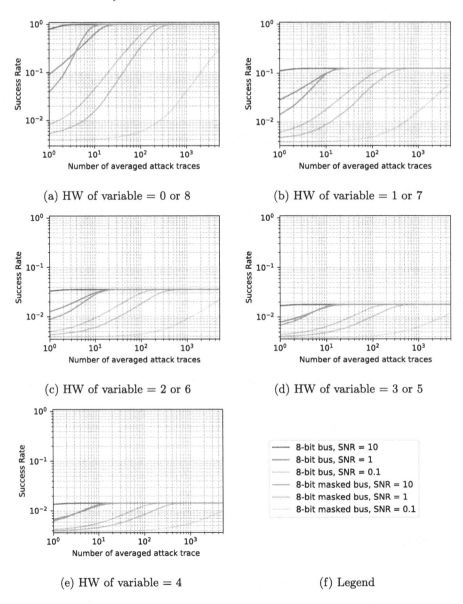

(a) HW of variable = 0 or 8

(b) HW of variable = 1 or 7

(c) HW of variable = 2 or 6

(d) HW of variable = 3 or 5

(e) HW of variable = 4

(f) Legend

Fig. 2. Success rate of a value-recovery attack against unprotected and masked implementations at different noise levels and for different target values.

nal that can be recovered asymptotically. The second one is the attack that recombines all these partial informations with SASCA, which remains unchanged. So no multiplicative effect takes place in this combination of countermeasures which can always be broken with a divide-and-conquer approach. As mentioned in introduction, this result is expected since the security of a PRF-

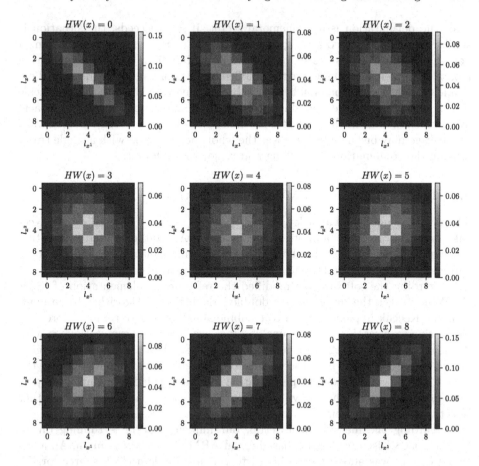

Fig. 3. Masked PDFs $f_x(l_{x^1}, l_{x^2} | x)$ for different $HW(x)$ values and SNR 10.

based re-keying scheme depends on the amount of side-channel signal that a leaking implementation provides. Therefore, a countermeasure aiming at amplifying the noise cannot be of any help to satisfy this assumption: it can only make the signal extraction more difficult, as would be provided by masking used as a stand-alone countermeasure. This conclusion holds for any number of shares.

4 Re-keying + Shuffling

Since combining re-keying with masking cannot lead to a strong (multiplicative) impact on the security of an implementation, we now consider shuffling as an alternative option. The situation is different in this case since in order to make the shuffling ineffective, the adversary has to recover the permutation π that is used to randomize the execution of the underlying operations in a single measurement. There is no possibility to combine multiple leakages for this part of the attack since the permutation is an ephemeral secret. If she succeeds, the situation is similar to an unprotected setting and the leakage of x can be averaged again. If not, the shuffling affects the shape of the leakage function, ultimately emulating a parallel implementation where the shuffled operations cannot be distinguished. While this ideal situation is not expected to happen [28], the question we tackle in this section is whether shuffling always adds some complexity to the attack. We next show that in the case of a low-noise MCU (e.g., an ARM Cortex M0), the leakage may be enough to recover the whole permutation with a single trace, making the combination of shuffling and re-keying irrelevant.

4.1   Implementation and Measurement Setup

The previous published attacks against re-keying schemes focused on the Keccak permutation [4,18] and its usage in the ISAP authenticated encryption scheme [3]. Next, we describe both our software implementation and the measurements setup that we keep as close to the one used in [3] as possible.

Regarding the software, we modified the reference implementation of ISAP [1]. We leveraged the shuffling with double indexing from Algorithm 1 and modified the Keccak implementation to combine shuffling and re-keying. More precisely, since a Keccak state contains 25 *lanes*, we generate permutations π with 25 elements and shuffle 25 independent operations.[7] The permutations are generated before the re-keying process and stored in memory. Therefore during the attack, the leakages l_{π_i} on the permutation indices π_i is independent of the permutation generation. They only result from the memory loadings and from other bijectively related leaking variables (e.g., memory addresses).

Regarding the measurement setup, our implementation is running on an STM32F0308 Discovery board, based on an ARM Cortex M0 as in [3]. An additional crystal was added to the board to provide stable a clock source for the side-channel measurements. Decoupling capacitors were also removed. We measured our traces thanks to the Tektronix CT-1 AC current probe and a Picoscope 5244D oscilloscope. The clock frequency of our MCU was set to the maximum value of 48 MHz and we sampled at 500 MSamples/s.

4.2   Leakage Modeling

In order to recover the permutation indices π_i, our adversary needs to obtain probabilities $\hat{p}(\pi_i|l)$. To do so, she uses the templates from Subsect. 2.2. More precisely, she first computes the SNR for each permutation index π_i [19]. Then, she selects the Points-Of-Interest for each of them by only considering samples above the noise floor. On average, we used $n = 450$ samples for each permutation index. For each of them, we then estimated a PDF with Eq. (1), with the number of subspace dimensions n' as a parameter.

---

[7] It is not always possible to find 25 independent operations within the Keccak round function. Yet, we will show that even in this best case (for the designer) where there are 25 independent operations, shuffling is ineffective.

4.3   Permutation Index Recovery

We first focus on an adversary attempting to recover each of the permutation indexes π_i within the permutation $\boldsymbol{\pi}$ independently, next denoted as $\mathcal{A}_1$. To do so, she uses the previously described templates. Namely, with a single leakage observation $\boldsymbol{l}$, she assumes a value $\hat{\pi}_i$ for the permutation index π_i with Eq. 3. On Fig. 4, we present the average SR_{π_i} of the first permutation within the shuffling implementation of ISAP described in Subsect. 4.1. We observe that by increasing the number of dimensions in the linear subspace n', the SR_{π_i} increases. Its maximum is of 99.18% with $n' = 15$ when all our 20,000 profiling traces are used. We can also see that the use of 5000 profiling traces and $n' = 7$ is enough to obtain the asymptotic SR values.

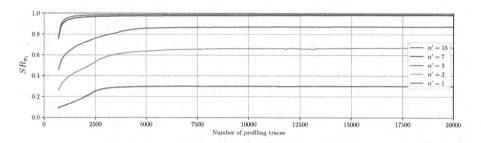

Fig. 4. Estimated SR_{π_i} for $1 \leq n' \leq 15$ and various number of profiling traces.

4.4   Full Permutation Recovery

We now discuss how to turn the information about the permutation indexes π_i into a full permutation recovery. To do so, we introduce the corresponding success rate $\mathrm{SR}_{\boldsymbol{\pi}}$ that is defined as

$$\mathrm{SR}_{\boldsymbol{\pi}} = \Pr[\pi_i = \hat{\pi}_i, \ \forall i]. \tag{7}$$

A first intuitive solution, denoted $\mathcal{A}_2$, is to derive an estimate for the full permutation $\hat{\boldsymbol{\pi}}$ by leveraging the $\mathcal{A}_1$ adversary and directly plugging the obtained π_i within $\hat{\boldsymbol{\pi}}$. The SR of these two adversaries are linked as $\mathrm{SR}_{\boldsymbol{\pi}} = \prod_i \mathrm{SR}_{\pi_i}$.

From this, we observe that even though the observed SR_{π_i} in Fig. 4 is close to 100%, it is not sufficient to recover the full permutation with overwhelming probability. Namely we have that $\mathrm{SR}_{\boldsymbol{\pi}} \approx 0.9918^{25} \approx 0.8139$.

In order to improve these results, the adversary $\mathcal{A}_3$ that we describe in Algorithm 2 takes advantage of a characteristic of permutations which are under attack. Namely, $\forall i, j$ such that $i \neq j$ we have $\pi_i \neq \pi_j$ and this constraint is not enforced with the straightforward divide & conquer adversary $\mathcal{A}_2$. A simple option to exploit this constraint is to enumerate the $\hat{\boldsymbol{\pi}}$'s from the most to the least probable, and to keep as guess the first one being a permutation.

Algorithm 2. Permutation adversary $\mathcal{A}_3$.

Input: Lists for probabilities $\hat{\mathsf{p}}(\pi_i|l)$ $\forall i$ and $\forall \pi_i$.
Output: Permutation guess $\hat{\pi}$ with $\hat{\pi}_i \neq \hat{\pi}_j$ $\forall i, j$ and $i \neq j$.

1: **for** $\hat{\pi} \leftarrow \text{Enumerate}(\hat{\mathsf{p}}(\pi_0|l), \hat{\mathsf{p}}(\pi_1|l), \ldots)$ **do**
2:     **if** $\hat{\pi}_i \neq \hat{\pi}_j$ $\forall i, j$ and $i \neq j$ **then**
3:        **return** $\hat{\pi}$

Various enumeration algorithms exist in the literature: $\mathcal{A}_3$ takes the key enumeration algorithm of [26] to instantiate Enumerate($\cdot$), which has the advantage to be optimal. The SR_π of this adversary is reported in Fig. 5 where the y-axis is $1 - \text{SR}_\pi$ in log-scale. The x-axis is the maximum number of permutations enumerated (i.e., the maximum number iterations of the loop) in Algorithm 2. The dashed horizontal lines are for a single iteration and correspond to $\mathcal{A}_2$. First, we observe that by enabling more enumeration steps, the SR increases. Second, we observe that the SR also increases with the number of dimensions n' in the template's linear subspace. Putting things together, for the best templates ($n' = 15$), we observe that SR_π starts from 0.814 if no enumeration is allowed and increases up to 0.995 when setting the maximum number of steps to 20. Enumerating more was useless in our case, since with high probability, a permutation was found with at most 20 steps. Hence, the computational cost of the enumeration is negligible compared to the rest of the attack.

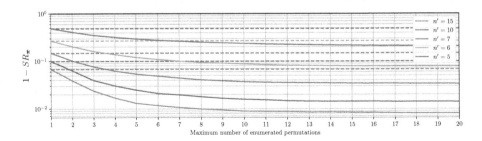

Fig. 5. $1 - \text{SR}_\pi$ for different subspace dimensions n' and as function of the enumeration depth. Dashed lines represent the value without enumeration.

Our experiments therefore illustrate that recovering a leaking permutation on the considered low-end platform is possible with low complexity. An adversary can then cancel the impact of the shuffling countermeasure, making analytical attacks against re-keying like [3,18] possible. We finally note that various other attacks could be applied against the shuffling and refer to [28] for a survey.

5   Conclusions

Single-trace attacks are an important threat against leakage-resilient PRFs such as used in the ISAP authenticated encryption scheme. A recent work of Kannwischer et al. suggested to avoid them by combining the re-keying scheme that leakage-resilient PRFs leverage with masking or shuffling. We first showed that combining such PRFs with masking is in general not a good idea as it just adds up the complexities to attack the two countermeasures separately. We then showed that combining these PRFs with shuffling, while theoretically appealing, can be practically challenging. For low-end embedded devices that are typical targets for such a combination (since they correspond to the targets of the single-trace attacks in [3,18]), implementing shuffling securely requires preventing multivariate side-channel attacks aiming at recovering the shuffling permutation (which are easy in low-noise settings). This second conclusion is not a general claim and shuffling could be effectively combined with re-keying on more noisy targets. But it shows that preventing single-trace attacks on low-end devices for which single-trace attacks are a concern is not trivial. Whether this can be achieved on the Cortex M0 device we analyzed is an interesting open question, which raises the challenge of hiding its leaky load/store operations. Overall, our results suggest that ISAP may not be the best option to ensure side-channel security on low-end devices and finds a more natural application to more parallel (possibly hardware) architectures. If aiming at exploiting a leakage-resilient PRF, leveraging the AES co-processors available on many Cortex-like chips seems more adequate, since they leak less and are faster [5,25].

Acknowledgments. François-Xavier Standaert is a senior research associate of the Belgian Fund for Scientific Research (F.R.S.-FNRS). This work has been funded in parts by the European Union through the ERC project SWORD.

References

1. ISAP code package. https://github.com/isap-lwc/isap-code-package. Accessed 10 Mar 2013
2. Belaïd, S., Grosso, V., Standaert, F.-X.: Masking and leakage-resilient primitives: one, the other(s) or both? Cryptogr. Commun. **7**(1), 163–184 (2014). https://doi.org/10.1007/s12095-014-0113-6
3. Bellizia, D., et al.: Mode-level vs. implementation-level physical security in symmetric cryptography. In: Micciancio, D., Ristenpart, T. (eds.) CRYPTO 2020. LNCS, vol. 12170, pp. 369–400. Springer, Cham (2020). https://doi.org/10.1007/978-3-030-56784-2_13
4. Bertoni, C., Daemen, J., Peeters, M., Van Assche, G.: The KECCAK reference. https://keccak.team/files/Keccak-reference-3.0.pdf
5. Bronchain, O., Momin, C., Peters, T., Standaert, F.: Improved leakage-resistant authenticated encryption based on hardware AES coprocessors. IACR Trans. Cryptogr. Hardw. Embed. Syst. **2021**(3), 641–676 (2021)
6. Bronchain, O., Standaert, F.-X.: Side-channel countermeasures' dissection and the limits of closed source security evaluations. IACR Trans. Cryptogr. Hardw. Embed. Syst. **2020**(2), 1–25 (2020)
7. Chari, S., Jutla, C.S., Rao, J.R., Rohatgi, P.: Towards sound approaches to counteract power-analysis attacks. In: Wiener, M. (ed.) CRYPTO 1999. LNCS, vol. 1666, pp. 398–412. Springer, Heidelberg (1999). https://doi.org/10.1007/3-540-48405-1_26

8. Chari, S., Rao, J.R., Rohatgi, P.: Template attacks. In: Kaliski, B.S., Koç, K., Paar, C. (eds.) CHES 2002. LNCS, vol. 2523, pp. 13–28. Springer, Heidelberg (2003). https://doi.org/10.1007/3-540-36400-5_3

9. Dobraunig, C., et al.: ISAP v2.0. IACR Trans. Symmetric Cryptol. **2020**(S1), 390–416 (2020)

10. Dobraunig, C., Eichlseder, M., Mangard, S., Mendel, F., Unterluggauer, T.: ISAP - towards side-channel secure authenticated encryption. IACR Trans. Symmetric Cryptol. **2017**(1), 80–105 (2017)

11. Dodis, Y., Pietrzak, K.: Leakage-resilient pseudorandom functions and side-channel attacks on Feistel networks. In: Rabin, T. (ed.) CRYPTO 2010. LNCS, vol. 6223, pp. 21–40. Springer, Heidelberg (2010). https://doi.org/10.1007/978-3-642-14623-7_2

12. Duc, A., Faust, S., Standaert, F.-X.: Making masking security proofs concrete. In: Oswald, E., Fischlin, M. (eds.) EUROCRYPT 2015. LNCS, vol. 9056, pp. 401–429. Springer, Heidelberg (2015). https://doi.org/10.1007/978-3-662-46800-5_16

13. Faust, S., Pietrzak, K., Schipper, J.: Practical leakage-resilient symmetric cryptography. In: Prouff, E., Schaumont, P. (eds.) CHES 2012. LNCS, vol. 7428, pp. 213–232. Springer, Heidelberg (2012). https://doi.org/10.1007/978-3-642-33027-8_13

14. Groß, H., Schaffenrath, D., Mangard, S.: Higher-order side-channel protected implementations of KECCAK. In: DSD, pp. 205–212. IEEE Computer Society (2017)

15. Grosso, Vincent, Poussier, Romain, Standaert, François-Xavier., Gaspar, Lubos: Combining leakage-resilient PRFs and shuffling. In: Joye, Marc, Moradi, Amir (eds.) CARDIS 2014. LNCS, vol. 8968, pp. 122–136. Springer, Cham (2015). https://doi.org/10.1007/978-3-319-16763-3_8

16. Herbst, C., Oswald, E., Mangard, S.: An AES smart card implementation resistant to power analysis attacks. In: Zhou, J., Yung, M., Bao, F. (eds.) ACNS 2006. LNCS, vol. 3989, pp. 239–252. Springer, Heidelberg (2006). https://doi.org/10.1007/11767480_16

17. Ishai, Y., Sahai, A., Wagner, D.: Private circuits: securing hardware against probing attacks. In: Boneh, D. (ed.) CRYPTO 2003. LNCS, vol. 2729, pp. 463–481. Springer, Heidelberg (2003). https://doi.org/10.1007/978-3-540-45146-4_27

18. Kannwischer, M.J., Pessl, P., Primas, R.: Single-trace attacks on Keccak. IACR Trans. Cryptogr. Hardw. Embed. Syst. **2020**(3), 243–268 (2020)

19. Mangard, S.: Hardware countermeasures against DPA – a statistical analysis of their effectiveness. In: Okamoto, T. (ed.) CT-RSA 2004. LNCS, vol. 2964, pp. 222–235. Springer, Heidelberg (2004). https://doi.org/10.1007/978-3-540-24660-2_18

20. Pereira, O., Standaert, F., Vivek, S.: Leakage-resilient authentication and encryption from symmetric cryptographic primitives. In: CCS, pp. 96–108. ACM (2015)

21. Rivain, M., Prouff, E., Doget, J.: Higher-order masking and shuffling for software implementations of block ciphers. In: Clavier, C., Gaj, K. (eds.) CHES 2009. LNCS, vol. 5747, pp. 171–188. Springer, Heidelberg (2009). https://doi.org/10.1007/978-3-642-04138-9_13

22. Standaert, F.-X., Archambeau, C.: Using subspace-based template attacks to compare and combine power and electromagnetic information leakages. In: Oswald, E., Rohatgi, P. (eds.) CHES 2008. LNCS, vol. 5154, pp. 411–425. Springer, Heidelberg (2008). https://doi.org/10.1007/978-3-540-85053-3_26

23. Standaert, F.-X., Malkin, T.G., Yung, M.: A unified framework for the analysis of side-channel key recovery attacks. In: Joux, A. (ed.) EUROCRYPT 2009. LNCS, vol. 5479, pp. 443–461. Springer, Heidelberg (2009). https://doi.org/10.1007/978-3-642-01001-9_26

24. Standaert, F.X., Pereira, O., Yu, Y., Quisquater, J.J., Yung, M., Oswald, E.: Leakage resilient cryptography in practice. In: Sadeghi, A.R., Naccache, D. (eds.) Towards Hardware-Intrinsic Security. Information Security and Cryptography, pp. 99–134. Springer, Heidelberg (2010). https://doi.org/10.1007/978-3-642-14452-3_5

25. Unterstein, F., Schink, M., Schamberger, T., Tebelmann, L., Ilg, M., Heyszl, J.: Retrofitting leakage resilient authenticated encryption to microcontrollers. IACR Trans. Cryptogr. Hardw. Embed. Syst. **2020**(4), 365–388 (2020)

26. Veyrat-Charvillon, N., Gérard, B., Renauld, M., Standaert, F.-X.: An optimal key enumeration algorithm and its application to side-channel attacks. In: Knudsen, L.R., Wu, H. (eds.) SAC 2012. LNCS, vol. 7707, pp. 390–406. Springer, Heidelberg (2013). https://doi.org/10.1007/978-3-642-35999-6_25

27. Veyrat-Charvillon, N., Gérard, B., Standaert, F.-X.: Soft analytical side-channel attacks. In: Sarkar, P., Iwata, T. (eds.) ASIACRYPT 2014. LNCS, vol. 8873, pp. 282–296. Springer, Heidelberg (2014). https://doi.org/10.1007/978-3-662-45611-8_15

28. Veyrat-Charvillon, N., Medwed, M., Kerckhof, S., Standaert, F.-X.: Shuffling against side-channel attacks: a comprehensive study with cautionary note. In: Wang, X., Sako, K. (eds.) ASIACRYPT 2012. LNCS, vol. 7658, pp. 740–757. Springer, Heidelberg (2012). https://doi.org/10.1007/978-3-642-34961-4_44

White-Box ECDSA: Challenges and Existing Solutions

Emmanuelle Dottax, Christophe Giraud, and Agathe Houzelot$^{(\boxtimes)}$

IDEMIA, Cryptography and Security Labs, Pessac, France
{emmanuelle.dottax,christophe.giraud,agathe.houzelot}@idemia.com

Abstract. White-box cryptography aims to protect secret keys when an algorithm is to be executed in an exposed environment, possibly fully controlled by an attacker. While this field enjoys a significant interest from researchers, a large majority of works focus on block ciphers, and asymmetric cryptography has been very little studied to date. This is in contrast with actual needs and usages by the industry. Indeed, most commercial white-box solutions offer asymmetric cryptography, and most notably the ECDSA signature. This paper provides a deeper comprehension on the challenges of such white-box ECDSA implementations. In particular, we highlight the existence of particularly devastating attacks, induced for instance by the lack of a reliable source of randomness in the white-box context. We also give an insight into the actual strategies for securing products in the field. To this end, we analyse the sole source of information – which is the patents filled by companies – and discuss how they respond to existing threats.

Keywords: White-box cryptography · ECDSA · Passive analysis · Active analysis

1 Introduction

Cryptography can be defined as the set of techniques enabling secure communication. For example, it is used to ensure that the information contained in a message is revealed only to those intended to have access to it. Cryptographic algorithms are designed to be resistant in the so-called *black-box* attack model, where attackers have only access to the inputs/outputs of the algorithm. However in practice, algorithms are rarely executed in a completely isolated environment and additional information is often leaked. Typically, cryptographic algorithms are widely implemented on embedded modules such as smart cards. In such environments, the attacker can perform passive and active analysis during the execution of the algorithm by using side-channel leakages [43,44] and physical disturbances [5,33] respectively. In such a *grey-box* model, specific countermeasures are implemented to counteract these attacks [12,22,41].

Nowadays, cryptographic algorithms tend to be implemented in even more exposed environments. Indeed, today's trend to increase user experience leads to

S. Bhasin and F. De Santis (Eds.): COSADE 2021, LNCS 12910, pp. 184–201, 2021.
https://doi.org/10.1007/978-3-030-89915-8_9

the deployment of security-related applications – like mobile payment, crypto-currency wallets, digital identity, etc. – in a wide variety of devices: laptops, mobile phones and diverse wearables. These devices offer different levels of security that cannot be controlled by application providers. In addition, they are "open" by nature, i.e. they provide the user with the opportunity to install any kind of applications. In a large majority of cases, this means one cannot completely eliminate the possibility that an attacker gains full control over the sensitive application. If so, he can potentially extract and analyse the code, scan the memory to recover manipulated variables, tamper the application execution, etc. Therefore, secret keys or other private data could be easily recovered if no specific countermeasures are implemented. The art of providing secure cryptographic functionalities in such an open environment is called *White-Box Cryptography* (WBC). It is the cornerstone of applications where a cryptographic key is used to protect assets, such as in Digital Rights Management (DRM) for example.

At the beginning of the 2000's, researchers suggested white-box solutions for symmetric cryptosystems such as DES and AES. Unfortunately, all published propositions [7,13,20,21,42,64] have been broken [8,24,25,34,45,48,63]. To stimulate the research, the WhibOx contests, a series of white-box competitions, have been organized as part of the CHES workshops. The first two contests in 2017 and 2019 [17,18] focused on implementing AES, and with 100 challenges and 900 breaks, tremendous interest for WBC was demonstrated since the first edition.

Nowadays, there is a growing need for white-box implementations of asymmetric cryptosystems, especially the Elliptic Curve Digital Signature Algorithm (ECDSA) [31] since it is used in many protocols (for instance in major crypto-currencies such as Bitcoin and Ethereum). This is illustrated by the last WhibOx contest which is targeting ECDSA implementations and gathers more than 50 challenges and 400 breaks only 10 days after its launch in May 2021 [19]. In addition, one can see that most WBC solutions available on the market [23,27,36,37,50,52,59,62] indeed propose the ECDSA signature algorithm as a service. However, when looking for publications on this topic in the literature, we found no relevant work: [4,29,65,66] target various asymmetric schemes but not ECDSA, and [14] operates in a specific context only (access to a server is required during signature computation). The documentation of above-mentioned industrial products also give no details about the techniques used to protect these implementations. The only option left to gain some information on the actual design of these products is thus to look for patents on this subject.

In this article, we first make a survey of known attack paths against ECDSA implementations and study how they extend in the white-box model. This allows us to identify powerful passive and active attacks that can be performed in this context. Then, we propose an overview of the most interesting techniques we have found in patents allowing one to counteract these attacks. In particular, we will assess the security of suggested methods against the attacks previously identified. Obviously, a patent is not as rigorous as a scientific article but we think that such information gives some interesting insight on the current advances in this field from a practical point of view.

The rest of this paper is organized as follows. In Sect. 2 we present the state-of-the-art attacks on ECDSA implementations in the grey-box model. In Sect. 3, we specify the objectives and capabilities of an attacker in the white-box model and we present the main attacks which can be mounted on an ECDSA implementation in this context. Section 4 exhibits the most efficient methods we found in public patents to reinforce the security of white-box ECDSA implementations. We discuss their characteristics and relevance with respect to different attacker models, and show in which conditions these proposals can be bypassed. Finally, Sect. 5 concludes this paper.

2   Grey-Box Inherited Attacks

ECDSA is a public key signature algorithm introduced in 1992 by Vanstone as a variant of DSA [60]. The parameters are a prime number q, an elliptic curve E over $\mathbb{F}_q$, a point G of prime order n and a cryptographic hash function H. The secret key d is randomly drawn from $[\![1, n-1]\!]$ and the public key consists of the point $Q = [d]G$ where $[d]G$ corresponds to the scalar multiplication of the point G by the scalar d. The ECDSA signature is described in Algorithm 1.

Algorithm 1: ECDSA signature

Input   : the message m
Output: the signature (r, s)

1 $e \leftarrow H(m)$
2 $k \xleftarrow{\$} [\![1, n-1]\!]$
3 $R = (x_R, y_R) \leftarrow [k]G$
4 $r \leftarrow x_R \bmod n$
5 $s \leftarrow k^{-1}(e + rd) \bmod n$
6 **if** $r = 0$ *or* $s = 0$ **then**
7 | Go to step 1
8 **end**
9 Return (r, s)

As discussed in [30], the security of this scheme is related to the difficulty of the Elliptic Curve Discrete Logarithm Problem (ECDLP), i.e. the difficulty of retrieving the scalar d from the points G and $Q = [d]G$. It also applies to the ephemeral point R since the knowledge of the scalar k generated in Step 2 of Algorithm 1 (also referred to as the *nonce*) allows an attacker to recover the private key d from the signature (r, s). To ensure that the ECDLP is diffi-cult to solve, there are several standards to define elliptic curves for a general cryptographic use, e.g. [31, 39, 46, 58].

However, there is a gap between the security of ECDSA in theory and the one of practical ECDSA implementations. If straightforwardly implemented, we will see in the following how the private key d can be easily recovered in the grey-box model by using passive or active analysis.

2.1   Passive Analysis

Unprotected implementations may leak information on the nonce k through side-channel analysis. The scalar multiplication is a target of choice as shown in [22] where it is explained that a single execution trace may lead to the full recovery of k. Countermeasures against these attacks are well known (e.g. use of regular algorithms [54]) but they may not be efficient against other kinds of side channel attacks. For instance, profiled analysis can be used to recover some bits of several nonces during several ECDSA executions [47]. This allows the generation of a system of equations that can be solved using lattice-based algorithms [11,38] or Bleichenbacher's Fourier analysis-based attacks [3]. To protect the implementations against these attacks, randomization techniques may be used on the scalar or on the point representation [12,22,41].

The scalar multiplication is not the only operation vulnerable to passive analysis during ECDSA execution. For instance, when the modular multiplication $rd \bmod n$ is computed during Step 5 of Algorithm 1, it may be possible to mount a side-channel analysis that directly targets the key d. Similarly, the leakages during the addition between e and rd can lead the attacker to obtain information on d. A way to prevent this is to mask the key during the computations [44].

2.2   Active Analysis

Disturbing a device executing an ECDSA signature may lead to the recovery of the private key d in several ways. The most obvious attack is to force the use of a weak elliptic curve during the scalar multiplication, that is a curve for which the discrete logarithm problem is easy to solve. To reach this goal, one can disturb the curve parameters, as for instance in [6]. Also, in some contexts, the curve parameters are given as input to the algorithm. It may thus be possible for an attacker to force the use of a weak curve without having to disturb the execution. To prevent such attacks, the consistency and/or the validity of all parameters must be checked before and after the computation.

Another possibility to compute the private key d consists in recovering two signatures of different messages m_1 and m_2 using the same nonce [61]. Indeed, the knowledge of $s_1 \equiv k^{-1}(e_1 + rd) \bmod n$ and $s_2 \equiv k^{-1}(e_2 + rd) \bmod n$, with $e_1 = H(m_1)$ and $e_2 = H(m_2)$, allows the recovery of k and thus d:

$$(e_1 - e_2)(s_1 - s_2)^{-1} \equiv (e_1 - e_2)(k^{-1}(e_1 - e_2))^{-1} \equiv k \bmod n. \qquad (1)$$

In the context of active analysis, the attacker can also force the algorithm to use a biased nonce, for instance by stucking a word of k at zero during several executions of the scalar multiplication. As explained in Sect. 2.1, the corresponding signatures can be used to obtain information on the key d using lattice-based algorithms.

The nonce k is not the only target of active analysis. Indeed, by flipping one bit of d during the computation of rd, it was shown in [28] that one can recover information on d by using the corresponding faulty signature. This attack was later extended in [32] to the exploitation of faults on one byte of d. A countermeasure against these fault attacks consists in verifying the integrity of d and of the computation of rd.

In this section, we gave an overview of the various attack paths on ECDSA implementations in the grey-box model. In the next one, we will see that the white-box context induces an even more powerful attacker model that comes with new threats.

3   White-Box Main Challenges

By nature, white-box implementations offer much more possibilities to an attacker. Besides trying to extract the key, he can try to lift the program to execute it on another device. Such a method, called *code lifting*, is sometimes sufficient to jeopardize the security of the application. He can also reverse the program to build the inverse functionality, which can be useful in some cases (e.g. encryption of private data). The expected security properties hence depend on the use-case.

The first white-box designs [20,21] have been proposed by Chow et al. in a DRM context but the security goals to achieve were not formally stated. A first attempt towards a theoretical model was proposed in 2009 by Saxena et al. in [55]. Later, Delerable et al. defined security notions that might be desired [26]: *unbreakability* (preventing key extraction), *one-wayness* (impossibility to inverse the cryptographic functionality), *incompressibility of programs* (force usage of a large program to limit possibilities to store and exchange it) and *traceability of programs* (a program is traceable if it is possible to identify the original implementation from illegal copies, even transformed).

As mentioned in the introduction, nowadays we find increasingly wide-ranging use-cases for WBC. In [1], Bock examines security notions especially in the case of mobile payment. In this context, traceability seems irrelevant as the legitimate user is the victim. Also, incompressibility is of poor interest given that applications on mobile phones are expected to be relatively compact and efficient (in particular for contactless operations). Nevertheless, code lifting is a real threat. Techniques for hardware and/or application *binding* [2] shall be used to prevent it. However, it seems reasonable to assume that, given enough time and energy, an attacker will succeed in bypassing those countermeasures. We shall thus expect that even in this case, a well designed white-box resists key extraction.

When implementing ECDSA in a white-box context, the grey-box attacks mentioned in Sect. 2 must be prevented, as they can be used to break a white-box implementation. In addition, as the white-box model enlarges the attack surface, more powerful attacks are available. They are presented in the rest of this section.

3.1 Passive Analysis

One of the main objectives when designing a white-box is to protect it against attackers having access to the memory. Techniques to prevent secret data from appearing in plain were introduced by Chow *et al.* in [21]. The principle is first to embed the key value into the algorithm, and then to introduce carefully crafted *encodings*. Informally, an operation *op* is replaced by $f^{-1} \circ op \circ f'$, where f and f' are bijections called respectively *input* and *output encodings*. The resulting function is implemented as a look-up table, thus preventing access to the function *op* and to the embedded key value. This technique may be used to conceal the secret values k and d of ECDSA. As it implies the use of a lot of memory, applying such a method on an operation as complex as a scalar multiplication while staying efficient becomes a real challenge. This explains the fact that white-box designers try to find out other ways to protect this step of ECDSA, as we shall see in Sect. 4.

As mentioned in Sect. 2, it is possible to extract secret values by observing side-channel leakages during the execution of a cryptographic algorithm. The white-box context offers a new channel that adds to the arsenal of the attacker: software execution traces [10]. Indeed, by instrumenting the binary, one can record traces of all accessed addresses and data over time. This is much more efficient than power or electromagnetic analysis for instance, as the measurements are completely noiseless. Possible countermeasures include the addition of random delays to compromise traces alignment, data masking and data splitting.

3.2 Active Analysis

A key issue faced by white-box designers is the impossibility to rely on a source of randomness. Indeed in the white-box model, such a source could be simply fixed to a constant value by the attacker. Such a disability reduces the efficiency of the countermeasures mentioned in the previous section but there are other disastrous consequences in the case of an ECDSA implementation. Indeed, disabling the source of randomness allows the following attack.

Fixing the Nonce. This attack consists in forcing the use of the same nonce during the signatures of two different messages. It allows the recovery of k by using (1). A natural solution is to generate the nonce from the only source of randomness the white-box has: its input, that is the hash of the message. Nevertheless, this solution allows the following two fault attacks.

Modifying the Hash. Let us assume that we generate the nonce k from the hash e of the message, i.e. we implement a function f unknown to the attacker such that $k = f(e)$. As the value e is used again during the computation of s, an attacker could run a "normal" execution of the algorithm on a message m, obtaining a signature $s \equiv k^{-1}(e + rd) \bmod n$, and then run it again on the same message, modifying e into $\tilde{e}$ just after the computation of k. The corresponding faulty signature $\tilde{s}$ will thus be equal to $k^{-1}(\tilde{e} + rd)$ since the same hash e was used for the computation of the nonce. The value k can thus be computed from the correct/faulty signatures and hashes:

$$(e - \tilde{e})(s - \tilde{s})^{-1} \equiv (e - \tilde{e})(k^{-1}(e - \tilde{e}))^{-1} \equiv k \bmod n. \tag{2}$$

The secret key d can then be recovered from k, r and s.

Modifying the First Part of the Signature. An adversary could also sign the same message m twice and disturb the computation of r the second time. Signing the same message twice implies using the same nonce twice, so the faulty signature is $\tilde{s} \equiv k^{-1}(e + \tilde{r}d) \bmod n$. The values of r and $\tilde{r}$ are known to the attacker since they are returned by the algorithm as the first part of the signature. Therefore, some secret information can be deduced:

$$(r - \tilde{r})(s - \tilde{s})^{-1} \equiv (r - \tilde{r})(k^{-1}d(r - \tilde{r}))^{-1} \equiv kd^{-1} \bmod n. \tag{3}$$

The adversary can then compute

$$e(kd^{-1}s - r)^{-1} \equiv d \bmod n. \tag{4}$$

While the attack on the first part of the signature can be performed by any adversary able to disturb the computation, there is a restriction for the attack on the hash: the attacker must know the result of his fault, i.e. the value of $\tilde{e}$. In both cases, the modifications can be anything from a bit flip to the change of e (resp. r) into a completely different value.

As discussed previously, no solution can be found in the literature to counteract these attacks. The patents registered by companies are therefore the only source of public information. In the next section, we study them in detail and try to underline which attacks they prevent (or not).

4   Existing Solutions

There is currently one published paper presenting an ECDSA white-box design [66], but it assumes having access to online services during the signature. Such a model is very restrictive and we rather consider generic white-boxes in the following.

In the last decade, several companies registered patents exposing different techniques to protect white-box ECDSA implementations. Of course, a patent is not comparable to a published article: some important details might be omitted and all techniques to reach overall security may not be found in the same patent. Also, the exact context and security model are usually not explained, which makes difficult the evaluation of the suggested techniques. However, these documents still give valuable information on methods implemented in the field. After a careful research, we found a dozen of such documents and studied them in detail before selecting the six most interesting patents in our context [9,16,35,49,53,56]. In this section, we expose the main ideas to counteract the different attacks discussed in Sect. 2 and 3.

In the white-box context, two phases can be distinguished. First, the so-called *offline* phase where secret values – as keys or masks – are generated and embedded in corresponding white-box programs. After deployment on the devices, the second phase consists in executing these programs to perform the cryptographic operation. In the following, we use the notation $WB[sk]$ to refer to a white-box program WB embedding a secret sk.

4.1   Countermeasures Against Passive Attacks

As discussed in Sect. 3, the traditional protection against passive attacks in the white-box model is the use of encodings. In the following, we assume all computations and intermediate variables manipulated by a white-box $WB[sk]$ are encoded, providing protection for the secret sk against all passive attacks we have seen. Ideally, the ECDSA implementation would consist of one such white-box taking as input the hash and computing the signature, but this is completely impractical (about 2^{232} GB for 256-bit inputs). Instead, different white-boxes are used to perform small groups of operations. For instance, the modular operations executed during the computation of s are usually included inside a white-box [16,49,53,56]. However, performing complex operations such as the scalar multiplication on encoded values can be very costly in terms of memory. This explains why encodings are replaced by masking techniques when possible. Homomorphic encryption is also used as another type of protection against passive attacks. It allows to perform operations on ciphertexts without revealing the plain values. In the following, we show how these techniques are used to protect white-box implementations and we expose their advantages and drawbacks.

Masking. The two main use-cases for masking techniques are the scalar multiplication and the inversion of k since they are very complex operations.

For instance in [49], the base point P and the secret key d are both multiplicatively masked by a random value t selected offline. Using the point $T = [t^{-1}]P$ for the scalar multiplication instead of P implies computing an ECDSA signature using the nonce kt^{-1}. It follows that k is not a sensitive value anymore since t is secret. Indeed, the attacker cannot recover t from the information available, that is a white-box embedding it and T. Finally, the modified key $\delta \equiv dt \bmod n$ is used instead of d to maintain the consistency of the signature. The computation of s is performed partly by a white-box $WB[\delta, t]$ computing $te + \delta r$ from e and r as shown in Algorithm 2.

Algorithm 2: ECDSA signature [49]

Input : the message m
Output: the signature (r, s)

// Precomputations:

1 $t \xleftarrow{\$} [\![1, n-1]\!]$
2 $T \leftarrow [t^{-1}]P$
3 $\delta \leftarrow dt$

// Signature:

4 $e \leftarrow H(m)$

5 $k \xleftarrow{\$} [\![1, n-1]\!]$
6 $R = (x_R, y_R) \leftarrow [k]T$
7 $r \leftarrow x_R \bmod n$
8 $u \leftarrow WB[\delta, t](r, e)$ // $u = te + tdr \bmod n$
9 $s \leftarrow k^{-1}u \bmod n$ // $s = k^{-1}t(e + dr) \bmod n$
10 **if** $r = 0$ *or* $s = 0$ **then**
11 | Go to step 5
12 **end**
13 Return (r, s)

Another possibility to protect the scalar multiplication against passive attacks is to use a white box taking the hash as input and computing $k + t$, with t a random mask that can be generated offline [56] or derived from e [53]. In such a case, R can be computed as $R = [k + t]P - T$ with $T = [t]P$ precomputed. However, the nonce also needs to be inverted for the computation of s and this is not easily feasible from $(k + t)^{-1}$. A common technique to overcome this problem is to use a second white-box that computes k from e again and masks it multiplicatively [9,53,56]. The result can be inverted in plain and multiplied again by the mask to give k^{-1}. An example of such an approach is given in [56] where the constant t and the corresponding point $T = [t]P$ are selected offline together with two symmetric encryption keys sk and sk'. Two white-boxes allow then to compute two different masked versions of k and a last one is used for the computation of s. If we denote by Enc_{sk} the encryption function with key sk then the white-boxes implement the following functions:

- $WB_0[sk, t](e) = Enc_{sk}(e) + t = k + t$.
- $WB_1[sk, sk'](e) = Enc_{sk}(e)Enc_{sk'}(e) = kk'$.
- $WB_2[sk', d](e, r, (kk')^{-1}) = Enc_{sk'}(e)(kk')^{-1}(e + rd) = k^{-1}(e + rd)$.

Algorithm 3 shows the different steps of this method.

Masking indeed prevents an attacker from directly reading the sensitive values in memory or performing a side-channel attack. However, one has to be careful with the implementation so that the mask cannot be recovered. In some cases, it may be difficult to get rid of it without revealing any secret information. Some operations, such as the ones used for the computation of s, may be difficult to secure. Masking is thus often combined with encodings [49,53,56].

Algorithm 3: ECDSA signature [56]

Input : the message m
Output: the signature (r, s)

// Precomputations:

1 $t \xleftarrow{\$} [\![1, n-1]\!]$
2 $T \leftarrow [t]P$
3 $(sk, sk') \xleftarrow{\$} [0, 2^{64} - 1]^2$

// Signature:

4 $e \leftarrow H(m)$
5 $v \leftarrow WB_0[sk, t](e)$ // $v = k + t$
6 $R \leftarrow [v]P - T$ // $R = [k]P$
7 $r \leftarrow x_R \bmod n$
8 $\hat{k} \leftarrow WB_1[sk, sk'](e)$ // $\hat{k} = kk'$
9 $\hat{k}_{inv} \leftarrow \hat{k}^{-1} \bmod n$ // $\hat{k}_{inv} = (kk')^{-1}$
10 $s \leftarrow WB_2[sk', d](e, r, \hat{k}_{inv})$ // $s = k^{-1}(e + dr)$
11 **if** $r = 0$ *or* $s = 0$ **then**
12 | Go to step 4
13 **end**
14 Return (r, s)

The later implies the use of a lot of memory and all the published white-box implementations relying on this technique have been broken. Therefore, some patents propose another idea to protect data against passive attacks: the use of homomorphic encryption. While it seems to be the safest solution, we will see that it also has some drawbacks.

Homomorphic Encryption. This type of encryption allows to perform some computations directly on encrypted data without having to decrypt it first. The supported operations depend on the encryption scheme, it can be both addition and multiplication or only one of them.

In the white-box context, sensitive data can be encrypted offline and never appear in plain. For instance, the authors of [35] use a pool of pre-encrypted randoms to compute the nonce, and none of these values is ever decrypted. Offline, scalars $(k_{i,0}, k_{i,1})$ are drawn for $1 \leq i \leq b$, b being the maximum bit length of a message, and the corresponding $(R_{i,0}, R_{i,1}) = ([k_{i,0}]P, [k_{i,1}]P)$ are computed. The scalars $(k_{i,0}, k_{i,1})$ are then encrypted, resulting in couples $(c_{i,0}, c_{i,1})$ that are stored on the device together with the generated points $(R_{i,0}, R_{i,1})$. The first step of the signature is the computation of $R = [k]P$ and c, the encrypted value of the nonce. If the value of the i-th bit of the message is denoted by m_i, the computations are as follows:

$$c = \sum_{i=1}^{b} c_{i,m_i} \text{ and } R = \sum_{i=1}^{b} R_{i,m_i}. \tag{5}$$

The way the second part of the signature is computed from c, r and e is not detailed. It is only mentioned that the encrypted value of s is obtained and not decrypted before being sent with r to the verifier, so the verification algorithm is not standard. This is the main drawback of using homomorphic encryption: one has to choose between using a decryption white-box or not respecting the standard by returning an encrypted value.

In [9], the first option is chosen. Paillier's homomorphic encryption [51], denoted by Enc, is used to protect sensitive data during computations and a decryption white-box allows the recovery of s in plain at the end of the algorithm. This white-box may be very costly and stands against one of the interests of homomorphic encryption, that is to avoid the use of look-up tables. Furthermore, it induces a security issue: an attacker could apply it on encrypted sensitive variables to recover their plain values. Another protection layer must thus be added. The inventors decided to mask the variables before their encryption. For instance, the value $Enc(dt)$ is used instead of $Enc(d)$ for the computation of s, with t a random mask that will be removed later on. This way, an adversary trying to apply the decryption white-box to $Enc(dt)$ would only recover the masked value of the key.

4.2   Countermeasures Against Active Attacks

We showed in Sect. 3 that a white-box implementation of ECDSA is particularly vulnerable to fault attacks. The usual countermeasures implemented for the grey-box model rely on redundancy and consistency checking. These techniques can also be used in the white-box model even if they are by essence memory consuming. An alternative is to link several values by encoding them together so that disturbing one of them also modifies the others with a high probability. The last option is to precompute the sensitive variables offline and embed them inside a white-box.

Redundancy and Checks of Consistency. A first fault attack that can be performed on ECDSA white-boxes consists in forcing the use of the same nonce twice. The fault can be induced either directly on k or on e when the nonce is computed from the hash, as shown in (2). An idea to reinforce the security against this attack is exposed in Algorithm 3 [56]. The white-box WB_1 does not take k as input but it computes it again from e. Similarly, WB_2 verifies the value $\hat{k}_{inv} = (kk')^{-1} \bmod n$ by deriving k and k' again and verifying $\hat{k}_{inv}kk' \equiv 1 \bmod n$. Hence, the fault on k has to be induced several times to keep the consistency between the variables. Regarding the fault on the hash, the difficulty of the attack depends on the implementation of WB_2. The modification has to occur inside the white-box and thus on encoded variables. In such a case, the adversary should not be able to recover the erroneous hash that he needs to perform the attack.

Another protection presented in [56] consists in storing a list of all messages that have been signed. This way, the attack on e cannot be performed since WB_0 would detect that the hash has already been used. However, this protection is not efficient against an adversary controlling the memory. Indeed, the adversary would only have to erase parts of the list or to restore the previous state of the white-box to be able to perform his attack.

Finally, the fault on the first part of the signature presented in (3) seems to be the most difficult to prevent. Indeed, this value necessarily appears in plain if the scalar multiplication is not encoded. Moreover, r is returned by the algorithm so the attacker always knows the result of the fault he induced. In [56], the inventors try to check the consistency of R without computing it again inside a white-box. They suggest two techniques: the secure delegation of calculus to a third party [15] and the technique of "small moduli". The later is not described in the patent but we assume that it is a reference to Shamir's method exposed in [40,57]. The idea would consist in computing $R = (x_R \bmod \rho n, y_R \bmod \rho n)$ in $\mathbb{Z}/\rho n\mathbb{Z}$ instead of $\mathbb{Z}/n\mathbb{Z}$ and in using a white-box to compute it again in $\mathbb{Z}/\rho\mathbb{Z}$ for ρ a small random. The white-box then checks the integrity of R by computing $(x_R \bmod \rho, y_R \bmod \rho)$ and by comparing it with the second computation. This technique is usually used in the grey-box context as a countermeasure against fault attacks. However in the white-box context, the adversary may be able to control the fault he induces on the first computation of R in $\mathbb{Z}/\rho n\mathbb{Z}$. He could thus add a multiple of ρ to its coordinates and the resulting faulty point would pass the verification. Hence, this technique prevents the use of random faults on R but it could still be bypassed. As for delegation of calculus to a third party, it may not be possible in some contexts.

Joint Encodings. The idea of joint encodings is to link several values together. For instance, if the encodings used in the scheme are bijections applied to bytes, one can jointly encode variables a and b by applying the bijections on a nibble of a concatenated with a nibble of b. This way, it shall be difficult for an adversary to modify a without disturbing b or to know the faulty results $\tilde{a}$ and $\tilde{b}$.

For instance, joint encodings can be used as described in [53]. Let $\alpha \geq 2$ be a security parameter. Offline, a function f and multiple functions g_i (for $0 \leq i \leq 2\alpha - 1$) are chosen. White-boxes WB_A^i and WB_B^j are created for $0 \leq i \leq 2\alpha - 1$ and $0 \leq j \leq \alpha - 1$. They takes e as input and return jointly encoded versions of $(f(e), g_i(e)) = (k, e_i)$ and $(g_{2j}(e), g_{2j+1}(e)) = (e_{2j}, e_{2j+1})$ respectively. At execution time, the white-boxes WB_A^i and WB_B^j are used to obtain two sets A and B. If we denote by $\overline{(x, y)}$ the joint encoding of (x, y), these sets can be defined as:

$$A = \{\overline{(k, e_i)}\}_i \text{ for } 0 \leq i \leq 2\alpha - 1,$$
$$B = \{\overline{(e_{2j}, e_{2j+1})}\}_j \text{ for } 0 \leq j \leq \alpha - 1. \tag{6}$$

Then, the set A is used to compute an encoded version of the variable $a = k + \sum_{i=0}^{2\alpha-1} c_i e_i$, with c_i being constants drawn offline. The point $[a]P = R + [\sum_{i=0}^{2\alpha-1} c_i e_i]P$ is then computed and we would like to extract R from it. To do so, the point $[\sum_{i=0}^{2\alpha-1} c_i e_i]P$ is recovered from the set B and is subtracted from aP. The computation of s is performed similarly to the scalar multiplication: two white-boxes are used to compute two distinct sets containing jointly encoded values depending on the nonce k and the hash e. These sets are then used separately to compute variables which, added together, give the value of s. Again, this scheme seems quite costly since many white-boxes have to be implemented. The technique of joint encodings in itself can be memory consuming since an operation requiring only k as input would take $\overline{(k, e_i)}$ instead. But depending on the context, it can be more advantageous than computing the nonce multiple times.

Offline r Computations. Since it is both difficult and costly to implement protections against faults on k or r computed in plain, the authors of [16] propose to embed them inside a white-box. Offline, several nonces k_i are drawn at random and the corresponding r_i are computed. One-time usage white-boxes $WB_i[k_i^{-1}, r_i, d](e)$ are created and couples (r_i, WB_i) are stored in the device.

To sign a message, a couple (r_i, WB_i) is selected. The hash e is given as input to WB_i, which only performs encoded modular operations to compute $s_i = k_i^{-1}(e + dr_i) \bmod n$.

To prevent replay attacks that lead to the recovery of k as shown in (1), it is proposed to erase the couple (r_i, WB_i) once it is used, but this protection is inefficient against an attacker having access to the memory. Indeed, such an adversary could extract a couple (r_i, WB_i) and use it twice on different messages. Finding a countermeasure seems to be a difficult task since a white-box cannot count on secure non-volatile memory to prevent its use on two different inputs. Hence, this patent does not seem to be applicable in contexts where the attacker has full access to the memory.

Embedding all the sensitive values into a white-box allows to efficiently protect them against extraction and faults but it implies to store many white-boxes, and thus use a lot of memory, or to have a regular connection to a server providing new tables. So this solution is definitely not adapted to every context.

We summarize in Table 1 the various attacks and the corresponding countermeasures presented in Sect. 3 and 4.

Table 1. Recap on attacks presented in this paper, associated countermeasures and main drawbacks.

Attack type	Countermeasures	Restrictions
Passive analysis	Masking and encoding	Memory consuming, security not proven.
	Homomorphic encryption	Implies either implementing a decryption white-box, or the output of encrypted signatures.
Active analysis		
Fixing the nonce	Computing the nonce from e	Enables the attack paths below.
Disturbing e or r	Redundancy and checks of consistency	Memory consuming, can be bypassed with two or more faults.
	Joint encodings on k and e	Memory consuming, does not protect r.
	Offline r computations	Enables new attack paths.

5   Conclusion

Over the last decades, ECDSA security has been constantly challenged and the range of attacks against its implementations has become very wide. We have seen in particular that the white-box context opens a path for very powerful attacks. The lack of a reliable source of randomness is a traditional issue in WBC, but it has a particular flavor for ECDSA implementations since the nonce (and thus the key) can be easily recovered if not drawn uniformly at random. We have shown that this weak point can be exploited by different means.

We have also presented the most efficient state-of-the-art techniques to protect an ECDSA white-box implementation against different kinds of attacks. We have seen how passive and active analyses can be counteracted by using encodings, redundancy and homomorphic encryption for instance. For each method, we have studied the efficiency and presented the limitations in terms of performances and security.

Our study shows that, even if it could be very costly in terms of memory and performance, one could use a combination of such countermeasures to prevent all attacks on ECDSA white-box implementations, except for the modification of the first part of the signature. Indeed, it seems that there is no solution to prevent this attack other than returning an encoded or encrypted s. This constitutes a strong limitation to the use of such a solution in the field, as any party involved in the system has to implement the corresponding function to get the plain signature. Finding a countermeasure in the general setting is therefore still a big challenge.

Acknowledgements. We would like to thank Hervé Chabanne for pointing out patents, and Guillaume Barbu, Laurent Castelnovi, Thomas Chabrier, Sarah Lopez, Nathan Reboud and Stphane Schneider for helpful comments on the preliminary version of this article.

References

1. Alpirez Bock, E., Amadori, A., Brzuska, C., Michiels, E.: On the security goals of white-box cryptography. Cryptogr. IACR Trans. Cryptogr. Hardw. Embed. Syst. **2020**(2), 327–357 (2020). https://tches.iacr.org/index.php/TCHES/article/view/8554
2. Alpirez Bock, E., Brzuska, C., Fischlin, M., Janson, C., Michiels, W.: Security reductions for white-box key-storage in mobile payments. In: Moriai, S., Wang, H. (eds.) ASIACRYPT 2020. LNCS, vol. 12491, pp. 221–252. Springer, Cham (2020). https://doi.org/10.1007/978-3-030-64837-4_8
3. Aranha, D.F., Novaes, F.R., Takahashi, A., Tibouchi, M., Yarom, Y.: LadderLeak: breaking ECDSA with less than one bit of nonce leakage. In: Ligatti, L., Ou, X., Katz, J., Vigna, G. (eds.) ACM CCS 2020, pp. 225–242. ACM Press, November 2020
4. Barthelemy, L.: Toward an asymmetric white-box proposal. Cryptology ePrint Archive, Report 2020/893 (2020). https://eprint.iacr.org/2020/893
5. Bellcore. New Threat Model Breaks Crypto Codes. Press Release, September 1996

6. Biehl, I., Meyer, B., Müller, V.: Differential fault attacks on elliptic curve cryptosystems. In: Bellare, M. (ed.) CRYPTO 2000. LNCS, vol. 1880, pp. 131–146. Springer, Heidelberg (2000). https://doi.org/10.1007/3-540-44598-6_8

7. Billet, O., Gilbert, H.: A Traceable block cipher. In: Laih, C.-S. (ed.) ASIACRYPT 2003, vol. 2894, LNCS, pp. 331–346. Springer, Heidelberg, November/December 2003

8. Billet, O., Gilbert, H., Ech-Chatbi, C.: Cryptanalysis of a white box AES implementation. In: Handschuh, H., Hasan, M.A. (eds.) SAC 2004. LNCS, vol. 3357, pp. 227–240. Springer, Heidelberg (2004). https://doi.org/10.1007/978-3-540-30564-4_16

9. Bockes, M.: White-box ECC implementation. Patent WO2020192968A1 (2020)

10. Bos, J.W., Hubain, C., Michiels, W., Teuwen, P.: Differential computation analysis: hiding your white-box designs is not enough. In: Gierlichs, B., Poschmann, A.Y. (eds.) CHES 2016. LNCS, vol. 9813, pp. 215–236. Springer, Heidelberg (2016). https://doi.org/10.1007/978-3-662-53140-2_11

11. Breitner, J., Heninger, J.: Biased nonce sense: lattice attacks against weak ECDSA signatures in cryptocurrencies. In: Goldberg, I., Moore, T. (eds.) FC 2019, vol. 11598, LNCS, pp. 3–20. Springer, Heidelberg, February 2019

12. Brier, É., Joye, M.: Weierstraß elliptic curves and side-channel attacks. In: Naccache, D., Paillier, P. (eds.) PKC 2002. LNCS, vol. 2274, pp. 335–345. Springer, Heidelberg (2002). https://doi.org/10.1007/3-540-45664-3_24

13. Bringer, J., Chabanne, H., Dottax, H.: White box cryptography: another attempt. cryptology ePrint Archive, Report 2006/468 (2006). https://eprint.iacr.org/2006/468

14. Casteigts, A.: White-Box Elliptic Curve Diffie-Hellman (2011). https://www.labri.fr/perso/acasteig/files/ecdh-report.pdf

15. Cavallo, R., Di Crescenzo, G., Kahrobaei, D., Shpilrain, V.: Efficient and secure delegation of group exponentiation to a single server. Cryptology ePrint Archive, Report 2015/206 (2015). https://eprint.iacr.org/2015/206

16. Chabanne, H., Prouff, E.: Method for electronic signing of a document with a predetermined secret key. Patent FR3063857A1 (2018)

17. CHES 2017: Capture the Flag Challenge - The WhibOx Contest - An ECRYPT White-Box Cryptography Competition. https://whibox-contest.github.io/2017/

18. CHES 2019: Capture the Flag Challenge - The WhibOx Contest Edition 2. https://whibox-contest.github.io/2019/

19. CHES 2021 Challenge - WhibOx Contest. https://whibox.io/contests/2021/

20. Chow, S., Eisen, P., Johnson, H., van Oorschot, P.C.: A white-box DES implementation for DRM applications. In: Feigenbaum, J. (ed.) DRM 2002. LNCS, vol. 2696, pp. 1–15. Springer, Heidelberg (2003). https://doi.org/10.1007/978-3-540-44993-5_1

21. Chow, S., Eisen, P., Johnson, H., Van Oorschot, P.C.: White-box cryptography and an AES implementation. In: Nyberg, K., Heys, H. (eds.) SAC 2002. LNCS, vol. 2595, pp. 250–270. Springer, Heidelberg (2003). https://doi.org/10.1007/3-540-36492-7_17

22. Coron, J.-S.: Resistance against differential power analysis for elliptic curve cryptosystems. In: Koç, Ç.K., Paar, C. (eds.) CHES 1999. LNCS, vol. 1717, pp. 292–302. Springer, Heidelberg (1999). https://doi.org/10.1007/3-540-48059-5_25

23. CryptoExperts SAS. White-Box Cryptography. https://www.cryptoexperts.com/technologies/white-box/

24. De Mulder, Y., Roelse, P., Preneel, B.: Cryptanalysis of the Xiao – Lai white-box AES implementation. In: Knudsen, L.R., Wu, H. (eds.) SAC 2012. LNCS, vol. 7707, pp. 34–49. Springer, Heidelberg (2013). https://doi.org/10.1007/978-3-642-35999-6_3

25. De Mulder, Y., Roelse, P., Preneel, B.: Cryptanalysis of the Xiao – Lai white-box AES implementation. In: Knudsen, L.R., Wu, H. (eds.) SAC 2012. LNCS, vol. 7707, pp. 34–49. Springer, Heidelberg (2013). https://doi.org/10.1007/978-3-642-35999-6_3

26. Delerablée, C., Lepoint, T., Paillier, P., Rivain, P.: White-box security notions for symmetric encryption schemes. Cryptology ePrint Archive, Report 2013/523, 2013. https://eprint.iacr.org/2013/523

27. Digital.ai. Application Protection. https://digital.ai/application-protection

28. Dottax, E.: Fault Attacks on NESSIE Signature and Identification Schemes. Technical report, NESSIE, October 2002. https://www.cosic.esat.kuleuven.ac.be/nessie/reports/phase2/SideChan_1.pdf

29. Feng, Q., He, D., Wang, H., Kumar, N., Choo, K.-K. R.: White-box implementation of Shamirs identity-based signature scheme. IEEE Syst. J. **14**, 1820–1829 (2019)

30. Fersch, M., Kiltz, E., Poettering, B.: On the provable security of (EC)DSA signatures. In: Proceedings of the 2016 ACM SIGSAC Conference on Computer and Communications Security (2016)

31. FIPS PUB 186–4. Digital Signature Standard. National Institute of Standards and Technology, July 2013

32. Giraud, C., Knudsen, E.W.: Fault attacks on signature schemes. In: Wang, H., Pieprzyk, J., Varadharajan, V. (eds.) ACISP 2004. LNCS, vol. 3108, pp. 478–491. Springer, Heidelberg (2004). https://doi.org/10.1007/978-3-540-27800-9_41

33. Giraud, C., Thiebeauld, H.: A survey on fault attacks. In: Quisquater, J.-J., Paradinas, P., Deswarte,Y., Kalam, A.E. (eds.) Smart Card Research and Advanced Applications VI (CARDIS 2004), pp. 159–176. Kluwer Academic Publishers (2004)

34. Goubin, L., Masereel, J.-M., Quisquater, M.: Cryptanalysis of white box DES implementations. In: Adams, C., Miri, A., Wiener, M. (eds.) SAC 2007. LNCS, vol. 4876, pp. 278–295. Springer, Heidelberg (2007). https://doi.org/10.1007/978-3-540-77360-3_18

35. Gouget, A., Vacek, J.: Method for generating a digital signature of an input message. Patent EP3709561A1 (2020)

36. intertrust. whiteCryption Secure Key Box. https://www.intertrust.com/products/application-protection/secure-key-box/

37. Irdeto. Cloakware. https://irdeto.com/whitebox-cryptography/

38. Jancar, J., Sedlacek, V., Svenda, P., Sys, M.: Minerva: the curse of ECDSA nonces. IACR Trans. Cryptogr. Hardw. Embed. Syst. **2020**(4), 281–308 (2020). https://tches.iacr.org/index.php/TCHES/article/view/8684

39. JORF n0241. Avis relatif aux paramètres de courbes elliptiques définis par l'État français, October 16 2011

40. Joye, M.: Protecting ECC against fault attacks: the ring extension method revisited. J. Math. Cryptol. **14**(1), 254–267 (2020)

41. Joye, M., Tymen, C.: Protections against differential analysis for elliptic curve cryptography — an algebraic approach —. In: Koç, Ç.K., Naccache, D., Paar, C. (eds.) CHES 2001. LNCS, vol. 2162, pp. 377–390. Springer, Heidelberg (2001). https://doi.org/10.1007/3-540-44709-1_31

42. Karroumi, M.: Protecting white-box AES with dual ciphers. In: Rhee, K.-H., Nyang, D.H. (eds.) ICISC 2010. LNCS, vol. 6829, pp. 278–291. Springer, Heidelberg (2011). https://doi.org/10.1007/978-3-642-24209-0_19

43. Kocher, P.C.: Timing attacks on implementations of Diffie-Hellman, RSA, DSS, and other systems. In: Koblitz, N. (ed.) CRYPTO 1996. LNCS, vol. 1109, pp. 104–113. Springer, Heidelberg (1996). https://doi.org/10.1007/3-540-68697-5_9

44. Kocher, P., Jaffe, J., Jun, B.: Differential power analysis. In: Wiener, M. (ed.) CRYPTO 1999. LNCS, vol. 1666, pp. 388–397. Springer, Heidelberg (1999). https://doi.org/10.1007/3-540-48405-1_25

45. T. Lepoint, M. Rivain, Y. De Mulder, P. Roelse, and B. Preneel. Two Attacks on a White-Box AES Implementation. In T. Lange, K. Lauter, and P. Lisonek, editors, SAC 2013, volume 8282 of LNCS, pages 265–285. Springer, Heidelberg, Aug. 2014

46. Lochter, M.: RFC 5639: ECC Brainpool Standard Curves and Curve Generation (2010). https://tools.ietf.org/pdf/rfc5639.pdf

47. Lomné, V., Roche, T.: A side journey to Titan (2021). https://ninjalab.io/wp-content/uploads/2021/01/a_side_journey_to_titan.pdf

48. Michiels, W., Gorissen, P., Hollmann, H.D.L.: Cryptanalysis of a generic class of white-box implementations. In: Avanzi, R.M., Keliher, L., Sica, F. (eds.) SAC 2008. LNCS, vol. 5381, pp. 414–428. Springer, Heidelberg (2009). https://doi.org/10.1007/978-3-642-04159-4_27

49. Muir, J., Sui, J., Murdock, D., Eisen, P.: System and method for protecting cryptographic assets from a white-box attack. Patent CA2792787C (2015)

50. PACE Anti-Piracy Inc., White-Box Works. https://www.paceap.com/white-box_cryptography.html

51. Paillier, P.: Public-key cryptosystems based on composite degree Residuosity classes. In: Stern, J. (ed.) EUROCRYPT 1999. LNCS, vol. 1592, pp. 223–238. Springer, Heidelberg (1999). https://doi.org/10.1007/3-540-48910-X_16

52. Quarkslab. Quarks Keys Protect. https://quarkslab.com/quarks-appshield-keys-protect/

53. Rietman, R., De Hoogh, S.R.: Elliptic curve point multiplication device and method for signing a message in a white-box context. Patent US020200119918A1 (2020)

54. Rivain, M.: Fast and regular algorithms for scalar multiplication over elliptic curves. Cryptology ePrint Archive, Report 2011/338 (2011). https://eprint.iacr.org/2011/338

55. Saxena, A., Wyseur, B., Preneel, B.: Towards security notions for white-box cryptography. In: Samarati, P., Yung, M., Martinelli, F., Ardagna, C.A. (eds.) ISC 2009. LNCS, vol. 5735, pp. 49–58. Springer, Heidelberg (2009). https://doi.org/10.1007/978-3-642-04474-8_4

56. Servant, V., Chabanne, H., Prouff, E.: Method for electronic signing of a document with a predetermined secret key. Patent FR3066845B1 (2018)

57. Shamir, A.: Method and apparatus for protecting public key schemes from timing and fault attacks . Patent US005991415A (1999)

58. Standards for Efficient Cryptography Group (SECG). SEC 2 Ver 2.0 : Recommended Elliptic Curve Domain Parameters. Certicom Research, January 27, 2010

59. Thales. Sentinel Portfolio. https://cpl.thalesgroup.com/software-monetization/white-box-cryptography

60. Vanstone, S.: Responses to NIST's proposal. Commun. ACM **35**, 50–52 (1992)

61. Vaudenay, S.: The security of DSA and ECDSA. In: Desmedt, Y.G. (ed.) PKC 2003. LNCS, vol. 2567, pp. 309–323. Springer, Heidelberg (2003). https://doi.org/10.1007/3-540-36288-6_23

62. Verimatrix. Whitebox Designer. https://www.verimatrix.com/products/whitebox/

63. Wyseur, B., Michiels, W., Gorissen, P., Preneel, B.: Cryptanalysis of white-box DES implementations with arbitrary external encodings. In: Adams, C., Miri, A., Wiener, M. (eds.) SAC 2007. LNCS, vol. 4876, pp. 264–277. Springer, Heidelberg (2007). https://doi.org/10.1007/978-3-540-77360-3_17
64. Xiao, Y., Lai, X.: A secure implementation of white-box AES. In: 2nd International Conference on Computer Science and its Applications, pp. 1–6. IEEE (2009)
65. Zhang, Y., He, D., Huang, X., Wang, D., Choo, K.-K. R., Wang, J.: White-Box implementation of the identity-based signature scheme in the IEEE P1363 standard for public key cryptography. IEICE Trans. Inf. Syst. E103.D(2),188–195 (2020)
66. Zhou, J., Bai, J., Jiang, M.S.: White-box implementation of ECDSA based on the cloud plus side mode. Secur. Commun. Netw. **2020**, 8881116:1–8881116:10 (2020)

Post-quantum Cryptography

On Using RSA/ECC Coprocessor for Ideal Lattice-Based Key Exchange

Aurélien Greuet[1], Simon Montoya[1,2(✉)], and Guénaël Renault[2,3]

[1] IDEMIA, Cryptography and Security Labs, Courbevoie, France
{aurelien.greuet,simon.montoya}@idemia.com
[2] LIX, INRIA, CNRS, École Polytechnique, Institut Polytechnique de Paris,
Palaiseau, France
{simon.montoya,guenael.renault}@lix.polytechnique.fr
[3] ANSSI, Paris, France
guenael.renault@ssi.gouv.fr

Abstract. Polynomial multiplication is one of the most costly operations of ideal lattice-based cryptosystems. In this work, we study its optimizations when one of the operands has coefficients close to 0. We focus on this structure since it is at the core of lattice-based Key Encapsulation Mechanisms submitted to the NIST call for post-quantum cryptography. In particular, we propose optimization of this operation for embedded devices by using a RSA/ECC coprocessor that provides efficient and secure large-integer arithmetic. In this context, we compare Kronecker Substitution, already studied in [AHH+19], with two specific algorithms that we introduce: KSV, a variant of this substitution, and an adaptation of the schoolbook multiplication, denoted SHIFT&ADD. All these algorithms rely on the transformation of polynomial multiplication to large-integer arithmetic. Then, thanks to these algorithms, existing secure coprocessors dedicated to large-integer can be re-purposed in order to speed-up post-quantum schemes. The efficiency of these algorithms depends on the component specifications and the cryptosystem parameters set. Thus, we establish a methodology to determine which algorithm to use, for a given component, by only implementing basic large-integer operations. Moreover, the three algorithms are assessed on a chip ensuring that the theoretical methodology matches with practical results.

1 Introduction

The emergence of academic and industrial projects on the design of a potential quantum computer that can break most of the current public-key cryptosystems with Shor's Algorithm [Sho97], led national agencies to study new proposals (e.g. [BSI]) and start standardization of quantum safe algorithms [Moo16,fCR18]. In particular, the National Institute of Standards and Technology (NIST) in 2016 launched a standardization call for post-quantum safe key exchange and signature [Moo16]. In July 2020, they announced seven finalists including four Key Encapsulation Mechanisms (KEMs) for a future standardization. Among

S. Bhasin and F. De Santis (Eds.): COSADE 2021, LNCS 12910, pp. 205–227, 2021.
https://doi.org/10.1007/978-3-030-89915-8_10

these four KEMs, three are based on lattice problems [MAA+20]. For the Chinese competition, the lattice-based KEM LAC [XYD+19], won the first prize in January 2020 [fCR20]. Hence international post-quantum cryptography standards are very likely to include lattice-based cryptosystems. Thus, optimizing and ensuring the practical security of these algorithms is an important area of research.

Constrained environments like smart cards can be very limited in terms of CPU frequency or amount of RAM, especially when compared to regular computers. Working on specific optimizations is often necessary to get an efficient implementation. These devices may embed dedicated hardware coprocessors to accelerate symmetric and asymmetric cryptographic computations. Moreover, these coprocessors offer security features (hardware and software countermeasures against faults and various leaks) and are Common Criteria EAL5+ or EAL6+ certified [Lom16]: they are not subject to "obvious" leaks, e.g. single trace attacks without prior learning phase are hard in practice. However, most of today's asymmetric coprocessors are designed for RSA or elliptic curve cryptography (ECC) and are not adapted for lattice-based cryptography. Performance, security and ease of deployment are part of the NIST selection criteria. Therefore, re-purposing existing secure components to optimize lattice-based KEM can facilitate the transition to quantum safe algorithms.

Motivation and Previous Works. Polynomial multiplication is one of the most costly operation for ideal lattice-based algorithms. A lot of research has been done on the design of efficient hardware to speed-up polynomial multiplication, see e.g. [YZMZBY+20, DFA+20, SRB20]. However, the transition period should rely on hybrid mechanisms, mixing both classical and post-quantum asymmetric cryptography. Thus, both large modular arithmetic and operations related with post-quantum cryptography, like polynomial multiplication, have to be handled.

Nowadays, hardware accelerating large modular arithmetic are designed and deployed. Then, re-purposing these coprocessors to optimize polynomial multiplication is relevant in terms of costs and ease of deployment for an hybrid cryptography world.

The previous work of Albrecht et al. in [AHH+19] optimizes Kyber 1st round algorithm with a RSA/ECC coprocessor, which handles large-integer arithmetic. They use and adapt techniques introduced in [Har07] which transform polynomial multiplication to an integer multiplication with Kronecker Substitution. The work of Wang et al. in [WGY20] re-use the Kronecker Substitution with such a coprocessor to optimize Saber algorithm.

More recently, an independent work of Bos et al. in [JWBJRCvV20] introduced Kronecker+, an algorithm using a variant of Nussbaumer allowing to combine with Kronecker Substitution. Theoretically, Kronecker+ allows a faster polynomial multiplication than Kronecker Substitution. However, the theoretical approach does not provide an estimation of the costs of the polynomial transformations required to apply Kronecker+, which does not ensure a faster algorithm in practice.

Contribution. In this paper we follow the approach initiated in [AHH+19] to improve polynomial multiplication for lattice-based KEMs using a RSA/ECC coprocessor. Such coprocessors usually provide a few basic operations on large integers: multiplication, addition, subtraction, right/left shift.

Our work focuses on the core operation: unreduced polynomial multiplication, i.e. without reduction mod q or $x^n + 1$. Indeed, optimizations for modular reductions can be used on top of any unreduced polynomial multiplication.

More precisely, our work focuses on the unreduced polynomial multiplication when one of the operands has small coefficients. To take advantage of this structure, we introduce a variant of Kronecker Substitution and an adaptation of the schoolbook multiplication, called SHIFT&ADD. Both methods allow to handle polynomial multiplication with operations on large integers.

Compared to Kronecker Substitution, its variant replaces large integer multiplications with additions, shifts and multiplications between a large integer and a coefficient. For small coefficients, the latter is expected to be cheaper than a regular multiplication. SHIFT&ADD handles polynomial multiplications with only integer additions and shifts. With SHIFT&ADD, the smaller the coefficients are, the fewer operations are performed.

Thereafter, we propose a methodology to help the comparison between Kronecker Substitution, its variant and SHIFT&ADD, for a given KEM and a given coprocessor. To this end, we give theoretical complexity estimates for the three algorithms, expressed in terms of basic operations like addition, multiplication, shift and evaluation. Then, by measuring the performance of these basic operations, a developer can determine the fastest algorithm without having to fully develop each algorithm.

Finally, we verify that practical results are in accordance with this methodology for seven parameter sets from the NIST PQC process. In particular, we show that for a given secure comparable component, SHIFT&ADD and Kronecker Substitution variant are faster than Kronecker Substitution as used in [AHH+19]. We also compare our results with reference software implementations for information purposes only: it is not our aim to compare the efficiency of our implementation with algorithms using specific CPU instructions set as one could find in e.g. [GKS20, CHK+20]. Hence, we are here interested by the challenge to re-purpose secure certified coprocessor deployed in several real-life components for an hybrid transition approach.

Organization. In Sect. 2 we introduce some notations and describe the three algorithms that we use to perform polynomial multiplication with a coprocessor. Section 3 is devoted to discuss the side-channel aspects of the proposed algorithms. In Sect. 4, we show how to determine the evaluation point and establish the complexity of the three algorithms in terms of basic coprocessor operations. Finally, in Sect. 5, we assess our algorithms with different set of parameters and show that our practical results are consistent with our theoretical study.

2   Algorithms

In this section we present the algorithmic material used in this work. We first detail some notations and well known algorithmic techniques that will be developed in our contributions presented at the end of this section.

2.1   Notation and Preliminaries

The arithmetic that we study comes naturally from the definition of the ideal lattice-based cryptography and is given as follows.

Rings. For an integer $q \geq 1$, let $\mathbb{Z}_q$ be the residue class group modulo q such that $\mathbb{Z}_q$ can be represented as $\{0, \ldots, q-1\}$. We define R_q being the polynomial ring $R_q = \mathbb{Z}_q[x]/(x^n + 1)$.

Modular Reduction. Let $a, b \in \mathbb{N}$, we denote by $a \mod {}^{(+)}b$ the unique integer $a' \equiv a \mod b$ such that $0 \leq a' < b$ and $a \mod {}^{(-)}b$ the unique integer $a' \equiv a \mod b$ such that $-\frac{b}{2} \leq a' < \frac{b}{2}$. In the following, we denote by $a \mod b = a \mod {}^{(+)}b$

Polynomials. A polynomial in R_q is represented by a polynomial of degree at most $(n-1)$ with coefficients in $\mathbb{Z}_q$. Given $f \in R_q$, we denote by f_i the coefficient associated with the monomial x^i.

Polynomial Representation. Polynomials are represented as byte strings. Let $f(x)$ be a polynomial of degree $n - 1$ with all its coefficients $0 \leq f_i \leq \beta$. Then, each coefficient is encoded on $\lfloor \log_2(\beta) \rfloor + 1$ bits. The coefficients are packed as a string of size $n(\lfloor \log_2(\beta) \rfloor + 1)$ bits to represent $f(x)$.

Let $g(x)$ be a polynomial of degree $n-1$ with all its coefficients $-\frac{\delta}{2} \leq g_i \leq \frac{\delta}{2}$. Then, each coefficient is encoded on $\lfloor \log_2(\delta) \rfloor + 1$ such that it is represented as $g_i \mod {}^{(+)}2^{\lfloor \log_2(\delta) \rfloor + 1}$. As previously, all the coefficients are packed as a string of size $n(\lfloor \log_2(\delta) \rfloor + 1)$ bits to represent $g(x)$.

Example 1. Let $f(x)$ be a polynomial with non-negative coefficients lower or equal to $q - 1 = 3328$, then each coefficient is encoded on $\lfloor \log_2(3328) \rfloor + 1 = 12$ bits:

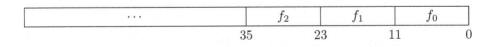

$\cdots$	f_2	f_1	f_0
35	23	11	0

Large Integer Operations. In the remainder of this paper , we introduce three algorithms: Kronecker Substitution (Algorithm 3), Kronecker Substitution Variant (Algorithm 4) and Shift&Add (Algorithm 5). For these algorithms the integer operations (multiplication, addition, subtraction, shift) are implicitly performed on large integers and correspond to the operations provided by a hardware coprocessor.

Number Theoretic Transform (NTT). NTT is an algorithm allowing to perform fast polynomial multiplication in R_q [Nus82,LN16]. Given a and $b \in R_q$, $a \times b$ is computed as $\text{NTT}^{-1}(\text{NTT}(a) \circ \text{NTT}(b))$, where $\circ$ is the coefficient-wise multiplication.

Theoretically, NTT has the best asymptotic complexity for multiplication in R_q. However, in constrained environments (e.g. smart cards), devices may have dedicated hardware to perform fast large-integer arithmetic. In this context, NTT can be outperformed by an algorithm relying on integer arithmetic, even if its theoretical complexity is worse than NTT.

In the following paragraph, we describe a well known technique coming from computer algebra that allows to perform polynomial multiplication with integer arithmetic.

Kronecker Substitution. The main idea of this substitution, introduced by Kronecker in [Kro82] and first applied in the univariate polynomial context by Schönhage in [Sch82], is to transform polynomial multiplication to an integer multiplication by evaluating the operands and to get back to the result using a radix conversion. More precisely if $f = \sum_{i=0}^{n-1} f_i X^i$ and $g = \sum_{i=0}^{n-1} g_i X^i$ are two polynomials with non-negative coefficients, by considering the product of their evaluations at an integer B we obtain the integer $\tilde{f}\tilde{g} = \left(\sum_{i=0}^{n-1} f_i B^i \right) \left(\sum_{i=0}^{n-1} g_i B^i \right)$, that can be expressed in the base B by radix conversion. Then one obtains the evaluation of fg at B, $\tilde{f}\tilde{g} = \sum_{j=0}^{2n-2} \left(\sum_{i=0}^{j} f_i g_{j-i} \right) B^j$, and thus deduces the value of each coefficient of the corresponding polynomial fg. This radix conversion is possible only if each of the resulting coefficients are smaller than B. The integer B is usually chosen as a power b^ℓ where b is equal to 2 or 10 depending on the context. In all cases, ℓ has to be chosen sufficiently large in order to make the radix conversion effective. More precisely, ℓ could be chosen as the smallest integer such that b^ℓ is greater than the maximum size of the coefficients of the resulting polynomial.

When some of the coefficients of the polynomials are negative, we have to adapt this reconstruction. In the following algorithms, we present the evaluation process and the radix conversion for a general polynomial of degree $n-1$. We take care of the sign of the coefficients by storing this information in a variable that is given as one of the outputs of the first algorithm. We explain more precisely this procedure in the following.

The integer obtained after evaluation at 2^ℓ of a polynomial of degree $n-1$, can be viewed as the concatenation of n integers of bitsize ℓ.

$\cdots$	$f(2^\ell)_2$	$f(2^\ell)_1$	$f(2^\ell)_0$
$3\ell - 1$	$2\ell - 1$	$\ell - 1$	0

EVALUATION. Algorithm 1 always returns a non-negative integer. Indeed, if the highest degree coefficient of a polynomial $g(x)$ is negative then the algorithm returns the evaluation of $-g(x)$. The parameter **neg** indicates, for the latter radix conversion, if the evaluation algorithm returned the evaluation of $g(x)$ or $-g(x)$. In the following we denote $f(2^\ell)_i = (f(2^\ell) >> (i\ell)) \& (2^\ell - 1)$.

Algorithm 1. EVALUATION

Input: $f(x) \in \mathbb{Z}[x]$ of degree $n - 1$,
     $\ell \in \mathbb{N}$
Output: $(-1)^{\text{neg}} \times f(2^\ell), \text{neg} \in \{0,1\}$

1: carry ← 0
2: if $f_{n-1} < 0$ then
3:     neg ← 1
4: else
5:     neg ← 0
6: end if
7: for $i = 0$ to $n - 1$ do
8:     tmp ← $(-1)^{\text{neg}} f_i$ + carry
       mod $^{(+)} 2^\ell$
9:     if tmp > $2^{\ell-1}$ then
10:         carry ← -1
11:     else
12:         carry ← 0
13:     end if
14:     $f(2^\ell) \leftarrow f(2^\ell) + \text{tmp} \times 2^{i\ell}$
15: end for

Algorithm 2. RADIX CONVERSION

Input: $r(2^\ell) = (r(2^\ell)_0, r(2^\ell)_1, \ldots,$
     $r(2^\ell)_{n-1})$ and $n, \ell, \text{neg} \in \mathbb{N}$
Output: $r(x) = r_0 + r_1 x + \ldots + r_{n-1} x^{n-1} \in \mathbb{Z}[x]$

1: carry ← 0
2: for $i = 0$ to $n - 1$ do
3:     $r_i \leftarrow r(2^\ell)_i + \text{carry} \mod^{(+)} 2^\ell$
4:     if $r_i > 2^{\ell-1}$ then
5:         $r_i \leftarrow (-1)^{\text{neg}+1}(2^\ell - r_i)$
6:         carry ← 1
7:     else
8:         $r_i \leftarrow (-1)^{\text{neg}} r_i$
9:         carry ← 0
10:     end if
11: end for

The following example presents Kronecker Substitution by using a decimal radix.

Example 2. Let $f(x) = 8x^2 + 3x + 2$ and $g(x) = -5x^2 - 4x + 1$. Note that the coefficients r_i of the result are such that $-\frac{10^2}{2} \leq r_i \leq \frac{10^2}{2}$. Hence, we evaluate f and g at 10^2 in order to compute $f(x) \times g(x)$ using integer multiplication: $f(10^2) = 080302$, $\text{neg}_f = 0$ and $g(10^2) = 050399$, $\text{neg}_g = 1$. After this evaluation, these two integers can be multiplied:

$$f(10^2) \times g(10^2) = 080302 \times 050399 = 4047140498$$

Since the evaluation was done at 10^2, the resulting polynomial can be interpolated by reading the coefficients 2 digits by 2 digits. The two first digits are $98 \geq \frac{10^2}{2}$, that represents the negative number $-(10^2 - 98) = -2$ and propagates a carry for the next coefficient. After that, we got $4 < 50$ plus the previous carry to obtain 5. And so on for the other coefficients. However, $\text{neg}_g = 1$, then reading the coefficients like this gives $-(f(x)g(x))$.

$$-(f(x) \times g(x)) = 40x^4 + 47x^3 + 14x^2 + (4+1)x - (10^2 - 98)$$
$$= 40x^4 + 47x^3 + 14x^2 + 5x - 2$$
$$f(x) \times g(x) = -40x^4 - 47x^3 - 14x^2 - 5x + 2$$

For sake of clarity, examples are given in 10-radix but in our algorithms and implementation, a power of 2 is used as the integer B. In the following Kronecker Substitution or KS refer to the Algorithm 3.

Algorithm 3. KRONECKER SUBSTITUTION

Input: $f(x) \in \mathbb{N}[x], g(x) \in \mathbb{Z}[x]$ and $\ell \in \mathbb{N}$
Output: $r(x) = f(x)g(x)$
  1: $(f(2^\ell), \text{neg}_f), (g(2^\ell), \text{neg}_g) \leftarrow$ evaluation of $f(x), g(x)$ at 2^ℓ
  2: $r(2^\ell) \leftarrow f(2^\ell)g(2^\ell)$
  3: $r(x) \leftarrow$ radix conversion of $(r(2^\ell), \text{neg}_f \oplus \text{neg}_g)$

2.2 Polynomial Multiplication Using the Structure

The polynomials arising in ideal lattice based cryptosystems are structured, we show in the sequel how to gain in efficiency by using them.

Notations. To perform an arithmetic operation using a hardware accelerator, the operands and an opcode for the operation to perform must be set into the coprocessor. When the choice of the operation depends on the value of a secret, we denote these sequences of instructions by $c \leftarrow \text{Op}(a, b)$, where $\text{Op} \in \{\text{Add}, \text{Sub}\}$ represents the opcode. This notation allows to simplify the constant-time implementation of an algorithm (see Sect. 2.2 below).

In the following algorithm descriptions, @var denotes the address of the variable var. Given a pointer ptr, *ptr stands for the value stored at address ptr. The bitwise exclusive-or is denoted by $\oplus$, the bitwise logical and by & and $a >> \ell$ (resp. $a << \ell$) stands for the logical right shift (resp. logical left shift) by ℓ bits of the value a.

Kronecker Substitution Variant. Classical Kronecker Substitution multiplies two integers of length $b^\ell \times n$, where b^ℓ is the evaluation point B and $n - 1$ the degree of the polynomials. As mentioned above, ℓ is determined by the maximum coefficient value of the result. In this variant, n multiplications are done on an integer of length $b^\ell \times n$ by an integer of length b^k with $k < \ell$.

A multiplication of two large integers is replaced with 3 multiplications of a large integer by a small coefficient and some additions and shifts. This technique is of interest when considering the multiplication of a polynomial with small coefficients by a generic polynomial. Such multiplications are used in some lattice-based key exchanges. Algorithm 4 multiplies two polynomials of degree $n - 1$ such that $(|fg(x)|)_i < 2^\ell$.

Algorithm 4. KRONECKER SUBSTITUTION VARIANT

Input: $f(x) \in \mathbb{N}[x], g(x) \in \mathbb{Z}[x]$ and $n, \ell \in \mathbb{N}$
Output: $r(x) = f(x)g(x)$
1: $(f(2^\ell), \mathbf{neg}_f) \leftarrow$ evaluation of $f(x)$ at 2^ℓ
2: **for** $i = n - 1$ to 0 **do**
3:    **if** $g_i \geq 0$ **then**
4:       Op $\leftarrow$ Add   // Addition will be performed line 9
5:    **else**
6:       Op $\leftarrow$ Sub   // Subtraction will be performed line 9
7:    **end if**
8:    $c \leftarrow |g_i|$
9:    $r(2^\ell) \leftarrow \text{Op}\left(r(2^\ell), c \times f(2^\ell)\right)$
10:   $r(2^\ell) \leftarrow r(2^\ell) << \ell$
11: **end for**
12: $r(x) \leftarrow$ radix conversion of $(r(2^\ell), \mathbf{neg}_f)$

Example 3. Let $f(x) = 8x^2 + 3x + 2$ and $g(x) = g_2 x^2 + g_1 x + g_0 = 5x^2 + 4x + 1$.

$$\text{Then, } f(10^2)g(10^2) = (f(10^2) \times g_2)(10^2)^2 + (f(10^2)g_1)10^2 + f(10^2)g_0$$
$$= (080302 \times 5)(10^2)^2 + (080302 \times 4)10^2 + 080302 \times 1$$
$$= 4015100000 + 32120800 + 080302 = 4047301102$$

The resulting polynomial is recovered with radix conversion like in classical Kronecker.

SHIFT&ADD. We now present an adaptation of the schoolbook polynomial multiplication, denoted SHIFT&ADD, where polynomials are represented as integers, after a Kronecker-like evaluation. It relies only on additions and left shifts. This technique is of interest when one of the operands has small coefficients.

The basic idea is explained in Example 4 while a full description is given in Algorithm 5.

Example 4. Let $f(x) = 9x^2 + 8x + 3$ and $g(x) = g_2 x^2 + g_1 x + g_0 = 2x^2 - 1$. Let $r = 0$. The computation of $f(x) \times g(x)$ is done as follows:

   Step 1. Evaluate f: $f(10^3) = 009008003$
   Step 2. Since $g_2 = 2$:
     1. $r \leftarrow r + f(10^3) \times \left(10^3\right)^2$;
     2. $r \leftarrow r + f(10^3) \times \left(10^3\right)^2$;
   Step 3. Since $g_1 = 0$, do nothing;
   Step 4. Since $g_0 = -1$, $r \leftarrow r - f(10^3) \times \left(10^3\right)^0$;

This leads to $f(10^3)g(10^3) = 2f(10^3)(10^3)^2 - f(10^3)$
$$= 2(009008003 \times (10^3)^2) - 009008003 = 18015996991997$$

By radix conversion, $f(x)g(x) = 18x^4 + (15+1)x^3 - (10^3 - (996+1))x^2 - (10^3 - (991+1))x - (10^3 - 997) = 18x^4 + 16x^3 - 3x^2 - 8x - 3$.

Algorithm 5. Shift&Add

Input: $f(x) \in \mathbb{N}[x], g(x) \in \mathbb{Z}[x]$ with all $g_i \in \{-\frac{\delta}{2}, \ldots, 0, \ldots, \frac{\delta}{2}\}$ and $n, \ell, q \in \mathbb{N}$
Output: $r(x) = f(x)g(x)$
1: $(f(2^\ell), \text{neg}_f) \leftarrow$ evaluation of $f(x)$
2: $\text{tmp} \leftarrow [\,]$ // dummy buffer for constant time implementation
3: **for** $i = n - 1$ to 0 **do**
4:      **if** $g_i \geq 0$ **then**
5:          $\text{Op} \leftarrow \text{Add}$ // addition will be done line 15
6:      **else**
7:          $\text{Op} \leftarrow \text{Sub}$ // subtraction will be done line 15
8:      **end if**
9:      **for** $j = 0$ to $\frac{\delta}{2} - 1$ **do**
10:          **if** $j < |g_i|$ **then**
11:              $\text{buff} \leftarrow @r(2^\ell)$ // Op in line 15 will be kept
12:          **else**
13:              $\text{buff} \leftarrow @\text{tmp}$ // Op in line 15 will be discarded
14:          **end if**
15:          $*\text{buff} \leftarrow \text{Op}\left(r(2^\ell), f(2^\ell)\right)$
16:      **end for**
17:      $r(2^\ell) \leftarrow r(2^\ell) << \ell$
18: **end for**
19: $r(x) \leftarrow$ radix conversion of $(r(2^\ell), \text{neg}_f)$

Isochronous Implementations. As it will be explained in Sect. 3, side-channel attacks must be taken into consideration. Hence, Algorithms 4 and 5 are intended to be isochronous: the execution time does not depend on a secret value. In the sequel we assume that for a given operands size, additions and subtractions have same execution time.

At each loop iteration, the same number of additions or subtractions and shifts are performed. However, the time taken to execute conditional assignments (lines 3 to 7 in Algorithm 4, lines 4 to 8 and lines 10 to 14 in Algorithm 5) can depend on the condition, that itself depends on a secret. Likewise, the computation of absolute value (line 8 in Algorithm 4 and line 10 in Algorithm 5) must be handled carefully to be isochronous.

We show in Algorithm 6 how to achieve the pointer selection for lines 10 to 14 in Algorithm 5. This pointer selection is done without branches and without table accesses. Thus, its execution time depends neither on any secret value nor on cache access. Since Algorithm 6 computes an absolute value and performs a conditional assignment, the same techniques can be used to make Algorithms 4 and 5 isochronous.

Algorithm 6. Isochronous pointers selection

Input: Coefficient $g_i \in \left\{ -\frac{\delta}{2}, \ldots, \frac{\delta}{2} \right\}$ encoded on $k = \lfloor \log_2(\delta) \rfloor + 1$ bits, $j \in \mathbb{N}$, $R =$ bitsize of CPU registers.

Output: buff $\leftarrow \begin{cases} @r(2^\ell) \text{ if } |g_i| < j \\ @\text{tmp else.} \end{cases}$

1: $s \leftarrow g_i >> (k-1)$ // 0 if $g_i \geq 0$, 1 else
2: $t \leftarrow (s \oplus 1) - 1$ // 0 if $g_i \geq 0$, $2^R - 1 = $ 0xFF...FF else
3: $t \leftarrow t \;\&\; \left(2^k - 1\right)$ // previous result on k bits
4: $\text{abs} = (t \oplus g_i) + s$ // $|g_i| = g_i$ if $g_i \geq 0$, $\overline{g_i} + 1 = \left(g_i \oplus \left(2^k - 1\right)\right) + 1$ else
5: $t \leftarrow \left((\text{abs} - j) >> (R - 1)\right) - 1$ // 0 if $|g_i| < j$, $2^R - 1 = $ 0xFF...FF else
6: $\text{switch} = @r(2^\ell) \oplus @\text{tmp}$
7: $\text{buff} = (\text{switch} \;\&\; t) \oplus \&r(2^\ell)$ // $@r(2^\ell)$ if $|g_i| < j$, $@\text{tmp}$ else

---

3   Considerations on Side-Channel Attacks

This work focuses on implementations on embedded devices, thus the side-channel aspect must be considered.

Simple Attacks. To avoid simple attacks like SPA, we make our multiplication algorithms isochronous: the execution time does not depend on any secret. For most of the hardware accelerators, large-integer arithmetic timings depend only on the operands size. Hence, we assume that the execution time of shift, addition, subtraction and multiplication on large integers does not depend on the processed data. Moreover, exploiting secure coprocessors leaks by SPA during their computation is hard in practice. Then, we assume that an hardware addition cannot be distinguished from a hardware subtraction with a simple power consumption or EM attack. In addition, in our experiments, the CPU is set to perform the multiplication and division between registers in constant time. These instructions are used to compute modular reductions.

Under these assumptions, it is clear that a straightforward implementation of Kronecker Substitution does not have any operation depending on the manipulated data.

In addition, we explained in Sect. 2.2 and showed in Algorithm 4 and 5 how to compute isochronous KSV and SHIFT&ADD, based on techniques described in Algorithm 6. With such techniques and since by assumption, addition cannot be distinguished from a subtraction, from an attacker point of view, the execution of the same instructions are performed at each loop iteration in Algorithm 5 regardless of the secret. Thus, SPA-like attack cannot reveal secret information.

Differential/Correlation Attacks. Several physical attacks against Post-Quantum cryptosystems have been studied [CCA+20]. Among them, some correlation attacks have been done on polynomial multiplication, see e.g. [EFGT17, OSPG18, RJH+18, RdCR+16, RRDC+16] and references therein.

These attacks are based on the fact that power consumption or electromagnetic emissions are correlated with the data being manipulated. Such attack targets an intermediate variable of the form $s \times m$, where s is a small part of the secret and m a known input, like a message or a public key. Since s is small and m is known, the attacker can make a guess on s, compute $s \times m$ and predict, for a given leakage model, the expected consumptions or emissions for a series of different m's. Then, using physical measurements, like power consumption traces, and statistical tools, the correct key guess can be found: it is likely to be the one for which the correlation between predictions and real measurements is the strongest.

Masking is the classical countermeasure against such attacks [MOP08]. The sensitive data is split in two shares, each share being manipulated individually. For multiplication in lattice-based cryptography, the secret polynomial s has a structure, e.g. small coefficients, that can be exploited for performance optimization. Hence, to keep this structure, one can split the known part: for a given public value m, consider a random m_1 and set $m_2 = m - m_1$. Then $s \times m$ can be computed as $(s \times m_1) + (s \times m_2)$, each $(s \times m_i)$ being processed independently. Since m_1 and m_2 are unknown and appear to be uniformly distributed, the computation of $(s \times m_i)$ can not be correlated to $s \times m$, so that order 1 attacks will fail [MOP08]. With this countermeasure, the overhead is roughly an extra polynomial addition and an extra polynomial multiplication.

In [RdCR+16], the additively-homomorphic property of R-LWE schemes is used to mask, by adding the encryption of a random message before the decryption process. This random message encryption can be precomputed, so that the overhead is only an extra addition.

Recall that our goal is to determine, given a lattice-based scheme and a device, the fastest polynomial multiplication. For both kind of masking, the overhead does not depend on the choice of the multiplication algorithm: if unmasked multiplication A is faster than unmasked multiplication B, then the same result holds for their masked versions. Then in the sequel, we focus on comparing the basic unmasked versions of polynomial multiplication algorithms.

4   Complexity

This section is devoted to compare the performance of Kronecker substitution (KS), Kronecker substitution variant (KSV) and SHIFT&ADD when using an existing RSA/ECC hardware accelerator. Hence, the complexity is given in terms of basic arithmetic operations performed by such accelerators: addition, multiplication and multiplication by a power of 2 (left shift) on large integers. Moreover, the number of evaluation differs between KS, KSV and SHIFT&ADD. Then, the evaluation step is considered in the following complexities. Since the cost of these operations depends on the operand sizes, we first determine the minimal value for the parameter ℓ.

Our work is focused on lattice-based key exchange submitted to the NIST PQC standardization process. The polynomial multiplication of these key exchanges is over $R_q = \mathbb{Z}_q[x]/(x^n+1)$. To compute such a multiplication, we first multiply over $\mathbb{Z}[x]$. The result is then reduced modulo x^n+1 and each coefficient is reduced modulo q. Since this reduction step is the same for the three methods, its cost is not relevant for a theoretical comparison between them. Hence, it is not included in the complexity computation. Likewise, radix conversion step is the same and is not included in the complexity. However, these costs are considered in the performance results of Sect. 5.

4.1 Choice of ℓ

As explained in Sect. 2, polynomial multiplication can be reduced to integer multiplication. To this end, the polynomials are evaluated at a point such that the result can be recovered by radix conversion. This evaluation point is determined by the maximum coefficient of the multiplication result.

In the following, we suppose that the polynomial evaluation is done by Algorithm 1. Then, each evaluated polynomial is represented as a non-negative integer.

Proposition 1. *Let f and g be polynomials of degree $n-1$ such that for all $i \in \{0, \ldots, n-1\}, 0 \le f_i \le \beta$ and $-\frac{\delta}{2} \le g_i \le \frac{\delta}{2}$. Then*

- *$\forall i \in \{0, \ldots, 2n-2\}, |(f(x)g(x))_i| < 2^{\ell-1}$, where $\ell = \lfloor \log_2(n\beta\delta) \rfloor + 1$.*
- *Each coefficient of $f(x)g(x)$ is encoded on at most ℓ bits.*
- *$\log_2(f(2^\ell)) < n\ell$ and $\log_2(|g(2^\ell)|) < n\ell$.*

Proof. Let $r(x) = f(x)g(x)$. Then $r(x)$ is of degree $2n-2$ and its k-th coefficient is $r_k = \sum\limits_{i=0}^{k} f_i g_{k-i}$. To prove the first assertion, we first consider the coefficients r_k for $k \le n-1$. Since for all i, $0 \le f_i \le \beta$ and $|g_i| \le \delta/2$, we get, for $k \le n-1$:

$$|r_k| = \left| \sum_{i=0}^{k} f_i g_{k-i} \right| \le \sum_{i=0}^{k} |f_i| \, |g_{k-i}| \le \sum_{i=0}^{k} \beta\frac{\delta}{2} \le \sum_{i=0}^{n-1} \beta\frac{\delta}{2} \le n\beta\frac{\delta}{2}.$$

For $k \ge n$, note that since f (resp. g) has degree $n-1$, $f_i = 0$ (resp. $g_i = 0$) for $i \ge n$. Hence,

$$|r_k| = \left| \sum_{i=0}^{k} f_i g_{k-i} \right| = \left| \sum_{i=0}^{n-1} f_i g_{k-i} + \sum_{i=n}^{k} f_i g_{k-i} \right| = \left| \sum_{i=0}^{n-1} f_i g_{k-i} \right| \le n\beta\frac{\delta}{2}.$$

Thus, for $k \in \{0, \ldots, 2n-2\}$, $|r_k| \le n\beta\frac{\delta}{2} < 2^{\lfloor \log_2(n\beta\frac{\delta}{2}) \rfloor + 1} = 2^{\ell-1}$. Each coefficient of the result is $-n\beta\frac{\delta}{2} \le r_k \le n\beta\frac{\delta}{2} < 2^{\ell-1}$, then to handle the negative case each coefficient of the result is at most encoded on ℓ bits.

We prove now the third assertion.

$$f(2^\ell) = \sum_{i=0}^{n-1} f_i 2^{i\ell} \le (2^\ell - 1)\sum_{i=0}^{n-1} 2^{i\ell} = (2^\ell - 1)\frac{2^{n\ell} - 1}{(2^\ell - 1)} = 2^{n\ell} - 1 < 2^{n\ell}$$

Thus, $\log_2\left(f(2^\ell)\right) \le n\ell$. Likewise, $\log_2\left(|g(2^\ell)|\right) \le n\ell$. $\square$

Remark 1. The previous proposition applies with polynomial $f(x)$ with non-negative coefficients. In our context, the negative coefficients of a polynomial in R_q can be replaced with their non-negative equivalent in $\{0, \dots, q-1\}$.

4.2   Complexity Estimates

In this section, we estimate the complexity of our multiplication algorithms. We express them in terms of the following basic operations. Let $E(n)$ be the evaluation complexity function for a polynomial of degree $n-1$. Let $M(x,y)$ and $A(x,y)$ be the multiplication and addition (or subtraction) of integers complexity functions depending on the bitsize of the inputs.

Example 5. Let a and b be two integers, let $x = \lfloor \log_2(a) \rfloor + 1$ and $y = \lfloor \log_2(b) \rfloor + 1$. Then the cost of computing $a \times b$ (resp. $a + b$) is $M(x,y)$ (resp. $A(x,y)$).

Likewise, $S(x,s)$ denotes the shift complexity function where x is the bitsize of the integer to shift on s bits.

Kronecker Substitution (KS)

Proposition 2. *Let $f(x)$ and $g(x)$ be two polynomials of degree $n-1$. Each coefficient of $f(x)$ is defined over $\mathbb{N}$ and each coefficient of $g(x)$ is defined over $\mathbb{Z}$. If for a given ℓ every coefficient $|(f(x)g(x))_i|$ is lower than $2^{\ell-1}$, then the multiplication complexity of $f(x)g(x)$ with Kronecker substitution is $2E(n) + M(n\ell, n\ell)$.*

Proof. Let $f(x)$ and $g(x)$ be polynomials of degree $n-1$. To compute $f(x) \times g(x)$ with Kronecker Substitution, the following steps are performed:

1. Evaluation of $f(x)$ and $g(x)$ at 2^ℓ. According to Proposition 1,
   $\log_2\left(f(2^\ell)\right) \leq n\ell$ and $\log_2\left(|g(2^\ell)|\right) \leq n\ell$.
2. Multiplication of two integers of bitsize $n\ell$.
3. Radix conversion of the coefficients.

Then, Kronecker Substitution complexity is $2E(n) + M(n\ell, n\ell)$.   □

Kronecker Substitution Variant (KSV)

Proposition 3. *Let $f(x)$ and $g(x)$ be polynomials of degree $n-1$. Each coefficient of $f(x)$ are defined over $\mathbb{N}$ and each coefficient of $g(x)$ are defined over $\mathbb{Z}$. If for a given ℓ every coefficient $|(f(x)g(x))_i|$ is lower than $2^{\ell-1}$ and all coefficients of $g(x)$ fit on k bits, then the polynomial multiplication complexity of $f(x)g(x)$ with Kronecker substitution variant is $E(n) + n(M(n\ell, k) + S(n\ell, \ell) + A(n\ell, n\ell))$.*

Proof. Let $f(x)$ and $g(x)$ be polynomials of degree $n-1$, such that each bit representation for g_i fits on k bits. Computing $f(x) \times g(x)$ with Kronecker Substitution Variant is done by doing:

1. The evaluation of $f(x)$ at 2^ℓ. Then, $\log_2\left(f(2^\ell)\right) \le n\ell$.
2. A "for" loop with n iterations, each step being:
   - A multiplication between an integer of bitsize $n\ell$ and a coefficients of bitsize k,
   - An addition or subtraction between two integers of size $n\ell$,
   - A ℓ-shift of an integer of bitsize $n\ell$.
3. A radix conversion of the coefficients.

Then the complexity of the multiplication using Kronecker Substitution Variant is $E(n) + n(M(n\ell, k) + S(n\ell, \ell) + A(n\ell, n\ell))$. ☐

Shift&Add

Proposition 4. *Let $f(x)$ and $g(x)$ be polynomials of degree $n - 1$ with coefficients in $\mathbb{Z}$. If for a given ℓ every coefficient $|(f(x)g(x))_i|$ is lower than $2^{\ell-1}$ and all coefficients of $g(x)$ belong to $\{-\frac{\delta}{2}, \ldots, 0, \ldots, \frac{\delta}{2}\}$, then the polynomial multiplication in* SHIFT&ADD *costs $E(n) + n(S(n\ell, \ell) + \frac{\delta}{2}A(n\ell, n\ell))$.*

Proof. Let $f(x)$, $g(x)$ be polynomials of degree $n - 1$. Algorithm SHIFT&ADD computes the multiplication as follow:

1. Evaluate $f(x)$ at 2^ℓ. Then, $\log_2\left(f(2^\ell)\right) \le n\ell$.
2. A "for" loop called n times. For the three cases, SHIFT&ADD computes:
   - $\frac{\delta}{2}$ additions or subtractions between two integers of size $n\ell$.
3. Radix conversion of the coefficients.

Then SHIFT&ADD complexity is $E(n) + n(S(n\ell, \ell) + \frac{\delta}{2}A(n\ell, n\ell))$. ☐

Complexities Comparison. Let $f(x)$ and $g(x)$ be polynomial of degree $n - 1$. Assume that the coefficients of $g(x)$ belong to $\{-\frac{\delta}{2}, \ldots, 0, \ldots, \frac{\delta}{2}\}$ and that for all $i \in \{0, \ldots, 2n - 1\}, |(f(x)g(x))_i| \le 2^{\ell-1}$. To choose the most efficient algorithm for polynomial multiplication we need to compare the three following complexities, depending on the component specification.

- SHIFT&ADD: $E(n) + n(S(n\ell, \ell) + \frac{\delta}{2}A(n\ell, n\ell)))$.
- Kronecker substitution: $2E(n) + M(n\ell, n\ell)$.
- Kronecker substitution variant: $E(n) + n(M(n\ell, k) + S(n\ell, \ell) + A(n\ell, n\ell))$.

In Sect. 5.2, we explain how to instantiate the different basic complexities in order to compare the above estimations. We focus our study on the execution time and do not provide memory consumption estimates.

4.3 Time-Memory Trade-Offs

The amount of RAM in embedded devices can be very limited. However, some devices allow a larger RAM consumption which can be utilized to speed-up our algorithms.

Polynomial Representation. In Sect. 2 we describe our compact polynomial representation. This representation is useful to optimize our memory consumption but not to access to the polynomial coefficients. The evaluation and radix conversion require a lot of accesses to the coefficients, thus representing these coefficients as a machine word (e.g. 32-bit) improves significantly the performance of these algorithms. Moreover, for some components, using a machine word representation allows to replace shift by pointers arithmetic.

Precomputation. In our context, polynomial multiplication is between $f(x)$ which is a random polynomial over R_q and $g(x)$ which has coefficients in $\{-\frac{\delta}{2}, \ldots, \frac{\delta}{2}\}$, where δ is close to 0. Then, we can precompute $\frac{\delta}{2} - 1$ multiples of $f(x)$: $2 \times f(x), \ldots, \frac{\delta}{2} \times f(x)$ to reduce the number of operation to one addition/subtraction and one shift of each iteration of SHIFT&ADD loop "for".

Positive Case. As mentioned above, one of the polynomials can have negative coefficients. That implies to handle carry propagation during the evaluation, radix conversion or the subdivision. The carry propagation requires an important amount of software implementation to be handled. However, KSV and SHIFT&ADD can perform the polynomial multiplication without negative coefficient and then without carry propagation. Indeed, as the cost of a supplementary evaluation/storage of $-f(x) \mod q$, which is the computation $q - f_i$ for all the coefficients of f, KSV (resp. SHIFT&ADD) multiplies (resp. add) $f(x)$ when the coefficient of $g(x)$ is non-negative and $-f(x) \mod q$ when the coefficient is negative.

4.4 Polynomial Subdivisions

RSA/ECC coprocessors perform large integers arithmetic with data in buffer whose size has a fixed limit. In our algorithms, after polynomial evaluation, the resulting integer is generally too large to fit in these buffers. In this case, a subdivision is performed on the polynomials before evaluation. Let $f(x) = f_I + f_S x^{n/2}$ and $g(x) = g_I + g_S x^{n/2}$, where f_I, f_S, g_I and g_S have degree $<n/2$. We consider the following methods to subdivide:

Naive: $f(x)g(x) = f_I g_I + (f_I g_S + f_S g_I)x^{n/2} + f_S g_S$
Karatsuba: $f(x)g(x) = f_I g_I + ((f_I + f_S)(g_I + g_S) - f_I g_I - f_S g_S)x^{n/2} + f_S g_S x^n$

Karatsuba performs fewer multiplications at the cost of extra additions, subtractions and memory usage. Depending on the coprocessor specification, it can be slower than the naive subdivision.

A. Greuet et al.

Impact on ℓ. Subdividing d times divides the value of n by 2^d. However, for the naive subdivision it does not reduce the value of $\ell = \lfloor \log_2(n\beta\delta) \rfloor + 1$. Indeed, after recombination the result's bitsize is the same as a multiplication without subdivision.

Karatsuba requires the multiplication $(f_I + f_S)(g_I + g_S)$, which increases the value of $\ell = \lfloor \log_2(n\beta\delta) \rfloor + 1$. In fact, let f_I, f_S have coefficients in $\{0, \ldots, \beta\}$ and g_I, g_S have coefficients in $\{-\frac{\delta}{2}, \ldots, \frac{\delta}{2}\}$. Then, $(f_I + f_S)$ have coefficients in $\{0, \ldots, 2\beta\}$ and $(g_I + g_S)$ have coefficients in $\{-\delta, \ldots, \delta\}$. Thus, $\ell' = \lfloor \log_2(\frac{n}{2} \cdot 2\beta \cdot 2\delta) \rfloor + 1 = \ell + 1$. More generally, if d subdivisions are required, then $\ell' = \ell + d$ must be used instead of ℓ.

Impact on the Complexities. Subdividing allows to perform a large integer multiplication by few multiplications, additions and subtractions on smaller integers. KS can require one more subdivision than KSV and SHIFT&ADD to avoid a lot of load, store and addition in software. Hence, to determine the most efficient algorithm, with the requirement of d subdivisions for KSV and SHIFT&ADD and d' subdivisions for KS, we only need to compare the following complexities, depending on the component specification.

- SHIFT&ADD: $E(n) + x^d \left(\frac{y}{x} A(\frac{n}{2^d}\ell, \frac{n}{2^d}\ell) + \frac{n}{2^d}(S(\frac{n}{2^d}\ell, \ell) + \frac{\delta}{2}A(\frac{n}{2^d}\ell, \frac{n}{2^d}\ell)) \right)$.
- Kronecker substitution: $2E(n) + x^{d'} \left(\frac{y}{x} A(\frac{n}{2^d}\ell, \frac{n}{2^d}\ell) + M(\frac{n}{2^{d+1}}\ell, \frac{n}{2^{d+1}}\ell) \right)$.
- Kronecker substitution variant: $E(n) + x^d(\frac{y}{x}A(\frac{n}{2^d}\ell, \frac{n}{2^d}\ell) + \frac{n}{2^d}[M(\frac{n}{2^d}\ell, k) + S(\frac{n}{2^d}\ell, \ell) + A(\frac{n}{2^d}\ell, \frac{n}{2^d}\ell)])$.

The values x and y are, respectively, the number of sub-multiplications and the number of additions (or subtractions) required by the subdivision method. Hence, for the naive subdivision $x = 4$ and $y = 3$ and for Karatsuba $x = 3$ and $y = 6$.

In this paper we use the naive or Karatsuba to subdivide but the subdivision can be achieved with other methods.

5 Assessment

5.1 Context

We evaluate three lattice-based algorithms: Saber, LAC and Kyber. They have been submitted to the NIST PQC standardization [DKRV19, XYD+19, ABD+19]. Saber and Kyber passed the 2nd round and they are finalists of the 3rd round. LAC did not pass the NIST 2nd round but won the Chinese cryptographic competition and thus remains relevant to study.

Parameters. In the following, the Kyber 1st round specifications are considered for Kyber512R1 and Kyber1024R1, in order to compare our results with the previous work in [AHH+19]. For the other schemes, 2nd round specifications are considered. However, Saber 3rd round parameters and the last two Kyber's 3rd round security levels parameters are the same as 2nd round. Our results come from a device with dedicated hardware coprocessor for large-integer operations (multiplication, addition, subtraction, right/left shift).

In the following results we consider the multiplication of $f(x)$ by $g(x)$ over $R_q = \mathbb{Z}_q[x]/(x^n + 1)$, where:

1. $f(x)$ is of degree $n-1$ with coefficients in $\{0, \ldots, q-1\}$.
2. $g(x)$ is of degree $n-1$ with coefficients in $\left\{\frac{-\delta}{2}, \ldots, \frac{\delta}{2}\right\}$.
3. The evaluation point is 2^ℓ, where the value of ℓ is given by Proposition 1.

Parameters for each candidate are represented in the following table.

Set/Param	n	q	δ	ℓ
Kyber512R1	256	7681	10	25
Kyber1024R1	256	7681	6	24
KyberR2	256	3329	4	22
Light Saber	256	2^{13}	10	25
Fire Saber	256	2^{13}	6	24
Lac128	512	251	2	18
Lac256	1024	251	2	19

Target. Assessments are done on a smart card component. Due to intellectual properties reasons, the component name or a detailed description cannot be given. However, details on our analysis are given, allowing it to be reproduced on any component embedding a similar coprocessor designed for large integer arithmetic. This component is used in real-life products like bank cards, passports, secure elements, etc. It embeds hardware accelerators for asymmetric cryptography computations, including large-integer arithmetic.

In the following, the chip is referred as "Component A".

Component A. The Component A is a ARM 32-bit architecture. Its asymmetric coprocessor can handle 2048-bit operands. The addition of two 2048-bit integers is done in less than ten cycles, while the multiplication takes several thousand cycles. Since the addition is several thousand times cheaper than the multiplication, SHIFT&ADD is expected to be faster than Kronecker Substitution when one operand has coefficients close to 0.

The coprocessor can also multiply a coefficient to a 2048-bit operand, that is of interest with Kronecker Substitution Variant. Then, KSV is expected to be faster than SHIFT&ADD and Kronecker Substitution when one operand has small coefficients but not too close to 0.

5.2 From Theory to Practice: A Methodology

In this section, we propose a methodology to determine, with a minimal amount of implementation, which polynomial multiplication algorithm is the fastest on a given component and for a given set of parameters. This is done by measuring the timings of basic operations (integer multiplication, addition and subtraction, shift and evaluation) and plugging them into the complexities from Sect. 4. Hence, this ease the algorithm choice without coding all the multiplication algorithms. This can help a developer to quickly decide which algorithm is the best choice.

We detail the methodology for Kyber512R1 parameters on component A. We focus on the comparison between Kronecker Substitution and SHIFT&ADD and between Kronecker Substitution Variant and SHIFT&ADD.

Component A's coprocessor can handle operands of about 2048 bits. For Kyber512R1 parameters $n = 256$ and $\ell = 25$, the polynomials after evaluation are of size $n\ell = 6400$ bits. Thus, we subdivide it to perform our algorithms (see Sect. 4.4).

On this component, the naive subdivision is more efficient than Karatsuba. For Kronecker Substitution we subdivide until the result $f(x)g(x)$ can fit in the coprocessor. That requires 3 subdivisions to get $\frac{n}{2^3}\ell = 800$ bitsize per operand. For SHIFT&ADD and KSV, we subdivide until the subdivisions of polynomial $f(x)$ can fit in the coprocessor. That requires 2 subdivisions of size 1600-bit. Then, KS requires one more subdivision than KSV and SHIFT&ADD to avoid a lot of load, store and addition in software. Indeed, KS result doubles the size of the operand while each iteration of KSV and SHIFT&ADD increases only by ℓ the result size, which can be handled without an important amount of software manipulation.

Naive subdivision transforms large arithmetic operations to 4^d smaller arithmetic operations, where d is the required depth. This leads to the following expressions for SHIFT&ADD, KS and KSV complexities:

$$\text{S\&A} : 4^2(\frac{n}{2^2}[\frac{\delta}{2}A(1600, 1600) + S(1600, \ell)]) + 12A(1600, 1600) + E(n)$$

$$\text{KS} : 4^3 M(800, 800) + 48A(1600, 1600) + 2E(n)$$

$$\text{KSV} : 4^2(\frac{n}{2^2}[M(1600, \ell) + S(1600, \ell) + A(1600, 1600)]) + 12A(1600, 1600) + E(n)$$

The value $12A(1600, 1600)$ and $48A(1600, 1600)$ are due to the recombination of the naive subdivision but they are negligible. Let $C(S\&A) = \frac{n}{2^2}(\frac{\delta}{2}A(1600, 1600) + S(1600, \ell)) + 3A(1600, 1600)$. We measure the execution time corresponding to $C(S\&A)$ as a reference. Then we measure $E(n)$, $M(800, 800)$ and $M(1600, \ell) + S(1600, \ell) + A(1600, 1600)$ and express them in terms of $C(S\&A)$. These measurements are obtained with an emulator. We get that:

$$E(n) \simeq 1.34 \times C(S\&A)$$

$$M(800, 800) \simeq 0.20 \times C(S\&A)$$

$$\frac{n}{2^2}(M(1600, \ell) + S(1600, \ell) + A(1600, 1600)) \simeq 0,86 \times C(S\&A).$$

It follows the following estimations for SHIFT&ADD, KS and KSV:

$$S\&A: 4^2 C(S\&A) + E(n) \simeq 17.34 \times C(S\&A)$$
$$KS: 4^3 M(800, 800) + 2E(n) \simeq 15.48 \times C(S\&A)$$
$$KSV: 4^2 (0.86 \times C(S\&A)) + E(n) \simeq 15.1 \times C(S\&A)$$

Hence, in this configuration, KSV is expected to be the fastest algorithm for these parameters.

Following this methodology, we get the expected ratios in Table 1 between Kronecker Substitution and SHIFT&ADD and between KSV and SHIFT&ADD, all measurements being obtained with emulators.

Table 1. Expected ratio based on basic operations performances for component A

	KS/S&A	KSV/S&A		KS/S&A	KSV/S&A
Kyber512R1	0.89	0.87	Fire Saber	1.17	1.1
Kyber1024R1	1.17	1.1	Lac128	1.45	1.37
KyberR2	1.26	1.2	Lac256	1.41	1.42
Light Saber	0.89	0.87			

5.3 Experiments

In the sequel, assessments are done using an emulator and we measure the performance of the following:

- algorithms relying on hardware coprocessors (KS, KSV, SHIFT&ADD)
- software implementation of schoolbook multiplication (Saber, Lac)
- software implementation of NTT (Kyber)

The NTT implementation used for Kyber512R1 and Kyber1024R1 is detailed in [LN16]. For KyberR2, the reference implementation of Kyber 2nd round is used [ABD+19]. We measure NTT performance with the requirement of frequency transformations of both polynomials (w/NTT(A)) or with only one frequency transformation (w/o NTT(A)).

Our hardware polynomial multiplications consider that the inputs are not in the NTT domain. Hence, in the case of a Kyber specification compliant implementation additional inverses NTT would have to be performed, which implies that a slower hardware polynomial multiplication than a NTT one.

For LAC software naive multiplication, we report the result for a C implementation and an optimized version in assembly (asm).

Software implementation results are given for information purposes and are not specifically optimized. Indeed, our objective is to provide algorithms which can be applied on many as possible components using a RSA/ECC coprocessors.

Therefore, optimizations for software polynomial multiplication using specific instructions set is out of our scope.

Our results are obtained by computing a complete polynomial multiplication over R_q with a compact representation as mentioned in Sect. 2. The following timings take into account the computation done by the CPU and the coprocessor. Moreover, any optimization of the reduction modulo q and $x^n + 1$ are done. For the same reason, we avoid any optimization which requires a specific software instructions set. However, software optimizations for modular reductions can be used on top of any polynomial multiplication algorithm.

Practical results are given in Table 2. As expected for the component A regarding Table 1, SHIFT&ADD is the fastest algorithm for 5/7 parameter sets and KSV is the fastest algorithm for the 2 others. Hence, for this component and these parameters, SHIFT&ADD or KSV are faster than the hardware multiplication introduced in [AHH+19].

Note that the theoretical ratios from Table 1 are not the exact same ratios between the practical results. This is because radix conversion and reduction over R_q are not taken into account in the theoretical complexity (see Sect. 4), while these operations are part of the timings in Table 2. Nevertheless, the fastest algorithm is always the expected one and proves that our methodology introduced in Sect. 5.2 is relevant.

Table 2. Polynomial multiplication over R_q cycle count on component A

Param/Algo	KS	KSV	S&A	NTT (w/w/o NTT(A))	NAIVE
Kyber512R1	588k	**556k**	594k	1139k/793k	N/A
Kyber1024R1	572k	539k	**500k**	1139k/793k	N/A
KyberR2	535k	512k	**441k**	998k/704k	N/A
Light Saber	580k	**546k**	585k	N/A	11691k
Fire Saber	563k	530k	**493k**	N/A	11440k
Lac128	1594k	1586k	**1285k**	N/A	15560k/1683k (asm)
Lac256	6209k	6310k	**4980k**	N/A	62340k/7494k (asm)

Table 3. Positive trade-off polynomial multiplication over R_q cycle count on component A

Param/Algo	KSV$_{\geq 0}$	S&A$_{\geq 0}$	KSV/KSV$_{\geq 0}$	S&A/S&A$_{\geq 0}$
KyberR2	362k	**326k**	1.41	1.35
Fire Saber	363k	**354k**	1.46	1.39
Lac256	4437k	**3455k**	1.42	1.44

Positive Time/Memory Trade-Off. The positive time/memory trade-off is presented in Sect. 4.3. This trade-off ensures that any carry propagation must be handled during polynomial multiplication, at cost of a supplementary storage ($n\ell$ bits). However, this trade-off only applies to KSV and S&A algorithms.

The Table 3 shows the practical results obtained on component A, with the highest security parameters of Kyber, Saber and LAC. Furthermore, $KSV_{\geq 0}$ (resp. $S\&A_{\geq 0}$) denotes the algorithm Kronecker Substitution Variant (resp. Shift&Add) using the positive trade-off. For the three parameters sets, a significant performance gain on hardware polynomial multiplication is achieved (at least 1.35), at cost of an additional storage of $n\ell$ bits.

6   Conclusion

In this paper, we pursue the work initiated in [AHH+19]. We propose two additional methods to compute polynomial multiplications using a RSA/ECC accelerator, when one operand has small coefficients. We introduce a methodology to compare the different methods, based on the implementation on a minimal set of basic functions. This methodology can help to quickly choose the most efficient multiplication algorithm on a given platform, depending on the cryptosystem parameters.

Then, we assess the polynomial multiplication algorithms for several NIST KEM candidates parameters on a smart card chip. The practical results are consistent with the expected behavior from our methodology. In our study, we show that hybrid cryptography can be realized with other methods than the Kronecker Substitution. Moreover, we show that the most optimized method for a given component can be determined with the implementation of few basic operations.

This attest that re-purposing standard asymmetric coprocessor to speed-up lattice-based cryptography is of interest especially in a context of hybrid cryptography deployment.

References

[ABD+19] Avanzi, R., et al.: CRYSTALS-Kyber (2019). https://csrc.nist.gov/ Projects/Post-Quantum-Cryptography/Round-2-Submissions

[AHH+19] Albrecht, M.R., Hanser, C., Hoeller, A., Pöppelmann, T., Virdia, F., Wallner, A.: Implementing RLWE-based schemes using an RSA Coprocessor. IACR Trans. Cryptogr. Hardware Embed. Syst. 169–208 (2019)

[BSI] BSI. Migration zu Post-Quanten-Kryptografie - Handlungsempfehlungen des BSI

[CCA+20] Chowdhury, S., Covic, A., Acharya, R.Y., Dupee, S., Ganji, F., Forte, D.: Physical security in the post-quantum era: a survey on side-channel analysis, random number generators, and physically unclonable functions. arXiv preprint arXiv:2005.04344, 2020. https://arxiv. org/abs/2005.04344

[CHK+20] Chung, C.-M.M., Hwang, V., Kannwischer, M.J., Seiler, G., Shih, C.J., Yang, B.Y.: NTT multiplication for NTT-unfriendly rings. Cryptology ePrint Archive, Report 2020/1397 (2020). https://eprint.iacr.org/2020/1397

[DFA+20] Dang, V.B., Farahmand, F., Andrzejczak, M., Mohajerani, K., Nguyen, D.T., Gaj, K.: Implementation and benchmarking of round 2 candidates in the NIST post-quantum cryptography standardization process using hardware and software/hardware co-design approaches. Cryptology ePrint Archive, Report 2020/795 (2020). https://eprint.iacr.org/2020/795

[DKRV19] D'Anvers, J.-P., Karmakar, A., Roy, S.S., Vercauteren, F.: Saber (2019). https://csrc.nist.gov/Projects/Post-Quantum-Cryptography/Round-2-Submissions

[EFGT17] Espitau, T., Fouque, P.-A., Gérard, B., Tibouchi, M.: Side-channel attacks on BLISS lattice-based signatures: exploiting branch tracing against strongSwan and electromagnetic emanations in microcontrollers. In: Proceedings of the 2017 ACM SIGSAC Conference on Computer and Communications Security, pp. 1857–1874 (2017)

[fCR18] Chinese Association for Cryptography Research. National cryptographic algorithm design competition (2018). https://www.cacrnet.org.cn/site/content/838.html

[fCR20] Chinese Association for Cryptography Research. Lac won first prize of the national cryptographic algorithm design competition (2020). https://m.cacrnet.org.cn/site/content/854.html

[GKS20] Denisa, O., Greconici, C., Kannwischer, M.J., Sprenkels, D.: Compact dilithium implementations on Cortex-M3 and Cortex-M4. Cryptology ePrint Archive, Report 2020/1278 (2020). https://eprint.iacr.org/2020/1278

[Har07] Harvey, D.: Faster polynomial multiplication via multipoint Kronecker substitution (2007)

[JWBJRCvV20] Bos, J.W., Renes, J., van Vredendaal, C.: Polynomial multiplication with contemporary co-processors: beyond Kronecker, Schönhage-Strassen & Nussbaumer. Cryptology ePrint Archive, Report 2020/1303 (2020). https://eprint.iacr.org/2020/1303

[Kro82] Kronecker, L.: Grundzüge einer arithmetischen theorie der algebraischen grössen. (abdruck einer festschrift zu herrn e. e. kummers doctorjubiläum. Journal für die reine und angewandte Mathematik **92**, 1–122 (1882)

[LN16] Longa, P., Naehrig, M.: Speeding up the number theoretic transform for faster ideal lattice-based cryptography. In: Foresti, S., Persiano, G. (eds.) CANS 2016. LNCS, vol. 10052, pp. 124–139. Springer, Cham (2016). https://doi.org/10.1007/978-3-319-48965-0_8

[Lom16] Lomne, V.: CHES Tutorial: Common Criteria Certification of a Smartcard: a Technical Overview (2016). https://iacr.org/workshops/ches/ches2016/presentations/CHES16-Tutorial1.pdf

[MAA+20] Moody, D., et al.: Status report on the second round of the NIST post-quantum cryptography standardization process. Technical report, National Institute of Standards and Technology, July 2020

[Moo16] Moody, D.: Post-Quantum Cryptography NIST's Plan for the Future (2016). https://csrc.nist.gov/CSRC/media/Projects/Post-Quantum-Cryptography/documents/pqcrypto-2016-presentation.pdf

[MOP08] Mangard, S., Oswald, E., Popp, T.: Power Analysis Attacks. Springer, Boston, MA (2007). https://doi.org/10.1007/978-0-387-38162-6

[Nus82] Nussbaumer, H.J.: Number theoretic transforms. In: Fast Fourier Transform and Convolution Algorithms, pp. 211–240. Springer, Heidelberg (1982). https://doi.org/10.1007/978-3-642-81897-4_8

[OSPG18] Oder, T., Schneider, T., Pöppelmann, T., Güneysu, T.: Practical CCA2-secure and masked ring-LWE implementation. IACR Trans. Cryptogr. Hardware Embed. Syst. 142–174 (2018)

[RdCR+16] Reparaz, O., de Clercq, R., Roy, S.S., Vercauteren, F., Verbauwhede, I.: Additively homomorphic ring-LWE masking. In: Takagi, T. (ed.) PQCrypto 2016. LNCS, vol. 9606, pp. 233–244. Springer, Cham (2016). https://doi.org/10.1007/978-3-319-29360-8_15

[RJH+18] Ravi, P., Jhanwar, M.P., Howe, J., Chattopadhyay, A., Bhasin, S.: Side-channel assisted existential forgery attack on Dilithium-A NIST PQC candidate (2018). https://eprint.iacr.org/2018/821

[RRDC+16] Reparaz, O., Roy, S.S., De Clercq, R., Vercauteren, F., Verbauwhede, I.: Masking ring-LWE. J. Cryptogr. Eng. 6(2), 139–153 (2016)

[Sch82] Schönhage, A.: Asymptotically fast algorithms for the numerical multiplication and division of polynomials with complex coeficients. In: EUROCAM (1982)

[Sho97] Shor, P.W.: Polynomial-time algorithms for prime factorization and discrete logarithms on a quantum computer. SIAM J. Comput. 26(5), 1484–1509 (1997)

[SRB20] Roy, S.S., Basso, A.: High-speed instruction-set coprocessor for lattice-based key encapsulation mechanism: saber in hardware. IACR Trans. Cryptogr. Hardware Embed. Syst. 2020(4), 443–466 (2020)

[WGY20] Wang, B., Gu, X., Yang, Y.: Saber on ESP32. In: Conti, M., Zhou, J., Casalicchio, E., Spognardi, A. (eds.) ACNS 2020. LNCS, vol. 12146, pp. 421–440. Springer, Cham (2020). https://doi.org/10.1007/978-3-030-57808-4_21

[XYD+19] Lu, X., Liu, Y., Jia, D., Xue, H., He, H., Zhang, Z.: LAC: lattice-based cryptosystems (2019). https://csrc.nist.gov/Projects/Post-Quantum-Cryptography/Round-2-Submissions

[YZMZBY+20] Zhu, Y., et al.: A high-performance hardware implementation of saber based on Karatsuba algorithm. Cryptology ePrint Archive, Report 2020/1037 (2020). https://eprint.iacr.org/2020/1037

Full Key Recovery Side-Channel Attack Against Ephemeral SIKE on the Cortex-M4

Aymeric Genêt[1,2], Natacha Linard de Guertechin[3], and Novak Kaluđerović[1(✉)]

[1] École Polytechnique Fédérale de Lausanne, Lausanne, Switzerland
{aymeric.genet,novak.kaluderovic}@epfl.ch
[2] Kudelski Group, Cheseaux-sur-Lausanne, Switzerland
[3] CYSEC SA, Lausanne, Switzerland
natacha.linard@cysec.com

Abstract. This paper describes the first practical single-trace side-channel power analysis of SIKE. While SIKE is a post-quantum key exchange, the scheme still relies on a secret elliptic curve scalar multiplication which involves a loop of a double-and-add procedure, of which each iteration depends on a single bit of the private key. The attack therefore exploits the nature of elliptic curve point addition formulas which require the same function to be executed multiple times. We show how a single trace of a loop iteration can be segmented into several power traces on which 32-bit words can be hypothesised based on the value of a single private key bit. This segmentation enables a classical correlation power analysis in an extend-and-prune approach. Further error-correction techniques based on depth-search are suggested. The attack is explicitly geared towards and experimentally verified on an STM32F3 featuring a Cortex-M4 microcontroller which runs the SIKEp434 implementation adapted to 32-bit ARM that is part of the official implementations of SIKE. We obtained a resounding 100% success rate recovering the full private key in each experiment. We argue that our attack defeats many countermeasures which were suggested in a previous power analysis of SIKE, and finally show that the well-known countermeasure of projective coordinate randomisation stops the attack with a negligible overhead.

Keywords: Sike · Side-channel analysis · Correlation power analysis · Single-trace attack · Post-quantum key exchange · Isogeny-based cryptography

1 Introduction

The advancement of theoretical quantum computing in the last three decades has brought algorithms which pose a threat to modern day cryptography. In particular, almost all public-key protocols that are currently used can be completely

S. Bhasin and F. De Santis (Eds.): COSADE 2021, LNCS 12910, pp. 228–254, 2021.
https://doi.org/10.1007/978-3-030-89915-8_11

broken with Shor's algorithm [45]. Practical quantum computers seem to be lagging behind their theoretical counterparts and there are still doubts about their feasibility [29]. In order to prepare for the potential threat of quantum computers, the National Institute of Standards and Technology (NIST) published a call for proposals for setting new standards in quantum-resistant cryptography. The proposed protocols are classical algorithms for classical computers and, as such, are prone to standard side-channel attacks, such as timing attacks, power analyses, or electromagnetic attacks. At the time of writing, the NIST standardisation process has reached the third round in which one of the alternative candidates is SIKE – "Supersingular Isogeny Key Encapsulation"; the main topic of this paper.

The development of isogeny-based cryptography protocols started in 1997 by Couveignes [16], only to be independently rediscovered in 2006 by Rostovsev and Stolbunov [43]. Their algorithm was resistant to known classical attacks, but a subexponential quantum attack was found by Childs et al. [11]. This attack was mitigated by Jao and De Feo [18] (and Plût [17]) where they proposed to use supersingular instead of ordinary elliptic curves in an algorithm called SIDH which later became SIKE. Due to the nature of supersingular elliptic curves, i.e., non-commutativity of the endomorphism ring, the previously mentioned attack is prevented. In addition to the lack of subexponential attacks in both classical and quantum settings, the new SIKE algorithm stood out in its simple structure reminiscent of the classical Diffie–Hellman protocol, but also, and more importantly, SIKE was more efficient and had lower key sizes. Over the years, SIKE was improved [3,6,7,15,49] and the current implementation stands competitive with respect to other NIST candidates in the third round. One of the main downsides of SIKE is its high run-time which currently qualifies the scheme as the slowest surviving candidate. However, this downside is compensated with the lowest key sizes among all quantum-resistant candidates. The trade-off between the cost-effectiveness of the key-size and the computational cost was studied in [33,34,40,47].

Our work follows the NIST recommendation to study side-channel attacks on post-quantum cryptographic schemes [1,38] and consists of the side-channel power analysis of the SIKE implementation adapted to the 32-bit ARM Cortex-M4 chip architecture. The Cortex-M4 implementation by Azarderakhsh et al. [44] is included in the official third round NIST submission of SIKE [27]. Both implementations are constant-time. The main differences lie in the low-level functions, such as multi-precision additions, multiplications, and modular reductions that have been rewritten in assembly in order to take full advantage of the Cortex-M4 capabilities. This allowed the authors to obtain a performance improvement of about $20\times$ when compared to the official implementation in C. Furthermore, this improvement comes at no security cost, at least from the point of view of our attack, as the power analysis can be easily adapted to the C implementation (when run on the same microcontroller).

The Cortex-M4 [23] is a low-power and low-cost embedded microcontroller from the ARM Cortex-M family, which is recommended by NIST for post-quantum cryptography evaluation [31,39]. As such, the Cortex-M4 should be used with care in cryptographic settings. In particular, Le Corre et al. [14] have assessed the leakage on a chip from the Cortex family and have shown how the power consumption is correlated with the operands and results from the pipeline registers. These properties will show to be useful in our own analysis.

1.1 Contributions

The main contribution of our paper is a full private key extraction using a side-channel power analysis of the Cortex-M4 implementation of SIKE with only a single trace, which therefore breaks confidentiality in a passive setting. In particular, we target the three point ladder with a straightforward vertical attack (i.e., with multiple traces and a fixed secret) and show how to extend it to the case of a horizontal attack (i.e., with a single trace and a secret which can therefore be ephemeral). Because the three point ladder is similar to an elliptic point scalar multiplication, our attack is completely analogous to a power analysis of the pre-quantum elliptic curve cryptography. This attack can be applied at any stage of the protocol: key generation, key encapsulation, and key decapsulation. Finally, we argue how our horizontal power analysis defeats many countermeasures that were mentioned in the power analysis of SIKE as presented in [50]; namely, starting with a random isomorphic curve, masking the scalar, splitting the key randomly, and using a window-based scalar multiplication. We recommend the well-known projective point coordinate randomisation, which stops our attack with a negligible performance overhead.

1.2 Related Work

Side-channel analysis of supersingular isogeny protocols was initially conducted in [32] in which the authors address concerns about power analysis without carrying out a practical experiment. The first paper to practically evaluate the side-channel vulnerabilities of SIKE is due to Zhang et al. [50]. In their study, the authors fully describe a practical vertical differential power analysis on the three point ladder of the key decapsulation procedure, and discuss potential countermeasures. However, since the authors rely on the fact that the private key is fixed across the measurements, the attack is applicable only to the semi-static settings of the SIKE protocol. We extend these results and target SIKE in ephemeral settings.

In the past, many papers have already mounted horizontal attacks against the classical Montgomery ladder in the case of elliptic curve cryptography, such as [4,12,41]. We apply similar techniques, but on the variant of the ladder with three points used in SIKE.

For the sake of completeness, let us also mention template attacks; a different kind of single-trace attacks in which an adversary profiles the power consumption. Such attacks have also been explored against the elliptic curve scalar multiplication, for instance in [19,36,51]. As opposed to horizontal correlation power analyses, template attacks require control over the input of the targeted procedure and sometimes even further interactions with the targeted device. Online template attacks [5] against classical elliptic curve cryptography require only one power trace of the target device, but additional power measurements on the same or a similar template device are needed. Our horizontal correlation power analysis does not rely on such a hypothesis and is executed purely offline. In comparison, our attack is based on an entirely different setup where, instead of correlating power traces with each others, we correlate Hamming weights of processed values. Our results show much stronger correlations due to the reliance on a specific leakage model, unlike the online template attack which is leakage-agnostic.

Other post-quantum algorithms have been targeted by power analyses. In a similar fashion, Aysu et al. [2] have attacked the lattice-based key exchanges of Frodo and NewHope with a horizontal correlation power analysis. Bos et al. have addressed this attack in [8] and proposed a profiled extend-and-prune approach. Recently, Sim et al. [46] have shown a single-trace ephemeral-key recovery against various lattice-based key exchanges. Finally, let us mention the work of Primas et al. [42] in which the first single-trace attack on lattice-based encryption was described using belief propagation. This work was recently extended by Kannwischer et al. [30] to a single-trace power analysis of the Keccak hash function, used in various applications, including the hash-based signature scheme SPHINCS+.

2   Background

We recall some of the definitions which will be used in this paper. For a more formal discussion the reader is advised to see [17] and [27].

2.1   SIDH – Supersingular Isogeny Diffie-Hellman

Let p be a prime of form $p = l_A^{e_A} l_B^{e_B} f \pm 1$, with l_A, l_B different primes, e_A, e_B non-zero integers, and f a small cofactor. For ease of exposition we assume that $f = 1$. We define the starting curve E_0 to be a curve over $\mathbb{F}_{p^2}$ of cardinality $(p \mp 1)^2 = (l_A^{e_A} l_B^{e_B})^2$ and isomorphic to

$$E(\mathbb{F}_{p^2}) \cong E[l_A^{e_A}] \oplus E[l_B^{e_B}] \cong \langle P_A, Q_A \rangle \oplus \langle P_B, Q_B \rangle,$$

where (P_A, Q_A) and (P_B, Q_B) are bases of $E[l_A^{e_A}]$ and $E[l_B^{e_B}]$ respectively. The public parameters of the protocol are

$$(p, E_0, P_A, Q_A, P_B, Q_B).$$

The protocol itself, as the name suggests, is similar to the classical Diffie–Hellman protocol. Each of the two parties (Alice and Bob) go through two phases: the public key generation, and the shared secret key computation.

Public Key Generation. Alice choses her private key $sk_A \in [0, l_A^{e_A})$, and computes the point $R_A = P_A + [sk_A]Q_A$. She then computes the isogeny $\phi_A : E_0 \rightarrow E_A$ of kernel $\langle R_A \rangle$. Finally she computes the images of points P_B, Q_B through ϕ_A, and sets her public key to be the triple

$$pk_A = (E_A, \phi_A(P_B), \phi_A(Q_B)).$$

Analogously, Bob sets $sk_B \in [0, l_B^{e_B})$ and computes $R_B = P_B + [sk_B]Q_B$, the isogeny $\phi_B : E_0 \rightarrow E_B$ of kernel $\langle R_B \rangle$, and $\phi_B(P_A)$ and $\phi_B(Q_A)$. His public key is

$$pk_B = (E_B, \phi_B(P_A), \phi_B(Q_A)).$$

Shared Secret Key Computation. In order to compute the shared secret, Alice computes $R'_A = \phi_B(P_A) + [sk_A]\phi_B(Q_A)$ and the isogeny $\phi'_A : E_B \rightarrow E_{BA}$ of kernel $\langle R'_A \rangle$. Bob computes $R'_B = \phi_A(P_B) + [sk_B]\phi_A(Q_B)$, and the isogeny $\phi'_B : E_A \rightarrow E_{AB}$ of kernel $\langle R'_B \rangle$. The final curves E_{BA} and E_{AB} are equal [35], and the j-invariant $j(E_{AB}) = j(E_{BA})$ constitutes the shared secret of Alice and Bob.

2.2 SIKE – Supersingular Isogeny Key Encapsulation

The textbook SIDH protocol, as explained above, is insecure [22] in the static (i.e., the key pair of both parties is fixed) or semi-static settings (i.e., the key pair of one of the two parties is fixed). In order to overcome this weakness, the Fujisaki–Okamoto transform [21] is introduced which allows defence against known attacks at the cost of a performance overhead and losing the possibility of having fully static public keys.

The public parameters, as in SIDH, are

$$pp = (p, E_0, P_A, Q_A, P_B, Q_B).$$

For efficiency reasons, we set $l_A = 2$, $l_B = 3$, and the starting supersingular curve is selected to be

$$E_0 : y^2 = x^3 + 6x^2 + x.$$

The protocol is asymmetrical, so we will assume that Bob is the *server* and Alice is the *client*. There are three phases: the public key generation, the key encapsulation, and the key decapsulation.

Public Key Generation. Bob starts by choosing a random string $s \in \{0,1\}^t$ ($t > 0$ public parameter) which will be used to create a random key K if he detects a cheating attempt from Alice. Then, as before, Bob chooses a random private key $sk_B \in [0, l_B^{e_B})$ and computes $R_B = P_B + [sk_B]Q_B$. After computing $\phi_B : E_0 \rightarrow E_B$ of kernel $\langle R_B \rangle$, and the images under ϕ_B of P_A and Q_A, Bob sets his public key to be

$$pk_B = (E_B, \phi_B(P_A), \phi_B(Q_A)).$$

Algorithm 1: PUBLIC KEY GENERATION

Procedure Public key generation(pp)

1    $sk_B \leftarrow [0, l_B^{e_B})$

2    $s \leftarrow \{0,1\}^t$

3    $R_B = P_B + [sk_B]Q_B$

4   Let $\phi_B : E_0 \to E_B$ be such that $\mathrm{Ker}(\phi_B) = \langle R_B \rangle$

    Output: $pk_B = (E_B, \phi_B(P_A), \phi_B(Q_A))$

Key Encapsulation. Alice generates a random message $m \in \{0,1\}^t$ ($t > 0$ public parameter) which plays the role of the secret in the following. Then, Alice computes her private key by setting

$$sk_A = G(m \,\|\, pk_B) \mod l_A^{e_A},$$

where G is a public cryptographic hash function (in practice, SHAKE256 is used). She proceeds by computing $R_A = P_A + [sk_A]Q_A$, the corresponding isogeny $\phi_A : E_0 \to E_A$, and the images under ϕ_A of P_B, Q_B. She sets

$$c_0 = pk_A = (E_A, \phi_A(P_B), \phi_A(Q_B)),$$

and proceeds by computing the common secret $j(E_{BA})$ and $c_1 = F(j(E_{BA})) \oplus m$, where F is also a cryptographic hash function that may or may not be different from G. Finally, Alice sends the concatenation of c_0 and c_1 as ciphertext (i.e., $ct = c_0 \,\|\, c_1$) to Bob and computes the key K to be used as $K = H(m \,\|\, ct)$ (where H is yet another cryptographic hash function which can be the same as G or F).

Algorithm 2: KEY ENCAPSULATION

Procedure Key encapsulation(pp, pk_b)

1    $m \leftarrow \{0,1\}^t$

2    $sk_A = G(m \,\|\, pk_B) \mod l_A^{e_A}$

3    $R_A = P_A + [sk_A]Q_A$

4   Let $\phi_A : E_0 \to E_A$ be such that $\mathrm{Ker}(\phi_A) = \langle R_A \rangle$

5    $pk_A = (E_A, \phi_A(P_B), \phi_A(Q_B))$

6    $R'_A = \phi_B(P_A) + [sk_A]\phi_B(Q_A)$

7   Let $\phi'_A : E_B \to E_{BA}$ be such that $\mathrm{Ker}(\phi'_A) = \langle R'_A \rangle$

8    $c_0 = pk_A$

9    $c_1 = F(j(E_{BA})) \oplus m$

10   $K = H(m \,\|\, ct)$

    Output: $ct = (c_0 \,\|\, c_1)$

Key Decapsulation. After receiving $ct = (c'_0 \,\|\, c'_1)$, Bob sets $pk'_A := c'_0$, computes $j(E'_{AB})$, and extracts $m' = F(j(E'_{AB})) \oplus c'_1$ as shown in Algorithm 3. Bob then computes

$$sk'_A = G(m' \| pk_B) \mod l_A^{e_A},$$

and proceeds by computing the corresponding public key pk''_A. Bob then checks that $pk''_A = pk'_A$, to confirm the truthfulness of Alice. In case the check passes, he sets $K = H(m' \,||\, ct)$, and $K = H(s \,||\, ct)$ otherwise.

Algorithm 3: KEY DECAPSULATION

Procedure Key decapsulation(ct)

1   $(E'_A, P'_B, Q'_B) = c'_0$
2   $R'_B = P'_B + [sk_B]Q'_B$
3   Let $\phi'_B : E'_A \to E'_{AB}$ be such that $\mathrm{Ker}(\phi'_B) = \langle R'_B \rangle$
4   $m' = F(j(E'_{AB})) \oplus c'_1$
5   $sk'_A = G(m' \,||\, pk_B) \mod l^{e_A}_A$
6   $R' = P_A + [sk'_A]Q_A$
7   Let $\phi' : E_0 \to E''_A$ be such that $\mathrm{Ker}(\phi') = \langle R' \rangle$
8   $pk''_A = (E''_A, \phi'(P_B), \phi'(Q_B))$
9   **if** $pk''_A = c_0$ **then**
     | $K \leftarrow H(m' \,||\, ct)$
     else
     | $K \leftarrow H(s \,||\, ct)$
     Output: K

2.3 Point of Attack

The attack takes place at step 2 of key decapsulation which is coloured in red. This operation is computed using the *"three point ladder"*. The input of the three point ladder is the public key of Alice and the execution depends on the private key of Bob. In the semi-static settings of the protocol, Bob executes the three point ladder with different inputs from different public keys of Alice (or other *client* parties) and with his own static private key. Our initial goal was to correlate the power traces from different executions of the three point ladder with the hamming weights of the corresponding public keys. This approach was successful, and we were actually able to obtain the full private key of Bob with only one power trace, i.e., from a measurement of only one communication with Alice. This allowed us to extend the attack to step 3 of Algorithm 1 and step 3 of Algorithm 2 coloured in blue, since these steps consist of the same three point ladder executed with, except for the secret keys, known inputs.

2.4 Correlation Power Analysis

A Correlation Power Analysis (CPA) [9] is a statistical known-text side-channel power analysis that aims to deduce a portion of a secret value across multiple power measurements. A CPA aims to use a correlation coefficient to quantify the link between power consumption and the values processed by a processing unit. In the scope of this paper, we consider two types of CPA:

- *Vertical* CPA, which targets a *fixed* secret value across different executions of the attacked algorithm by collecting *multiple* power traces that correspond to multiple executions of the *same* operation.
- *Horizontal* CPA, which targets an *ephemeral* secret value using a *single* power trace that correspond to *multiple* operations. These operations must be similar to allow the segmentation of the power trace into multiple ones to simulate a vertical CPA.

In a typical threat model for CPA, the adversary has the capability of measuring the power consumption of a target device which acts as a black-box key decapsulating device. The algorithm inputs are not required to be manipulated but are supposed to be accessible by the target device. As a result, a CPA attack is completely passive (i.e., non-intrusive) and can be mounted even during a trusted communication between two honest parties.

To assess correlation between the processed values and the power samples, the Pearson's Correlation Coefficient (PCC) is computed. Let $n > 0$ be the number of measurements, each of which consists of $S > 0$ power samples. Then, let $T(s) \in \mathbb{R}^n$ be a vector of power samples synchronised at a same instant $0 \le s < S$, and $M \in \mathbb{N}^n$ a vector of the Hamming weight of the processed values.

$$\mathrm{PCC}(M, T(s)) = \frac{\mathrm{Cov}(M, T(s))}{\sqrt{\mathrm{Var}(M)\mathrm{Var}(T(s))}}.$$

The overall attack consists of the following steps:

1. Find an operation in the attacked procedure which involves:
   (a) A (small) portion of a secret value which is the same across all measurements.
   (b) A known input (resp. output).
   In the following, we refer to the result of this operation as the *intermediate value*.
2. Collect $n > 0$ power traces consisting of $S > 0$ power samples each, i.e., $T(s)$ for $0 \le s < S$, that correspond to the computation of the intermediate value with different inputs (resp. outputs).
3. Take a guess for the portion of the secret value involved in the intermediate value computation.
4. Compute the vector of intermediate values from the known inputs (resp. outputs) and the secret value guess, and derive its corresponding vector of Hamming weight M.
5. For each vector of power samples at a same time, i.e., $T(s)$ for each $0 \le s < S$, compute $\mathrm{PCC}(M, T(s))$.
   This results in a vector of PCC at each moment in time.

Using a large enough $n > 0$ given the signal-to-noise ratio of the power consumption, a strong PCC at any point in time indicates a valid guess, while a weak PCC at every point in time can rule out said guess.

Figure 1 gives a visual example of a CPA. In this example, the portion of the secret value is only one bit, resulting thus in two possible intermediate values. The PCC computation takes one of the two Hamming weight vectors M sketched on the left of the figure, and each vector of power samples at a same timing instant shown on the right, to produce each point in the corresponding PCC plot below. Since the PCC plot for the bit guess of one shows a spike, the corresponding bit for the secret value is successfully recovered.

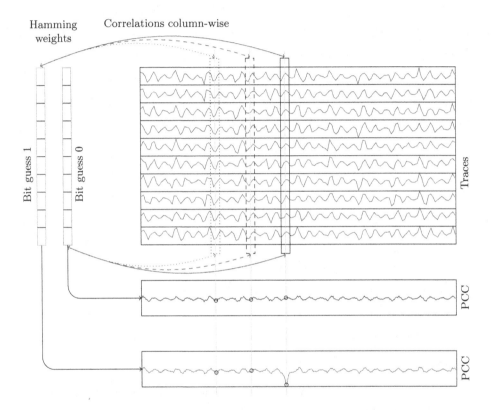

Fig. 1. Visual example of a CPA. Correlations between two arrays of Hamming weights and the power traces are plotted in the bottom. A strong correlation indicates that the bit value associated to these power traces is 1.

3 Side-Channel Analysis

In this chapter, we explain how to exploit the link between power consumption and processed data in order to recover private key bits.

3.1 The Three Point Ladder

The main point of attack is the three point ladder. This is a function which takes as input an elliptic curve E and two points P and Q on that curve. These may be thought of as $pk_A = (E_A, \phi_A(P_B), \phi_A(Q_B))$ or (E_0, P_A, Q_A) etc. The three point ladder computes the point $R = P + [sk]Q$ where sk is the private key of the computing party.

Montgomery Representation. The curve E over the field $\mathbb{F}_{p^2}$ is represented in Montgomery representation [37] as

$$E : \beta Y^2 Z = X^3 + \alpha X^2 Z + X Z^2, \qquad \text{for some } \alpha, \beta \in \mathbb{F}_{p^2}.$$

In SIKE, we are only interested in curves where $\beta = 1$ so the curves which we work with depend on a single parameter α.

Montgomery curves allow for compact representation of points, up to sign, by using only the X and the Z coordinates. In particular, a point $S = [X_S : Y_S : Z_S] \neq [0 : 1 : 0]$ can be represented by a single field element $x_s = X_S/Z_S \in \mathbb{F}_{p^2}$. The value $[X_S : Z_S] = [x_s : 1]$ uniquely defines $\{\pm S\}$, and we write $S = [x_s : 1]$.

The triple (E, P, Q) containing a curve and two points is represented as three field elements (x_Q, x_P, x_{Q-P}), where $Q = [x_Q : 1]$, $P = [x_P : 1]$, $Q - P = [x_{Q-P} : 1]$; the coefficient α defining the curve E can be obtained from these values with a couple of modular multiplications, squarings and a single inversion.

The main ingredient of the three point ladder is a double-and-add function xDBLADD. It takes as input a triple of points $S, T, U \in E$ in Montgomery representation such that $U = S - T$, the curve defining coefficient α, and outputs $(2S, T + S, U)$. The ladder takes as input $Q, Q - P, P$ and computes $P + [sk]Q$ by going through the bits of sk starting from the least significant, as shown in Algorithm 4.

Algorithm 4: THREE POINT LADDER

Procedure Three point ladder (x_Q, x_P, x_{Q-P})

```
1    prev_bit = 0
2    S = [xQ : 1], T = [xQ−P : 1], U = [xP : 1]
3    α = curve_coefficient(S, T, U)
4    for i ← 0 to bitlength(sk) − 1 do
5        current_bit = sk[i]
6        if (current_bit ≠ prev_bit) then
7            swap(T, U)
8        (S, T, U) = xDBLADD(S, T, U, α)
9        prev_bit = current_bit
10   if (prev_bit) then
11       swap(T, U)
     Output: U
```

The goal of the attack is to measure the power consumption of the xDBLADD operation and to deduce if the function was executed with or without the swap at step 7. We may assume that we know the private key up to bit $i - 1$, by induction. We also know the starting points $Q, P, Q - P$ since they are public. Therefore, we may obtain the two possible inputs for xDBLADD, and we know how they relate to the value of the ith bit of the private key. The two inputs and their Hamming weights are computed and the power trace of certain instructions within xDBLADD is correlated with the Hamming weights. Thanks to CPA, this allows us to distinguish when the ith bit is zero or one.

Double-and-Add. Despite the involvement of a (random) bit of the private key, xDBLADD is a deterministic function. The inputs and outputs of each sub-procedure in xDBLADD depend only on the original inputs of the function. As a result, an educated guess on the original inputs allow us to infer the results of all the operations involved in xDBLADD.

The function consists of 7 multiplications and 4 squarings of $\mathbb{F}_{p^2}$ elements, and multiple field additions, subtractions, and modular reductions. Each $\mathbb{F}_{p^2}$ multiplication and each squaring contain two multi-precision additions of $\mathbb{F}_p$ elements, referred to as "mp_addfast". This multi-precision addition is the operation on which our attack is focused. In total, there are $11 \times 2 = 22$ mp_addfast functions, out of which only 10 have inputs which differ in case of a swap at step 6 of the three point ladder. The code of xDBLADD and the squaring and multiplication functions can be found in Fig. 5.

Multi-precision Addition. In the Cortex-M4 implementation of SIKE, the mp_addfast is written in assembly. The function computes the addition of two $\mathbb{F}_p$ elements. Depending on the size of p, each field element is saved in an array of $n \in \{14, 16, 20, 24\}$ 32-bit words. Each mp_addfast executes $2n$ load instructions (LDMIA), n store instructions (STMIA), and n additions (ADDS, ADCS). These are executed in batches of four consecutive additions, due to the limited number of available registers on the Cortex-M4. The code of the mp_addfast function can be found in Fig. 6.

3.2 Vertical Attack

In a vertical attack against SIKE, we measure multiple executions of the three point ladder in which Bob's private key is fixed, but the client public key inputs are different. From these traces, we concentrate only on a single mp_addfast instruction per xDBLADD, i.e., per bit of the private key. Within the mp_addfast, we can decide to focus even further on the first addition instruction. We can thus compute the two possible outputs of the first ADDS depending on the (timing-constant) swap, for each public key, and then correlate the two vectors of Hamming weights of these outputs with the power traces using the CPA procedure from Sect. 2.4. This process can be repeated for each bit of Bob's private key, as the correctness of each guess depends on the correctness of previous ones, resulting thus in an *extend-and-prune* attack.

3.3 Horizontal Attack

In the horizontal attack scenario, we can measure only one power trace for a single execution of the three point ladder. The same approach as in the vertical attack cannot be used because there would not be enough data to obtain strong correlations. We can work out this issue and re-obtain *"verticality"* by combining the power traces of all 10 mp_addfast functions within each xDBLADD. This way, we obtain 10 power traces with which we can correlate pairs of inputs – similarly as in a vertical attack with 10 power traces.

We can further improve this attack. A multi-precision addition takes two $\mathbb{F}_p$ elements as input and gives one as output. Each one of the $2n$ 32-bit input words is loaded once and then used in the addition instruction, and the n 32-bit output words are stored. In total, there are $3n$ words which pass through the pipeline registers and whose Hamming distance from the previous word in the pipeline are related to the power consumption.

For each of the $3n$ words, we compute the PCC between the 10 power traces and the 10 pairs of hamming weights of 32-bit words accounting for the two guesses of the current bit of the private key. For each word, a spike in the correlation is expected at a different position depending on the instruction which uses this particular word. The locations of spikes can be deduced from the shape of the power traces. Once the $3n$ pairs of correlations are computed, we can add them up such that the locations of the expected spikes are aligned. We expect to end up with two correlations for each guess of the private-key bit, with a clear spike in the correlation plot of the correctly guessed value.

In presence of noise in power measurement, the private key guesses may be erroneous. A single wrong guess of a bit of the private key leads to completely inconclusive results, because the following guesses depend on the correctness of the previous bits. Therefore, it is of particular importance that no erroneous guesses are made in the process of key extraction. We propose two measures to approach this problem.

Depth Search. When the guess of a single bit gives inconclusive results, we can proceed by making four guesses for the next two bits in hope of finding a correlation coefficient with a notable spike. In particular we can make a guess for k consecutive bits, obtaining in total 2^k different combinations. For each combination we compute a PCC for each of the k bits. In total there are $2(2^k - 1)$ correlation coefficients, not counting repetitions. We then add up all the PCCs for each k-bit combination and we guess the current sk bit to be the trailing bit of the combination with the strongest correlation.

Increasing Verticality. We can increase verticality (i.e., the amount of power traces in the horizontal settings) by computing correlations for bits in windows of k. If, for one bit, 10 mp_addfast functions can be measured from a single xDBLADD, then, for k bits, there will be $k \times 10$ traces of mp_addfast functions from the k consecutive xDBLADD functions. In total, 2^k hypotheses need to be

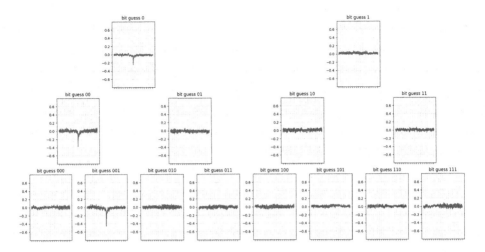

Fig. 2. Depth search.

made (one per bit), and 2^k correlation coefficients are computed for $10k$ power traces (Fig. 2).

Finally, rather than performing the attack on contiguous windows of k bits, we select only one bit of Bob's private key to be the trailing bit of the k-bit combination with the strongest correlation. This way, we can re-run the process starting from the bit right afterwards as a way to correct errors due to the potential proximity of strong correlations. This process resembles the error-correction procedure introduced in [19].

Also, we mention that other operations, such as fpmul_mont and fpsub, can be measured and combined to increase verticality. While these are dissimilar operations and may leak information differently than mp_addfast, they may still add information to the overall selection of Bob's private bits.

4   Experimental Results

In order to validate the horizontal attack described in Sect. 3, we reproduced the key recovery on a programmable board which runs an adapted version of reference implementation of SIKE [44].

4.1   Hardware Setup

The experiment comprises the following equipment:

- The ChipWhisperer toolkit [25], that includes:
  - A (NAE-CW308T-)STM32F3 board which includes an ARM Cortex-M4 microcontroller (the victim).
  - A ChipWhisperer-Lite board which is solely used to communicate with the STM32F3 in serial through USB.

- A ChipWhisperer (NAE-)CW308 UFO board which interfaces the signals between the ChipWhisperer-Lite and the STM32F3.
– A high-definition oscilloscope with the following specifications:
  - An analog bandwidth of at least 500 MHz.
  - A sampling rate of 250 samples per microsecond (i.e., 250 MS/s).
  - A resolution of 16 bits per sample.
  - A memory of 50,000 samples per acquisition.
– A general-purpose computer which runs an operating system compatible with the ChipWhisperer framework [26].

The STM32F3 is plugged into the CW308 UFO, which is itself connected to the ChipWhisperer-Lite with a 20-pin cable. The oscilloscope measures the power consumption in AC through a passive probe connected to the SHUNTL[1] pin on the CW308 UFO, and whose measurement is triggered by reacting to the active-high GPIO04/TRIG (see Footnote 1) pin also with a passive probe (both probes are grounded to the GND pins on the CW308 UFO). The computer is simply connected to the ChipWhisperer-Lite with a USB to micro-USB cable.

The reasoning behind such a setup was to overcome the limitations of memory of the ChipWhisperer-Lite by means of an oscilloscope with better specifications.

4.2   Target Implementation

The attacked implementation is the official SIKE implementation adapted for (32-bit) ARM Cortex-M4 microcontrollers [44], which is part of the official submission package and is constant in timing. We attacked SIKE instantiated with a prime of 434 bits (i.e., SIKEp434); a choice that we elaborate in this section.

In our experiment, we wrote a small piece of software that interfaces the serial communication from the ChipWhisperer framework to the SIKE library. The code allows the computer to program the STM32F3 remotely through USB and simulate the key exchange while power consumption is measured.

Concretely, the software uses ChipWhisperer's SimpleSerial protocol [24] to program different commands to which the STM32F3 reacts. The computer uses these commands to communicate data to the STM32F3 by serially transmitting, first, the byte of the command in ASCII, then, the data of length specified for the command. When the procedure corresponding to the command ends, the STM32F3 responds with the letter z followed by a code returned by the procedure, which concludes the protocol exchange. Two custom commands of were introduced in the scope of this experiment – command k which sets Bob's private key used in the three point ladder, and the command p which sends Alice's public key and executes the three point ladder procedure of SIKE.

We made additional modifications in the SIKE implementation to ease the collection and the pre-processing of the traces. Note that these adjustments were made for efficiency purpose and are by no means necessary for our attack to work.

---

[1] We refer to the official NAE-CW308 UFO datasheet to find the mentioned pins: http://media.newae.com/datasheets/NAE-CW308-datasheet.pdf.

In other words, we emphasise that the attack can be mounted on the original implementation of SIKE presented in [44] without any difficulty.

The list of adjustments are the following:

- A GPIO pin (PA12[2], a.k.a., the trigger) is toggled when the double-and-add operation of the three point ladder enters into an mp_addfast procedure that depends on the swap.
- An idle delay of about 1 ms was introduced in between each mp_addfast call, and of about 1 s after each loop iteration of the three point ladder.

Limitations of the Software. While the introduction of a trigger GPIO and multiple delays results in an unrealistic attack scenario, we emphasise on the fact that the attack is still possible on an unmodified SIKE implementation. The process of segmenting the power traces, as well as the correlation and Hamming weights computations can be done *offline*, after the power traces have been sampled. In a plain attack, as opposed to our experiment, the traces acquisition will be synchronised on serial communication. Then, the targeted operations need to be identified within the full resulting power trace (e.g., using cross-correlation techniques, as in [19]), so the sub-power traces corresponding to the attacked instructions can be manually segmented and carefully aligned to perform the CPA. This cumbersome process is not the main focus of our study and was therefore duly skipped.

Other SIKE Instances. To achieve various levels of security, the original SIKE submission [27] presents four different parameters sets; each of which with a prime of different size (i.e., a p with a bit-length of 434, 503, 610, and 751). While instantiating SIKE with a larger prime offers stronger security guarantees against theoretical cryptanalysis, larger instances present a wider attack surface in a single-trace power analysis. This property was also observed by Bos et al. [8], and is due to the increased number of instructions executed which, therefore, yield more power measurements. As a result, our attacked instance (SIKEp434) is expected to be the hardest to attack with a single trace.

Also, the compressed instances of SIKE are prone to the same horizontal attack, because the starting points of the three point ladder are deterministically obtained from the compressed public key.

4.3   Collection of Traces

Our experiment simulated a portion of the SIKE key exchange between Alice (the computer) and Bob (the STM32F3); namely, the key decapsulation procedure. Our attack scenario can be summarised with the following steps:

---

[2] We refer to the official CW308T-STM32F3 datasheet to find the mentioned pins: https://media.newae.com/datasheets/NAE-CW308T-STM32F_datasheet.pdf.

1. On the computer, generate Bob's key pair at random, and send Bob's private key to the STM32F3 (with the command **k**).
2. Given Bob's public key, generate Alice's key pair at random.
3. Send a public key to the STM32F3 (with the command **p**) during which the oscilloscope measures the power consumption of:
   - only the *second* mp_addfast call involved in steps 6 and 8,
   - and both mp_addfast call involved in steps 16, 17, 18, and 19,

   of the xDBLADD procedure (see Fig. 5) as used in the three point ladder.

Once triggered, the oscilloscope was configured to sample the power consumption at a rate of 250 MS/s during a period of 20 µs. As a result, a power trace for a single execution of mp_addfast includes 5,000 power samples.

This attack scenario was repeated a total of 460 times to obtain at most 1 million traces. Each of these experiments includes the power traces of the 10 mp_addfast calls from the loop iterations for all the 217 bits of Bob's private key. Hence, $460 \times 10 \times 217 = 998,200$ different power traces were acquired during that experiment.

For reference, Fig. 3 (top) shows the average power consumption of an mp_addfast execution captured by our oscilloscope.

4.4 Traces Polishing

Because our initial results turned out to be inconclusive due to a serious level of noise in the acquisition (see top of Fig. 3), we processed the collected power traces with a denoising technique, in the hope that such a processing would increase the success rate of our CPA.

In our case, we applied a wavelet denoising compression, as initially explored in [48], to down-sample the power traces. This compression actually aims to decompose the signal into two sub-signals; approximation and details. Applied to a signal in one dimension, the approximation corresponds to the low frequencies of the signal, while the details contain the high frequencies. By keeping the approximation only, each application halves the number of samples (minus a few points due to a windowed convolution). Best results were experimentally obtained when Daubechies 3 wavelets ('db3') were used recursively three times to reduce the number of samples from 5,000 to 623. The average of the resulting traces is shown in Fig. 3.

The denoised traces and public data are made accessible at https://github. com/COSADE-anonymous-submission/SIKE-HPA-2021.

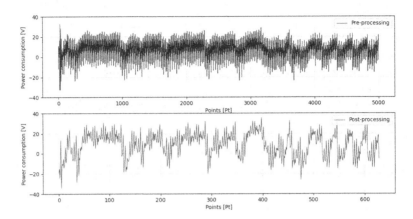

Fig. 3. Result of the discrete wavelet transform with Daubechies 3 wavelets ('db3').

4.5   Horizontal CPA Procedure

Using the denoised power traces, we performed a horizontal CPA on each iteration of the loop in the three point ladder. Each time, a single bit of Bob's private
key is attacked. This process can then be repeated across all the bits of the key.

Since a single bit is hypothesised at each step of the horizontal attack, there
are only two hypotheses to consider:

– The points P and $Q - P$ were swapped (the bit is different from the previous
bit).
– The points P and $Q - P$ were left un-swapped (the bit is the same as the
previous bit).

A strong correlation between the power traces for one loop iteration and the
values corresponding to one of the two hypotheses indicates the correctness of
the hypothesised bit. As the attack moves forward, a successful recovery of the
first bits allows the recovery of the next ones. Therefore, a full-key recovery can
be incrementally mounted in an extend-and-prune manner.

Power Traces Segmentation. Due to the ephemeral settings of the protocol,
we have access to only a single trace per loop iteration involving a single bit
of Bob's private key. Therefore, in order to apply a classical CPA, we need to
obtain verticality, i.e., find a way to obtain a certain amount of multiple different
power samples which are linked to a same portion of the private key. In our case
study, we segmented the power trace that corresponds to an iteration of the
three point ladder into 10 different power traces, each of which corresponding
to an `mp_addfast` execution, for which, given either hypothesis, the full input
and output (and thus, relevant Hamming distances information) are known. As
a result, our horizontal CPA will amount to a vertical CPA with 10 power traces
and 2 hypotheses.

CPA Enhancements. To further improve the success of our attack, we have inspected the targeted function for which the power traces were collected. Particularly, the power traces correspond to the `mp_addfast` function which adds two input $\mathbb{F}_p$ elements and returns a single $\mathbb{F}_p$ element (see Fig. 6). Because, in our experiment, p is 434-bit long, each element is saved as an array of $\lceil 434/32 \rceil = 14$ words of 32 bits. This results in exactly 14 addition instructions, hence 14 leakage points, in a single `mp_addfast` power trace.

Moreover, we considered the leakage model from a Cortex-M4 microcontroller as explained in [14]. Because the power consumption leaks in the Hamming distance between the pipeline registers, we actually obtain *three* leakage points on a power trace per instruction:

(1) the Hamming distance between the first inputs of the current and the previous instruction,
(2) the Hamming distance between the second inputs of the current and the previous instruction, and
(3) the Hamming distance between the output of the current and the previous instruction.

This results in an additional segmentation of $3 \times 14 = 42$ points of leakage. For each point of leakage, a PCC is computed with the 10 `mp_addfast` power traces and the 10 Hamming distances.

We expect each of these PCCs to produce a spike at a different point in time in the correlation plot which we try to recover. The location of the spike corresponds to the position at which the associated 32-bit word is processed by a pipeline register. Each of these leakage points is constant throughout the `mp_addfast` executions and the three point ladder loop (assuming the power traces are properly aligned, which can be automated using basic peak alignment methods). These positions can even be identified by analysing the spike structure of the power trace (using, e.g., cross-correlation techniques).

Finally, the 42 PCCs at each point of leakage are added together to produce a larger spike. This consists of aligning all correlation plots on their leakage points and adding them together. We expect the difference of added correlation coefficients to be large enough to correctly validate the private bit.

4.6 Results

Among the 460 trials, our experimental results returned a resounding success rate of 100% in recovering the full key. None of the improvements described in Sect. 3.3 were even required. An example of the corresponding CPA is shown in Fig. 4 where six bits are shown to be successfully recovered. This proof of concept shows that, even in ephemeral settings, the official ARM implementation of SIKE is vulnerable to classical power analysis techniques.

All the code used to derive our results is shared on https://github.com/nKolja/SIKE-HPA-2021.

5   Countermeasures

The attack arises as a consequence of the three point ladder being a deterministic function with predictable inputs. Each value going through the pipeline registers can be reduced to only two cases. These inputs depend on the public triple x_Q, x_P, x_{Q-P} (which define $Q = [x_Q : 1]$, $P = [x_P : 1]$, $Q - P = [x_{Q-P} : 1]$), the bits of Bob's private key up to the step at which the instruction in question is being executed (which we may assume to be known by induction), and the two possibilities for the current bit of the private key.

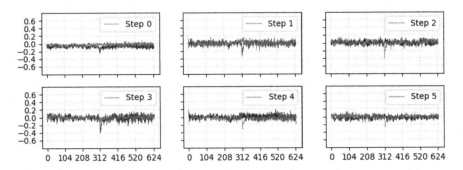

Fig. 4. Addition of shifted PCC results with 10 segments of a single power trace. Each step corresponds to a different bit. The blue curve corresponds to a bit hypothesis of zero, while the red curve corresponds to bit hypothesis of one. (Color figure online)

5.1   Recommended Countermeasure

A simple and low-cost countermeasure, which was also mentioned in [13,20, 50] consists of randomising the coordinates that define the starting points, i.e., generate three random non-zero field elements r_Q, r_P, r_{Q-P} and set

$$Q = [x_Q r_Q : r_Q], \quad P = [x_P r_P : r_P], \quad Q - P = [x_{Q-P} r_{Q-P} : r_{Q-P}].$$

The increase in complexity comes from generating three random $\mathbb{F}_{p^2}^*$ elements and three field multiplications. This is negligible with respect to the overall cost of the three point ladder. The execution of the protocol is still correct because the points $Q, P, Q - P$ are not changed, but the input of xDBLADD, seen as three pairs of $\mathbb{F}_{p^2}$ elements is now randomised. Since the values r_Q, r_P, r_{Q-P} are secret, we cannot predict the loaded and stored values in the pipeline registers, and thus cannot apply the same attack anymore.

Point randomisation is in general still vulnerable to refined power analysis, as shown in [20,32]. Such power analysis constitutes in finding a point P such that one of its coordinates is 0, so that randomisation would not change this coordinate. Feeding P to the attacked device would lead to some of the coordinates being known in the computation of the ladder. However, the only points that have a zero in the X or Z coordinates are $[0 : 1 : 0]$ (i.e., the point at infinity) and $[0 : 0 : 1]$, a point of order 2. Neither of these points can be a part of a public key or an input of the three point ladder, so they can be avoided by a simple sanity check.

5.2   Other Countermeasures

In addition to the randomised projective coordinates described above, the authors of [50] proposed a series of countermeasures (based on [20,28]) against CPA on SIKE that we aim to evaluate in the case of a horizontal attack. However these countermeasures are either too expensive, or do not offer additional protection against horizontal attacks. We also comment atomic elliptic curve algorithms.

1. **Masking the base point Q**
   The starting point Q is masked with a random point R in order to obtain $Q \leftarrow Q + R$. The final point $P + [sk](Q + R)$ of the three point ladder is then adjusted by subtracting $[sk]R$.
   Masking the base point prevents both a vertical and a horizontal attacks but cannot be done without leaving Montgomery representation. As a result, such a countermeasure requires at least a square root computation over the field $\mathbb{F}_{p^2}$, which is very expensive.

2. **Random isomorphic elliptic curve**
   The point Q is mapped to a random elliptic curve E' where the scalar multiplication is computed. The result is then mapped back to the original curve E in order to obtain $[sk]Q$ which is then added to P.
   Such a countermeasure is unfortunately limiting, since the number of curves of isomorphic to E is low, and finding a non-trivial isomorphism is not trivial. In particular, mapping Q to an isomorphic elliptic curve does not provide enough security against a horizontal attack due to the possibility of testing all isomorphic curves.

3. **Masking the scalar sk**
   The secret key sk is masked with a random value r by setting $sk \leftarrow sk + r \cdot \mathrm{ord}(Q)$.
   If the masking is different at each execution and big enough, the vertical attack can be conceivably prevented with this countermeasure. However, the horizontal attack is simply extended by $r \cdot \mathrm{ord}(Q)$ bits and recover a value congruent to the actual sk $(\mathrm{mod}\ \mathrm{ord}(Q))$. Besides, the execution of the three point ladder would be a factor of $\log(r)$ slower.

4. **Random key splitting**
   The private key sk is divided randomly as $sk = sk_1 + sk_2$. Then two three point ladders are computed in order to obtain $(P + [sk_1]Q) + [sk_2]Q$.
   While splitting sk differently across executions produces measurements of dissimilar operations in a vertical attack, this countermeasure is not effective against a horizontal attack, as both shares can be independently recovered.

5. **Window-based countermeasure**
   Instead of making a binary choice for swapping at each step of the three point ladder, a 3-bit window is used, and two additions and three doublings are computed per window.

While a window-based method increases the complexity of a vertical attack, such a countermeasure is ineffective in the settings of a horizontal attack, as the number of guesses per CPA iteration simply increases from 2^1 to 2^3. Besides, similarly as with the base point masking, this countermeasure is not cost-efficient, as the new ladder will require to leave the Montgomery representation, requiring at least one computation of a square root over $\mathbb{F}_{p^2}$.

6. **Atomic three point ladder**

   The authors of [10] propose atomic algorithms for preventing simple side-channel analysis. An atomic algorithm is made out of a sequence of instructions which are indistinguishable from a side-channel point of view.

   At the first look, the three point ladder might seem to be atomic, however the assumption in [10] that modular operations are side-channel equivalent fails in the Cortex-M4 environment. While we are not able to distinguish a single pair of modular additions with two different inputs, we are able to distinguish 10 tuples of modular additions with two different 10-tuples of inputs, which breaks indistinguishability.

6   Conclusion

The report describes a CPA on SIKE in ephemeral settings that recovers Bob's entire private key using a single power trace of the three point ladder in the key decapsulation procedure. The attack was experimentally verified on an STM32F3 which features a Cortex-M4 microcontroller in the context of the ChipWhisperer framework. A countermeasure based on point randomisation is finally suggested.

The impact of this attack on the security of SIKE is critical when the reference implementation is adapted in an unprotected manner to a Cortex-M4 microcontroller. This is especially important, because of the exceptionally leaky nature of such microcontrollers, thanks to the findings of [14]. Due to the simplicity of the CPA, countermeasures are required to be deployed when the reference implementation of SIKE is used in an embedded environment.

We emphasise on the fact that the three point ladder attacked in the key decapsulation is not the only point of attack of the SIKE protocol and that *each* use of the three point ladder (even in the key generation, and key encapsulation) requires to be protected when exposed to power analyses. Also, for future study, we propose to investigate the secret isogeny computation which is independent from the scalar multiplication.

A   Appendix

We include the code of the xDBLADD, fp2mul_mont, fp2sqr_mont and mp_addfast functions from [44]. Minor changes, such as variable naming, have been made to the code in order to adapt it to the names used in this paper. The lines of code 3,6,7,8,9,10,11,15,16,17,18,19 and the mp_addfast (highlighted in red) correspond to the targeted instructions.

```
void xDBLADD(point_proj_t Q, point_proj_t P, point_proj_t QP, const
    f2elm_t A24)
{ // Simultaneous doubling and differential addition.
  // Input: projective Montgomery points Q=(Q->X:Q->Z), P=(P->X:P->Z),
  //   Q-P=(QP->X:QP->Z), and Montgomery curve constant A24=(A+2)/4.
  // Output: projective Montgomery points Q <- 2*Q, and P <- Q+P.

  f2elm_t t0, t1, t2;
```

1	`fp2add(Q->X, Q->Z, t0);`
2	`fp2sub(Q->X, Q->Z, t1);`
3	`fp2sqr_mont(t0, Q->X);`
4	`fp2sub(P->X, P->Z, t2);`
4.5	`fp2correction(t2);`
5	`fp2add(P->X, P->Z, P->X);`
6	`fp2mul_mont(t0, t2, t0);`
7	`fp2sqr_mont(t1, Q->Z);`
8	`fp2mul_mont(t1, P->X, t1);`
9	`fp2sub(Q->X, Q->Z, t2);`
10	`fp2mul_mont(Q->X, Q->Z, Q->X);`
11	`fp2mul_mont(t2, A24, P->X);`
12	`fp2sub(t0, t1, P->Z);`
13	`fp2add(P->X, Q->Z, Q->Z);`
14	`fp2add(t0, t1, P->X);`
15	`fp2mul_mont(Q->Z, t2, Q->Z);`
16	`fp2sqr_mont(P->Z, P->Z);`
17	`fp2sqr_mont(P->X, P->X);`
18	`fp2mul_mont(P->Z, QP->X, P->Z);`
19	`fp2mul_mont(P->X, QP->Z, P->X); //In practice 19 is outside of xDBLADD`

```
}
```

```
void fp2mul_mont(const f2elm_t a,
    const f2elm_t b, f2elm_t c)
{ // GF(p^2) multiplication.
  // Inputs: a = a0+a1*i and b =
  b0+b1*i.
  // Output: c = c0+c1*i.
  felm_t t1, t2;
  dfelm_t tt1, tt2, tt3;
  digit_t mask;
  unsigned int i;

  mp_addfast(a[0], a[1], t1);
  mp_addfast(b[0], b[1], t2);

  fpmul_mont(a[0], b[0], c[0]);
  fpmul_mont(a[1], b[1], tt2);
  fpmul_mont(t1, t2, c[1]);

  fpsub(c[1],c[0],c[1]);
  fpsub(c[1],tt2,c[1]);

  fpsub(c[0],tt2,c[0]);
}
```

```
void fp2sqr_mont(const f2elm_t a,
    f2elm_t c)
{ // GF(p^2) squaring.
  // Inputs: a = a0+a1*i.
  // Output: c = c0+c1*i.
  felm_t t1, t2, t3;

  mp_addfast(a[0], a[1], t1);
  fpsub(a[0], a[1], t2);
  mp_addfast(a[0], a[0], t3);
  fpmul_mont(t1, t2, c[0]);
  fpmul_mont(t3, a[1], c[1]);
}
```

Fig. 5. xDBLADD, fp2mul_mont and fp2sqr_mont from [44].

```
void __attribute__ ((noinline, naked))
    mp_addfast(const digit_t* a, const digit_t* b
    , digit_t* c)
{ // Multiprecision addition, c = a+b.
  asm(

        "push  {r4-r9,lr}            \n\t"
        "mov r14, r2                 \n\t"

        "ldmia r0!, {r2-r5}          \n\t"
        "ldmia r1!, {r6-r9}          \n\t"

        "adds r2, r2, r6             \n\t"
        "adcs r3, r3, r7             \n\t"
        "adcs r4, r4, r8             \n\t"
        "adcs r5, r5, r9             \n\t"

        "stmia r14!, {r2-r5}         \n\t"

        "ldmia r0!, {r2-r5}          \n\t"
        "ldmia r1!, {r6-r9}          \n\t"

        "adcs r2, r2, r6             \n\t"
        "adcs r3, r3, r7             \n\t"
        "adcs r4, r4, r8             \n\t"
        "adcs r5, r5, r9             \n\t"

        "stmia r14!, {r2-r5}         \n\t"

        "ldmia r0!, {r2-r5}          \n\t"
        "ldmia r1!, {r6-r9}          \n\t"

        "adcs r2, r2, r6             \n\t"
        "adcs r3, r3, r7             \n\t"
        "adcs r4, r4, r8             \n\t"
        "adcs r5, r5, r9             \n\t"

        "stmia r14!, {r2-r5}         \n\t"

        "ldmia r0!, {r2-r3}          \n\t"
        "ldmia r1!, {r6-r7}          \n\t"


        "adcs r2, r2, r6             \n\t"
        "adcs r3, r3, r7             \n\t"

        "stmia r14!, {r2-r3}         \n\t"

        "pop  {r4-r9,pc}             \n\t"


    :
    :
    :
    );

}
```

Fig. 6. mp_addfast from [44].

References

1. Apon, D.: Passing the final checkpoint! NIST PQC 3rd round begins (2020). https://meetings.ams.org/math/fall2020se/meetingapp.cgi/Paper/1656. https://www.scribd.com/document/474476570/PQC-Overview-Aug-2020-NIST
2. Aysu, A., Tobah, Y., Tiwari, M., Gerstlauer, A., Orshansky, M.: Horizontal side-channel vulnerabilities of post-quantum key exchange protocols. In: 2018 IEEE International Symposium on Hardware Oriented Security and Trust (HOST), pp. 81–88 (2018). https://doi.org/10.1109/HST.2018.8383894
3. Azarderakhsh, R., Jao, D., Kalach, K., Koziel, B., Leonardi, C.: Key compression for isogeny-based cryptosystems. Cryptology ePrint Archive, Report 2016/229 (2016). https://eprint.iacr.org/2016/229
4. Azouaoui, M., Poussier, R., Standaert, F.-X.: Fast side-channel security evaluation of ECC implementations. In: Polian, I., Stöttinger, M. (eds.) COSADE 2019. LNCS, vol. 11421, pp. 25–42. Springer, Cham (2019). https://doi.org/10.1007/978-3-030-16350-1_3
5. Batina, L., Chmielewski, L., Papachristodoulou, L., Schwabe, P., Tunstall, M.: Online template attacks. J. Cryptogr. Eng. 9(1), 21–36 (2017). https://doi.org/10.1007/s13389-017-0171-8
6. Bos, J.W., Friedberger, S.J.: Arithmetic considerations for isogeny based cryptography. Cryptology ePrint Archive, Report 2018/376 (2018). https://eprint.iacr.org/2018/376
7. Bos, J.W., Friedberger, S.J.: Faster modular arithmetic for isogeny based crypto on embedded devices. Cryptology ePrint Archive, Report 2018/792 (2018). https://eprint.iacr.org/2018/792
8. Bos, J.W., Friedberger, S.J., Martinoli, M., Oswald, E., Stam, M.: Assessing the feasibility of single trace power analysis of Frodo. In: Cid, C., Jacobson, M., Jr. (eds.) SAC 2018. LNCS, vol. 11349, pp. 216–234. Springer, Cham (2018). https://doi.org/10.1007/978-3-030-10970-7_10
9. Brier, E., Clavier, C., Olivier, F.: Correlation power analysis with a leakage model. In: Joye, M., Quisquater, J.-J. (eds.) CHES 2004. LNCS, vol. 3156, pp. 16–29. Springer, Heidelberg (2004). https://doi.org/10.1007/978-3-540-28632-5_2
10. Chevallier-Mames, B., Ciet, M., Joye, M.: Low-cost solutions for preventing simple side-channel analysis: side-channel atomicity. IEEE Trans. Comput. 53(6), 760–768 (2004). https://doi.org/10.1109/TC.2004.13
11. Childs, A., Jao, D., Soukharev, V.: Constructing elliptic curve isogenies in quantum subexponential time. J. Math. Cryptol. 8(1), 1–29 (2014). https://doi.org/10.1515/jmc-2012-0016
12. Clavier, C., Feix, B., Gagnerot, G., Roussellet, M., Verneuil, V.: Horizontal correlation analysis on exponentiation. In: Soriano, M., Qing, S., López, J. (eds.) ICICS 2010. LNCS, vol. 6476, pp. 46–61. Springer, Heidelberg (2010). https://doi.org/10.1007/978-3-642-17650-0_5
13. Coron, J.-S.: Resistance against differential power analysis for elliptic curve cryptosystems. In: Koç, Ç.K., Paar, C. (eds.) CHES 1999. LNCS, vol. 1717, pp. 292–302. Springer, Heidelberg (1999). https://doi.org/10.1007/3-540-48059-5_25
14. Corre, Y.L., Großschädl, J., Dinu, D.: Micro-architectural power simulator for leakage assessment of cryptographic software on ARM Cortex-M3 processors. Cryptology ePrint Archive, Report 2017/1253 (2017). https://eprint.iacr.org/2017/1253
15. Costello, C., Longa, P., Naehrig, M.: Efficient algorithms for supersingular isogeny Diffie-Hellman. Cryptology ePrint Archive, Report 2016/413 (2016). https://eprint.iacr.org/2016/413

16. Couveignes, J.M.: Hard homogeneous spaces. Cryptology ePrint Archive, Report 2006/291 (2006). https://eprint.iacr.org/2006/291
17. De Feo, L., Jao, D., Plût, J.: Towards quantum-resistant cryptosystems from supersingular elliptic curve isogenies. J. Math. Cryptol. **8**(3), 209–247 (2014). https://doi.org/10.1515/jmc-2012-0015. https://www.degruyter.com/view/journals/jmc/8/3/article-p209.xml
18. De Feo, L., Jao, D., Plût, J.: Towards quantum-resistant cryptosystems from supersingular elliptic curve isogenies. Cryptology ePrint Archive, Report 2011/506 (2011). https://eprint.iacr.org/2011/506
19. Dugardin, M., Papachristodoulou, L., Najm, Z., Batina, L., Danger, J.-L., Guilley, S.: Dismantling real-world ECC with horizontal and vertical template attacks. In: Standaert, F.-X., Oswald, E. (eds.) COSADE 2016. LNCS, vol. 9689, pp. 88–108. Springer, Cham (2016). https://doi.org/10.1007/978-3-319-43283-0_6
20. Fan, J., Guo, X., De Mulder, E., Schaumont, P., Preneel, B., Verbauwhede, I.: State-of-the-art of secure ECC implementations: a survey on known side-channel attacks and countermeasures. In: 2010 IEEE International Symposium on Hardware-Oriented Security and Trust (HOST), pp. 76–87 (2010). https://doi.org/10.1109/HST.2010.5513110
21. Fujisaki, E., Okamoto, T.: Secure integration of asymmetric and symmetric encryption schemes. In: Wiener, M. (ed.) CRYPTO 1999. LNCS, vol. 1666, pp. 537–554. Springer, Heidelberg (1999). https://doi.org/10.1007/3-540-48405-1_34
22. Galbraith, S.D., Petit, C., Shani, B., Ti, Y.B.: On the security of supersingular isogeny cryptosystems. In: Cheon, J.H., Takagi, T. (eds.) ASIACRYPT 2016. LNCS, vol. 10031, pp. 63–91. Springer, Heidelberg (2016). https://doi.org/10.1007/978-3-662-53887-6_3
23. Holdings, A.: Cortex-M4 specifications. https://developer.arm.com/ip-products/processors/cortex-m/cortex-m4
24. NewAE Technology Inc.: SimpleSerial - ChipWhisperer Wiki (2017). https://wiki.newae.com/SimpleSerial
25. NewAE Technology Inc.: CHIPWHISPERER — NewAE Technology (2021). https://www.newae.com/chipwhisperer
26. NewAE Technology Inc.: GitHub - newaetech/chipwhisperer: ChipWhisperer - the complete open-source toolchain for side-channel power analysis and glitching attacks (2021). https://github.com/newaetech/chipwhisperer
27. Jao, D., et al.: Supersingular isogeny key encapsulation (2017). https://sike.org/
28. Joye, M., Tymen, C.: Protections against differential analysis for elliptic curve cryptography — an algebraic approach —. In: Koç, Ç.K., Naccache, D., Paar, C. (eds.) CHES 2001. LNCS, vol. 2162, pp. 377–390. Springer, Heidelberg (2001). https://doi.org/10.1007/3-540-44709-1_31
29. Kalai, G.: The argument against quantum computers (2019). https://arxiv.org/abs/1908.02499
30. Kannwischer, M.J., Pessl, P., Primas, R.: Single-trace attacks on Keccak. IACR Cryptol. ePrint Arch. 2020, 371 (2020). https://eprint.iacr.org/2020/371
31. Kannwischer, M.J., Rijneveld, J., Schwabe, P., Stoffelen, K.: pqm4: testing and benchmarking NIST PQC on ARM Cortex-M4. In: Workshop Record of the Second PQC Standardization Conference (2019). https://cryptojedi.org/papers/#pqm4
32. Koziel, B., Azarderakhsh, R., Jao, D.: Side-channel attacks on quantum-resistant supersingular isogeny Diffie-Hellman. In: SAC (2017)

33. Kwiatkowski, K.: Towards post-quantum cryptography in TLS (2019). https:// blog.cloudflare.com/towards-post-quantum-cryptography-in-tls/
34. Langley, A.: Post-quantum confidentiality for TLS (2018). https://www. imperialviolet.org/2018/04/11/pqconftls.html
35. Leonardi, C.: A note on the ending elliptic curve in SIDH. Cryptology ePrint Archive, Report 2020/262 (2020). https://eprint.iacr.org/2020/262
36. Medwed, M., Oswald, E.: Template attacks on ECDSA. In: Chung, K.-I., Sohn, K., Yung, M. (eds.) WISA 2008. LNCS, vol. 5379, pp. 14–27. Springer, Heidelberg (2009). https://doi.org/10.1007/978-3-642-00306-6_2
37. Montgomery, P.: Speeding the Pollard and elliptic curve methods of factorization. Math. Comput. **48**, 243–264 (1987)
38. Moody, D.: Let's get ready to rumble - The NIST PQC "competition" (2018). https://csrc.nist.gov/presentations/2018/let-s-get-ready-to-rumble-the-nist-pqc-competiti
39. Moody, D.: Round 2 of the NIST PQC "competition" - What was NIST thinking? (2019). https://csrc.nist.gov/presentations/2019/round-2-of-the-nist-pqc-competition-what-was-nist
40. Paquin, C., Stebila, D., Tamvada, G.: Benchmarking post-quantum cryptography in TLS. Cryptology ePrint Archive, Report 2019/1447 (2019). https://eprint.iacr. org/2019/1447
41. Poussier, R., Zhou, Y., Standaert, F.-X.: A systematic approach to the side-channel analysis of ECC implementations with worst-case horizontal attacks. In: Fischer, W., Homma, N. (eds.) CHES 2017. LNCS, vol. 10529, pp. 534–554. Springer, Cham (2017). https://doi.org/10.1007/978-3-319-66787-4_26
42. Primas, R., Pessl, P., Mangard, S.: Single-trace side-channel attacks on masked lattice-based encryption. In: Fischer, W., Homma, N. (eds.) CHES 2017. LNCS, vol. 10529, pp. 513–533. Springer, Cham (2017). https://doi.org/10.1007/978-3-319-66787-4_25
43. Rostovtsev, A., Stolbunov, A.: A public-key cryptosystem based on isogenies. Cryptology ePrint Archive, Report 2006/145 (2006). https://eprint.iacr.org/2006/145
44. Seo, H., Anastasova, M., Jalali, A., Azarderakhsh, R.: Supersingular isogeny key encapsulation (SIKE) round 2 on ARM Cortex-M4. Cryptology ePrint Archive, Report 2020/410 (2020). https://eprint.iacr.org/2020/410
45. Shor, P.W.: Polynomial-time algorithms for prime factorization and discrete logarithms on a quantum computer. SIAM J. Comput. **26**(5), 1484–1509 (1997). https://doi.org/10.1137/s0097539795293172
46. Sim, B., et al.: Single-trace attacks on message encoding in lattice-based KEMs. IEEE Access **8**, 183175–183191 (2020). https://doi.org/10.1109/ACCESS.2020. 3029521
47. Weibel, A.: Round 2 hybrid post-quantum TLS benchmarks (2020). https://aws. amazon.com/blogs/security/round-2-hybrid-post-quantum-tls-benchmarks/
48. Xavier, C., Hervé, P.: Improving the DPA attack using wavelet transform (2005). https://www.researchgate.net/publication/228717434_Improving_the_DPA_attack_using_Wavelet_transform
49. Zanon, G.H.M., Simplicio, M.A., Pereira, G.C.C.F., Doliskani, J., Barreto, P.S.L.M.: Faster isogeny-based compressed key agreement. In: Lange, T., Steinwandt, R. (eds.) PQCrypto 2018. LNCS, vol. 10786, pp. 248–268. Springer, Cham (2018). https://doi.org/10.1007/978-3-319-79063-3_12

50. Zhang, F., et al.: Side-channel analysis and countermeasure design on ARM-based quantum-resistant SIKE. IEEE Trans. Comput. **69**(11), 1681–1693 (2020). https://doi.org/10.1109/TC.2020.3020407

51. Zhang, Z., Wu, L., Mu, Z., Zhang, X.: A novel template attack on WNAF algorithm of ECC. In: Tenth International Conference on Computational Intelligence and Security, CIS 2014, Kunming, Yunnan, China, 15–16 November 2014, pp. 671–675. IEEE Computer Society (2014). https://doi.org/10.1109/CIS.2014.66

Resistance of Isogeny-Based Cryptographic Implementations to a Fault Attack

Élise Tasso[1,2]([⊠]), Luca De Feo[3], Nadia El Mrabet[4], and Simon Pontié[1,2]

[1] CEA Tech, Centre CMP, Équipe Commune CEA Tech - Mines Saint-Étienne,
F-13541 Gardanne, France
[2] Université Grenoble Alpes, CEA, Leti, F-38000 Grenoble, France
{elise.tasso2,simon.pontie}@cea.fr
[3] IBM Research, Zürich, Switzerland
cosade21@defeo.lu
[4] Mines Saint-Étienne, CEA-Tech, Centre CMP, F-13541 Gardanne, France
nadia.el-mrabet@emse.fr

Abstract. The threat of quantum computers has sparked the development of a new kind of cryptography to resist their attacks. Isogenies between elliptic curves are one of the tools used for such cryptosystems. They are championed by SIKE (Supersingular isogeny key encapsulation), an "alternate candidate" of the third round of the NIST Post-Quantum Cryptography Standardization Process. While all candidates are believed to be mathematically secure, their implementations may be vulnerable to hardware attacks. In this work we investigate for the first time whether Ti's 2017 theoretical fault injection attack is exploitable in practice. We also examine suitable countermeasures. We manage to recover the secret thanks to electromagnetic fault injection on an ARM Cortex A53 using a correct and an altered public key generation. Moreover we propose a suitable countermeasure to detect faults that has a low overhead as it takes advantage of a redundancy already present in SIKE implementations.

Keywords: Post-quantum cryptography · SIKE · Elliptic curve ·
Isogeny · Fault injection attack

1 Introduction

Starting in 1994 with Shor's factorization algorithm [24], quantum computers have been shown to threaten classic asymmetric cryptography. Thus the National Institute of Standards and Technology launched the Post-Quantum Cryptography Standardization Process in December 2016 [20]. Research teams worldwide had begun to work on algorithms that can be implemented on classical computers but resist quantum computer attacks before and thus continued to study encryption and signature protocols as required by the NIST. These protocols are

© Springer Nature Switzerland AG 2021
S. Bhasin and F. De Santis (Eds.): COSADE 2021, LNCS 12910, pp. 255–276, 2021.
https://doi.org/10.1007/978-3-030-89915-8_12

based on various mathematical tools, including lattices, error correcting codes, multivariate polynomial equations, hash functions and isogenies between elliptic curves. We will focus here on the Supersingular Isogeny Key Encapsulation (SIKE) [14], the only candidate based on isogenies. More precisely, SIKE is a key encapsulation mechanism (KEM) based on the Supersingular Isogeny Diffie-Hellman (SIDH) key exchange proposed by Jao and De Feo in 2011 [15]. It is now an alternate candidate in the third round of the standardization process, meaning that it is deemed promising enough by the NIST to pursue research on it. It has indeed the smallest key size by far among the third round candidates [1], but is comparatively slow. Like the other candidates, SIKE is believed to be mathematically secure, but vulnerabilities may appear in its implementations. A further interesting characteristic is its regularity, which makes hardware attacks more challenging. Hardware attacks assume that the attacker has physical access to the device where the algorithm is being executed. There are two categories of such attacks. In a passive attack, the attacker is only able to observe the execution of the algorithm on the target. They may measure the computation time, the power consumption or the electromagnetic emanation of the circuit and try to deduce information about the keys or exchanged messages. These are called side-channel attacks. In an active attack, they may disrupt the execution of the algorithm by creating power or clock glitches, illuminating the target with a laser beam or injecting an electromagnetic field to get information. These are called fault attacks. Attacks of both kinds have been found to affect SIKE.

Galbraith et al. discussed in 2016 some attacks based on the leakage of partial knowledge of the key [11]. In 2017, Gélin and Wesolowski presented a loop-abort attack by injecting a random fault in the isogeny computation loop counter during the computation of the shared key [12]. There already exists countermeasures to avoid loop abort attacks, for instance as presented in [22]. The same year, Ti published a paper about another way to do a fault attack on a static key variant of SIDH [27]. Koziel et al. [17] proposed a refined power analysis on the three-point Montgomery differential ladder during the shared secret computation and during the isogeny computation. Countermeasures are proposed for both. In 2018, Koppermann et al. [16] also attacked the shared secret computation, but with a differential power attack on the scalar multiplication during the kernel generator computation. A countermeasure to such an attack is the randomisation of the projective representations of the points [4]. The latest known attack is by Zhang et al. [30]: a differential power attack and differential electromagnetic attack, also on the scalar multiplication during the isogeny kernel generator computation. We classify these attacks in different categories as seen in Table 1 below.

In the implementation of SIKE we can distinguish two phases: a first one that uses only classical elliptic curve cryptography algorithms, where a scalar multiplication on elliptic curve points is performed, and a second one that performs isogeny computations and evaluations. We classify attacks depending on their target, the first or the second phase. To the best of our knowledge, there has

Table 1. Classification of known hardware attacks on SIKE depending on their type, if they are experimentally verified or not, and depending on the part of the algorithm that is attacked.

Gélin et al. (2017) [12]	Fault injection	Simulated	Isogeny
Koziel et al. (2017) [17]	Side-channel attack	Theoretical	Scalar multiplication, isogeny
Ti, 2017 [27]	Fault injection	Theoretical	Isogeny
Koppermann et al. (2018) [16]	Side-channel attack	Experimentally verified	Scalar multiplication
Zhang et al. (2020) [30]	Side-channel attack	Experimentally verified	Scalar multiplication

not been any experimentally verified attack specific to the isogeny phase, thus we want to investigate whether Ti's 2017 theoretical fault injection attack [27] is exploitable in practice. The goal of this attack is to recover the static key, which is a private key used more than once over a long period of time. After reviewing some background information about isogenies and SIDH/SIKE, we will present Ti's attack. Then, we shall describe the experimental setups used in our investigation to finally analyse possible countermeasures.

Contributions. We provide the first experimental realization of Ti's 2017 theoretical fault attack by carrying out an attack campaign in a laboratory. We induced faults on the SIKE round 3 implementation optimized for ARM64 on a system on chip (SoC) with four cortex A53 cores by using electromagnetic fault injection. This provides an experimental understanding of the threat on SIKE caused by Ti's attack. At last, we propose two new countermeasures against this attack: one concerns the protocol and the other is a verification at the end of the public key generation.

2 Preliminaries

In this section we are going to present a few mathematical and cryptographic notions, in particular, the SIDH cryptosystem and the key encapsulation in SIKE that will be of use when analysing Yan Bo Ti's attack in Sect. 3. We shall start with a primer on isogeny-based cryptography.

2.1 Isogenies Between Elliptic Curves

For basic definitions concerning elliptic curves and isogenies between elliptic curves, we refer the reader to [25]. An introduction to isogenies as used in cryptography can be found in [8].

The elliptic curves used in SIKE are represented as Montgomery curves [18].

Definition 1. *Let K be a finite field such that $char(K) \neq 2$ and $A, B \in \mathbb{F}_{p^2}$ such that $B(A^2 - 4) \neq 0$. The Montgomery (elliptic) curve $E_{A,B}$ consists of a point at infinity O and the set of points $(x, y) \in \mathbb{F}_{p^2}$ such that*

$$By^2 = x^3 + Ax^2 + x.$$

In particular, $B = 1$ in SIKE.

One advantage of Montgomery curves is to provide algorithms to compute scalar multiplications more efficiently [7,18]. Indeed, let us consider the multiplication by an integer k on an elliptic curve E:

$$[k] : E \to E$$
$$P \mapsto \underbrace{P + P + \ldots + P}_{k \text{ times}}.$$

The automorphism of $E \ominus : P \mapsto -P$ can be used to quotient E and thus get a map $x : E \to \mathbb{P}^1 \cong E/\langle \ominus \rangle$. We have $x(P) = x(Q)$ if and only if $P = Q$ or $P = -Q$. It is then possible to define an induced multiplication on $\mathbb{P}_1$ for all $k \in \mathbb{Z}$ such that $x(P) \mapsto x([k]P)$. Hence, instead of performing scalar multiplications on points of the curve, one can use the x-coordinates of the points only. Montgomery provides more efficient formulas for point multiplication using the x-coordinates. For efficiency reasons, this coordinate $x = X/Z$ of Montgomery curves is represented projectively with $(X : Z)$, see [7,18].

As shown in [6], the A coefficient of a Montgomery curve can be recovered using three distinct non-zero x-coordinates of points P, Q and R such that $R = P - Q$ with the following formula (see also algorithm cfpk in [14]):

$$A = \frac{(1 - x_P x_Q - x_P x_R - x_Q x_R)^2}{4 x_P x_Q x_R} - x_P - x_Q - x_R. \tag{1}$$

In SIKE, an elliptic curve is encoded by such an x-coordinate triplet.

An invariant can be defined for these elliptic curves [7].

Definition 2. *Let E be a Montgomery curve as above. Then the j-invariant of E is*

$$j(E) = \frac{256(A^2 - 3)^3}{A^2 - 4}.$$

This allows us to create equivalence classes of elliptic curves, see [25, § III.1].

Proposition 1. *Two elliptic curves are isomorphic over the algebraic closure of their definition field if and only if they have the same j-invariant.*

Maps can be defined between these equivalence classes. Let E and F be two elliptic curves defined over a finite field K. An isogeny ϕ between E and F is a non-trivial group morphism between E and F. We will often use the "morphism aspect" of this definition i.e. that for all points P and Q on E,

$$\phi(P + Q) = \phi(P) + \phi(Q).$$

Moreover, we consider in SIKE a special kind of isogenies called separable isogenies that are uniquely determined by their kernel. This kernel C is necessarily finite. Knowing C, there are formulas by Vélu [28] showing how to compute the equation of the target elliptic curve of the isogeny, denoted by E/C. Hence, referring to the kernel of an isogeny amounts to referring to the isogeny itself. As only separable isogenies appear in SIKE, we define the degree $\deg(\phi)$ of ϕ as the size of its kernel. We shall now define the dual of an isogeny.

Definition 3 (Dual isogeny [25, § III.6]**).** *Let $\phi : E \to F$ be an isogeny. Then there is a unique isogeny $\hat{\phi} : F \to E$ called the dual isogeny of ϕ such that*

$$\hat{\phi} \circ \phi = [\deg(\phi)]_E \text{ and } \phi \circ \hat{\phi} = [\deg(\phi)]_F.$$

The dual isogeny has the following properties.

- For all isogenies $\phi : E \to F$ and $\psi : F \to G$, we have $\widehat{\psi \circ \phi} = \hat{\phi} \circ \hat{\psi}$.
- $\deg(\hat{\phi}) = \deg(\phi)$
- $\hat{\hat{\phi}} = \phi$

Having described the necessary mathematical tools, we will now present the scheme that is at the crux of SIKE.

2.2   The SIDH Key Exchange

The supersingular isogeny Diffie-Hellman (SIDH) key exchange [15] is a Diffie-Hellman-like key exchange that is a building block of SIKE.

Alice and Bob are two parties who would like to share a key. Let e_2 and e_3 be two positive integers that define a prime p such that $p = 2^{e_2} 3^{e_3} f \pm 1$, f being a small cofactor (p is of that form in the SIKE specifications [14]). Let E be a supersingular elliptic curve defined over $\mathbb{F}_{p^2}$. Let $P_2, Q_2 \in E[2^{e_2}]$ (i.e. $2^{e_2} P_2 = 2^{e_2} Q_2 = O$) and $P_3, Q_3 \in E[3^{e_3}]$ be bases of these respective torsions, R_2 such that $R_2 = P_2 - Q_2$ and $R_3 = P_3 - Q_3$. These parameters are public. Alice and Bob both have a secret key which is a uniformly distributed random integer, respectively $\mathrm{sk}_2 \in [0, 2^{e_2} - 1]$ and $\mathrm{sk}_3 \in [0, 3^{e_3} - 1]$. The associated secret isogenies ϕ_A and ϕ_B are such that

$$\mathrm{Ker}(\phi_A) = \langle P_2 + \mathrm{sk}_2 Q_2 \rangle \text{ and } \mathrm{Ker}(\phi_B) = \langle P_3 + \mathrm{sk}_3 Q_3 \rangle.$$

We denote by E_A (respectively E_B) the target curve of ϕ_A (respectively ϕ_B), E_{AB} the target curve of ϕ'_A with kernel $\langle \phi_B(P_2) + \mathrm{sk}_2 \phi_B(Q_2) \rangle$ and E_{BA} the target curve of ϕ'_B with kernel $\langle \phi_A(P_3) + \mathrm{sk}_3 \phi_A(Q_3) \rangle$. The following diagram shows how the shared key is constructed.

First, Alice and Bob generate each their private keys, sk_2 and sk_3. Then, they compute their public keys, respectively $(x_{\phi_A(P_3)}, x_{\phi_A(Q_3)}, x_{\phi_A(R_3)})$ and $(x_{\phi_B(P_2)}, x_{\phi_B(Q_2)}, x_{\phi_B(R_2)})$ and exchange them. At last, they both determine the j-invariant of E_{AB} or E_{BA}, depending on the party. It can be shown that E_{AB} and E_{BA} are isomorphic, thus $j(E_{AB}) = j(E_{BA})$, which is used as shared key.

Now we shall see how the public keys are computed in the key generation steps thanks to Algorithm 1 (Algorithm $\mathtt{isogen}_l$ in [14, § 1.3.6]).

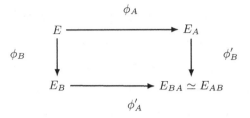

Fig. 1. The SIDH key exchange [15].

Input : A private key sk_A.
Output: A public key pk_A.
1 $x_S \leftarrow x_{(P_2+\mathrm{sk}_2 Q_2)}$ // `ladder3pt` [14, App. A, Alg. 8]
2 $(x_1, x_2, x_3) \leftarrow (x_{P_3}, x_{Q_3}, x_{R_3})$ // `init_basis`[1]
3 **for** i **from** 0 **to** $e_2 - 1$ // Tree traversal loop
4 **do**
5   (a) Compute a 2-isogeny
6

$$\phi_i : E_i \rightarrow E'$$
$$(x, ...) \mapsto (f_i(x), ...)$$

7   such that $\mathrm{Ker}(\phi_i) = \langle 2^{e_2-i-1} S \rangle$.
8   (b) $E_{i+1} = E'$
9   (c) $x_s = f_i(x_S)$
10   (d) $(x_1, x_2, x_3) \leftarrow (f_i(x_{x_1}), f_i(x_{x_2}), f_i(x_{x_3}))$
11 **end**
12 Return (x_1, x_2, x_3).
Algorithm 1: SIKE public key computation with 2-isogenies [14, § 1.3.6].

Remark 1. Optimized implementations of SIDH use a slightly more involved algorithm, performing scalar multiplications and isogeny evaluations according to a predetermined binary tree topology in the tree traversal loop starting at Line 3 of Algorithm 1, as described in [14, § 1.3.8]. The choice of algorithm does not impact the feasibility of Ti's attack.

In the following section, we present key encapsulation in SIKE using the concepts of SIDH.

2.3 SIKE

SIKE is a key encapsulation mechanism (KEM). A KEM is used to securely exchange a symmetric key for data encryption using asymmetric cryptography. Figure 2 shows its different elements. It is composed of three algorithms:

---
[1] https://github.com/microsoft/PQCrypto-SIDH/blob/97c1/src/sidh.c#L10

1. Keygen generates a pair of long term secret and public keys.
2. Encaps takes as input the public key and outputs a random symmetric key K and an encapsulation c of said key.
3. Decaps takes as input the secret key, the public key and c and outputs the symmetric key K.

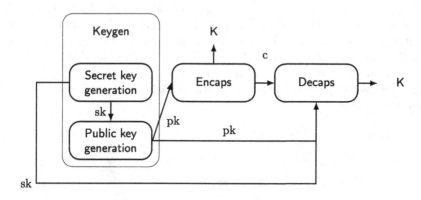

Fig. 2. Description of a Key Encapsulation Mechanism (KEM).

We use the notions of Sect. 2.2 to explain how the concepts of SIDH are used in SIKE. In SIKE, an IND-CPA PKE scheme is built using the same operations as in SIDH, similar to how the "hashed ElGamal" PKE is obtained from the Diffie–Hellman key exchange. The SIKE IND-CCA KEM is built from the PKE scheme using a transformation of Hofheinz, Hövelmanns and Kiltz [13]. The secret key and the public key generation in Keygen are performed exactly as in SIDH. Encaps and Decaps are based on operations from SIDH but also use hash functions and XOR operations. An ephemeral scalar and the associated isogeny are generated in Encaps. This scalar cannot be called "secret" key because it will be recovered by the other party in Decaps. Each time the parties want to compute a shared key K, this scalar is generated anew. However, this is not necessarily the case for the key material in Keygen. Ti's attack takes advantage of this static key, as we will see in the next section. Using this ephemeral scalar and the public key pk, a shared secret j (a j-invariant) is computed. The "secret" scalar and a hash of j are then used to compute the symmetric key K and an encapsulated key c as a ciphertext. In Decaps, the ciphertext is then decrypted with the secret key to recover K and K is validated by recomputing the "secret" scalar and the associated isogeny.

Remark 2. Since Round 2 [14], SIKE specifies two variants, called *uncompressed* and *compressed*. For efficiency reasons, the roles of 2 and 3 are swapped between the two: in the uncompressed version, the public key is computed using 3-isogenies, while the ciphertext is computed using 2-isogenies. In the compressed version, key generation is done by computing 2-isogenies and encapsulation by computing 3-isogenies. The key material used inside the encapsulation is generated anew at each call of Encaps, while the public key produced by Keygen is generated once and can be reused for multiple encapsulations.

3   Ti's Theoretical Fault Attack

As seen in Table 1, there are no experimental validations of attacks on SIKE specific to isogenies. Ti's attack imposes few constraints on the faults to inject, thus it is a good candidate for practical exploitation, even on systems where controlling the produced faults is difficult. This is why we decided to tackle Ti's attack and put it in practice on a modern SoC.

First, we will explain present Ti's attack scenario. The overview of the attack is described in Fig. 3.

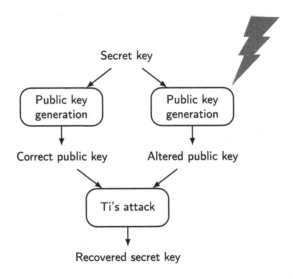

Fig. 3. Schematic representation of Ti's attack scenario.

Attack Scenario. We consider an attack scenario where the victim holds a public-private SIKE key pair, and where the attacker is permitted to retrigger public key generation **from the same secret**, injecting a fault to produce an altered public key (with some probability of success that we shall determine later). To mount the attack, a single altered public key is sufficient.

In a KEM, Keygen generates a fresh secret key and outputs the public key at the same time, hence it is a design mistake to enable a regeneration of the public key. It is however difficult to ensure that all developers will respect the KEM API and avoid generating more than once a public key from the same secret. Hence a countermeasure intrinsic to the public key generation would be useful.

Moreover, avoiding secret reuse is simply not possible in a multipartite exchange [2] where Bob has to use his secret key to generate multiple triplets of points to send to Alice and Charlie, for instance. Hence if the attacker injects a fault during the computation of the triplet Bob wants to send to Alice, they can still recover a correct triplet of Bob's by intercepting the communication from Bob to Charlie. Thus a countermeasure intrinsic to public key generation is strictly necessary for multipartite key exchange (Fig. 4).

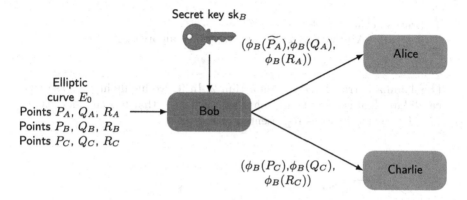

Fig. 4. Ti's attack in a multipartite key exchange setting.

In Ti's article, the starting curve E_0 is defined on $\mathbb{F}_{p^2}$ with $p = 2^{e_2} 3^{e_3} f \pm 1$ where f is a small cofactor as in Sect. 2.2. Normally, when the key generation is not under attack, the images of three fixed public points P_3, Q_3 and R_3 by the secret isogeny ϕ are computed to get the public key (line 10 of Algorithm 1). The attacker will force the computation of the image of a random point by ϕ. The result is an altered point $\phi(\widetilde{P_3})$, $\phi(\widetilde{Q_3})$ or $\phi(\widetilde{R_3})$.

Ti uses the following lemma to show that it is possible to recover the secret key via this point.

Lemma 1. *Let p be a prime number such that $p = 2^{e_2} 3^{e_3} f \pm 1$, where f is a small positive integer and e_2 and e_3 are positive integers such that $2^{e_2} \approx 3^{e_3}$, the same form as in the SIKE specifications [14]. Let E_1, E_2 and E' be supersingular elliptic curves defined over $\mathbb{F}_{p^2}$. Suppose that $\phi : E_1 \rightarrow E_2$ is an isogeny of degree 2^{e_2} with a cylic kernel and let P and Q be generators of $E_1[2^{e_2}]$. For any $X \in E_1[2^{e_2}]$, let $\psi : E_2 \rightarrow E'$ be an isogeny with kernel generated by $\phi(X)$. Then there exists an isogeny $\theta : E' \rightarrow E_1$ of degree 2^ϵ where ϵ is a positive integer such that $\epsilon \leqslant e_2$ and $\hat{\phi} = \theta \circ \psi$.*

Proof. See [27].   □

Input : $\phi(P_3)$, $\phi(Q_3)$ or $\phi(R_3)$ and
M, an altered point that can be $\phi(\widetilde{P_3})$, $\phi(\widetilde{Q_3})$ or $\phi(\widetilde{R_3})$.
Output: $\hat{\phi}$

1 $\lambda = 3^{e_3} f$
2 Compute A_{e_2}, the parameter of the final Montgomery curve $E_{A_{\mathrm{acc}}}$, using algorithm **cfpk** of section 1.2.1 in [14].
3 $T = \lambda M$ on E_{e_2}
4 **if** $\mathrm{ord}(T) = 2^{e_2}$ **then**
5 | $\langle T \rangle = \ker(\hat{\phi})$
6 **else**
7 | Brute force for θ such that $\hat{\phi} = \theta \circ \psi$

Algorithm 2: Ti's key recovery algorithm.

This lemma is translated to Algorithm 2. In it, we highlight the case where the candidate dual isogeny ψ has maximum order, so that θ is the identity map (Fig. 5). The general case is represented in Fig. 6.

Fig. 5. T has maximal order.   **Fig. 6.** T does not have maximal order.

If the kernel generator T has maximal order, i.e. 2^{e_2}, then the isogeny with kernel $\langle T \rangle$ has degree 2^{e_2} and is the dual of ϕ since an isogeny and its dual have the same degree. If, however, T does not have maximal order, an additional isogeny θ of degree $2^{e_2 - \mathrm{ord}(T)}$ will be needed so that $\theta \circ \psi$ is the dual of ϕ. Recovering ϕ knowing the dual is then possible using its definition.

Remark 3. What is the size of the search space for θ's kernel? Do note that we study here a public key generation with a secret isogeny of degree 2^{e_2}. First, to be able to carry out the attack, we need the altered point to be on E_0. Assuming the altered x-coordinate (recall we are using Montgomery curve arithmetic, see Sect. 2) behaves like a random element of $\mathbb{F}_{p^2}$, the probability that it corresponds to a point X on E_0 is approximately $\frac{1}{2}$. Moreover, as E_0 is supersingular, $E_0(\mathbb{F}_{p^2}) \simeq (\mathbb{Z}/(p+1)\mathbb{Z})^2$. Hence there is a basis (A, B) of $E_0(\mathbb{F}_{p^2})$ such that A and B are of order $p+1$ and $3^{e_3} B = S$, where $S \in E_0$ is the secret kernel generator of ϕ and $\mathrm{ord}(S) = 2^{e_2}$. Let $X \in E_0(\mathbb{F}_{p^2})$ such that $X = aA + bB$ where $a, b \in \mathbb{Z}/(p+1)\mathbb{Z}$. Then $T = 3^{e_3} \phi(X) = a 3^{e_3} \phi(A) + b \phi(3^{e_3} B)$ and thus $T = a\phi(3^{e_3} A)$ using the definition of B. The order of $3^{e_3} A$ is 2^{e_2}, and so the order of $\phi(3^{e_3} A)$ is also 2^{e_2}. The order of T is then $2^{e_2 - \mathrm{val}_2(a)}$, where $2^{\mathrm{val}_2(a)}$ is the maximum power of 2 dividing a. The order of T is maximal if $\mathrm{val}_2(a) = 0$ i.e.

if a is odd. The probability of a being odd is $\frac{1}{2}$. T is of order 2^{e_2-1} if a is even but not divisible by 4. The probability for this is $\frac{1}{4}$. In the worst case, $\mathrm{val}_2(a) = e_2$, and the brute force to compute θ is the longest. But the probability of such an event is low: only $\frac{1}{2^{e_2+1}}$. Hence the probability to have no θ to compute is $\frac{1}{4}$, to have a θ of degree 2 to compute is $\frac{1}{8}$ and the worst case, which corresponds to a brute force of the dual isogeny, has probability $\frac{1}{2^{e_2+2}}$ to occur. The expected value of the search space for θ is then given by $\sum\limits_{i=0}^{e_2} \frac{1}{2^{i+1}} \cdot 2^i = \frac{e_2+1}{2}$, which is quite low. All in all, there is a 50% chance that the attack will fail, a 25% chance that the attacker will not need to search for θ, a 12.5% chance that he will have to find θ among the isogenies of degree 2^1 and a 6.25% that he will have to find θ among the isogenies of degree 2^2, etc. Thus it is clear that the probability for the attacker to succeed within a reasonable time is close to 50%. Do note that the reasoning is similar if the attack is performed to find a secret 3^{e_3}-isogeny, and that there is again a 50% chance for the attack to fail and a nearly 50% chance for it to succeed in a reasonable amount of time. These results are valid for a fault at line 2 of Algorithm 1. A fault on x_1, x_2 or x_3 after executing line 10 of Algorithm 1 for the i-th time will modify the probability distribution of $\mathrm{val}_2(\mathrm{ord}(T))$. Indeed, T will have at most a 25% chance to have order 2^{e_2-i} (or 3^{e_3-i}, depending on the case): the distribution is the same, but shifted by i on the $\mathrm{val}_2(\mathrm{ord}(T))$ axis.

Remark 4. Some implementations of SIKE use compressed public keys (for instance [14]). There are different variants of the compression available, for instance in [3,5,19,21,29]. We focus on the one presented in [19], which is the one used in the round 3 submission of SIKE [14]. There are three main steps to compress a public key:

1. Compute the basis of the 3^{e_3}-torsion of E_A.
2. Pull it back to E_0 with the dual of the secret isogeny.
3. Compute the coordinates of P_3, Q_3 and R_3 in that basis on E_0.

These coordinates are the same as the coordinates of $\phi(P_3)$, $\phi(Q_3)$ and $\phi(R_3)$ in the 3^{e_3}-torsion of E_A, and they are the compression of the public key. In this case, we would have to adapt Ti's attack to compute the image of incorrect points by the dual instead of images of the basis. Thus we would have to create a fault during the computation of the image of the basis by the dual. The impact of the different compression methods on the feasibility of the attack should thus be studied in the future. In the rest of this work, we will focus on the non-compressed version of SIKE.

Remark 5. Ti's attack is possible on both 2-isogenies and 3-isogenies. In practice, the attacker will attack 2-isogenies or 3-isogenies depending on what is used in Keygen. We chose to focus our experiments on the attack of only one type of isogenies. When altering point initializations with fault injections, an effect can be to uninitialize some words. In the studied SIKE implementation, the allocated memory space for a point is first filled with zero words. All these zero words are then overwritten by data from constant parameter set coordinates (init_basis at Line 2 of Algorithm 1). The expected effect of fault injection is to skip an instruction during this overwriting to obtain altered point coordinates. An overwriting by zero of a zero word has no effect thus it is easier to alter points initialized with few zero words. When looking at the non-compressed SIKE p434 parameter set, one notices that the points P_3 and Q_3 in the ternary torsion have more zero words in their coordinates so it is more difficult to alter these points. Hence we decided to attack a public key generation with computations of the images of P_3 and Q_3 by 2-isogenies, starting by the non-compressed version, with the goal of attacking the compressed version later.

4   Experimental Setups

Before performing real-life electromagnetic fault attacks, we decided to simulate these attacks using software only. Indeed, fault injection attacks are long and complex to carry out [10], thus we chose to validate the attack with a simulation before the laboratory experiments. There were two steps:

- first, we used Sagemath [26] to simulate fault injection **and** to recover the secret isogeny with an implementation of Algorithm 2 and
- then we emulated the target in C and injected the fault by debugging, while recovering the secret with the same Sage implementation of Algorithm 2.

We are going to subsequently describe the second step, as it is the most realistic simulation of the two, and then the experimental setup for the real-life fault injection.

4.1   Fault Injection Simulation with C

For that second step, we simulate the fault injection by debugging with GDB the optimized round 3 ARM64 implementation of SIKE [14] with curve p434 (non compressed version) using QEMU as an emulator of our target. The emulator is a tool to study the execution of the ARM64 application on an Intel processor. We compiled the SIKE sources from the path Additional_Implementations/ARM64/SIKEp434 in the round 3 SIKE archive with gcc 7.2.1 and the optimization level 3 [14][2].

First, we programmed a tool to generate the key material, i.e. the private key and the public key. Our public key generation tool is a simple encapsulation of the function EphemeralKeyGeneration_A of said ARM64 SIKE implementation. Then we could perform the fault injection simulation, which consists in debugging the public key generation program executed by the emulator with debugger GDB. The input is Alice's secret key. 300 fault attacks are launched by executing EphemeralKeyGeneration_A and skipping a different instruction

---

[2] The original ARMv8-A software implementation is also available in the SIDH Microsoft library at https://github.com/microsoft/PQCrypto-SIDH/tree/f43c9f74.

for each experiment. We only observed the program's behaviour when skipping one of the first 300 instructions. Indeed, the "instruction skip" fault model is easy to implement in GDB with the command "set $pc=$pc+4" and is a very simplified but satisfying model before the implementation of a real attack, as shown in [9] and [23].

This fault injection simulation was done for two different random secret keys. Among the 300 instructions that were skipped, 85 are particularly interesting because they are load/store pairs of instructions that copy the coordinates x_{P_3}, x_{Q_3} and x_{R_3} in the accumulator of line 2 of Algorithm 1. They correspond to the second `init_basis` function call at the beginning of function `EphemeralKeyGeneration_A` in `sidh.c`[3]. 28 of these instructions have no impact on the public key when skipped. The 57 remaining instructions modify the public key when skipped. Out of these 57, 8 instructions yield an x that does not correspond to a point on the target curve because it is impossible to compute y. For the 49 other instructions, it is possible to compute y. Table 2 shows the order of T and the attack successes for these 49 instructions. Recovering the secret was limited to points T with $\log_2(\mathrm{ord}(T)) \geq 210$ to limit brute force computations and, as stated in theory in Remark 3, we notice that the obtained $\log_2(\mathrm{ord}(T))$ are close to e_2. Thus 45 to 48 instructions yield the secret key, and this shows that different faults enable secret key recovery, and is encouraging for the set up of a laboratory fault attack campaign.

Table 2. Number of altered instructions during the second call to `init_basis` yielding the secret key.

$\log_2(\mathrm{ord}(T))$	<208	209	210	211	212	213	214	215	216
Instructions yielding T for secret key #1	0	1	0	1	3	4	10	21	9
Instructions yielding secret key #1	/	/	0	1	3	4	10	21	9
Instructions yielding T for secret key #2	0	4	0	3	3	2	14	16	7
Instructions yielding secret key #2	/	/	0	3	3	2	14	16	7

Sensitive instructions yielding the secret key were also identified outside of the second call to `init_basis`. We focused the study on the first 300 instructions of the function `EphemeralKeyGeneration_A`. 11 additional instructions were identified after calls to the `init_basis` functions. A lot of instruction skips generated altered points that could not be exploited to recover the secret. For example, altering the points used to compute the secret kernel generates three altered points in the public key but this alteration of the secret isogeny cannot be exploited by the attack. Table 3 shows the order of T computed from altered points. Each instruction skip that yields the secret key generates a unique altered point. Again, as expected in Remark 3, the obtained $\log_2(\mathrm{ord}(T))$ are close to e_2.

---

[3] https://github.com/microsoft/PQCrypto-SIDH/blob/f43c9f74/src/sidh.c#L51.

Table 3. Number of altered instructions in the 300 first instructions of EphemeralKeyGeneration_A yielding the secret key.

$\log_2(\mathrm{ord}(T))$	<208	209	210	211	212	213	214	215	216
Altered point yielding T for secret key #1	1	2	0	1	4	6	19	53	136
Instructions yielding secret key #1	/	/	0	1	3	5	12	27	11
Altered point yielding T for secret key #2	1	4	0	4	3	4	31	46	128
Instructions yielding secret key #2	/	/	0	3	3	3	19	19	9

4.2 Carrying Out the Fault Injection in a Laboratory

After having shown that it is possible to simulate Ti's attack, we now present an experimental version. The target is a system on chip (SoC) equipped with four ARM Cortex-A53 cores and including a Yocto Linux operating system. While it is difficult to skip a chosen instruction because of a poorly predictable latency of execution in SoCs [10], we have seen in Sect. 3 and with the simulation in Sect. 4.1 that we only need to alter the beginning of the key generation and do not need to choose precisely the time for the fault injection. Thus we can expect a successful attack on such a target. As seen in Sect. 3, we specifically target key generation, thus we only take this part of the code from the optimized version for ARMv8-A of the SIKE round 3 submission, ignoring decapsulation. We force computations to run on a single CPU of the quad-core, and we fix the CPU clock to the maximum frequency, i.e. 1.2 GHz. We choose electromagnetic injection to create faults, because it is relatively cheap, and because it does not require a complex sample preparation, like removing the circuit packaging. Our setup for the campaign can be seen in Fig. 7.

To launch attacks, the control computer executes a campaign script that manages the communication with the target and the other devices (target power supply, oscilloscope, pulse generator and motorized stage). The key generation implemented on the target has been modified so that the state of a GPIO (general purpose input/output, here output pin) of the target changes just before the public key computation. The fault injection is then triggered by the target when this rising edge appears on the GPIO. The fault is induced by an electromagnetic disturbance generated with a tension pulse generator. The width in nanoseconds, the amplitude in volts and the delay of the pulse, i.e. the time between the rising edge corresponding to the public key computation and the injection of said pulse can all be controlled. The tension pulse is then transmitted as an electromagnetic disturbance to the target through an electromagnetic probe. The probe can be moved with the motorized stage to find the optimal position for fault injection, that is to say the position where it is indeed possible to modify the execution of the algorithm and perform our attack. This induces unwanted currents inside the target. The results of the algorithm computations after injection may be affected and are retrieved and analysed by the computer. In case of application or kernel crash, the power supply is used to reboot the target.

During our campaign, the probe does not move and the pulse width is set at 6 ns. This position and the width are propitious for fault injection according

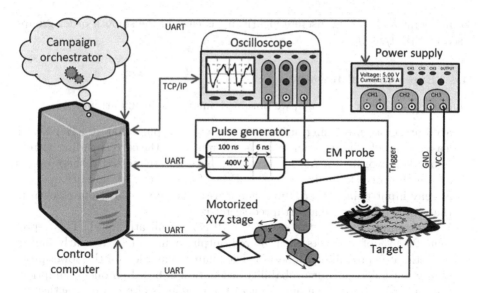

Fig. 7. Campaign setup.

to [10]. The amplitude varies from 300 to 360 V with a 20 V step and the delay between the start of the public key generation and the fault injection varies from 100 to 600 ns with a 20 ns step. Per such configuration, 10,000 attempts are made. Hence 1,040,000 attemps were made in total. The campaign lasted for 4.5 days.

4.3   Analysis

To analyse the results produced by either the simulation or the real fault attack, we use a Sagemath tool and follow the steps described in Sect. 3. In the proof of Ti's attack the order of the candidate dual generator can be maximal or not, and in the latter case, a brute force is necessary to get a θ isogeny to "go back" to the starting elliptic curve. To ensure that the computations do not take "too much time", i.e. that the number of candidates for θ when performing the brute force is small, the order of generator T should be as close to the maximum order, 2^{e_2}, as possible. In that case, the degree of θ (the size of its kernel) will be small. When computing T and checking its order, we will thus only keep points that yield generators T with a "nearly" maximum order, higher or equal to 2^{e_2-6}. Assuming that the altered point is on E_0 (Remark 3), meaning that we can compute T, the probability to get a point T with such order is more than 99%. We then compute a candidate ψ for the dual of the secret isogeny. Depending on the order of T, we will then determine θ or not, and then we will compute the images of P_3, Q_3 and R_3 by the reconstructed secret isogeny to get a reconstructed public key and check that the attack went well. Recovering the secret scalar associated to this secret isogeny is also possible because we know its kernel point and solving discrete logarithms is easy in the smooth order groups used by SIDH/SIKE.

4.4 Experimental Results

During the 4.5 days campaign, we obtained among 1,040,000 attempts:

- 8706 attempts producing at least one altered output point (0.84%) i.e. at least one point whose x-coordinate is different from the corresponding correct public key coordinate. At this point, we have not yet tested if these points are on the correct public key curve. Even if our goal is an alteration of the isogeny input point, other faults might arise and prevent us from recovering the secret, for example a corrupted secret kernel.
- 1780 attempts yielding the secret key (0.17% of all attempts). This represents 20.45% of attempts with altered output point, which is nearly half of the estimated probability in Sect. 3. The main explanation for this lower probability must be that our probability estimation is based on one assumption: the x-coordinate of the input point of the isogeny is altered. In practice, we also induced other faults. Table 4 shows $\log_2(\text{ord}(T))$ with T computed using faulted output points for the 1780 attempts (see line 3 of Algorithm 2). As anticipated, the order of most of these points is high (Table 6 shows the number of attempts we ignored because they yielded a point T with an order too small for us to want to continue the attack) and thus, brute force for θ is fast.

Table 4. Attacks yielding the secret by altering P_3, Q_3 or R_3.

$\log_2(\text{ord}(T))$	210	211	212	213	214	215	216
Number of successful attempts with altered $\phi(P_3)$	5	6	64	80	115	273	82
Number of successful attempts with altered $\phi(Q_3)$	11	14	60	52	188	371	93
Number of successful attempts with altered $\phi(R_3)$	4	19	12	10	58	75	219

Table 5. Attacks altering P_3, Q_3 or R_3 and getting $\text{ord}(T) \geq 210$ but not yielding the secret.

$\log_2(\text{ord}(T))$	210	211	212	213	214	215	216
Number of unsuccessful attempts with altered $\phi(P_3)$	0	2	5	30	176	512	2169
Number of unsuccessful attempts with altered $\phi(Q_3)$	0	2	4	28	83	572	2174
Number of unsucessful attempts with altered $\phi(R_3)$	0	2	5	33	82	621	2124

Remark 6. Do note that for each (amplitude, delay) configuration, we check if either P, Q or R has been altered. Sometimes, for a given configuration, more than one of these points is altered and matches our condition (yielding the secret,

Table 6. Attacks yielding T but its order is too small for us to want to continue the attack.

$\log_2(\mathrm{ord}(T))$	1	206	207	208	209
Number of attempts with altered $\phi(P_3)$	155	1	4	0	3
Number of attempts with altered $\phi(Q_3)$	350	0	0	5	69
Number of attempts with altered $\phi(R_3)$	225	0	0	3	1

yielding a T of order greater than 210 but not the secret (Table 5), yielding a T with an order strictly smaller than 210). Thus for instance the line for attempts with an altered $\phi(P_3)$ matching the chosen condition also includes attempts where two points including $\phi(P_3)$ are altered and match it, and attempts where the three points are altered and match it.

Figure 8 is a heat map representing the percentage of successful attempts i.e. those that yield Alice's secret key depending on the (delay, amplitude) configuration. After one campaign, injections of pulses with a 360 V amplitude and a delay of 440 ns seem to be the best choice to recover the secret key: there is a 0.62% chance to recover the secret key in this configuration. Do note that the maximum amplitude delivered by our pulser is 400 V, and that the number of reboots increases when approaching that limit, thus slowing the campaign. There are few configurations where there is no chance to recover the secret. This confirms than the required accuracy on the induced fault is low and compatible with practical fault injection.

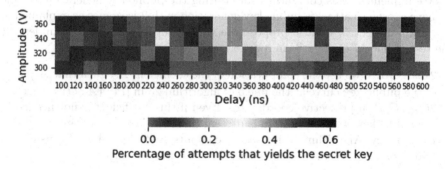

Fig. 8. Percentage of successful attempts depending on the amplitude and delay.

Remark 7. The reader might wonder why the best success rate is only 0.62% experimentally while the theoretical success rate of the attack is around 50% as seen in Remark 3. This is due to the low repeatability of electromagnetic fault injection [10]: a lot of attempts at altering the algorithm's execution does not induce faults, or at least not in a way that enables us to perform the attack (e.g. a reboot).

5   Countermeasures

As discussed in Sect. 3, it is difficult to make sure that people implementing the SIKE protocol will adhere to the specified API and avoid computing twice the public key. Moreover, it is not possible to avoid computing more than one public key using the same secret in a multipartite setting. Thus we propose a countermeasure that shall work in this setting too.

Let us consider the round 3 optimized implementation of SIKE. The starting curve E_0 is pushed successively through the isogenies of small degrees (update of the curve line 8 of Algorithm 1 and Algorithm 3) to be used for the computation of the kernel generator of the next isogeny (line 7 of Algorithm 1 and Algorithm 3). Let us compute the coefficient A of this last target elliptic curve. We call it A_{e_2}. But we can also compute the coefficient by using the x-coordinates of the public key. Let us call the result of this computation A_{x_1,x_2,x_3}. If at least one image of a point different of P_3, Q_3 and R_3 is computed, then the probability to recover the correct elliptic curve coefficient using the x-coordinates at the end will be very low: most of the time, we will have $A_{x_1,x_2,x_3} \neq A_{e_A}$. Algorithm 3 is a modified version of the public key generation Algorithm 1 with the added countermeasure.

We would like to know the probability of not detecting a faulted point. Suppose that there is only one faulted point. Then according to Equation (1) in Sect. 2.1, A is a polynomial of degree 2 in x_P for instance. Hence it has two roots in $\mathbb{F}_{p^2}$. One is the correct x_P. The probability to get the wrong one is then $\frac{1}{p^2}$, as there is only one value that is a root and that is not the correct abscissa. Looking at the size of p, it is a very low probability.

We implement this countermeasure during the public key generation. While we have chosen to attack a public key generation with 2-isogenies as explained in Remark 5 of Sect. 3, we also propose the variant for 3-isogenies. We implement the test of line 12 of Algorithm 3 as follows.

- **2-isogenies:** we use the computation of the coefficient A_{e_2} such that $A_{e_2} = \frac{A}{C}$ of the public key curve at the line 5 of algorithm 23 in [14]: $(A : C) = (4A_{24}^+ - 2C_{24} : C_{24})$ in projective coordinates. Even if this coefficient is not needed in the public key, its computation is present in SIKE. We take advantage of this redundancy. Algorithm 10 is used to compute coefficient A_{x_1,x_2,x_3} using the triplet of x-coordinates of the public key. We want to check that

$$(CA_{x_1,x_2,x_3} : C) = (4A_{24}^+ - 2C_{24} : C_{24}).$$

Thus we check that

$$4A_{24}^+ = A_{x_1,x_2,x_3}C_{24} + 2C_{24}.$$

If not, then we detect a problem during the public key generation. This costs four additions, one multiplication and one call to get_A.

Input : A private key sk_A.
Output: A public key pk_A.

1   $x_S \leftarrow x_{(P_A + sk_A Q_A)}$; // ladder3pt [14, App. A, Alg. 8]
2   $(x_1, x_2, x_3) \leftarrow (x_{P_B}, x_{Q_B}, x_{R_B})$; // init_basis[4]
3 **for** i from 0 to $e_A - 1$; // Tree traversal loop
4 **do**
5   (a) Compute an l_A-isogeny
6

$$\phi_i : E_i \to E'$$
$$(x, ...) \mapsto (f_i(x), ...)$$

7   such that $\text{Ker}(\phi_i) = \langle l_A^{e_A - i - 1} S \rangle$.
8   b) $E_{i+1} = E'$
9   c) $x_S = f_i(x_S)$
10   d) $(x_1, x_2, x_3) \leftarrow (f_i(x_1), f_i(x_2), f_i(x_3))$
11 **end**
    // A_{e_2} can be retrieved after the computation of E_{e_2}.
12 $A_{x_1, x_2, x_3} = \text{get\_A}(x_1, x_2, x_3)$
13 **if** $A_{x_1, x_2, x_3} \neq A_{e_2}$ **then**
14   return 0 // fault detected, do not return the altered public key
15 **else**
16   return $pk_A = (x_1, x_2, x_3)$.// return the public key
17 **end**

Algorithm 3: SIKE public key computation with countermeasure.

– **3-isogenies:** we use the computation of the coefficient A_{e_2} such that $A_{e_2} = \frac{A}{C}$ of the public key curve at the line 5 of algorithm 24 in [14]: $(A : C) = (2(A_{24}^+ + A_{24}^-) : (A_{24}^+ - A_{24}^-))$ in projective coordinates. Even if this coefficient is not needed in the public key, its computation is present in SIKE. Algorithm 10 is used to compute coefficient A_{x_1, x_2, x_3} using the triplet of x-coordinates of the public key. We want to check that

$$(CA_{x_1, x_2, x_3} : C) = (2(A_{24}^+ + A_{24}^-) : (A_{24}^+ - A_{24}^-)).$$

Thus we check that

$$(A_{24}^+ - A_{24}^-)A_{x_1, x_2, x_3} = 2(A_{24}^+ + A_{24}^-).$$

If not, then we detect a problem during the public key generation.
This costs three additions and substractions, one multiplication and one call to get_A.

A call to get_A costs seven additions and subtractions, one squaring, four multiplications and one inversion. It is possible to get rid of the inversion and obtain a faster verification by manipulating the equality we check using the formula of A in Eq. (1) as computed by get_A.

---

[4] https://github.com/microsoft/PQCrypto-SIDH/blob/97c1/src/sidh.c#L10.

The number of operations to add to implement the countermeasure is very small compared to the number of operations necessary to generate the public key, thus the overhead is low. We added the countermeasure in function `EphemeralKeyGeneration_B`[5] of the implementation described in Sect. 4 with ARMv8-A assembly optimizations and then measured on a Cortex-A53 a 1.5% overhead during the public key generation with 3-isogenies. In our naive implementation of the countermeasure, we use the existing `get_A` function which includes a division to obtain the affine representation of the A coefficient. This normalization is not necessary to compare the two coefficients. The overhead could thus be further reduced by avoiding the division. The verification can also be done during and after the tree traversal step of Algorithm 3. But considering the probability to detect a fault at the end of the public key computation, it does not seem necessary.

6   Conclusion

We have shown that Ti's 2017 fault injection attack on the key generation step of SIKE is exploitable in practice though electromagnetic injection on a SoC. While it is complex to generate faults on a SoC, Ti's attack does not require a high precision when performing it, which simplifies the experimental verification in a laboratory. In a 4.5 days campaign, 0.17% of the attack configurations yielded the secret key for at least one of the altered public key points, which corresponds to around one configuration that enables us to recover the secret key every 3 min and 18 s. This attack requires both the real public key of Alice and an altered version. While the attack scenario is unlikely to apply to implementations of SIKE that respect the KEM API, it occurs in a multipartite setting. We thus propose a countermeasure which consists in computing the public key curve coefficient by using two different methods. This countermeasure has both a small overhead and a high probability to detect a fault. It remains to be seen if the attack is still feasible when the public keys are compressed.

References

1. Alagic, G., et al.: Status report on the second round of the NIST post-quantum cryptography standardization process. US Department of Commerce, NIST (2020)
2. Azarderakhsh, R., Jalali, A., Jao, D., Soukharev, V.: Practical supersingular isogeny group key agreement. IACR Cryptol. ePrint Arch. **2019**, 330 (2019)
3. Azarderakhsh, R., Jao, D., Kalach, K., Koziel, B., Leonardi, C.: Key compression for isogeny-based cryptosystems. In: Proceedings of the 3rd ACM International Workshop on ASIA Public-Key Cryptography, pp. 1–10 (2016)
4. Coron, J.-S.: Resistance against differential power analysis for elliptic curve cryptosystems. In: Koç, Ç.K., Paar, C. (eds.) CHES 1999. LNCS, vol. 1717, pp. 292–302. Springer, Heidelberg (1999). https://doi.org/10.1007/3-540-48059-5_25

---

[5] https://github.com/microsoft/PQCrypto-SIDH/blob/97c1/src/sidh.c/#L123.

5. Costello, C., Jao, D., Longa, P., Naehrig, M., Renes, J., Urbanik, D.: Efficient compression of SIDH public keys. In: Coron, J.-S., Nielsen, J.B. (eds.) EUROCRYPT 2017. LNCS, vol. 10210, pp. 679–706. Springer, Cham (2017). https://doi.org/10.1007/978-3-319-56620-7_24

6. Costello, C., Longa, P., Naehrig, M.: Efficient algorithms for supersingular isogeny Diffie-Hellman. In: Robshaw, M., Katz, J. (eds.) CRYPTO 2016. LNCS, vol. 9814, pp. 572–601. Springer, Heidelberg (2016). https://doi.org/10.1007/978-3-662-53018-4_21

7. Costello, C., Smith, B.: Montgomery curves and their arithmetic. J. Cryptogr. Eng. 8(3), 227–240 (2017). https://doi.org/10.1007/s13389-017-0157-6

8. De Feo, L.: Mathematics of isogeny based cryptography. CoRR abs/1711.04062 (2017). http://arxiv.org/abs/1711.04062

9. Dehbaoui, A., Dutertre, J.M., Robisson, B., Tria, A.: Electromagnetic transient faults injection on a hardware and a software implementations of AES. In: 2012 Workshop on Fault Diagnosis and Tolerance in Cryptography, pp. 7–15. IEEE (2012)

10. Gaine, C., Aboulkassimi, D., Pontié, S., Nikolovski, J.P., Dutertre, J.M.: Electromagnetic fault injection as a new forensic approach for SoCs. In: 2020 IEEE International Workshop on Information Forensics and Security (WIFS), pp. 1–6. IEEE (2020)

11. Galbraith, S.D., Petit, C., Shani, B., Ti, Y.B.: On the security of supersingular isogeny cryptosystems. In: Cheon, J.H., Takagi, T. (eds.) ASIACRYPT 2016. LNCS, vol. 10031, pp. 63–91. Springer, Heidelberg (2016). https://doi.org/10.1007/978-3-662-53887-6_3

12. Gélin, A., Wesolowski, B.: Loop-abort faults on supersingular isogeny cryptosystems. In: Lange, T., Takagi, T. (eds.) PQCrypto 2017. LNCS, vol. 10346, pp. 93–106. Springer, Cham (2017). https://doi.org/10.1007/978-3-319-59879-6_6

13. Hofheinz, D., Hövelmanns, K., Kiltz, E.: A modular analysis of the Fujisaki-Okamoto transformation. In: Kalai, Y., Reyzin, L. (eds.) TCC 2017. LNCS, vol. 10677, pp. 341–371. Springer, Cham (2017). https://doi.org/10.1007/978-3-319-70500-2_12

14. Jao, D., et al.: SIKE: supersingular isogeny key encapsulation (2020). https://sike.org/files/SIDH-spec.pdf

15. Jao, D., De Feo, L.: Towards quantum-resistant cryptosystems from supersingular elliptic curve isogenies. In: Yang, B.-Y. (ed.) PQCrypto 2011. LNCS, vol. 7071, pp. 19–34. Springer, Heidelberg (2011). https://doi.org/10.1007/978-3-642-25405-5_2

16. Koppermann, P., Pop, E., Heyszl, J., Sigl, G.: 18 seconds to key exchange: limitations of supersingular isogeny Diffie-Hellman on embedded devices. IACR Cryptology ePrint Archive 2018, 932 (2018)

17. Koziel, B., Azarderakhsh, R., Jao, D.: Side-channel attacks on quantum-resistant supersingular isogeny Diffie-Hellman. In: Adams, C., Camenisch, J. (eds.) SAC 2017. LNCS, vol. 10719, pp. 64–81. Springer, Cham (2018). https://doi.org/10.1007/978-3-319-72565-9_4

18. Montgomery, P.L.: Speeding the pollard and elliptic curve methods of factorization. Math. Comput. 48(177), 243–264 (1987)

19. Naehrig, M., Renes, J.: Dual isogenies and their application to public-key compression for isogeny-based cryptography. In: Galbraith, S.D., Moriai, S. (eds.) ASIACRYPT 2019. LNCS, vol. 11922, pp. 243–272. Springer, Cham (2019). https://doi.org/10.1007/978-3-030-34621-8_9

20. NIST: Submission requirements and evaluation criteria for the post-quantum cryptography standardization process, December 2016. https://csrc.nist.gov/CSRC/media/Projects/Post-Quantum-Cryptography/documents/call-for-proposals-final-dec-2016.pdf
21. Pereira, G.C., Doliskani, J., Jao, D.: x-only point addition formula and faster torsion basis generation in compressed SIKE. IACR Cryptol. ePrint Arch. 2020, 431 (2020)
22. Proy, J., Heydemann, K., Berzati, A., Cohen, A.: Compiler-assisted loop hardening against fault attacks. ACM Trans. Archit. Code Optim. (TACO) 14(4), 1–25 (2017)
23. Proy, J., Heydemann, K., Majeric, F., Cohen, A., Berzati, A.: Studying EM pulse effects on superscalar microarchitectures at ISA level. arXiv preprint arXiv:1903.02623 (2019)
24. Shor, P.W.: Algorithms for quantum computation: discrete logarithms and factoring. In: Proceedings 35th Annual Symposium on Foundations of Computer Science, pp. 124–134. IEEE (1994)
25. Silverman, J.H.: The Arithmetic of Elliptic Curves. GTM, vol. 106. Springer, New York (2009). https://doi.org/10.1007/978-0-387-09494-6
26. The Sage Developers: SageMath, the Sage Mathematics Software System (Version 8.1) (2017). https://www.sagemath.org
27. Ti, Y.B.: Fault attack on supersingular isogeny cryptosystems. In: Lange, T., Takagi, T. (eds.) PQCrypto 2017. LNCS, vol. 10346, pp. 107–122. Springer, Cham (2017). https://doi.org/10.1007/978-3-319-59879-6_7
28. Vélu, J.: Isogénies entre courbes elliptiques. CR Acad. Sci. Paris, Séries A 273, 305–347 (1971)
29. Zanon, G.H.M., Simplicio, M.A., Pereira, G.C.C.F., Doliskani, J., Barreto, P.S.L.M.: Faster isogeny-based compressed key agreement. In: Lange, T., Steinwandt, R. (eds.) PQCrypto 2018. LNCS, vol. 10786, pp. 248–268. Springer, Cham (2018). https://doi.org/10.1007/978-3-319-79063-3_12
30. Zhang, F., et al.: Side-channel analysis and countermeasure design on ARM-based quantum-resistant SIKE. IEEE Trans. Comput. 69(11), 1681–1693 (2020)

Physical Unclonable Functions

Analysis and Protection of the Two-Metric Helper Data Scheme

Lars Tebelmann[1]([✉])[iD], Ulrich Kühne[2][iD], Jean-Luc Danger[2][iD],
and Michael Pehl[1][iD]

[1] TUM Department of Electrical and Computer Engineering, Chair of Security in
Information Technology, Technical University Munich, Munich, Germany
{lars.tebelmann,m.pehl}@tum.de
[2] Télécom Paris, Paris, France
{ulrich.kuhne,jean-luc.danger}@telecom-paris.fr

Abstract. To compensate for the poor reliability of Physical Unclonable
Function (PUF) primitives, some low complexity solutions not requiring
error-correcting codes (ECC) have been proposed. One simple method is
to discard less reliable bits, which are indicated in the helper data stored
inside the PUF. To avoid discarding bits, the Two-metric Helper Data
(TMH) method, which particularly applies to oscillation-based PUFs,
allows to keep all bits by using different metrics when deriving the PUF
response. However, oscillation-based PUFs are sensitive to side-channel
analysis (SCA) since the frequencies of the oscillations can be observed by
current or electromagnetic measurements. This paper studies the security
of PUFs using TMH in order to obtain both reliable and robust PUF
responses. We show that PUFs using TMH are sensitive to SCA, but can
be greatly improved by using temporal masking and adapted extraction
metrics. In case of public helper data, an efficient protection requires
the randomization of the measurement order. We study two different
solutions, providing interesting insights into trade-offs between security
and complexity.

Keywords: PUF · Side-channel analysis · Two-metric helper data ·
LFSR-based protection · Permutation · Countermeasures

1 Introduction

Physical Unclonable Functions (PUFs) have become an important security primitive, which can greatly enhance authentication mechanisms in digital devices. A
good PUF provides a unique identifier, which does not have to be programmed
in non-volatile memory (NVM) and hence is not sensitive to memory hacking.

This work was partly funded by the German Ministry of Education and Research in the
project SecForCARs under grant number 01KIS0795 and under the SPARTA project,
which has received funding from the European Union's Horizon 2020 research and
innovation programme under grant agreement number 830892.

S. Bhasin and F. De Santis (Eds.): COSADE 2021, LNCS 12910, pp. 279–302, 2021.
https://doi.org/10.1007/978-3-030-89915-8_13

This identifier corresponds to the value returned by a function that exploits slight technological differences from the fabrication process, and which stay constant during life time of a component. The extraction can be done in many different ways, such as measuring the delay – giving rise to the delay PUF [17] – and the initial state of SRAM cells – the SRAM PUF [7]. In particular, a PUF has the property of *unclonability*: the outputs depend on process variations only, i.e., copying a device from the same blueprint does not yield the same PUF response.

One of the main drawbacks of PUFs is the reliability, as the bit error rate (BER) of their output can be in the range of 3 to 15% [9]. The most common way to improve the reliability is the use of error-correcting codes (ECC) [6,10]. It requires to generate a public word during the enrollment phase, termed helper data, which enables correction of faulty PUF bits during the reconstruction phase. Alternatively, the reliability can be improved if the PUF output contains an indication of the bit reliability. For example, oscillation-based PUFs such as the Ring Oscillator (RO) PUF [17] or Loop PUF [2] use the sign of a frequency difference as secret, while the difference's magnitude provides reliability information regarding the probability of bit flips. A first approach is to discard unreliable bits [15]. In this work, we examine an improved method, called the Two-metric Helper Data (TMH) scheme [3], that does not loose unreliable bits. By reconstructing under two different metrics, it can make the use of ECC unnecessary.

PUFs have been attacked by side-channel analysis (SCA) in different ways, e.g., targeting the post-processing stage [13,19]. Oscillation-based PUFs have been attacked by observing the electromagnetic (EM) emanations from the RO PUF [11,12,16] and the Loop PUF [18]. To face this threat, protections based on randomization have been proposed, such as using a random path for the RO PUF [11] and temporal masking for the Loop PUF [18]. While helper data manipulation has been used as an attack vector [1,4,5], the impact of the helper data algorithm for SCA has been neglected so far.

Contribution: We show that the TMH scheme [3] is prone to yet unexplored SCA attacks. As a consequence, new protection mechanisms are needed. In particular:

1. We present a novel attack against the TMH scheme, which makes use of the *magnitude* – in contrast to the *sign* – of the frequency differences in oscillator-based PUFs. The feasibility of the attack is shown for a 63-bit Loop PUF.
2. We provide two different approaches for countermeasures that combine modification of the TMH metrics with randomization of the Loop PUF challenge order. We show trade-offs between security and cost.
3. We deeply analyze the security of the proposed solutions, showing that the low-complexity solution – while requiring less randomness – may be attacked, although with higher effort than without the protection.

Structure: The remainder of this work is organized as follows: Sect. 2 explains the TMH method. Sections 3 and 4 provide the threat model and the security analysis of the TMH respectively. Protections are presented in Sect. 5, their security analysis in Sect. 6 and a conclusion is drawn in Sect. 7.

2 Two-Metric Helper Data Method

The TMH is a method that enhances the reliability level of PUFs to generate secret responses used as cryptographic key [3]. It applies specially to delay PUFs, whose responses contain reliability information. Oscillator-based PUFs, such as the RO PUF [17] and the Loop PUF [2] use the sign of a frequency difference df as response bit. The magnitude of the difference provides reliability information. Using this information, the TMH method can allow for highly reliable responses without the use of ECC decoders in the post-processing stage.

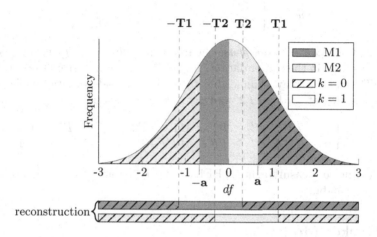

Fig. 1. Choice of metric and extraction of PUF bit value from the frequency difference df according to [3].

For this purpose, in the *enrollment phase*, the distribution of all df on a device is estimated under the assumption that it follows a Gaussian normal distribution with mean $\mu = 0$ and variance σ^2, i.e., $df \sim \mathcal{N}(0, \sigma^2)$. The distribution is divided into octiles defined by the points $-T1, -a, -T2, T2, a, T1$ (and $\pm\infty$) as depicted in Fig. 1. For each octile the upper and lower bounds x and y are adapted such that, the cumulative distribution function (CDF) $\Phi(\cdot)$ defined by the integral over the probability density function (PDF) $\phi(\cdot)$ complies to

$$\Phi(x) - \Phi(y) = \int_y^x \phi(x)dx = \frac{1}{8}. \tag{1}$$

The Two-metric Helper Data (TMH) method derives its name from the fact that based on the octiles two metrics $M1$ and $M2$ define the mapping of the frequency difference df to the PUF bit k as:

$$M1 : k = \begin{cases} 0, T2 \leq df \vee df < -T1 \\ 1, -T1 \leq df < T2 \end{cases} \quad M2 : k = \begin{cases} 0, T1 \leq df \vee df < -T2 \\ 1, -T2 \leq df < T1 \end{cases}. \tag{2}$$

Note that from the definition of the octiles $\int_{-T1}^{T2} \phi(x)dx = \int_{-T2}^{T1} \phi(x)dx = 1/2$, i.e., the values for k are equiprobable and no bias is induced by the TMH. For the frequency difference df_C of a particular challenge C the metric is chosen and stored as helper data w_C, for which the reconstruction from a perturbed $df'_C = df_C + \delta$ is more reliable. In other words, the metric is stored as helper data, for which a deviation δ from the enrollment value is less likely to cause a change of the PUF bit during reconstruction. From Fig. 1 metrics $M1$ and $M2$ are least stable around $-T1/T2$ and $-T2/T1$ respectively, thus the selection of the appropriate helper data is done according to the following intervals:

$$w_C = \begin{cases} M2, & -a < df_C \vee 0 < df_C \leq a \\ M1, & -a \leq df_C \leq 0 \vee a < df_C \end{cases}. \tag{3}$$

During the *reconstruction phase* the frequency difference df'_C is mapped with the metric stored in the helper data w_C to k'_C. As the bounds from the enrollment $\pm T1$, $\pm T2$ and $\pm a$ may change due to environmental conditions, the device estimates a new set $\pm T1'$, $\pm T2'$ and $\pm a'$ for reconstruction i.e.,

$$k'_C = \begin{cases} 1, & -T1' \leq df'_C < T2' \,\&\, M1 \vee -T2' \leq df'_C < T1' \,\&\, M2 \\ 0, & -T2' \geq df'_C \geq T1' \,\&\, M2 \vee -T1' \geq df'_C \geq T2' \,\&\, M1 \end{cases}. \tag{4}$$

For typical noise measurements a BER of $< 10^{-6}$ is achieved [3], i.e., $k'_C = k_C$ with high probability.

3   Attacker Model

Throughout the paper we adopt an attacker model where the attacker has physical access to the targeted device. In particular, the attacker has read access to the helper data of the PUF, i.e., it is known which metric $M1$ and $M2$ of the TMH scheme is used to derive a particular PUF bit. The assumption of public helper data is generally accepted when designing PUF-based key storage as (i) the helper data should not leak about the secret [14] and (ii) storing the helper data in a protected NVM would render the PUF approach useless as the secret could directly be stored. In theory, access to the helper data could be hampered, e.g. if it is stored by fuses, that are difficult to read out. Limited helper data represents the worst case scenario for an attacker, which is why we also investigate the possibility of an attack without helper data knowledge. However, the security of the system must not depend on the concealment of the helper data.

Furthermore, the attacker is able to perform passive physical attacks such as side-channel measurements during the reconstruction phase of the PUF. This includes power measurements as well as EM measurements above the package. We neglect semi-invasive attacks such as localized EM SCA, which have been applied to RO PUFs [11,12,16], but require a high level of sophistication due to decapsulation of chips, and expensive measurement equipment in terms of micro near-field probes. The bar for mounting these kinds of attacks can be raised by adding sensors that detect opening of the package and thus impede direct access to the die. As we focus on sequentially evaluated PUFs like the Loop PUF, the application of semi-invasive means does not promise any advantage compared to non-invasive attacks that would justify the additional effort.

For all considerations, the attacker is able to acquire multiple measurements of the reconstruction phase for the same PUF device. That means for the countermeasures proposed in Sect. 5 that the attacker can compare measurements with different randomization to establish a relationship among measurements. The number of measurements can practically be limited by the time and storage capacities of the adversary, but we assume no countermeasures to limit the number of reconstructions.

4   Analysis of the Two-Metric Helper Data Method

In this section, we describe a side-channel vulnerability of the original TMH method given an attacker without helper data access. We propose a modification of the TMH from Sect. 2 that improves the scheme regarding mitigation of the vulnerability. Subsequently, we show that even with the improved method an attack with helper data knowledge still succeeds in recovering the secret. The findings emphasize the need for additional countermeasures, which are proposed in Sect. 5.

4.1   SCA Attack Vector of the Two-Metric Helper Data Method

For oscillation-based PUFs, the use of the sign of frequency difference df can be targeted by side-channel analysis. In case of the RO PUF, attacks target the comparison of frequencies [12] and the resolution of single oscillators or counters using localized EM measurements [11]. Even if components are placed close to each other, EM attacks succeed due to *geometric leaks* [16], making an effective protection against SCA difficult.

A possible improvement regarding side-channel resistance is the so-called Loop PUF [2] that uses a single RO configured by challenges. In order to generate a PUF bit k, a challenge C and its complement $\neg C$, where each bit is flipped, generate the frequencies f_C and $f_{\neg C}$. The sign of the difference $df = f_C - f_{\neg C}$ is then taken as the PUF bit. While the original Loop PUF design is vulnerable to SCA, because the frequencies can be measured sequentially, a simple and effective countermeasure called *temporal masking* can be applied [18]. It randomizes the order of the two challenges to derive df, therefore an attacker is not able to deduce the sign of df anymore. The required randomness is derived from the counter's least significant bit (LSB), in other words from the oscillators phase jitter, enabling a self-protected PUF design.

In the following and without loss of generality, we assume that the frequency differences df processed by the TMH stem from a Loop PUF that is protected by the *temporal masking* scheme. With this approach the underlying PUF primitive is protected against SCA and we can focus on the properties of the TMH. First, note that for the TMH method the bit value is not given by the sign of df but by its magnitude. Revisiting Fig. 1 and Eqs. (2) and (3), which establish the bit value according to the metrics and df, if the absolute value of df is greater than the threshold a, the bit value is always $k = 0$. Furthermore for absolute values of df around 0, the bit value is $k = 1$. Thus an attacker observing the frequencies and their difference in the side-channel can easily derive the bit value even in presence of the temporal masking countermeasure. This is only possible because the TMH uses the magnitude instead of the sign to derive the PUF bits.

4.2   Formalization of the Attack Success

In the following, we provide theoretical insights into the success probability that an attacker can achieve by formally modelling the side-channel observations.

The noise $\mathcal{N}_{attack}$ that the attacker is confronted with is a combination of the noise from measurements $\mathcal{N}_{meas.} \sim \mathcal{N}(0, \sigma_{meas.})$ and the inherent noise $\mathcal{N}_{osc.} \sim \mathcal{N}(\mu_{osc.}, \sigma_{osc.})$ of the oscillation frequency f that occurs from measurement to measurement. Assuming that the noise terms are normally distributed and additive, the overall noise is expressed as

$$\mathcal{N}_{attack} = \mathcal{N}_{meas.} + \mathcal{N}_{osc.} \sim \mathcal{N}(\mu_{adv.}, \sigma_{adv.}), \tag{5}$$

where $\sigma_{adv.} = \sqrt{\sigma_{meas.}^2 + \sigma_{osc.}^2}$[1]. Assuming that environmental conditions change slowly, any perturbation is constant among the different frequencies. Thus, offsets $\mu_{osc.}$ of the oscillators are cancelled out when calculating the frequency difference $df = f_C - f_{\neg C}$, and it follows that $\mu_{adv.} = 0$.

The following notation is adopted for the PDF of a normally distributed variable with mean μ and standard deviation σ

$$\phi^\star(x; \mu, \sigma) := \frac{1}{\sigma} \phi\left(\frac{x-\mu}{\sigma}\right) = \frac{1}{\sigma\sqrt{2\pi}} e^{-\frac{1}{2}\left(\frac{x-\mu}{\sigma}\right)^2}, \tag{6}$$

where $\phi(x)$ is the standard normal distribution.

The attacker mimics the reconstruction process by estimating bounds $\pm T1^\star$, $\pm T2^\star$ and $\pm a^\star$ from the observed values $df^\star$ and guesses $\hat{k}_C$ using Eq. (4). Note, that for $\sigma_{meas.} = 0$ this corresponds to the reconstruction procedure on the device as only $\sigma_{osc.}$ is present compared to the enrollment, i.e., $T1^\star = T1'$, $T2^\star = T2'$ and $a^\star = a'$. In this case, the attacker has the same information as the device and the attack will succeed. We will investigate how the attack success is affected if the attacker observes $\sigma_{meas.} > 0$. Without loss of generality we can set $\sigma_{osc.} = 0$ in the following such that $\sigma_{adv.} = \sigma_{meas.}$ is the additional noise the attacker observes. In other words, the device will reconstruct based on the same bounds as during enrollment, i.e., $T1' = T1$, $T2' = T2$ and $a' = a$, while the attacker does so based on the noisy versions $T1^\star$, $T2^\star$ and $a^\star$. In the following, we will investigate the success probability

$$Pr_{success}(df_C, \sigma_{adv.}) = Pr[\hat{k}_C = k_C | df_C, \sigma_{adv.}] \tag{7}$$

---

[1] Note that the device observes only $\sigma_{osc.}$ during reconstruction, i.e., the attacker is always in a worse position compared to the reconstruction.

that defines whether an attacker can retrieve the correct PUF bit for a challenge C. The assumption is that the device sees df_C for reconstruction, while the attacker observes df_C^* drawn from the normal distribution $\phi^*(df^*; df_C, \sigma_{adv.})$. Besides a relationship of attack success and Signal-to-Noise Ratio (SNR), Eq. (7) also provides insights whether certain values df_C can be more easily attacked.

Weighting the success probability by the occurrence of the df, which follows – per assumption from Sect. 2 – a normal distribution that for the sake of simplicity we assume to be transformed into a standard normal distribution for $\sigma_{osc.} = 0$, yields the average success probability

$$\overline{Pr}_{success}(\sigma_{adv.}) = \int_{-\infty}^{\infty} Pr_{success}(df, \sigma_{adv.}) \cdot \phi^*(df; 0, 1) \, ddf. \tag{8}$$

4.3 Exploiting the Two-Metric Helper Data Method

In this section, we investigate the side-channel vulnerability of the TMH introduced in Sect. 2 and provide insights into how attacks with and without helper data knowledge differ. Subsequently, we introduce an extension of the TMH in Sect. 4.4 that impedes attacks without helper data knowledge.

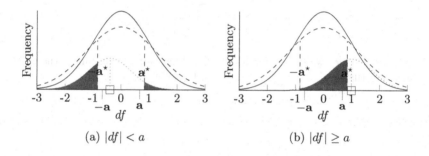

(a) $|df| < a$ (b) $|df| \geq a$

Fig. 2. Visualization of the attack failure for attacker without helper data.

Attacker Without Helper Data Knowledge. In a first step we will show that even if an attacker does not know the helper data, i.e., whether metric $M1$ or $M2$ is applied, the TMH leaks side-channel information. From Fig. 1 the attacker needs to observe the magnitude of the frequency difference df^* regarding a^*: if $|df^*| > a^*$, the guessed PUF bit is $\hat{k}_C = 0$, otherwise $\hat{k}_C = 1$ and the success probability is

$$Pr_{success}^{no\,HD}(df, \sigma_{adv.}) = 1 - Pr[\hat{k}_C \neq k_C]$$
$$= 1 - \left(Pr\left[|df^*| \leq a^* \mid |df| > a \right] + Pr\left[|df^*| > a^* \mid |df| \leq a \right] \right)$$
$$= 1 - \begin{cases} \int_{-a^*}^{-a^*} \phi^*\left(df^*; df, \sigma_{adv.}\right) ddf^* + \int_{a^*}^{\infty} \phi^*\left(df^*; df, \sigma_{adv.}\right) ddf^*, & -a \leq df < a \\ \int_{-a^*}^{a^*} \phi^*\left(df^*; df, \sigma_{adv.}\right) ddf^*, & -a > df \geq a \end{cases},$$
$$\tag{9}$$

i.e., the probability that the estimated PUF bit $\hat{k}_C$ does not match the correct k_C. Figures 2a and 2b depict the distributions of $df/df^\star$ from which device and attacker derive their bounds $a/a^\star$ as solid and dashed curves respectively. The dotted red curve represents the distribution of observed values $df_C^\star$ for an enrolled value df_C marked as square. Consequently, the filled area below the dotted curve marks a failed attack according to Eq. (9).

Figure 3a depicts the success probability depending on the enrolled value of df for different levels of noise $\sigma_{adv.}$. Around $df^\star = |a^\star|$, the attacker faces the biggest uncertainty, which is in accordance with intuition as the additional noise changes the retrieved PUF bit most easily close to the decision boundary. Note that the attack does not change whether the *temporal masking* [18] is applied or not – in both cases, the magnitude reveals the PUF bit.

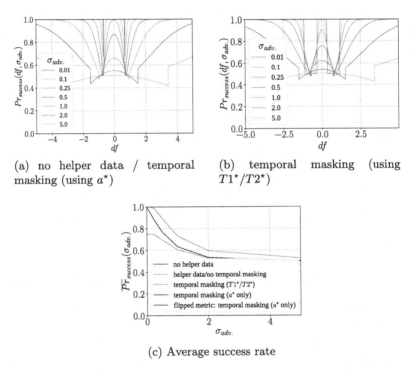

(a) no helper data / temporal masking (using $a^\star$)

(b) temporal masking (using $T1^\star/T2^\star$)

(c) Average success rate

Fig. 3. Simulation of the attack success probability for different levels of attacker noise $\sigma_{adv.}$. (a)–(b) Depeding on enrolled value df. (c) Integrated success probability according to the occurrence of df.

In Fig. 3c the overall success rate for varying noise levels $\sigma_{adv.}$ is depicted according to Eq. (8). In case the helper data is known, but no temporal masking is applied the TMH can be attacked even more easily highlighting that the TMH scheme without further protection enables SCA. Note that without temporal masking the frequency difference df would be revealed independently of the helper data scheme, therefore the notion is rather of theoretical interest and we provide the details in Appendix A. However, the results show that the reliability information of the TMH improves the attack compared to the scenario without helper data knowledge.

Attacker with Helper Data Access and Temporal Masking. Finally, we consider the case where the temporal masking is activated and the attacker cannot trust the sign of the observed frequency difference df_C. The attacker is still able to estimate bounds $\pm T1^\star$ and $\pm T2^\star$, but due to the randomization of the sign there may be a small estimation error. We neglect this effect in the following as it can be considered as an additional noise term in $\sigma_{adv.}$.

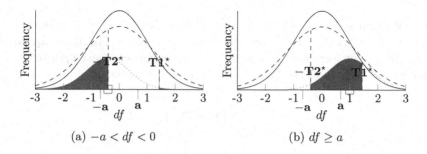

(a) $-a < df < 0$ (b) $df \geq a$

Fig. 4. Visualization of the attack failure with known helper data and temporal masking, where the sign of $df^\star$ is flipped compared to df for metric $M1$.

From an attackers point of view there are two possible approaches towards the temporal masking scheme. First, any helper data knowledge can be ignored, i.e., the bound $a^\star$ is used on the absolute values $|df^\star|$ – the attack success rate is the same as if no helper data was known. Second, the attacker can try to exploit the helper data by using the bounds $T1^\star$ and $T2^\star$. However, it has to be considered that the sign of the observation could be flipped. Taking metric $M1$ as an example, the average over the usage of $-T1^\star$ and $T2^\star$ (as defined by $M1$ in Fig. 1) and $-T2^\star$ and $T1^\star$ (reflecting a sign flip depicted in Fig. 4) gives

$$P_1(df, \sigma_{adv.}) = Pr[\hat{k}_C \neq k_C | w_C = M1, df > a]$$

$$= \frac{1}{2} \left[\int_{-T1^\star}^{T2^\star} \phi^\star (df^\star; df, \sigma_{adv.}) \, \mathrm{d}df^\star + \int_{-T2^\star}^{T1^\star} \phi^\star (df^\star; df, \sigma_{adv.}) \, \mathrm{d}df^\star \right]. \quad (10)$$

Accordingly the other intervals from the enrollment are dealt with. From Fig. 4 the resulting error can be seen if the observed $df^\star$ has flipped sign. Figure 3b highlights that the intervals between $-T1^\star$ and $-T2^\star$ and $T1^\star$ and $T2^\star$ are most prone to errors. For increasing attacker noise $\sigma_{adv.}$ the intervals $[-T1^\star, T2^\star]$ and $[-T2^\star, T1^\star]$ overlap increasingly, i.e., the average error in Fig. 3c converges towards the error for the case without helper data. However, even in the noise-free case and for low-noise scenarios the attack using $T1^\star$ and $T2^\star$ yields worse results compared to only using the helper data or $a^\star$. Thus, with temporal masking activated, the attacker will use the bounds $\pm a^\star$, and no additional information is achieved from the helper data.

4.4 SCA-Hardening for the Two-Metric Helper Data Method

A straightforward improvement of the TMH is to modify the mapping of the metrics. If the bit value with metric M2 is inverted compared to Eq. (2), i.e.,

$$M1 : k = \begin{cases} 0, T2 \le df \vee df < -T1 \\ 1, -T1 \le df < T2 \end{cases} \quad M2 : k = \begin{cases} 1, T1 \le df \vee df < -T2 \\ 0, -T2 \le df < T1 \end{cases},$$

(11)

the PUF response is related to the sign of df as shown in Fig. 5. Note that the choice of the metric, i.e., the helper data, is maintained according to Eq. (3). As the magnitude no longer reveals information the temporal masking protects the TMH scheme as long as the helper data is unknown to the adversary.

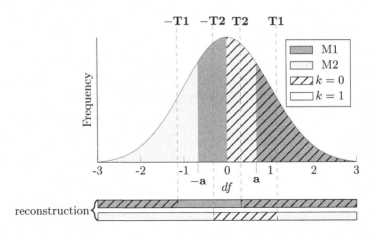

Fig. 5. Choice of metric and extraction of PUF bit value from the frequency difference df with new metric $M2$.

However, in case of known helper data, the attacker can still learn about the secret despite the temporal masking countermeasure. As the sign of $df_C^\star$ is randomly altered by the temporal masking, consider the absolute values $|df^\star|$ and estimate the parameters $\pm a^\star$, $\pm T1^\star$ and $\pm T2^\star$ as described in Sect. 4.2. Again, the attacker uses the bounds $\pm a^\star$ and combines the helper data and the values of $|df_C^\star|$ to estimate the PUF bit as

$$\hat{k}_C = \begin{cases} 0, \left(|df_C^\star| > a^\star \wedge w_C = M1\right) \vee \left(|df_C^\star| \le a^\star \wedge w_C = M2\right) \\ 1, \left(|df_C^\star| > a^\star \wedge w_C = M2\right) \vee \left(|df_C^\star| \le a^\star \wedge w_C = M1\right) \end{cases}.$$

(12)

Using Eq. (12), the attacker achieves the same success probability as for the non-flipped metric. However, using the sign instead of the magnitude to derive PUF bits, the following improvements are achieved:

1. Attacks without helper data are impeded completely.
2. The Hamming weight of the key is not leaked for unknown helper data, because the attacker cannot distinguish regions that map to 0 or 1.

Yet, the attacker is able to retrieve PUF bits even under noisy measurements. Furthermore, from the knowledge of the likelihood of a correct estimate, a smart guessing strategy can be derived: In Eq. (12), the closer the values of $|df_C^\star|$ is to the boundary $a^\star$, where 0 and 1 change, the lower is the reliability of the estimate. In the remainder of this section we will provide practical results from side-channel measurements to verify the possibility of a successful SCA attack.

4.5   Experimental Setup

We confirm the side-channel evaluation of the TMH scheme using an field programmable gate array (FPGA) implementation of a 63-bit Loop PUF, similar to [18]. The Loop PUF is implemented on an Artix-7 (XC7A100TFTG256) running at $f_{clk} = 100$ MHz. The use of a ChipWhisperer 305 Artix FPGA Target (CW305) SCA board facilitates the analysis as power measurements can be directly acquired using the SMA jack X4. We measure the voltage drop of the FPGA's internal supply voltage VCC$_{\text{int}}$ over a 100 mΩ shunt amplified by the board's 20 dB low-noise amplifier. A PicoScope 6402D USB oscilloscope acquires measurements at a sampling frequency of $f_s = 1.25$ GHz.

At the beginning of each challenge, a trigger signal allows optimal alignment of the measurements, which are transformed into the frequency domain after acquisition. The counter values after each challenge are read back for offline-verification of the SCA measurements. From the maximum of the frequency signals, the counter values and their differences are estimated. The attack from Sect. 4.4 is carried out by first performing an enrollment on the actual counter values averaged over ten runs. From the enrollment, a set of reference helper data is generated, which is used throughout the attack. The measurements of challenge pairs $(C, \neg C)$ are randomized to emulate the temporal masking countermeasure.

4.6   Practical Attack Results

For the following practical results, the TMH is derived on measured frequencies, i.e. the attacker has an additional "noise term" due to the difference of frequencies during enrollment and measurement.

Table 1 depicts the results for two different campaigns of ten Loop PUF runs each recorded on the same device. Enrollment is performed on the average of the actual counter values of the campaign, while attacks are carried out on single runs from the measured frequencies. The smart guessing changes first bits derived from frequency difference $|df_C^\star|$ close to $a^\star$ and is stopped at 20 bit to limit the time used for the attack. The median guessing complexity is around 16 bits in both campaigns, indicating that an attack can break the TMH even with the improved construction from Sect. 4.4 with reasonable effort.

Table 1. Remaining entropy in bit after smart guessing on 63-bit Loop PUF using TMH with flipped metric $M2$ and temporal masking.

Campaign	Remaining entropy in bits									
#1	7.3	9.1	15.7	16.6	16.6	17.0	17.5	>20	>20	>20
#2	10.5	11.4	13.1	13.7	14.4	15.6	16.8	19.5	>20	>20

5   Protection of the Two-Metric Helper Data Scheme

According to Sect. 4 an attacker with helper data knowledge and side-channel observations of frequencies can easily break the TMH scheme. However, the matching of frequency differences and helper data is needed. Consequently, the protection is to *hinder the matching*. This is achievable through randomization of the measurement order or, equivalently, the order of applying challenge pairs. Possible solutions are to generate challenge pairs in a randomized order or to store a randomized mapping of helper data and challenges in protected NVM. In a PUF scenario with publicly stored helper data no protected memory shall be used. Further, by Kerckhoffs's principle, the attacker knows how the challenges are generated and applied. Therefore, this section investigates methods to randomly permute challenge pairs during reconstruction.

5.1   Attack Vector on the Protection Mechanism

We consider the case of a flipped metric as introduced in Sect. 4.4 and temporal masking enabled. Thus, the attacker measures frequency differences df of the Loop PUF without knowing the sign. Even if we randomize the order of the different df, she still knows *which* frequency differences are used. Thus, a divide and conquer strategy is possible: In a first step, the attacker brings the frequencies into the correct order; In a second step, she mounts the attack from Sect. 4.6 on the ordered data. The attack succeeds if the first step yields only few possible mappings between helper data and frequency differences: For each possible mapping, the attack from Sect. 4 is to be performed for which the remaining entropy after a single measurement is determined by noise. As a consequence, the difficulty of the attack is mainly determined by the complexity to bring the frequencies into the correct order.

Realistic Loop PUFs generate $M > 3$ secret bits from M challenge pairs $(C, \neg C)$ and their corresponding df values. In such a case $M! > 2^M$ different permutations of df exist and permutation suffices to protect the secret. The difficulty is to develop an algorithm, which generates the permutations or a subset of permutations efficiently and unpredictably.

5.2   True Random Number Generator Based Protection

We first development a countermeasure that randomizes the order of challenge pairs $\mathfrak{C}_i = (C_i, \neg C_i)$ using a True Random Number Generator (TRNG). For this purpose at least M random numbers of length $R \geq \lceil log_2(M) \rceil$ bit are needed to index $\mathfrak{C}_i$ and to select the corresponding challenge pair. In this case, an attacker with SCA knowledge observes a random permutation of frequency differences, which hinders matching of helper data with observations and, eventually, the attack in Sect. 4.

Two questions have to be addressed: (i) What is a suitable choice of R to mitigate SCA attacks while retaining a low implementation overhead and (ii) how to map from random values to a unique sequence of challenge pairs? We discuss the former together with the problem of colliding random numbers in Sect. 6.1. An efficient method to solve the latter problem is given in algorithmic form and as block diagram in Fig. 6. It requires two $\lceil log_2(M) \rceil$-bit adders, two $\lceil log_2(M) \rceil$-bit counters, an R-bit comparator and $M \cdot (\lceil log_2(M) \rceil + R)$ bit of storage capability. The permutation generator, which is related to Lehmer encoding, takes as an input M distinct randomly chosen R-bit numbers stored in T-RAM. The index RAM (I-RAM) is initialized with zero. By iterating with counters A and B over all $\frac{M \cdot (M-1)}{2}$ pairs of random numbers and incrementing always the entry in I-RAM that corresponds to the index of the larger random number, the I-RAM finally contains a permutation of the values $0, ..., M-1$. The sorting algorithm defines – independent of the number of random bits R– the permuted order of $\mathfrak{C}_1$ to $\mathfrak{C}_M$. Please note, that the order is unpredictable for the attacker but can be resolved by the device in order to match frequency differences and helper data.

The TRNG-based approach described so far has one significant drawback: It requires a relatively large number of random bits. This raises the question, if a more lightweight protection mechanism is possible.

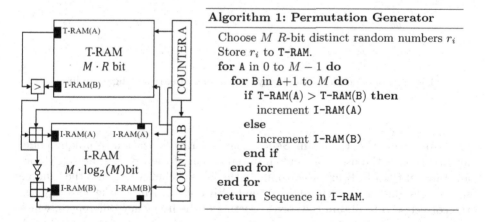

Algorithm 1: Permutation Generator

Choose M R-bit distinct random numbers r_i
Store r_i to T-RAM.
for A in 0 to $M-1$ **do**
    for B in A+1 to M **do**
        if T-RAM(A) > T-RAM(B) **then**
            increment I-RAM(A)
        else
            increment I-RAM(B)
        end if
    end for
end for
return Sequence in I-RAM.

Fig. 6. Block diagram and algorithm of permutation generator

5.3   Towards a Lightweight Protection of the TMH Method

The TRNG-based approach from Sect. 5.2 exclusively focuses on the complexity of guessing the sorting of the frequency differences. However, in a practical setting, frequency differences as well as their relations to each other are not constant between multiple reconstructions of the PUF response due to PUF noise. This limits the attacker's capability to establish a relationship between observed frequency differences from different reconstructions. In parallel, the measurement complexity can limit the applicability of the attack. This leads to the question if a more lightweight approach with less random bits compared to Sect. 5.2, and lower implementation complexity is feasible that retains a sufficient level of protection. This section introduces such an approach with the implementation shown in Fig. 7. It uses a combination of the linear feedback shift register (LFSR) seed (b_0 to b_5), the LFSR feedback polynomial (in red), an additive mask (in green), and clock shifting (in blue). We discuss an LFSR with six state bits b_0 to b_5, because our target application is a Loop PUF with 64 stages. Hence, 63 challenges[2] have to be permuted, and the $2^N - 1$ states of an $N = 6$-bit LFSR directly represent the index of a challenge, which makes the approach very lightweight. The discussion focuses on a 6-bit LFSR as the Loop PUF with more than 64 stages would be too slow and less stages ease the attack. For other applications longer LFSR length could be considered, i.e., the method is generally applicable.

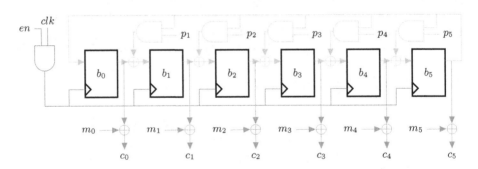

Fig. 7. Combined low-complexity countermeasure. (Color figure online)

Entropy from the Random Seed. The first randomization technique under investigation is the use of a random initialization of the LFSR state bits. Since all states of the LFSR are used to index the $2^N - 1$ challenge pairs, the random seed corresponds to a cyclic shift of the LFSR output. An attacker has to guess the correct seed to obtain the correct sorting of the frequency differences, which introduces $log_2(2^N - 1) \approx N$ bit of entropy – 5.98 bit in case of the 6-bit LFSR.

---

[2] From the 64 Hadamard challenges the pair of the all-zero and the all-one challenge shall not be used to derive secret bits, c.f. [2,18] for further details.

Entropy from the Random Shifts. The second protection mechanism is a multi-bit shift of the LFSR output. The LFSR is read out only after every n-th shift, where n is selected once per reconstruction. In Fig. 7 the enable signal en is set for n cycles after which the values of the c_i are used to determine challenge index. As the LFSR output is cyclic the shift by n has to be relative prime to the period of the LFSR $2^N - 1$ in order to reach all states of the LFSR, i.e., to index all challenge pairs. In case of the 6-bit LFSR, from Euler's totient function $\varphi(63)$ there are 36 values for n corresponding to approximately 5.12 bits of guessing entropy for the attacker.

Note that shifting the LFSR output has two possible drawbacks: First, the method delays the indexing of the challenge pairs. This is, however, not critical, since the next index is calculated in parallel to the much slower measurement of the Loop PUF. Second, an attacker can observe through a side-channel how frequently the LFSR is clocked. However, the SNR for the attacker is likely too small, to observe the LFSR: When the LFSR is clocked in parallel to the Loop PUF, the attacker has to observe both the Loop PUF frequency and the LFSR in parallel and the attacker can observe the clocking only $2^N - 1$ times, i.e., once per frequency difference, since for the next reconstruction another n is chosen. An additional hiding countermeasure could be to randomize the point in time, when the LFSR starts shifting during the measurement time of the Loop PUF.

Entropy from the Random Mask. The third method to add randomness is to mask the output by applying an additive 6-bit mask to the LFSR state corresponding to 6 bits of entropy. By adding a mask we introduce the index zero, i.e., the index of a challenge pair, which is not used, while another index – the one equal to the mask – disappears. We therefore map the zero index to the missing index in our analysis[3].

Entropy from the Random Polynomials. As a fourth and last method different feedback polynomials are randomly chosen for the LFSR. For the case of $N = 6$ there are six irreducible polynomials [8] that add another $\log_2(6) \approx 2.6$ bit of entropy.

Summary of Countermeasure. The idea of the combined countermeasure is to increase the complexity for an attack while maintaining a low complexity of the countermeasure. Summing the entropy values of the four protection mechanisms, 19.7 bit of entropy are achieved for an 6-bit LFSR. While the brute-force complexity below 20 bit would not prevent an attack, recall that the attacker has to perform the smart guessing attack from Sect. 4.6 up to $2^{19.7}$ times if the different sequences are indistinguishable. Considering that a single run of the attack takes more than an hour, even with a 100-fold parallelization, the attack on the

---

[3] We also investigated inserting a zero randomly at the beginning or end of the state before masking. For index zero we selected the Loop PUF under the all zero/all one challenge. However, the results were equivalent to the ones shown in this work.

different sequences would take approximately one year, which can be considered a reasonable protection level for a lightweight solution. However, the practical security analysis in Sect. 6 shows that an adversary can distinguish sequences generated by the lightweight countermeasure, which reduces the entropy and allows for an attack.

6 Security Analysis

The attacker can observe absolute values of frequency differences, but due to temporal masking the sign of the differences is unknown. The goal is to enable the attack from Sect. 4 by reconstructing the order of the frequency differences. Since the adversary does not have direct information regarding the correct ordering, she can enable an attack by labeling the observed frequencies with symbols. Then she brings the symbols into an order that might have been generated by the protection mechanism. An attacker wins if she can guess or identify the correct ordering of the frequencies since then and only then she can sort the frequency differences according to the helper data.

6.1 Security Analysis of the TRNG-Based Protection

If a TRNG outputs only distinct random numbers, the protection mechanism in Sect. 5.2 does not reveal information about the sorting. However, in practice collisions, i.e., sampling the same random number twice, are possible. Options to overcome this problems include to put the frequency differences for which collisions appear into a predefined order or to re-sample in case of a collision. The former leads to a higher probability for specific permutations that gives additional information to an attacker. To prevent possible statistical attacks exploiting permutations with distinct probabilities, we suggest to ensure distinct random numbers through re-sampling.

The probability that collisions of at least two random numbers appear is defined by the Birthday Paradox. However, it is less important if collisions appear than how many bits are required when generating a set of distinct random numbers if we resolve the collisions through re-sampling. Let us assume that the random numbers r_i are sampled sequentially and that the current r_i is re-sampled until the TRNG provides a number not yet used. Further, let us assume an ideal TRNG providing R-bit outputs such that all 2^R possible sequences are equally likely. Under this assumptions the probability of a collision $p_{re,R}(i)$ for the i-th random number with $2^R \geq i \geq 0$ is linked by

$$p_{re,R}(i) = \frac{i}{2^R} \Leftrightarrow E_{re,R}(i) = \frac{1}{1 - \frac{i}{2^R}} = \frac{2^R}{2^R - i}$$

with the expected number of samples to receive a yet unused random number $E_{re,R}(i)$. As a consequence, the average number of required random bits $E_{bits,M}(R)$ when sampling all random numbers r_i, $i \in \{0, ..., M-1\}$ is

$$E_{bits,M}(R) = R \cdot \sum_{i=0}^{M-1} \frac{2^R}{2^R - i}, \tag{13}$$

which has a minimum in R. For a given M the minimum defines the optimal choice of R regarding the expected amount of TRNG bits needed. We suggest to use this optimum for the permutation generator from Sect. 5.2: Under consideration of re-sampling for the case of $M = 63$ the minimum is reached at $R = 8$, i.e., on average $E_{bits,63}(8) \approx 577.23$ bits are needed.

6.2   Security Analysis of the Lightweight LFSR

In this section, we analyze the quality of the lightweight countermeasure from Sect. 5.3 in order to show its limitations and to point towards possible solutions. We discuss the different countermeasures individually and show practical evaluation results of individual and combined countermeasures. In the following, we interpret the Galois LFSR state from Fig. 7 as integers, e.g., $[1, 0, 0, 0, 0, 0]$ corresponds to 1. For simplicity of explanation we treat the case of a 6-bit LFSR.

Attack Strategy. Assume an attacker taking two measurements from two distinct reconstructions of the same Loop PUF. The randomized seed, shift size, mask, and polynomial are fixed for each reconstruction. The attacker defines the frequency differences of the PUF as symbols $s_i \in 1, ..., N$. She knows that there is a native order $\mathbf{s}_{nat} = [s_1, ..., s_N]$ of the symbols, which matches the sorting of the helper data. Further, the frequency differences $\mathbf{s}_{obs}$ she observes are sorted by a permutation described by a permutation matrix $\mathbf{A}$.

From the $2^{19.7}$ bit of entropy Sect. 5.3, more than $850k$ permutation matrices exist and the attacker's task is to find the correct one corresponding to one of her observations. If one or more randomization options are disabled, the number of permutations decreases accordingly. The attacker uses a differential approach on the observed sequences $\mathbf{s}_{obs,1}$ and $\mathbf{s}_{obs,2}$. She resorts each of the sequences with all possible sub-sequences. For the correct permutation matrices $\mathbf{A}_1$ and $\mathbf{A}_2$ of two noise-free measurements it holds that

$$(\mathbf{s}_{obs,1} = \mathbf{s}_{nat}\mathbf{A}_1 \wedge \mathbf{s}_{obs,2} = \mathbf{s}_{nat}\mathbf{A}_2) \Rightarrow \mathbf{s}_{nat} = \mathbf{s}_{obs,1}\mathbf{A}_1^{-1} = \mathbf{s}_{obs,2}\mathbf{A}_2^{-1}.$$

However, the reverse argumentation does *not* hold, i.e., if two matrices $\mathbf{A}_1^\star$ and $\mathbf{A}_2^\star$ exist such that $\mathbf{s}_{cand} = \mathbf{s}_{obs,1}\mathbf{A}_1^{\star-1} = \mathbf{s}_{obs,2}\mathbf{A}_2^{\star-1}$ the candidate solution $\mathbf{s}_{cand}$ is not necessarily $\mathbf{s}_{nat}$. In the following we determine how many solutions $\mathbf{s}_{cand}$ exist, i.e., how much entropy the attacker faces.

For noisy measurements, a direct matching of the resorted sequences is not reasonable. However, we show that the attack is still applicable by correlating the two observed and transformed sequences $\mathbf{s}_{obs,1}\mathbf{A}_1^{\star-1}$ and $\mathbf{s}_{obs,2}\mathbf{A}_2^{\star-1}$.

Confusion from Random Seed. Randomizing the seed corresponds to a cyclic shift of the LFSR. The permutation matrix $\mathbf{R}_m$ for a cyclic shift by m bit is

$\mathbf{R}_m = \mathbf{R}_1^m$, where $\mathbf{R}_1$ is the permutation matrix of the shift by one bit. Same applies to the inverse, i.e., $\mathbf{R}_m^{-1} = \left(\mathbf{R}_1^{-1}\right)^m$. Consequently, if two observations have the shifts α and β from their seeds, the relative shift of the sequences corresponds to a κ-bit shift with $\kappa = \alpha - \beta$. The native sequence follows from inverting the respective shifts, i.e., $\mathbf{s}_{obs,\alpha}\mathbf{R}_\alpha^{-1}$ and $\mathbf{s}_{obs,\beta}\mathbf{R}_\beta^{-1}$. Every candidate $\mathbf{s}_{cand,n}$ that fulfills

$$\mathbf{s}_{cand,n} = \mathbf{s}_{obs,\alpha}\mathbf{R}_\alpha^{-1}\mathbf{R}_n = \mathbf{s}_{obs,\beta}\mathbf{R}_\beta^{-1}\mathbf{R}_n = \mathbf{s}_{nat}\mathbf{R}_n$$

is a solution. Since the LFSR is cyclic with period $2^N - 1$, the attacker cannot distinguish $2^N - 1$ different sequences.

Confusion from Random Shift. Similarly to the previous argumentation, the shift by multiple bits is a permutation with a permutation matrix $\mathbf{T}$. Let $\mathbf{T}_\alpha$ corresponds to the permutation of the LFSR state sequence under shifts by α, and $\mathbf{T}_\beta$ corresponds to the permutation of the LFSR state sequence under shifts by β. Since all shift sizes are relative prime to the LFSR length $2^N - 1$, their product modulo $2^N - 1$ is relative prime to the LFSR length. The multiplication of matrices $\mathbf{T}_\alpha$ and $\mathbf{T}_\beta$ therefore results in a valid shift. Thus, for each pair of observations there exists a pair of matrices $\mathbf{T}_k$, $\mathbf{T}_l$ so that

$$\mathbf{s}_{obs,i}\mathbf{T}_\alpha^{-1}\mathbf{T}_k = \mathbf{s}_{obs,i}\mathbf{T}_\beta^{-1}\mathbf{T}_l,$$

and the attacker cannot distinguish different shift widths.

Confusion from Random Masks. A mask is implemented as a bitwise XOR onto the LFSR state with the all-zero result mapped to the mask value. Different from the previous methods, two permutations M_α and M_β inserted by the mask are unique. As a consequence, if different masks are used to permute the state sequence of the LFSR, the resulting symbol orders can be distinguished since only for the correct pair of masks and – as the experiments show – few exceptions

$$\mathbf{s}_{obs,\alpha}\mathbf{M}_\alpha^{-1} = \mathbf{s}_{obs,\beta}\mathbf{M}_\beta^{-1}$$

holds. Consequently, the entropy spent through this countermeasure does *not* contribute to the confusion of the attacker. In addition, the experiments in the last part of this section reveal that the mask, when combined with the random shift, effectively reduces the uncertainty for an attacker.

Confusion from Random Polynomial. Similar to the mask case, polynomials do not lead to an increased confusion of the attacker but rather allow for a better attackability of the LFSR. The reason is, that the permutation matrices P_α and P_β from different feedback polynomials are very distinct. Therefore,

$$\mathbf{s}_{obs,\alpha}\mathbf{P}_\alpha^{-1} = \mathbf{s}_{obs,\beta}\mathbf{P}_\beta^{-1}$$

only holds for the correct permutation and – as the experiments show – for few exceptions.

Practical Evaluation. We verify the theoretical insights with experimental data from synthetic symbols as well as on the measurement data of campaign #1 used in Table 1. All experiments assume temporal masking, i.e., the absolute values of frequency differences are used. An attack is limited to the measurements of a single Loop PUF, but can employ measurements from multiple reconstructions. Each pair of two reconstructions in the campaign is analyzed. For the attack, resorted frequency differences from two reconstructions are correlated in order to find their correct ordering. A correlation of 1 would be a perfect match of sequences, which only occurs for synthetic data. As frequency differences differ from measurement to measurement, for experimental data the correlations depend on the noise level. For fair comparison we present results for highest and lowest correlation, i.e., for lowest and highest noise seen by the attacker. This best and worst case have correlations of 0.97 and 0.91 for our measurements. Please note, that the attack requires only two single-shot measurements of the Loop PUF.

The synthetic symbols and measured frequency differences are permuted in software with different permutation strategies from Sect. 5.3 enabled. In accordance with the attack strategy, the attacker pre-computes all inversions to map from some permutation back to the native sorting. For the 6-bit LFSR a list with more than $850k$ inversions is generated. Then, the attacker permutes the two observed sequences of symbols w.r.t. to the pre-computed inversion list and correlates the result. Clearly, the result between the two correct inversions is $\rho_0 = 1$ in case of a noise free sequence and $\rho_0 = 0.91$ and $\rho_0 = 0.97$ in case of the selected noisy sequences. The complete attack takes on a commodity computer[4] in the range of seconds if only one permutation strategy is enabled up to less than 70 min with all four protection mechanisms enabled.

Table 2. Attack results on lightweight protection mechanism. Noisy data from power measurements of Loop PUF frequencies, noise free data from synthetically generated symbols. **R, T, M, P** correspond to random seed, randomly selected shift width, random mask, and randomly selected polynomial.

Enabled countermeasure				Used data								
				Noise free			Noisy; correlation 0.97			Noisy; correlation 0.91		
R	**T**	**M**	**P**	Min	Median	Max	Min	Median	Max	Min	Median	Max
x	–	–	–	63	63	63	63	63	63	63	63	63
–	x	–	–	36	36	36	36	36	36	36	36	36
–	–	x	–	1	1	1	1	2	8	1	8	27
–	–	–	x	1	1	1	1	1	6	1	1	1
x	x	–	–	2,268	2,268	2,268	2,268	2,268	2,268	2,268	2,268	2,268
x	x	x	–	378	378	756	378	378	3,780	378	2,268	10,584
x	x	–	x	2	2	13,608	2	4	13,608	2	4	13,608
x	x	x	x	2	4	2,268	2	4	11,340	4	13	870,912

---

[4] Intel(R) Core(TM) i7-6700 CPU; 3.40 GHz; 4 cores; 16 GB RAM.

Table 2 summarizes the results for different levels of countermeasures enabled, namely random seed (**R**), randomly selected shift (**T**), random mask (**M**), and randomly selected feedback (**P**). Each experiment is repeated ten times for each set of enabled countermeasures and minimum, maximum, and median number of indistinguishable sequences are provided. A sequence is included into the set of possible candidates if it yields a correlation $\rho \geq \rho_0 - \varepsilon$ with the data. The correlation threshold ρ_0 considers the noise level of the data sets and setting $\varepsilon = 10^{-6}$ prevents rounding errors. The values indicate, how many times the attacker would have to run the attack on the TMH scheme in Sect. 4.4 under different mappings between helper data and frequency differences.

We provide some remarks regarding the results in Table 2:

1. Except for all countermeasures enabled, the minimum value is the same for the noise conditions, and minimum and median are close. The small deviations indicate that the attack is quite robust against noise.
2. The maximum for noisy data and only polynomials (**P**) enabled is 6 and the maximum value for random seed, shift width, and feedback enabled (**R, T, P**) is always $13,608 = 36 \cdot 63 \cdot 6$, both corresponding to the theoretical maximum according to Sect. 5.3. The reason for these cases is, that by random chance twice the same polynomial has been selected and the attacker does not know which one. Conversely, if distinct polynomials are used, the distinction of two sequences is easier, which suggest that the polynomial countermeasure should not be used in combination.
3. In case that the mask is enabled, the median and maximum numbers of indistinguishable sequences increase, and at the same time the minimum number decreases, compared to the same setting without mask, i.e., (**R, T, P**) vs. (**R, T, M, P**), and (**R, T**) vs. (**R, T, M**). While the increased median and maximum values indicate a susceptibility of the attack towards noise, the increase of the minimum value reveals that masking is an unsuited permutation strategy and lowers the overall protection similar as the use of random polynomials.

Summarizing, the best combination of protection mechanisms is the use of random seeds (**R**) and randomly selected shifts (**T**) for which the attacker faces $63 \cdot 36 = 2,268$ indistinguishable sequences when observing ten different pairs of Loop PUF measurements. While we showed that the attack is independent of the noise level, an attacker could combine N_{meas} measurements to construct $N_{meas}!$ different pairs for an attack. From each pair, processed in parallel, she could take the $2,268$ most likely results or drop results, which have more than $2,268$ equally high correlations. The resulting up to $N_{meas}! \times 2,268$, sequences could be used in parallel to match helper data and frequency differences and to run the attack from Sect. 4.6. This eventually demonstrates that the lightweight countermeasure hardly provides sufficient protection to the TMH method. Nevertheless, the discussion highlights pitfalls, e.g., regarding combined permutations, and provides indicators on how to develop improved lightweight protection mechanisms in the future.

7 Conclusion

This paper studies the security of a PUF using the TMH method in the presence of SCA attacks. While TMH can greatly enhance the reliability without resorting to ECC, we show that the used metrics need to be modified in order to achieve a high level of security when the helper data is unknown to the attacker. In case of public helper data, it appears that the TMH method has important security weaknesses. Two protections are proposed relying on randomization of the challenge order. The first one, which takes advantage of a TRNG, provides excellent security but requires a significant number of random bits. The second and less costly solution is relying on an LFSR, but only adds a limited security enhancement. The limitations of the approaches highlight the need for more efficient protections in terms of complexity and security. In particular, we are interested in minimizing the number of random bits and in interleaving challenges during oscillation measurements.

A Attacker with Helper Data Access and No Temporal Masking

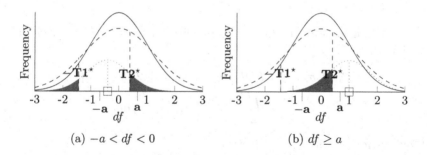

(a) $-a < df < 0$ (b) $df \geq a$

Fig. 8. Visualization of the attack failure for attacker with helper data knowledge. As an example metric $M1$ is used, but no temporal masking is effective.

We assume that the attacker can read the helper data, but the temporal masking countermeasure is not activated. We show how this additional information affects the attack highlighting that the TMH scheme without further protection enables SCA. This notion is rather of theoretical interest as without temporal masking, the frequency difference df would be revealed independently of the helper data scheme. However, the results show that the reliability information of the TMH can also be exploited by the attacker and improves the attack compared to the scenario without helper data knowledge.

Figures 8a and 8b depict the attack scenario assuming helper data knowledge. As an example, the use of metric $M1$ is depicted, where an attacker can use the bounds $-T1^{\star}$ and $T2^{\star}$ instead of $\pm a^{\star}$ if no helper data is known. Compared to Figs. 2a and 2b, the red area below the distribution of observed values is significantly smaller. This indicates that the attacker benefits from the reliability information encoded in the helper data and is formalized in the following.

Assuming metric $M1$ and the value $df > a$ during enrollment the actual PUF bit is $k_C = 0$ according to Eqs. (2) and (3). The attacker will know that $M1$ is the metric but any observed value $T1^* \le df'_C < T2^*$ is decoded as $\hat{k}_C = 1 \ne k_C$. In other words any perturbation $T1^* - df < \epsilon < T2^* - df$ will lead to an error in the attack. Now for $df^* \sim \mathcal{N}(df, \sigma_{adv.})$, the probability for this event is

$$P_1(df, \sigma_{adv.}) = Pr[\hat{k}_C \ne k_C | w_C = M1, df > a]$$

$$= \int_{-T1^*}^{T2^*} \phi^* (df^*; df, \sigma_{adv.}) \, ddf^*. \tag{14}$$

The boundaries $-T1^*$ and $T2^*$ depend on the noise the attacker faces[5], thus Eq. (14) establishes a relationship between the SNR and failure probability. Similarly, for the case when the metric is $M1$ and $k_C = 1$, the failure probability is:

$$P_2(df, \sigma_{adv.}) = Pr[\hat{k}_C \ne k_C | w_C = M1, -a \le df \le 0]$$

$$= \int_{-\infty}^{-T1^*} \phi^* (df^*; df, \sigma_{adv.}) \, ddf^* + \int_{T2^*}^{\infty} \phi^* (df^*; df, \sigma_{adv.}) \, ddf^*. \tag{15}$$

In an analogous way the failure probability for metric $M2$ with $k_C = 0$ is defined as

$$P_3(df, \sigma_{adv.}) = Pr[\hat{k}_C \ne k_C | w_C = M2, df < -a]$$

$$= \int_{-T2^*}^{T1^*} \phi^* (df^*; df, \sigma_{adv.}) \, ddf^*, \tag{16}$$

and for metric $M2$ with $k_C = 1$ it results in

$$P_4(df, \sigma_{adv.}) = Pr[\hat{k}_C \ne k_C | w_C = M2, 0 < df \le a]$$

$$= \int_{-\infty}^{-T2^*} \phi^* (df^*; df, \sigma_{adv.}) \, ddf^* + \int_{T1^*}^{\infty} \phi^* (df^*; df, \sigma_{adv.}) \, ddf^*. \tag{17}$$

From the probabilities in Eqs. (14) to (17), which define the entire support of df, the overall success probability to recover a PUF bit is given by

$$Pr_{success}(df, \sigma_{adv.}) = 1 - \sum_{i=1}^{4} P_i(df, \sigma_{adv.}). \tag{18}$$

---

[5] Note: For the standard normal distribution $\mu = 0$, $\sigma = 1$, the resulting value are $|\pm T1| = 0.31863936$, $|\pm a| = 0.67448975$ and $|\pm T2| = 1.15034938$. Depending on σ, the value are scaled accordingly. Notably the points that define the octiles are not equidistant.

Figure 9 depicts the success probability for different levels of noise $\sigma_{adv.}$ an attacker faces and depending on the enrollment value df. The results show that $df \approx \pm a$ and $df \approx 0$ contain most uncertainty for the attacker, i.e., it is most likely that the estimated value for the PUF bit k'_C is wrong. The attacker faces the highest uncertainty for values of df close to the boundary between $\hat{k} = 0$ and $\hat{k} = 1$. On the one hand, this means the attack will not yield a 100% success rate for all PUF bits. On the other hand, the attacker is provided with reliability information for the attack results that allow for developing a smart guessing strategy.

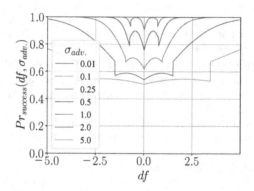

Fig. 9. Helper data/no temporal masking: Simulation of the attack success probability for different levels of attacker noise $\sigma_{adv.}$.

References

1. Becker, G.T.: Robust fuzzy extractors and helper data manipulation attacks revisited: theory versus practice. IEEE Trans. Dependable Secure Comput. **16**(5), 783–795 (2019). https://doi.org/10.1109/TDSC.2017.2762675
2. Cherif, Z., Danger, J., Guilley, S., Bossuet, L.: An easy-to-design PUF based on a single oscillator: the loop PUF. In: 2012 15th Euromicro Conference on Digital System Design, pp. 156–162, September 2012. https://doi.org/10.1109/DSD.2012.22
3. Danger, J.L., Guilley, S., Schaub, A.: Two-metric helper data for highly robust and secure delay PUFs. In: 2019 IEEE 8th International Workshop on Advances in Sensors and Interfaces (IWASI), pp. 184–188. IEEE (2019)
4. Delvaux, J., Verbauwhede, I.: Attacking PUF-based pattern matching key generators via helper data manipulation. In: Benaloh, J. (ed.) CT-RSA 2014. LNCS, vol. 8366, pp. 106–131. Springer, Cham (2014). https://doi.org/10.1007/978-3-319-04852-9_6
5. Delvaux, J., Verbauwhede, I.: Key-recovery attacks on various RO PUF constructions via helper data manipulation. In: 2014 Design, Automation Test in Europe Conference Exhibition (DATE), pp. 1–6 (2014). https://doi.org/10.7873/DATE.2014.085

6. Dodis, Y., Reyzin, L., Smith, A.: Fuzzy extractors: how to generate strong keys from biometrics and other noisy data. In: Cachin, C., Camenisch, J.L. (eds.) EUROCRYPT 2004. LNCS, vol. 3027, pp. 523–540. Springer, Heidelberg (2004). https://doi.org/10.1007/978-3-540-24676-3_31

7. Guajardo, J., Kumar, S.S., Schrijen, G.-J., Tuyls, P.: FPGA intrinsic PUFs and their use for IP protection. In: Paillier, P., Verbauwhede, I. (eds.) CHES 2007. LNCS, vol. 4727, pp. 63–80. Springer, Heidelberg (2007). https://doi.org/10.1007/978-3-540-74735-2_5

8. Houghton, A.: Error Coding for Engineers. Springer, Boston (2001). https://doi.org/10.1007/978-1-4615-1509-8

9. Katzenbeisser, S., Kocabaş, Ü., Rožić, V., Sadeghi, A.-R., Verbauwhede, I., Wachsmann, C.: PUFs: myth, fact or busted? A security evaluation of physically unclonable functions (PUFs) cast in silicon. In: Prouff, E., Schaumont, P. (eds.) CHES 2012. LNCS, vol. 7428, pp. 283–301. Springer, Heidelberg (2012). https://doi.org/10.1007/978-3-642-33027-8_17

10. Maes, R., Van Herrewege, A., Verbauwhede, I.: PUFKY: a fully functional PUF-based cryptographic key generator. In: Prouff, E., Schaumont, P. (eds.) CHES 2012. LNCS, vol. 7428, pp. 302–319. Springer, Heidelberg (2012). https://doi.org/10.1007/978-3-642-33027-8_18

11. Merli, D., Heyszl, J., Heinz, B., Schuster, D., Stumpf, F., Sigl, G.: Localized electromagnetic analysis of RO PUFs. In: 2013 IEEE International Symposium on Hardware-Oriented Security and Trust (HOST), pp. 19–24, June 2013. https://doi.org/10.1109/HST.2013.6581559

12. Merli, D., Schuster, D., Stumpf, F., Sigl, G.: Semi-invasive EM attack on FPGA RO PUFs and countermeasures. In: 6th Workshop on Embedded Systems Security (WESS 2011). ACM, March 2011. https://doi.org/10.1145/2072274.2072276

13. Merli, D., Stumpf, F., Sigl, G.: Protecting PUF error correction by codeword masking. IACR Cryptology ePrint Archive 334 (2013). http://eprint.iacr.org/2013/334

14. Pehl, M., Hiller, M., Sigl, G.: Secret key generation for physical unclonable functions, pp. 362–389. Cambridge University Press (2017). https://doi.org/10.1017/9781316450840.014

15. Schaub, A., Danger, J., Guilley, S., Rioul, O.: An improved analysis of reliability and entropy for delay PUFs. In: 21st Euromicro Conference on Digital System Design, DSD 2018, Prague, Czech Republic, 29–31 August 2018, pp. 553–560 (2018). https://doi.org/10.1109/DSD.2018.00096

16. Shiozaki, M., Fujino, T.: Simple electromagnetic analysis attacks based on geometric leak on an ASIC implementation of ring-oscillator PUF. In: Proceedings of the 3rd ACM Workshop on Attacks and Solutions in Hardware Security Workshop, ASHES 2019, pp. 13–21. ACM, New York (2019). https://doi.org/10.1145/3338508.3359569

17. Suh, G.E., Devadas, S.: Physical unclonable functions for device authentication and secret key generation. In: 44th ACM/IEEE Proceedings of the Design Automation Conference (DAC 2007), pp. 9–14 (2007)

18. Tebelmann, L., Danger, J.-L., Pehl, M.: Self-secured PUF: protecting the loop PUF by masking. In: Bertoni, G.M., Regazzoni, F. (eds.) COSADE 2020. LNCS, vol. 12244, pp. 293–314. Springer, Cham (2021). https://doi.org/10.1007/978-3-030-68773-1_14

19. Tebelmann, L., Pehl, M., Sigl, G.: EM side-channel analysis of BCH-based error correction for PUF-based key generation. In: Proceedings of the 2017 Workshop on Attacks and Solutions in Hardware Security, ASHES 2017, pp. 43–52. ACM, New York (2017). https://doi.org/10.1145/3139324.3139328

Enhancing the Resiliency of Multi-bit Parallel Arbiter-PUF and Its Derivatives Against Power Attacks

Trevor Kroeger[1]([✉]), Wei Cheng[2], Sylvain Guilley[2,3], Jean-Luc Danger[2], and Naghmeh Karimi[1]

[1] CSEE Department, University of Maryland Baltimore County, Baltimore, MD 21250, USA
{trevor.kroeger,naghmeh.karimi}@umbc.edu
[2] LTCI, Télécom Paris, Institut Polytechnique de Paris, 91120 Palaiseau, France
{wei.cheng,sylvain.guilley,jean-luc.danger}@telecom-paris.fr
[3] Secure-IC S.A.S., 35510 Cesson-Sévigné, France
sylvain.guilley@secure-ic.com

Abstract. Embedded systems utilize Physically Unclonable Functions (PUFs) for authentication and identification purposes. However, modeling PUFs' behavior via machine-learning methods has received utmost attention. Current research on modeling PUFs mainly targets a single PUF instance (PUF producing a single-bit response per query). It is admittedly more challenging to attack multi-bit parallel PUFs (with $M > 1$ PUF instances). In this work, we first target a multi-bit (mainly $M = 2$-bit) parallel arbiter-PUF using its power traces, then introduce a hybrid countermeasure, combining Dual Rail Logic and Randomized Initialization Logic mechanisms, to thwart such attack. In addition, we explore Randomized Arbiter Swapping and Randomized Response Masking mitigation techniques for providing further protection for parallel PUFs against modeling attacks. To mimic the PUFs' behavior in real silicon, we add noise artificially in our simulations. The results confirm the high success of the launched attack for the unprotected-PUF, and the resiliency of our countermeasures.

Keywords: Physically unclonable functions · Side-channel attack · Machine learning · Modeling attack · Parallel PUFs

1 Introduction

The fabrication of Integrated Circuits (IC) suffers from unavoidable imperfections. Such drawbacks can be leveraged within carefully designed circuits which harness these distinct variations for generating unpredictable unique values despite the similarity of their gate-level netlists. These circuitries, aka Physically Unclonable Functions (PUFs), map their input bits (referred to as a challenge hereafter) to a unique bit vector, so-called response. A PUF can be embedded in

S. Bhasin and F. De Santis (Eds.): COSADE 2021, LNCS 12910, pp. 303–321, 2021.
https://doi.org/10.1007/978-3-030-89915-8_14

an IC to generate hardware fingerprints and in turn to enable device authentication. Such reproducible fingerprints, so-called Challenge-Response Pairs (CRPs) can also be used for security parameters, for example secret keys in cryptographic modules [18]. Test and methodologies to assess the security of PUFs have recently been standardized at international level, in ISO/IEC 20897 [16].

Thanks to their ease of implementation and small size, PUFs are broadly deployed in radio-frequency identifiers (RFIDs), smart cards, and low-cost internet of Things (IoT) devices. Indeed, PUFs have been proven to be highly useful such that they have found their way into critical systems such as autonomous vehicles [8] as well as cryptocurrencies [22], and in chip onboarding schemes [14].

PUFs are categorized into strong and weak groups. A weak PUF simply refers to a PUF with highly limited number of (or no) CRPs, e.g., SRAM-PUF. Weak PUFs are typically used for key generation. However, they are susceptible to invasive attacks that monitor the internal structure of the PUF [23], as well as cloning attacks where the response can be easily replicated due to the limited number of responses [17]. On the other hand, strong PUFs have an exponential number of challenge response pairs. The arbiter-PUF [4] is an archetype of strong PUFs suitable for authentication purposes [18].

Although PUFs are abundantly useful they are not infallible. One such drawback is their susceptibility to the modeling attacks where an adversary tries to build a model that mimics the behavior of the target PUF. PUFs can be modeled through their CRPs [24] or via their side-channel leakage, in particular their power consumption [3,12]. To alleviate such vulnerability, several countermeasures have been proposed in literature including new PUF designs like the XOR-PUF [32], the Feed-Forward PUF [13], and Challenge Obfuscation schemes [9,29]. Besides, it has been suggested to use a fake PUF along with the genuine PUF and sneakly query the fake PUF intermittently [5]. However, these countermeasures are tailored against the attacks that exploits CRPs, and fall short when the adversary takes the power side-channel into account since the exploited leakage in power consumption is independent of the challenges [2,11].

Arbiter-PUFs and their derivatives are highly popular as a candidate for device authentication. To decrease their area and power overhead, they can be implemented as single instance, i.e., as a 1-bit response generator. This instance is queried multiple times with different challenges to generate an R-bit response. However, such implementation has been shown to be vulnerable against power analysis attacks [11]. Thereby, this paper expands the knowledge of power side-channel based modeling attacks by investigating the vulnerability of the arbiter-PUFs composed of multiple single-bit response arbiter-PUFs ($M = 2$-bit in particular) operating in parallel as parallelization may contribute to hinder the modeling of a PUF behavior through observing its power side-channel. To the best of our knowledge, there is no research in open literature on these multi-bit response parallel PUFs with respect to their assailability to power side-channel modeling attacks. This paper shows that these PUFs are in fact vulnerable (in the presence of realistic noise) especially if simple attack enhancements are made such as averaging multiple repeated power trace captures to increase the signal-to-noise ratio (SNR) of the target device's traces. Finally, to mitigate such vulnerability we propose a hybrid countermeasure that benefits from hiding the current leakage through the use of complementary Dual Rail Logic and response confusion with Randomized Initialization Logic. We also evaluate swapping and masking countermeasures. The contributions of this paper are as follows:

- Successful power-based modeling attacks on parallel multi-bit response arbiter-PUFs;
- Investigation into the attack validity in the presence of realistic noise and data extraction methods;
- Presentation of a number of lightweight countermeasures to thwart the modeling attack in the parallel PUFs based on equalizing the power consumption using Dual-Rail Logic, as well as randomizing the response;
- Assessment of the efficiency of the proposed countermeasures at different noise levels.

2   Background on Arbiter-PUFs

The arbiter-PUF is broadly used due to its ease of implementation, its effectiveness in producing unique values and its large space of its CRPs [7]. This PUF creates a base for many other PUF variants such as XOR-PUF [32], Feed-Forward PUF [13], etc. Each instance of an arbiter-PUF is composed of a pair of delay chains and one arbiter (as simple as an SR latch), and generates one response bit per challenge, in a single query [4] based on the process-variation induced race between two identical paths (top and bottom paths in Fig. 1). The difference in the propagation delay of these paths determines the PUF response to each challenge. Only the sign of this difference (not the exact amount) determines the response bit for each challenge.

Note that a full implementation of a PUF, embedded in a chip for generating keys or authentication purposes, would contain a storage mechanism following the PUF's output; denoted as system component in Fig. 1 and is mainly realized as a Flip-Flop to store the result of the PUF before the downstream components use the response. However, these system components create power side-channels that can be exploited to extract information, which we call *power leakages* in this work, and accordingly may be exploited by an adversary in order to model the PUF's behaviors. These leakages play an important role in the overall power consumption of the PUF, and in turn the underlying chip [6]. The derivatives of arbiter-PUFs, e.g., XOR-PUFs and Feed-Forward PUFs all follow the same scenario regarding the inclusion of system components which jeopardizes their security against power side-channel attacks.

3   Related Works

Most modeling countermeasures are for CRP-based modeling attacks which attempt to predict the PUF's response for previously unseen challenges: they can consist in design-level protection [9,28,29] or in mode-of-operation hindering [30]

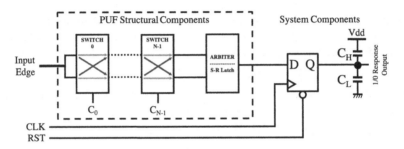

Fig. 1. Structure of an arbiter-PUF [4]. This includes both the PUF structural components as well as the system components (the target of the modeling attacks).

(here: a lockdown technique). However these methods fall short when confronted with power-based modeling attacks performed in this work [10,11,20]. In fact due to the implementation of power-based modeling attacks (namely: the leakage upon response sampling is spied on), the challenge is unused in the modeling of the PUF's behavior and therefore the size of the PUF does not matter [20].

Literature is not devoid of power-based modeling countermeasures. In [25] the authors share a method for a duplicate arbiter implementation on the arbiter-PUF. In this proposed work a second arbiter is used with the top and bottom traces reversed so that it creates the leakage from the opposite response value simultaneously. This hides the leakage from the arbitration unit of the PUF. The authors of [2] describe a mitigation technique which utilize overlapping delay chains to obfuscate the side channel information. The goal of this is to introduce algorithmic (or intentional) noise such that the modeling algorithm will not be able to coherently model the PUF.

These mitigations fail to consider the system components, shown in Fig. 1, used for storing the response for usage which as we will discuss later on are the principle component of attack. Therefore these countermeasures provide scant protection from what we discuss here.

4   Motivation

As mentioned earlier, arbiter-PUFs (and their derivatives) are mainly realized as a single-bit response circuitry (Fig. 1) which is queried multiple times to generate multi-bit responses. However, such implementation not only imposes low throughput but also an individual response leakage which is discernible as only one PUF is active in each point of time which is devoid of algorithmic noise.

To create greater algorithmic noise in the critical components designers can choose parallel multi-bit response PUFs. As shown in Fig. 2, deploying multi-bit parallel PUFs makes the attack more difficult as in this case there are more variations in the output traces that have to be discerned for an attack to be successful compared to a single-bit PUF. Parallelization of the PUF chains does not affect the uniformity and uniqueness of PUFs, and its effect on PUFs' reliability is negligible.

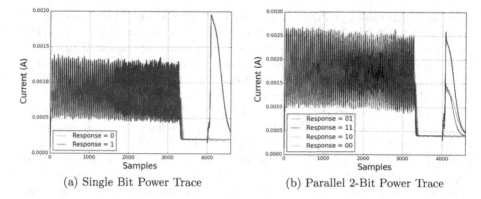

(a) Single Bit Power Trace   (b) Parallel 2-Bit Power Trace

Fig. 2. The noiseless power traces segregated into their response values of a single-bit response arbiter-PUF and that of a parallel multi-bit (M = 2-bit) response arbiter-PUF.

PUFs are valued for their small implementation size and power consumption in comparison to traditional cryptographic algorithms [18]. Designers hoping to use these to their advantage have limitations on the number of parallel instances. Therefore a smaller number of parallelizations are more likely to be used.

In the following sections, we target a 2-bit parallel PUF and show that attacking is indeed feasible. Accordingly, we introduce potential countermeasures to thwart such an attack.

5   Threat Model and Attack Methodology

We assume that the adversary has physical access and the ability to record the power traces of a device with an embedded multi-bit arbiter-PUF. It is also assumed that the attacker knows the number of parallel PUF instances. The attacker typically models the chip in the enrollment phase when it is still "open" to readily query with known challenges (for CRP-based modeling attacks). He launches a power side-channel based modeling attack subsequently to retrieve valuable secrets in the post-customization phase. To improve the SNR, the adversary can replay each challenge multiple times, collect the corresponding traces and average them to reduce the noise, and in turn increase the focus on the power associated solely with the usage of the PUF [2]. Since actual hardware runs relatively fast, the adversary can amass many traces to average and increase the SNR. After creating the model, this attacker reintroduces the PUF into the supply chain so that it can be deployed in a critical system and compromise it afterwards.

Attack Methodology: Power-based modeling attacks opt to characterize the target PUF's behavior via its power side-channel. These attacks involve the collection of a series of power traces corresponding to the operation of the target PUF when it is queried , i.e. when the input transition is propagating through the switches (in case of targeting an arbiter-PUF). These traces are then used to train a Machine Learning (ML) algorithm such that the resulting model mimics the target PUF's behavior [3,12]. Modeling a PUF via its power traces is more applicable than via its CRPs as the former requires fewer traces compared to the large number of the CRPs that the latter requires to model the PUF accurately [11]. Moreover, the PUF output is typically cut through anti-fuses following the Enrollment phase of the PUF [15] making CRP-based attacks almost impossible. Such limiting access to the CRPs is performed as a countermeasure against the adversary who aims at using the CRPs to model the PUF behavior. Accordingly, in this paper we focus on the power-based modeling attacks. It is noteworthy to mention that in the power based attack when the system component is targeted, the size of the challenge bitstream does not matter to the attacker since the challenge is not used when building the PUF model through its power side-channel. This means that the relation between the challenge and response is unnecessary to discern but rather it is the relation between the power and the response that is of interest. More details can be found in [20].

We assume that the adversary exploits the leakage produced from the Flip-Flop, shown as the system component in Fig. 1, which is used to store the PUF's result before the downstream components use it. There are several advantages for targeting this leakage namely that the Flip-Flop is sequential, synchronized, and has considerable capacitive loading which in turn induces higher observable leakage. The presence of such leakage has already been confirmed in real silicon devices [31].

After collecting enough power traces, we use Support Vector Machine (SVM), a supervised ML scheme, to train a model that mimics the PUF's behavior. As mentioned earlier, before training the model we apply the averaging technique to increase the SNR by repeating each measurement multiple times and computing the average of all measurements related to the same challenge. The averaged traces are used for training the model. We repeat the averaging scheme during the evaluation phase to increase the accuracy of predicting the response.

6   Proposed Countermeasures

We propose two sets of countermeasures, each including two schemes, to mitigate the power side-channel based modeling attacks discussed earlier. The first set opts to reduce the SNR of the power trace leakage from the Flip-Flop, while the second set consists of random masking or switching the PUF's response bits before storing in the Flip-Flop, thereby confusing/poisoning the model during training phase.

Reducing the SNR of Flip-Flop Leakage: To thwart power based modeling attacks by reducing the SNR of the Flip-Flops' leakage, we propose the marrying of two mitigation techniques, namely Dual Rail Logic (DRL) and Randomized Initialization Logic (RIL) implementations.

The DRL makes use of two complimentary Flip-Flops connected to the Q and $\bar{Q}$ output pins of the PUF's arbiter (i.e., the S-R latch in Fig. 1). Indeed, the standard implementation (unprotected) would have one Flip-Flop fed with the Q output of the arbitration unit to feed the system circuitry that utilizes the PUF's response. However, as discussed, this Flip-Flop produces unavoidable leakage. Placing a second Flip-Flop after the $\bar{Q}$ output of the arbitration unit, balances the leakage and prevents exploiting such leakage for modeling the PUF. This countermeasure is inspired by [21, § 7.3]. The loading on the outputs of the Flip-Flops also needs to be balanced. Accordingly, in this research we consider differences between the output capacitors of the deployed Flip-Flops, i.e., $C_{H1}, C'_{H1}, C_{L1}, C'_{L1}$ in Fig. 3. The capacitance values were chosen regarding the relatively high load of the DFF which is generally a system bus, and the process mismatch. The same specification holds for the lower PUF as well. To increase the randomness of the leakage in the response we propose the RIL countermeasure. Increased randomization is a common technique for thwarting modeling attacks [27]. To do so, we initialize each Flip-Flop with a random value before querying the PUF. Such random initialization hides the leakage as monitoring the switching from "0" to "1" or "1" to "0" (which can be exploited by the adversary to predict the PUF's response) may not benefit any more since observing a transition or not depends on the initial random value of the Flip-Flop (which is unknown to the adversary) as well. In parallel PUFs the random value for each PUF should be unique to prevent revealing the response to an adversary inadvertently. *Note that we use the above two methods together and refer to them together as DRILL.* This method can be used in both cases of single and parallel PUFs. However, in case of parallel PUFs, we propose to equip the circuits with the following countermeasures on top of the ones mentioned above.

It can also be surmised that the parallelization of the PUF can be considered as a countermeasure itself. For instance increasing the parallelization will increase the algorithmic noise that occurs during the PUF operation, thus decreasing the SNR and accordingly making the output less discernible (particularly in presence of noise).

Confusing and Poisoning the Modeling Algorithm: To enhance the resiliency of the parallel PUFs against the power-based modeling attack even more, we propose 2 countermeasures aiming at confusing and poisoning the inputs to the ML algorithms. The first method is referred to as Randomized Arbiter Swapping (RAS) hereafter, and the second is introduced as Randomized Response Masking (RRM), where both methods utilize a Random Number Generator (RNG).

Specifically, the RAS scheme poisons the PUF output via swapping the different bits of PUFs responses which other based on a value generated with a RNG. This makes differentiating the "01" from "10" responses highly difficult,

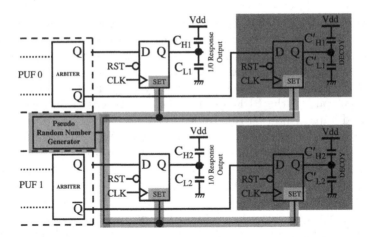

Fig. 3. The DRL (highlighted in blue) and RIL (highlighted in yellow) implemented on a standard 2-bit response parallel arbiter-PUF. (Color figure online)

if not impossible, in our 2-bit parallel PUF as depending on the generated random value, the outputs of the PUFs may swap for some challenges but remain intact for other ones. This countermeasure is shown in Fig. 4 and is realized with multiplexers which swap the outputs (shuffle them when $M > 2$) of the arbitration units based on the RNG value. Note that by swapping the outputs the entropy of the response increases but the uniformity is unchanged, provided that the PUF is unbiased.

In the RRM, the arbiters' responses are masked as being XORed with random values generated by an on-chip RNG. Figure 5 shows this implementation. Since this scheme is applied to both response bits of our 2-bit parallel PUF, it can diminish the modeling success rate significantly, i.e., the ML algorithm has 1 out of 4 chance for predicting the response correctly. Since the unmasking of the response is intended to be reversed the result will have the same response as PUF.

Note that in both of the above countermeasures, the randomization effects are reversed in software to extract the true PUF's response before using it for authentication. The software and hardware should follow the same RNG schemes. In this paper, we assume that the mask generator is secure and the method for sharing with the trusted hardware is secure as well. This means that there is no second order attack focused on the mask and the response.

7   Experimental Setup

Simulation Details: We targeted various instances of the single bit arbiter-PUF, 2-bit, and 4-bit response parallel arbiter-PUF circuitries, each with 64 challenge bits, using 15,000 random challenges and recording both responses and power traces. The capacitance values used were considered to be the worst case

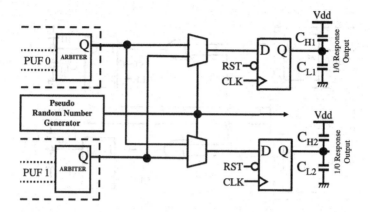

Fig. 4. The RAS countermeasure implemented within the PUF. Software is used to descramble the outputs.

loading condition for attacking, this was done to ensure that the side-channel modeling countermeasures were effective in this scenario. The capacitance values are shown in Table 1. If the capacitances are perfectly balanced then the attack will be extremely difficult as there is little differentiation in the leakages; here we consider imbalances which produce a worst case for our protections.

Table 1. Loading Capacitance Values for our PUFs. All have 2-bit responses except the single-bit one. For the PUF equipped with DRILL, each line shows the capacitors of one rail.

	C_{H1}	C_{L1}	C_{H2}	C_{L2}
Single-Bit PUF	200 fF	250 fF	N/A	N/A
Unprotected PUF	200 fF	250 fF	150 fF	200 fF
PUF + DRILL	200 fF	250 fF	150 fF	200 fF
	150 fF (')	200 fF (')	100 fF (')	150 fF (')
PUF + RAS	200 fF	250 fF	150 fF	200 fF
PUF + RRM	200 fF	250 fF	150 fF	200 fF

For the parallel PUFs both unprotected and protected circuitries were simulated in the transistor level using Synopsys HSPICE and a 45nm NANGATE technology [1]. Process variation was realized through Monte-Carlo simulations with Gaussian distributions: transistor gate length L: $3\sigma = 10\%$, threshold voltage V_{TH}: $3\sigma = 30\%$, and gate-oxide thickness t_{OX}: $3\sigma = 3\%$ reflecting a 45 nm process in commercial use.

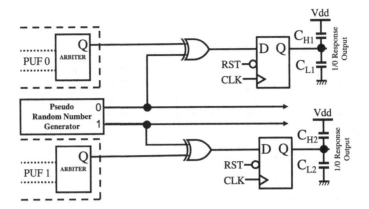

Fig. 5. The RRM countermeasure implemented on the outputs of the PUF arbiters. Software is used to unmask the outputs.

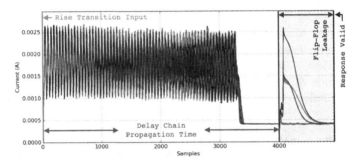

Fig. 6. Timing of the sampling window used to collect the power traces of the Unprotected 2-bit response parallel arbiter-PUF (with a 64-bit challenge). The Flip-Flop's leakage is highlighted.

Data Extraction: A set of collected power traces (sampled at 1ps) from the simulated 2-bit unprotected arbiter-PUF are shown in Fig. 6. Before sampling, the arbiter-PUF is given its challenge and the circuit has the opportunity to settle to a steady state before being queried for a response. The sampling of the power trace starts when the arbiter-PUF is given a rising transition and continues whilst the transition propagates through the chain of switches. Sampling is pursued during arbitration and the registration of the response in the Flip-Flop. Once registered, the response bit becomes valid and the sampling of the power trace ceases.

Adding Noise: In real silicon, noise occurs naturally as the PUF is embedded in a chip which may contain multiple other IP blocks producing their own current draw and fluctuations. Those circuitries entail additional "algorithmic" noise, which increases the difficulty of exploiting the target PUF's current leakage to build a model that mimics its behavior. Accordingly, in this paper to realize traces that reflect the effects of real silicon experiments more precisely, artificial noise is added to the power traces post simulation. The noisy trace (Y) is produced by adding the Gaussian noise N to the original trace (X):

$$Y = X + N \quad where \ N \sim \mathcal{N}(0, \sigma^2). \quad (1)$$

where we realize different standard deviations as $\sigma \in \{2.5e{-}4, 9.5e{-}4, 16e{-}4,$ $32e{-}4, 64e{-}4\}$. The signal-to-noise ratio (SNR) decreases with higher level of noise. The SNR is considered as a measure of attack feasibility, and is commonly used in side-channel analysis for this reason. It is assessed as the ratio of inter-variance and intra-variance [21, § 4.3.2] as below:

$$SNR = \frac{Var(Signal)}{Var(Noise)}. \quad (2)$$

For a 2-bit parallel PUF, the SNR can be assessed via the following equation, where $\mathcal{L}_{00}$, $\mathcal{L}_{01}$, $\mathcal{L}_{10}$, and $\mathcal{L}_{11}$ relate to the cases with '00', '01', '10', and '11' responses, respectively.

$$SNR = \frac{Var([\mathbb{E}(\mathcal{L}_{00}), \mathbb{E}(\mathcal{L}_{01}), \mathbb{E}(\mathcal{L}_{10}), \mathbb{E}(\mathcal{L}_{11})])}{\mathbb{E}([Var(\mathcal{L}_{00}), Var(\mathcal{L}_{01}), Var(\mathcal{L}_{10}), Var(\mathcal{L}_{11})])}. \quad (3)$$

Indeed, Eq. 3 presents the full SNR between all response possibilities. Recent research targeting a real arbiter-PUF shows that a plausible SNR is 1.81 [7]. We refer to this as a comparison point in our experiments.

Modeling Accuracy: In this paper, the accuracy of the modeling attack is defined as:

$$Accuracy = \frac{Predicted \ Correctly}{Total \ Tested}. \quad (4)$$

Note that the ideal accuracy when modeling a resilient PUF is equal to the probability of each response occurrence, i.e., 50% for a single PUF and 25% in case of 2 parallel PUFs.

All experiments are based on using 1000 traces for training and 5000 traces for testing.

8 Experimental Results

Single PUF Results: As a baseline for the parallel multi-bit PUF, the results for attacking a single-bit PUF are shown in Fig. 7. As shown, the accuracy of the attack is *approx* 100% until the noise level becomes quite high. The SNR for $\sigma = 32e{-}4$ (the noise for the last successful attack) is 0.079 which is far below the SNR of 1.81 seen in a real circuit [7]. This confirms the high vulnerability of single-bit PUFs against power based modeling attacks and motivates using parallel PUFs.

Parallel Multi-bit PUF Results: Figure 8 depicts the resiliency of the 2-bit response parallel PUF against modeling attack in different noise levels. At a first glance, the 2-bit parallel PUF seems secure as for the noise level of $32e{-}4$ and

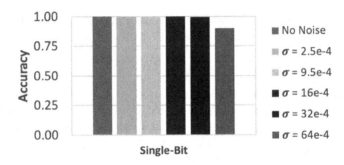

Fig. 7. The attack accuracy targeting a 1-bit response arbiter-PUF for various noise levels. Ideally the accuracy, from a design standpoint, for a 1-bit PUF is 50%.

beyond, the modeling accuracy is significantly lower than the single PUF counterpart shown in Fig. 7. However, we resemble the case in which the adversary uses a simple averaging technique in which the same challenge is fed multiple times and the recorded traces are averaged. In that case, as shown in the right side of Fig. 7, the 2-bit response PUF can be compromised as simple as the single PUF, i.e., the 2-bit PUF can be modeled with ≈100% accuracy for SNR of $\sigma = 16e-4$ or less, and the drop occurs at $\sigma = 32e-4$ which presents 94.8% accuracy. Investigating the SNR values gives a better picture in this case. The maximal SNR values for these cases are displayed in Table 2; when sigma is 16e−4 or lower (with averaging) the SNR is higher than then 1.81 (our baseline in real silicon) and as expected the attack accuracy is 100%. For sigma beyond this value, although not 100% but our attack was still quite successful. As expected, with averaging of 10 traces the SNR increases around 10 times. This confirms the ease of attack when averaging technique is applied.

Table 2. The maximum SNR when the Flip-Flops are queried in the unprotected parallel PUF with & without averaging.

	$\sigma = 2.5e-4$	$\sigma = 9.5e-4$	$\sigma = 16e-4$	$\sigma = 32e-4$	$\sigma = 64e-4$
Non-averaging	9.713419	0.658853	0.232567	0.062253	0.016153
Averaging	94.948925	6.666043	2.344949	0.589082	0.146669

The takeaway from these results is that the parallel multi-bit PUF is indeed vulnerable to power side-channel based modeling attacks when the SNR is even lower than that seen in real silicon. This is because the entropy introduced by the side-channel leakage of an M-bit response PUF is not really M bit as expected but rather is equal to the smaller quantity (where $X \in \{0,1\}^M$ and w_H is the Hamming weight function):

$$H(w_H(X)) = -\sum_{i=0}^{M} \frac{1}{2^M} \binom{M}{i} \log_2 \left(\frac{1}{2^M} \binom{M}{i} \right) \text{ bit,} \tag{5}$$

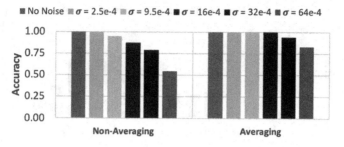

Fig. 8. The attack accuracy targeting an unprotected 2-bit response PUF for various noise levels with & without using averaging scheme during the attack. Ideally the accuracy, from a design standpoint, for a 2-bit PUF is 25%.

resulting in the entropy of 1.5 for $M = 2$. Moreover, although an accuracy of 75% would be expected for the 2-bit PUF corresponding to entropy of 1.5, it is only the imbalance and mismatch of the Flip-Flops and their capacitive loads which allow the adversary to discriminate the state "01" from "10". The results also show that the averaging scheme is highly effective in improving SNR as one would expect.

Reducing the SNR of the Target Flip-Flop's Leakage: To mitigate the attack, the proposed countermeasure shown in Fig. 3 was implemented. The modeling attack accuracy in presence of this DRILL countermeasure is shown in Fig. 9. As depicted the DRILL countermeasure is effective at mitigating the attack when the noise level is $\sigma = 9.5e-4$ and beyond if averaging scheme is not applied, while benefiting from averaging scheme results in a more successful attack and increasing the accuracy to 100% for $\sigma = 2.5e-4$ and to 95.7% for $\sigma = 9.5e-4$, respectively. Even with averaging, our DRILL countermeasure is highly successful for noises with $\sigma > 9.5e-4$. Note that all SNR values reported in Table 3, are much lower than the real-silicon baseline (i.e., 1.81) we referred to earlier.

Table 3. The maximum SNR for the proposed DRILL Protected PUF with and without averaging.

	$\sigma = 2.5e-4$	$\sigma = 9.5e-4$	$\sigma = 16e-4$	$\sigma = 32e-4$	$\sigma = 64e-4$
Non-averaging	0.034776	0.00476	0.002327	0.001941	0.001105
Averaging	0.185653	0.025787	0.011142	0.004322	0.001901

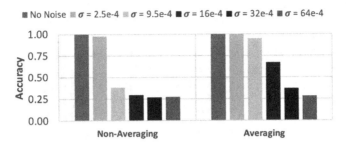

Fig. 9. The attack accuracy when the 2-bit response parallel PUF is protected with the proposed DRILL countermeasure. Ideally the accuracy, from a design standpoint, for a 2-bit PUF is 25%.

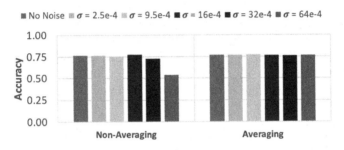

Fig. 10. The modeling accuracy when the 2-bit response PUF is only protected with RAS scheme. Ideally the accuracy, from a design standpoint, for a 2-bit PUF is 25%.

The takeaway point from these results is that the proposed DRILL countermeasure does mitigate the attack. However, we need to improve its resiliency at low noise levels.

Confusing and Poisoning Countermeasure Results: To further mitigate the modeling attacks, we implemented the proposed countermeasures of RAS (shown in Fig. 4) and RRM (depicted in Fig. 5). The accuracy of modeling attack when the PUF is only equipped with RAS is shown in Fig. 10. As depicted, in almost all cases, regardless if the averaging scheme is used or not, the accuracy is ≈75%. This is because, with such swapping, only the cases in which the responses equal to "01" or "10" are protected, but the "11" and "00" cases are still differentiable. Although this protection may seem not effective in 2-bit response PUFs, its inclusion in the PUFs with more response bits is promising. For example, for a 3-bit response PUF, the leakage of 6 out of 8 response cases (all 3-bit combinations of responses except "000" and "111") is reduced when the RAS scheme is adopted.

To improve the resiliency of the parallel-PUF against modeling attacks, we inserted our RAS scheme on top of the DRILL protection. Figure 11 depicts the related modeling accuracies. As shown the results are very promising. Even when the attacker uses the averaging scheme, the accuracy does not exceed 60%.

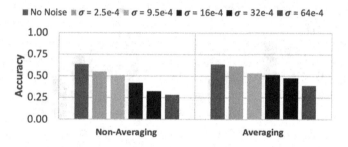

Fig. 11. The accuracy of modeling the 2-bit response PUF when RAS scheme is applied on top of DRILL countermeasure. Ideally the accuracy, from a design standpoint, for a 2-bit PUF is 25%.

The takeaway point from these observation is that the combination of RAS and DRILL countermeasures can highly protect the multi-bit PUF against modeling attacks.

We further applied the RRM (shown in Fig. 5). The results (not shown for the sake of space) confirm that this countermeasure is highly successful in thwarting the modeling attack, with the accuracy consistently being at 25% in all noise levels.

4-bit Parallel PUF Results: To assess the parallelization as a natural countermeasure, we launched similar attacks on a 4-bit parallel PUF. The power traces when the Flip-Flops are registering their responses is shown in Fig. 12. As shown the hamming weight of the response is clearly discernible, while the trace for the individual response is less distinguishable.

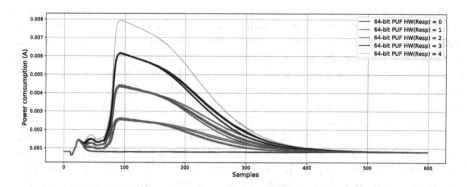

Fig. 12. Superimposing 50 traces of the 64-bit PUF in 4-bit parallel settings. Note that *HW(Resp)* denotes the Hamming weight of a 4-bit response *Resp*.

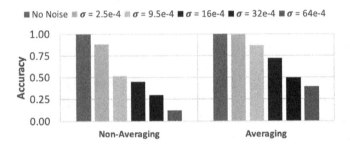

Fig. 13. The attack accuracy targeting a 4-bit response arbiter-PUF for various noise levels. Ideally the accuracy, from a design standpoint, for a 4-bit PUF is 6.25%.

The results of attacking are shown in Fig. 13. Compared to the 2-bit results in Fig. 8, we can clearly see that the individual 4-bit responses were less distinguishable, thus the attack is less accurate at predicting the responses of a 4-bit response parallel PUF. In fact, with noise levels' greater than $\sigma = 2.5\mathrm{e}{-}4$ the response is not modelable, and the accuracy of modeling is less than 75%.

9   Discussions

In the attack of the multi-bit arbiter PUF, we considered slight variations between PUFs, realized as small differences between output capacitances of the response flip-flops due to process mismatch. Indeed, these variations increase the adversary's ability to successfully attack the PUF through its power traces. It is interesting to note that the technological imbalance which is the essence of the PUF, can reduce the efficiency of the protections, notably when using multi-bit responses. For the simulation results, we used variation values that are typical in real designs. Moreover, even though the capacitances C_{H1} and C_{H2} are rigorously equal, an attacker resorting to small-sized electromagnetic probes (instead of powerline fluctuations measurements with an ammeter/oscilloscope) could make a difference depending on the provenance (H1 vs H2) of the leakage [19]. Thus, in the sequel, we should consider that somehow, the adversary manages to collect even slightly different signals originating from either capacitance.

The use of multi-bit arbiter PUF does not only provide intrinsic security enhancement against side-channel observations but also against invasive attacks which manage to monitor the PUF while it is challenged [26]. Such attacks are very powerful as they require the knowledge of the PUF layout and its position within the chip, as well as a perfect synchronization with the challenges. Few PUFs (and actually few security IPs in general) resist such attacks. However, we notice that the use of parallel PUFs, provided the M instances are sufficient apart, allow to thwart this attack, since the imaging sensor has a small aperture size.

Finally, we wish to remind the reader that in this work the randomly generated variables used in mask generation and arbiter swapping are not exploited by the attacker. This is the case if they are generated before the arbitration time and the attack is at first order.

10   Conclusion and Future Directions

We investigated the resiliency of parallel multi-bit response arbiter-PUFs against power side-channel based modeling attacks. The results confirm the vulnerability of such PUFs against the power based modeling attacks, especially when the adversary benefits from the averaging technique. We proposed a number of countermeasures based on hiding the power consumption by equalizing the power for different response values as well as randomizing the relation between the power consumption and response bits. We also showed that increasing the number of bits in multi-bit responses naturally improve the security against power modeling attacks. The results confirmed the efficacy of the proposed countermeasures in thwarting the power based modeling attacks in parallel arbiter-PUFs. All findings can be extended to the arbiter-PUF derivatives considering their architecture. We plan to extend this research by investigating the findings on real silicon, and for larger multi-bit response implementations.

Acknowledgments. This work has benefited from a funding via the bilateral project APRIORI (*Advanced Privacy of IOT Devices through Robust Hardware Implementations*), from FR-DE cybersecurity 2020 call (MESRI-BMBF), managed by ANR from the French side.

References

1. Nangate 45nm open cell library. http://www.nangate.com
2. Aghaie, A., Moradi, A.: TI-PUF: toward side-channel resistant physical unclonable functions. TIFS **15**, 3470–3481 (2020)
3. Mahmoud, A., et al.: Combined modeling and side channel attacks on strong PUFs. IACR Crypt. ePrint Arch. **2013**, 632 (2013)
4. Gassend B., et al.: Silicon physical random functions. In: CCS, pp. 148–160 (2002)
5. Gu, C., et al.: A modeling attack resistant deception technique for securing PUF based authentication. In: AsianHOST, pp. 1–6 (2019)
6. Merli, D., et al.: Side-channel analysis of PUFs and fuzzy extractors. In: Trust and Trustworthy Computing, pp. 33–47 (2011)
7. Fukushima, K., et al.: Delay PUF assessment method based on side-channel and modeling analyzes: the final piece of all-in-one assessment methodology. In: IEEE Trustcom/BigDataSE/ISPA, pp. 201–207 (2016). https://doi.org/10.1109/TrustCom.2016.0064
8. Jiang, Q., et al.: Two-Factor Authentication Protocol Using Physical Unclonable Function for IoV. In: IEEE/CIC ICCC, pp. 195–200 (2019)
9. Zalivaka, S.S., et al.: Reliable and modeling attack resistant authentication of arbiter PUF in FPGA implementation with trinary quadruple response. IEEE TIFS **14**(4), 1109–1123 (2019)
10. Kroeger, T., et al.: Cross-PUF attacks on arbiter-PUFs through their power side-channel. In: ITC (2020)

11. Kroeger, T., et al.: Effect of aging on PUF modeling attacks based on power side-channel observations. In: DATE, pp. 454–459 (2020)
12. Rührmair, U., et al.: Efficient power and timing side channels for physical unclonable functions. In: CHES, pp. 476–492 (2014)
13. Alkatheiri, M.S., Zhuang, Y.: Towards fast and accurate machine learning attacks of feed-forward arbiter PUFs. In: IEEE Conference on Dependable and Secure Computing, pp. 181–187 (2017). https://doi.org/10.1109/DESEC.2017.8073845
14. Danger, J.-L., Guilley, S., Pehl, M., Senni, S., Souissi, Y.: Highly reliable PUFs for embedded systems, protected against tampering. In: Vo, N.-S., Hoang, V.-P., Vien, Q.-T. (eds.) INISCOM 2021. LNICSSITE, vol. 379, pp. 167–184. Springer, Cham (2021). https://doi.org/10.1007/978-3-030-77424-0_14
15. Gao, Y., et al.: Obfuscated challenge-response: A secure lightweight authentication mechanism for PUF-based pervasive devices. In: PerCom Workshops, pp. 1–6 (2016)
16. Guilley, S., Hamaguchi, S., Kang, Y.: ISO/IEC 20897–1:2020. Information security, cybersecurity and privacy protection - Physically unclonable functions - Part 1: Security requirements (2020). https://www.iso.org/standard/76353.html
17. Helfmeier, C., Boit, C.: Cloning Physically Unclonable Functions. In: HOST, pp. 1–6 (2013). https://doi.org/10.1109/HST.2013.6581556
18. Herder, C., et al.: Physical unclonable functions and applications. Tutorial. Proc. IEEE 102(8), 1126–1141 (2014)
19. Immler, V., Specht, R., Unterstein, F.: Your rails cannot hide from localized EM: how dual-rail logic fails on FPGAs. In: Fischer, W., Homma, N. (eds.) CHES 2017. LNCS, vol. 10529, pp. 403–424. Springer, Cham (2017). https://doi.org/10.1007/978-3-319-66787-4_20
20. Kroeger, T., Cheng, W., Guilley, S., Danger, J., Karimi, N.: Making obfuscated PUFs secure against power side-channel based modeling attacks. In: DATE (2021)
21. Mangard, S., Oswald, E., Popp, T.: Power Analysis Attacks: Revealing the Secrets of Smart Cards. Springer, Cham (2006)
22. Mars, A., Adi, W.: New concept for physically-secured e-coins circulations. In: Adaptive Hardware and Systems, pp. 333–338 (2018)
23. Nedospasov, D., Seifert, J., Helfmeier, C., Boit, C.: Invasive PUF analysis. In: FDTC, pp. 30–38 (2013). https://doi.org/10.1109/FDTC.2013.19
24. Rührmair, U., Sölter, J.: PUF modeling attacks: an introduction and overview. In: DATE, pp. 1–6 (2014). https://doi.org/10.7873/DATE.2014.361
25. Rührmair, U., et al.: Power and timing side channels for PUFs and their efficient exploitation. IACR Cryptol. ePrint Arch. 2013, 851 (2013)
26. Tajik, S., et al.: Photonic side-channel analysis of arbiter PUFs. J. Cryptol. 30(2), 550–571 (2017)
27. Tebelmann, L., et al.: Self-secured PUF: protecting the loop PUF by masking. In: COSADE, Lugano, 5–7 October (2020)
28. Vijayakumar, A., Kundu, S.: A novel modeling attack resistant PUF design based on non-linear voltage transfer characteristics. In: DATE, pp. 653–658 (2015). https://doi.org/10.7873/DATE.2015.0522
29. Wang, Q., Gao, M., Qu, G.: A machine learning attack resistant dual-mode PUF. In: Great Lakes Symposium on VLSI, pp. 177–182 (2018). https://doi.org/10.1145/3194554.3194590
30. Yu, M.M., Hiller, M., Delvaux, J., Sowell, R., Devadas, S., Verbauwhede, I.: A lockdown technique to prevent machine learning on PUFs for lightweight authentication. IEEE Trans. Multi Scale Comput. Syst. 2(3), 146–159 (2016). https://doi.org/10.1109/TMSCS.2016.2553027

31. Yu, Y., et al.: Profiled deep learning side-channel attack on a protected arbiter PUF combined with bitstream modification. Cryptology ePrint Archive, Report 2020/1031 (2020). https://eprint.iacr.org/2020/1031
32. Zhou, C., Parhi, K.K., Kim, C.H.: Secure and reliable XOR arbiter PUF design: an experimental study based on 1 trillion challenge response pair measurements. In: Proceedings of the 54th Annual Design Automation Conference 2017. DAC 2017, Association for Computing Machinery, New York (2017). https://doi.org/10.1145/3061639.3062315

Author Index

Printed in the United States
by Baker & Taylor Publisher Services